The AI IT Security Implementation & Strategy™

Running the Program the Audit Proved You Needed

Stephen R. Jordan

SRJ Consulting & Services Publishing

Copyright

The AI IT Security Implementation & Strategy™

Running the Program the Audit Proved You Needed

The Operating Discipline for AI Library™, Volume VI

Pillar II: AI Risk Governance & Security™

Volumes are numbered by operating sequence, the natural order in which the disciplines build inside a business.

Copyright

Published by SRJ Consulting & Services LLC, Frisco, Texas. SRJConsulting Services.com.

Names: Jordan, Stephen R. (Stephen Ray), 1960- author.

Title: The AI IT Security Implementation & Strategy: running the program the audit proved you needed / Stephen R. Jordan.

Other titles: Artificial intelligence information technology security implementation and strategy

Description: First edition. | Frisco, Texas: SRJ Consulting & Services Publishing, [2026] | Series: Operating discipline for AI library. Pillar 2: AI risk governance & security; v. 6. | Includes bibliographical references.

Identifiers: ISBN: 9798996940257 (Paperback) | 9798996940271 (Hardcover) | 9798996940264 (ePub)

Subjects: LCSH: Artificial intelligence--Security measures--Management. | Computer security--Management. | Artificial intelligence--Risk management. | Information technology--Security measures. | Data protection--Management. | Business enterprises--Data processing--Security measures. | Corporate governance. | BISAC: COMPUTERS / Security / General. | COMPUTERS / Artificial Intelligence / General. | BUSINESS & ECONOMICS / Corporate Governance.

Classification: LCC: HD30.2 .J676 2026 | DDC: 658/.0563--dc23

Trademarks

sessment™, AI Readiness Maturity Scale™, Expand, Refine, or Pause Decision Protocol™, AI Governance Maturity Scale™, The AI Efficiency Scorecard™, The AI ROI Formula™, and the AI Governance Framework Crosswalk™. All other trademarks referenced are the property of their respective owners.

The title mark, The AI IT Security Implementation & Strategy™, is used in full wherever the Volume refers to itself. Other trademark symbols appear in this front matter and in the Appendix, and are omitted from chapter prose so the reading is not interrupted. The absence of a symbol in the body text does not waive any right in the mark.

Disclaimer

This Volume provides general operational and management frameworks intended to support executive decision-making. It is sold with the understanding that neither the author nor the publisher is rendering legal, financial, regulatory, compliance, tax, or technical advice specific to any organization or situation.

References to solution categories, architectural patterns, operating rhythms, and control designs are provided for general operational guidance only. No vendor, product, or service is named, endorsed, or recommended anywhere in this Volume. The regulatory and threat environment around AI security continues to develop rapidly, and readers should verify current requirements against the applicable authorities in their jurisdiction and industry before acting.

Reading this Volume does not establish a consulting, professional services, or advisory relationship with SRJ Consulting & Services LLC or with the author. Engagement of professional services requires a separate written agreement.

References to specific regulatory frameworks, security standards, professional audit standards, and supervisory guidance (including but not limited to the NIST AI Risk Management Framework, ISO/IEC 42001, ISO/IEC 27001, the EU AI Act, the SEC cybersecurity disclosure rules, GDPR, HIPAA, OWASP LLM Top 10, OWASP Agentic Top 10, OWASP MCP Top 10, OWASP AIVSS, MITRE ATLAS, HITRUST AI, and Google SAIF) reflect the author's pro-

AI Disclosure

This Volume was produced with AI assistance. The text was developed through extensive use of AI tools, with substantial editorial review, structural revision, and final approval by the author. All figures, diagrams, scorecards, and illustrations were generated using AI tools under the direction of the author, who reviewed and approved each one for accuracy and appropriateness. The academic sources in the References section were located using AI-assisted literature search and were verified against the published record before inclusion. The author retains full responsibility for the content, analysis, frameworks, judgments, and conclusions presented in this work. The Volume is an original English-language work; no portion was machine-translated from another language.

Cover design by Muhammad Shakir Tahir, Book Bloom Studio.

First Edition

Dedication

For the security leaders who ran the audit, produced the evidence, answered the board honestly, and then went back to their desks on Tuesday morning to find that nothing in the program actually governed what the machines were doing.

This one is for the Tuesday.

Acknowledgments

This Volume exists because a specific complaint kept surfacing in the same shape across very different organizations.

The complaint was never that the audit was wrong. Security leaders who ran the work in Volume V produced findings they believed, a risk register they could defend, and a regulatory crosswalk that held up under scrutiny. The complaint was that the audit ended and the program did not begin. The binder was accurate on the day it was dated and aging by the end of that week. The findings named the exposure without naming who would close it, on what cadence, with what authority to stop a system that had started acting badly.

My thanks go to the CISOs, deputy CISOs, GRC directors, SOC managers, third-party risk leads, and privacy officers who described that gap plainly rather than defensively. Several of them read early sections and told me where the sequencing was wrong, where a control assumed a maturity their organizations did not have, and where a twelve-month plan was really a thirty-six-month plan wearing a shorter label. Those corrections shaped the operating models in Chapters 3, 6, 9, and 12 more than any other input.

Thanks also to the General Counsels who explained, carefully and more than once, why an attestation about AI behavior is a different legal object than an attestation about a control, and to the underwriters who were candid about what their AI exclusions actually exclude. Both conversations changed how this Volume treats the accountability question.

Any errors in judgment, sequencing, or emphasis are mine.

Stephen R. Jordan

Frisco, Texas, 2026

Executive Summary

Volume V answered a question that has arrived in nearly every boardroom and audit committee where AI is running at scale: can you prove your AI exposure is known, controlled, and governed? The AI IT Security Audit™ produced the four-layer AI inventory, the Non-Human Identity Inventory, the Agent Boundary Matrix, the AI Vendor Tier Map, the AI Data Flow Map, the Regulatory Crosswalk, and the Defensible AI Security Baseline. Dated, scored, and signed, that evidence base survives the regulator, the enterprise customer, the insurance carrier, and the audit committee.

Then the audit ends, and a different problem starts. The evidence was true on the date it was produced. The environment it described mutates weekly. Volume VI is built for what happens next.

This Volume converts the audit's artifacts into an operating program across the four domains a CISO is accountable for: Security Governance and Risk Management, Security Operations, Third-Party and Supply Chain Risk, and Data Protection and Privacy. Each domain receives three chapters in the same sequence. The first names what AI is breaking in that domain, working from the specific artifacts Volume V handed over. The second names how AI rebuilds the domain's capability, because the same technology creating the exposure is the only thing operating at the speed required to govern it. The third names where the market is now, which solution categories matter, whether the department itself survives in its current form, what the twelve-month target operating model looks like with owners and budget lines, and whether that domain ends up needing more security or less.

The horizon is deliberately one year. Multi-year transformation plans get written, presented, funded in year one, and defunded in year two when the sponsoring executive changes roles or the threat picture moves. Every target operating model in this Volume is scoped to four quarters, with the milestone the CISO will name to the board at the end of each one. Where a capability genuinely requires longer to mature, the Volume says what Year One makes possible rather than pretending the work compresses.

The frameworks this Volume adds to the Library are the operating instruments the audit did not produce. The AI Security Operating System™ is the umbrella that holds the four domains in one program rather than four parallel projects. The Human Supervision Matrix™ documents which actions machines may take alone, which require human confirmation, and what evidence is required before autonomy expands. The Red-Button Protocol™ makes suspension a rehearsed capability with a measured time-to-stop rather than a paragraph in a policy. The Shadow AI Sanctioning Pathway™ converts rogue demand into governed capability instead of driving it further underground. Adaptive AI Trust Scores™ make vendor trust a managed variable rather than a binary annual assessment. The Non-Human Identity Pyramid™ provides the tiered governance model for the identity population that now outnumbers the human one. The AI Decision Provenance Chain™ answers the accountability question when no human decided.

No vendor is named anywhere in this Volume. The solution landscape is described in categories and architectural patterns, because the category outlives the vendor and the reader has to make a procurement decision that survives a market consolidation.

The answer to the question every board eventually asks, whether AI means the enterprise needs more security or less, is delivered four times in this Volume, once per domain, with the reasoning shown. The short version is that the answer is more, in every domain, but transformed. The work changes shape. The headcount changes composition. The controls move from periodic to continuous.

What does not change is that someone has to be accountable, and the point of this Volume is to make sure that someone has a program to be accountable with.

Contents

Introduction

You Proved It. Now Run It.

The audit is done. The binder exists. The board saw the slides, asked reasonable questions, and nodded at the right moments. The CISO delivered. The findings were real, the risk register was honest, and the regulatory crosswalk held up under scrutiny. For that moment in the boardroom, the work was complete and the posture was proven.

Then Tuesday morning arrived.

And nothing in your security program actually governs what AI is doing in your enterprise right now. Not the inventory that's been sitting static for four months. Not the risk register that hasn't been touched since the audit closed. Not the vendor questionnaires that went out last quarter to supply chain partners who have since quietly enabled AI features nobody reviewed. The binder proved the posture at a point in time. The enterprise kept moving. And the gap between those two things is growing every single day.

This is the specific problem this book was written to solve. Not the audit. The audit is done. The problem is what comes after it, which is the part nobody has written a real operating manual for. Agents are making decisions nobody approved. Non-human identities are accumulating access nobody audits. Models are processing data in ways no privacy team has mapped. The second intelligence layer inside your enterprise is running, and the security program built to govern human decisions and static documents is watching it happen without the tools, the rhythms, or the decision rights to do anything about it.

That's not a failure of effort. It's a failure of operating model.

The people who completed Volume V of The AI IT Security Library did genuinely hard work. Cataloguing AI systems across a mid-to-large enterprise is not a small task. Building a risk register that reflects real findings against real regulatory requirements takes months of honest, difficult effort. Producing a board-ready deliverable that maps AI risk to business impact requires a level of cross-functional coordination that most security teams aren't naturally built for. If you did that work, or led the team that did it, you earned the result. The audit was real. The posture was proven.

Static evidence ages. That's the part nobody warned you about clearly enough.

A regulator who picks up that binder six months from now won't see a thorough organization that completed a rigorous assessment. They'll see an organization that completed a rigorous assessment and then stopped. The gap between what the binder says and what the environment actually looks like isn't just a technical discrepancy. It's documented proof that governance wasn't operating after the audit closed. You didn't just fail to update the inventory. You created a paper trail that shows exactly when you stopped paying attention. That's the liability you're carrying right now, and it grows every week the operating model doesn't catch up to the audit evidence.

This book picks up exactly where the audit left off. Not to re-prove the posture. To run it, every single day, in a way that keeps the evidence current, keeps the board answered, and keeps the security function relevant in an enterprise where machine reasoning is now making consequential decisions alongside human ones.

Think about what that actually means in practice. Consider a hypothetical security director at a large healthcare organization. She spent six months leading her team through a comprehensive AI security audit. They inventoried 61 AI systems, documented 94 risk findings, and produced a regulatory crosswalk that satisfied her compliance team and impressed the audit committee. The CISO presented the finished binder to the board in March. By June, her organization had deployed three new clinical decision-support agents, a vendor had updated their patient scheduling platform with an embedded AI feature that changed how appointment data was processed, and two service accounts tied to retired pilot projects were still active with permissions nobody had reviewed. When a state health regulator requested her current AI inventory in August, she submitted the March binder. The examiner's first question was whether it was current. She said yes. It wasn't. That single word created a documentation liability that took her legal and compliance teams four months to manage. The audit didn't fail her. The absence of an operating model did. Note: this is a hypothetical scenario illustrating a pattern that is playing out across regulated industries right now, not a real case study.

That scenario isn't unusual. It's the default outcome when an audit closes without an operating model to replace it. The binder becomes the program, the program stops moving, and the enterprise keeps deploying AI at a pace that governance cycles weren't designed to match. Proving the posture was the hard part. Operating it is the part that keeps you defensible when the regulator calls, when the board asks the budget question, or when an agent makes a decision that someone needs to account for.

You picked up this book at exactly the right moment.

The Operating System This Book Installs

This is an operating manual. Not a framework overview. Not a principles document. Not a survey of AI risk categories that leaves you to figure out the execution on your own. Every chapter in this book is built around the same commitment: name the owner, set the cadence, and identify the executive decision each artifact feeds. If a chapter doesn't deliver that, it hasn't earned its place in the book.

Before the four domains begin, this introduction installs the machinery they all run on.

The first piece of that machinery is the AI Security Operating System. This is the governance rhythm that keeps audit evidence current instead of aging into liability. It runs across five time horizons: daily, weekly, monthly, quarterly, and annual. Each horizon has a specific function. Daily rhythms catch what changes overnight in an AI environment that doesn't pause between business hours. Weekly rhythms aggregate signals and surface anomalies that individual daily checks don't connect. Monthly rhythms run the artifact reviews that keep the risk register, the inventory, and the compliance mapping current. Quarterly rhythms feed the board and the executive committee with the posture updates that answer the budget and accountability questions. Annual rhythms rebuild the operating model itself, incorporating what changed in the regulatory environment, the threat landscape, and the enterprise's own AI deployment profile. These five horizons aren't arbitrary. They're designed to close the structural gap between how fast AI environments change and how slowly traditional governance cycles move. Governance that reviews quarterly what changes daily isn't governance. It's documentation. The AI Security Operating System is what bridges that gap with a rhythm that actually matches the asset it's governing.

The second piece is Decision Rights. This is where most AI governance efforts fail quietly and completely. The question of who approves an AI agent, who can suspend it, and who is accountable when it acts cannot be answered for the first time during an incident. By then, the agent has already made the decision, the data has already flowed, and the board is already asking questions that nobody prepared an answer for. The Decision Rights RACI built into this book spans the CISO, General Counsel, Chief Privacy Officer, Chief Data Officer, Chief Financial Officer, and business unit leaders. It answers three specific questions for every AI system in scope: who approves it before deployment, who has authority to suspend it without a committee meeting, and who carries accountability when it acts in a way that causes harm or regulatory exposure. Those three questions have to be answered before the agent is deployed. Not after. The RACI isn't a governance formality. It's the pre-authorization structure that makes the kill switch real instead of theoretical.

The third piece is operated artifact discipline. Every artifact this book installs has three attributes: an owner, a cadence, and the executive decision it feeds. Not a general owner like "the security team." A specific role. Not a vague cadence like "regularly updated." A specific frequency. Not a broad purpose like "supports governance." A specific decision that a specific executive makes because the artifact exists and stays current. This discipline is what separates a security program that runs from a security program that documents. The artifact without an owner doesn't get updated. The artifact without a cadence gets updated when someone remembers. The artifact without a named executive decision gets filed and forgotten. All three attributes have to be present for the artifact to function as a living governance tool rather than a static record.

The contract with you as a reader is equally explicit. This book contains no vendor names. None. The moment a vendor name appears in a governance operating manual, the book becomes a sales document, and the trust breaks. Every recommendation in these pages is written in terms of solution categories and architectural patterns. You'll know what type of tool to evaluate, what capability it needs to deliver, and what operating requirement it has to meet. The selection is yours to make based on your environment, your budget, and your existing stack. That's how it should be.

There's also no security 101 in this book. No AI hype primer. No chapter explaining what large language models are or why prompt injection is a risk category. You already know. You sat through the briefings, read the threat reports, and fielded the questions from your board. This book assumes you're operating at the CISO, director, or manager level and writes to that assumption without apology. Every page is written for someone who needs to know what to do, who owns it, and what decision it feeds. Not for someone who needs to be convinced that AI security matters.

What this book does, specifically, is install four operating models across the four domains where CISOs are measured. It does that through twelve chapters organized into four parts, each following the same arc. And it does it in a way that answers the question every board is asking right now, which is the one that matters most for your budget, your team, and your career.

What the Audit Handed You, and In What Condition It Arrives

The handoff from Volume V is the most important twenty minutes of work in this book, and most readers will skip it because they ran the audit themselves and believe they know what it produced. They know what it produced. What they generally do not know is the condition each artifact is in by the time implementation starts, and that condition determines the first quarter of the program more than any strategic decision they will make.

Ten artifacts crossed over. The four-layer AI inventory names sanctioned, shadow, embedded, and agentic AI. The Non-Human Identity Inventory enumerates every identity capable of taking action. The Agent Boundary Matrix documents what each agent is permitted to do. The AI Vendor Tier Map classifies vendors by access depth. The AI Data Flow Map traces sensitive data through every AI system that touches it. The Regulatory Crosswalk maps obligations to controls. The Defensible AI Security Baseline scores seven security areas across four maturity levels. The Four-Page Board Pack communicates all of it upward. Alongside those sit the risk register entries and the compliance gap analysis the audit produced along the way.

Each of those arrives stale, and they arrive stale at different rates, which is the observation that shapes everything downstream. The Regulatory Crosswalk decays slowly because regulations publish on a schedule. The AI inventory decays weekly because business units adopt tools continuously and nothing in the audit installed a mechanism to catch that. The Non-Human Identity Inventory decays whenever an integration is built, which in most enterprises is more often than anyone tracks. The Vendor Tier Map decays whenever a vendor ships an AI feature, which requires no contract change and generates no notification the security organization reads.

That differential decay is the first thing to measure and the last thing most programs measure. The instinct is to begin with the highest-severity finding, which is a defensible instinct and the wrong sequence. A control built on a stale population produces a coverage claim that is wrong by an unmeasured margin, and the enterprise will not discover the margin until an incident occurs in the part of the population the inventory missed. Measure the drift first. Sample fifteen systems, check whether each still exists, whether the model version changed, whether data access expanded, and whether the security organization would have known. That percentage is the number that tells you whether you are building on a record or on a memory.

The second thing the audit could not hand over is authority. Every artifact describes a state; none of them assign a right. The audit named that AI systems act without documented human decision, and it could not resolve who is accountable when they do, because that resolution requires six executives in a room agreeing to carry something. The absence of that resolution is why so many post-audit programs produce excellent instrumentation attached to nothing, and it is why the ninety-day sequence in Chapter 13 puts the ratification session before the tooling. Instrumentation without authority produces a program that can see everything and stop nothing.

The Fourth Attack Surface

Security programs have organized themselves around three attack surfaces for twenty years, and the organization has held because the three were exhaustive. Infrastructure, where servers and networks are compromised. Applications, where software is exploited. Data, where information is stolen. Every control the enterprise owns maps to one of the three, every budget line traces to one of them, and every security leader can locate any given finding inside the taxonomy without thinking about it.

There is now a fourth, and it is the one the audit found the enterprise had no coverage for. Decisions are an attack surface. An AI system that approves a credit application, adjudicates a claim, prices a contract, routes a shipment, flags a transaction, or authorizes a payment has become the point at which a business outcome is determined, and an attacker who influences that determination has achieved the objective without touching the other three surfaces. No server was compromised. No application was exploited. No data left the building. The enterprise made a decision it would not otherwise have made, acted on it, and generated no alert in doing so.

The distinction is not academic, because the three established surfaces each have a mature detection discipline and the fourth has almost none. Infrastructure compromise produces host telemetry. Application exploitation produces request anomalies. Data theft produces egress. Decision manipulation produces a correct-looking output from a system operating within its permissions, consumed by a business process that has no mechanism for questioning it. Every instrument in this Volume that seems unfamiliar, from behavioral baselining of reasoning to recorded objectives to provenance for machine decisions, exists because the fourth surface needs the detection discipline the first three already have.

What follows from this for a CISO is a budget argument as much as a technical one, and it is worth making explicitly to the CFO. The security program is currently funded to defend three surfaces and is being asked to defend four, and the fourth is the one where the enterprise's most consequential outcomes are now produced. That is not a case for a proportional increase. It is a case for a specific capability the existing spend does not cover, which is exactly what the twelve-month models in this Volume are built to fund.

The four surfaces do not replace each other and the fourth does not diminish the first three. An enterprise that redirects its infrastructure security budget toward AI decision integrity has traded a mature defense for an immature one and will discover the error the ordinary way. The correct posture is additive, and the Volume is organized around building the fourth capability inside the four CISO domains that already own the other three, rather than standing up a parallel function that competes with them for the same executives and the same money.

The Chain That Runs Through All Four Domains

One question sits underneath every domain in this Volume, and naming it here saves the reader from discovering it four separate times. The security question for AI systems is no longer whether an attacker can compromise the model. It is whether an attacker can manipulate a system that already holds legitimate authority. Those are different problems with different controls, and the second one is where the enterprise's actual exposure now sits.

The distinction matters because every traditional access control answers a question that agentic systems have made insufficient. Identity and access management asks whether the actor is authorized. That question is necessary and it stops being sufficient the moment the actor is a system that formulates its own approach to a goal. An agent holding valid credentials, operating inside its permitted scope, calling tools it is allowed to call, can still take an action nobody authorized, because the objective it was pursuing arrived through a channel the enterprise did not control. No credential check catches that. The credentials were fine.

Six elements have to be answerable for every consequential machine action, and this Volume refers to them together as the Agent Authority Chain. Identity: which system acted. Intent: what objective it was pursuing. Authority: who delegated the right to pursue that objective, with what scope and what expiry. Context: what information influenced the reasoning, and whether that information came from a trusted source. Action: what the system actually did, including which tools it invoked and which other agents it delegated to. Impact: what changed in the enterprise as a result.

Most organizations can currently answer two of the six. Identity is usually recorded because the identity provider records it. Action is usually recorded because the tool logs it. Intent, authority, context, and impact are the four that go unrecorded, and they are the four that a regulator, a plaintiff, or a board will ask about after something goes wrong. The chain is not a new control category to purchase. It is the specification for what the instruments in this Volume have to produce between them.

Each Part carries one link of the chain as its primary responsibility. Governance owns authority, because delegation is a decision right. Security operations owns action and the detection of intent that has been hijacked. Third-party risk owns context, because most untrusted context arrives through a vendor's tool or another organization's agent. Data protection owns impact, because impact in an AI estate is usually a change to what the enterprise knows. The chain is what keeps those four programs describing one system rather than four.

The Road Ahead: Four Domains, Same Arc

The board's question is always some version of the same thing. "Now that we've deployed AI, do we need more security or less? And what exactly are we funding?" It sounds like a budget question. It's actually an accountability question. They want to know whether the security function is keeping pace with what the enterprise is deploying, whether the investment is justified, and whether the CISO standing in front of them has a real answer or a slide deck full of principles.

This book answers that question four times, once per domain, with a 1-Year Target Operating Model at the end of each one.

The four domains are Security Governance and Risk Management, Security Operations, Third-Party and Supply Chain Risk, and Data Protection and Privacy. These are the domains where CISOs are measured, where directors build their functions, and where managers run the day-to-day work. They're also the four domains where AI is simultaneously creating the most new risk and offering the most operational leverage. Every part of this book lives at that intersection.

Each domain gets three chapters, and every set of three follows the same arc. The first chapter handles the handoff from the audit. It takes the findings, the inventory, and the risk register from Volume V and shows exactly what governance inherited in that domain and why it's already under pressure. It names the specific problems AI is causing the domain right now, not in theory but in the operating reality of a mid-to-large enterprise running AI at scale. The second chapter flips the lens. It shows how AI is strengthening security in that domain, what the new detection capabilities look like, where machine speed outperforms human review, and how the security function can use AI to do work that wasn't possible before. The third chapter is the operating model chapter. It covers the current state of the domain, the solution categories that matter, the operating rhythms that keep it current, and the 1-Year Target Operating Model that answers the board's question for that specific domain.

The arc is the same across all four parts because the underlying logic is the same. AI is causing new problems and creating new capabilities simultaneously, and the operating model has to account for both. The security function that only sees the risk without capturing the operational leverage will spend more and deliver less. The security function that only sees the leverage without governing the risk will be exposed the moment an agent makes a consequential decision nobody approved.

The answer to the board's question, proven four times over across these four domains, is more security. But transformed.

Not more of the same controls. Not more headcount doing the same work. A fundamentally different function, one that governs machine judgment instead of operating manual controls, supervises autonomous reasoning instead of monitoring human behavior, and treats accuracy and accountability as security properties alongside confidentiality and integrity. The security leader who builds that function doesn't get replaced by AI. They become the executive who makes AI governable. That's a different job than the one most security programs were built to do, and it's a more important one.

Consider what that transformation looks like inside each domain. In Security Governance and Risk Management, the shift is from sampling compliance to running continuous compliance. Quarterly reviews governing daily AI behavior is a structural mismatch that creates documented gaps. The operating model this book installs closes that gap with a governance rhythm that matches the speed of the asset. Risk registers become living documents with owners and update cadences, not snapshots that age between audit cycles. Decision rights get ratified before agents are deployed, not improvised when something goes wrong.

In Security Operations, the shift is from detecting breaches to supervising machine reasoning. The SOC built to catch unauthorized access and data exfiltration wasn't designed to detect prompt injection, training data corruption, or context manipulation. Machine reasoning can be corrupted without triggering a single traditional alert. The operating model this book installs adds a supervision layer where humans govern what machines investigate, and where anomalies in AI behavior get the same detection attention as anomalies in network traffic.

In Third-Party and Supply Chain Risk, the shift is from annual questionnaires to continuous monitoring. A vendor questionnaire sent in January doesn't capture the AI feature that vendor quietly enabled in March. The supply chain that mutates weekly can't be governed by a process that samples annually. The operating model this book installs treats vendor AI feature changes as a distinct risk category with its own detection process, its own escalation path, and its own artifact discipline.

In Data Protection and Privacy, the shift is from protecting databases to governing enterprise memory. Privacy programs built around data collection and storage weren't designed to handle inference, the ability of AI models to derive sensitive attributes from non-sensitive inputs, or enterprise memory, the persistent context that AI agents accumulate over time and that no erasure request was designed to reach. The operating model this book installs treats both as governed assets with their own classification, their own retention policy, and their own erasure path.

Four domains. Four operating models. One arc. And one central lesson running through every chapter of this book.

Enterprise security is no longer protecting information. It is governing organizational intelligence.

AI created a second intelligence layer inside your enterprise. Autonomous agents that make decisions. Models that reason across data at a speed no human review process can match. Persistent memory that accumulates context over time and shapes future outputs in ways that no traditional data map captures. That second intelligence layer is running right now, in your environment, making consequential decisions alongside human ones. The security function that doesn't adapt its operating model to govern that layer will become progressively less relevant, not more. The security function that does adapt becomes the most important strategic function in the enterprise, because it's the one that makes machine judgment accountable.

That's what this book builds. Not a compliance program dressed up with AI terminology. Not a vendor evaluation guide with governance language layered on top. A real operating model, built for practitioners at the CISO, director, and manager levels, that installs the rhythms, the decision rights, the artifact discipline, and the 1-Year Target Operating Model that answers the board's question with owners, cadences, and budget lines.

The audit proved the posture. This book operates it. Every day, in every domain, with every artifact named and every decision fed. That's the commitment this book makes to you, and it starts in the next chapter.

Part I: Security Governance and Risk Management

What the Audit Handed Governance, and What It Could Not Hand Over

Governance received the most complete set of artifacts of any domain in the audit, and it is the domain least equipped to keep them current. That is the tension the next three chapters work inside. The AI inventory, the risk register entries, the compliance gap analysis, and the regulatory crosswalk all arrived in governance's hands because governance is where evidence goes to be organized. What did not arrive with them was a mechanism for keeping any of it true past the week it was produced.

The specific failure is not that governance functions are lazy or under-resourced, though many are both. The failure is architectural. Every governance instrument in a mature security program was designed around an assumption that the thing being governed changes slowly enough that a quarterly review catches material change before it becomes material loss. Policies get reviewed annually. Risk registers get updated at committee. Control testing runs on a sampling cycle. That machinery works when a system's behavior in March is a reasonable predictor of its behavior in June, and it produces confident, well-formatted, wrong answers when it is not.

AI systems break that assumption in three separate ways, and a governance function that only sees one of them will build a program that closes one third of the gap. Model versions change under the enterprise without a change ticket, because the change happened at the provider. System behavior drifts as retrieval corpora grow and agent memory accumulates, without any version changing at all. And the population of AI systems in scope expands through business unit adoption that never touched procurement, which means the inventory is stale in a direction nobody is measuring. Any one of those makes a quarterly cadence insufficient. All three together make it decorative.

The accountability problem sits underneath all of it and is the one that eventually reaches the General Counsel. When a system acts and the action produces loss, the governance function is asked who approved it, who owned it, and who is answerable. In most enterprises running AI at any meaningful scale today, that question produces a pause, then a search, then a reconstruction, then an answer that is honest but not documentary. A reconstruction is not evidence. It is testimony about what people remember deciding, which is exactly the artifact that fails in a regulatory examination and in discovery.

Chapter 1 names what AI is breaking in this domain, working from the audit's own artifacts rather than from generic risk categories. Chapter 2 names how the same technology becomes the only instrument fast enough to govern itself, which is uncomfortable and also true. Chapter 3 names where the market is, which solution categories matter, whether the GRC department survives in its current form, what twelve months of funded work looks like quarter by quarter, and whether governance ends up needing more security or less.

Chapter 1: Governance Inherits the Audit

Everything AI Is Breaking in the Domain That Owns Accountability

CHAPTER 1 OUTCOMES

At the end of this chapter, you will be able to:

1. Explain why an accurate audit binder stops governing on the day it is signed.
2. Name what governance received in the handoff and the condition each artifact arrives in.
3. Identify the velocity mismatch between daily AI change and quarterly governance machinery.
4. Locate the accountability vacuum that opens when no human made the decision.
5. Distinguish shadow AI demand from shadow AI risk, and register both.
6. Assign an owner, a cadence, and a stop authority to every finding the audit produced.

A BINDER IS EVIDENCE. A PROGRAM IS A CONTROL.

The Handoff: What Governance Received and Why the Binder Is Already Aging

The audit is done. The binder exists. Someone printed it, someone bound it, and someone walked it into a board meeting and presented it as proof that your organization understands its AI security posture. And for that moment, it was true. The inventory was accurate. The risk register reflected real findings. The compliance gap analysis mapped to real regulatory requirements. The regulatory crosswalk was current. That binder, on the day it was delivered, represented months of honest, difficult work.

That was then.

The problem with a completed audit isn't that it was wrong. The problem is that it was right at a specific point in time, and AI environments don't hold still long enough for that to matter. Every day that passes between the audit's completion and the moment a regulator, a board member, or an incident response team picks it up, the binder drifts further from reality. Not because anyone failed. Because AI systems mutate continuously, and a static document can't keep up with a moving target.

This is what governance inherited. Not a finished product. A starting point with an expiration date that's already passing.

To understand why this matters so much, you have to understand what "mutate" actually means in an AI environment. It doesn't mean the system crashed or someone changed a configuration file. It means an agent that was scoped to read customer records last quarter now has write access nobody formally approved. It means a model that was deployed for one business unit is now being called by three others through an API that wasn't in the original inventory. It means a vendor updated their product and quietly enabled an AI feature that processes data in a way your compliance gap analysis never considered. None of these changes required a change ticket. None of them triggered an alert. They just happened, the way AI environments do, because the people building and using these systems are moving fast and governance cycles weren't designed to match that speed.

So the binder sits there. Accurate as of six months ago. Increasingly disconnected from what's actually running.

A regulator who receives static evidence doesn't see a thorough organization that completed a rigorous audit. They see an organization that completed a rigorous audit and then stopped. The gap between what the binder says and what the environment actually looks like isn't just a technical discrepancy. It's documented proof that governance was not operating. You didn't just fail to update the inventory. You created a paper trail showing exactly when you stopped paying attention.

That's the liability you're carrying right now. Not the gaps the audit found. The gap between the audit and today.

Consider a hypothetical security director at a mid-sized financial services firm. She spent eight months leading her organization through a comprehensive AI security audit. Her team catalogued 47 AI systems, built a risk register with 112 findings, and produced a regulatory crosswalk that mapped every significant gap to the relevant control framework. The board saw it. The audit committee praised it. The CISO presented it to the regulator as evidence of mature AI governance. Three months later, her organization deployed two new AI agents to automate parts of the loan approval process. Neither agent was added to the inventory. Neither was assessed against the risk register. The vendor managing one of them pushed an update that changed how it handled applicant data. When an examiner asked for the current AI inventory eight months after the original audit, she handed over the original binder. The examiner's first question was: "Is this current?" She said yes. It wasn't. That single word created a documentation liability that took her legal and compliance teams four months to manage. The audit didn't fail her. The absence of an operating model did. Note: this is a hypothetical scenario illustrating a pattern common across regulated industries, not a real case study.

The audit was the proof. The operating model is the practice. And right now, for most governance teams, the operating model doesn't exist yet.

Converting the audit artifacts into operated instruments isn't optional, and it isn't a project for next quarter. Each artifact needs three things before it functions as a living governance tool rather than a historical record. It needs an owner, a specific named role accountable for its accuracy, not "the security team" but a person with a title and a calendar. It needs an update trigger, a defined event or cadence that causes the artifact to be reviewed and revised, not "when something changes" but a specific frequency or condition. And it needs an escalation path, a defined route from the artifact owner to the executive who acts on what the artifact reveals. Without all three, the artifact is decoration. With all three, it's governance.

Start with the AI inventory. Assign it to a specific manager, not a team. Set a monthly review cadence with a defined scope: any new AI system deployed, any existing system that received a vendor update, any agent whose access scope changed. Define the escalation path: material changes go to the security director within 48 hours, the director surfaces them to the CISO weekly. That's an operated inventory. The binder version has none of those three things, which is why it aged the moment the audit closed.

Do the same for the risk register. Assign it to the GRC manager. Set a trigger: any new AI system added to the inventory automatically generates a risk assessment within 14 days. Any existing finding that hasn't been reviewed in 90 days gets flagged for the director. Escalation path: findings that move from medium to high risk go to the CISO before the next board cycle, not at it. The compliance gap analysis and regulatory crosswalk get the same treatment. Owner, update trigger, escalation path. Every artifact. This week, not next quarter.

That's Monday morning's work. Not because it's easy, but because every day it doesn't happen, the liability grows and the binder gets harder to defend.

FIGURE 1.2 **The Handoff**

What governance received from the audit, and the condition it arrives in.

1 THE EVIDENCE BASE

Arrives as: a dated snapshot.

The four-layer inventory, the identity inventory, and the crosswalk were true on the date produced. Nothing in the binder updates itself.

2 THE FINDING REGISTER

Arrives as: an observation list.

Findings name the exposure without naming who closes it, on what cadence, with what authority to stop a system behaving badly.

3 THE REGULATORY CROSSWALK

Arrives as: a point-in-time map.

The mapping held under scrutiny on the audit date. The obligations move, and the crosswalk does not move with them.

4 THE BASELINE

Arrives as: a signed standard.

A defensible baseline proves what was true. It does not prove the estate still matches it this quarter.

THE AUDIT ENDED. THE PROGRAM DID NOT BEGIN.

The Velocity Mismatch: Governing Daily Change With Quarterly Machinery

Governance was built for a specific kind of technology. Technology that changed slowly, required formal change requests, and was operated by humans who made deliberate decisions at deliberate speeds. Quarterly reviews made sense for that environment. A system that was stable last quarter was probably stable this quarter. A risk that was low three months ago was probably still low today. The governance machinery matched the asset it was governing.

AI broke both of those assumptions at once, and governance hasn't caught up.

The velocity mismatch is structural, not procedural. It's not that governance teams are moving slowly because they're lazy or under-resourced. It's that the machinery they're using was designed for a different class of asset. Quarterly governance reviews, annual risk assessments, semi-annual vendor audits, these cadences were calibrated for technology that changed on a human schedule. AI doesn't operate on a human schedule. It changes continuously, at machine speed, in ways that don't generate the signals that traditional governance processes were built to detect.

Think about what actually happens between governance cycles. An agent that was scoped and approved in January gets called by a new workflow in February that nobody formally reviewed. A model that was assessed as low risk in Q1 gets fine-tuned in Q2 in a way that changes its behavior on edge cases nobody tested. A business unit deploys an AI tool under a SaaS contract that procurement approved without a security review because the dollar threshold didn't trigger one. By the time the quarterly governance committee meets, the environment they're reviewing is three months old. They're making decisions about a system that no longer exists in the form they're looking at.

That's not a minor timing issue. That's a governance committee certifying a posture that's already outdated before the meeting ends.

The failure is structural, which means patching the process won't fix it. Adding an agenda item to the quarterly meeting doesn't solve a quarterly meeting problem. Sending more frequent emails to business units doesn't close the gap between daily AI deployment and monthly governance visibility. The machinery has to be rebuilt to match the asset, not adjusted to approximate it.

What that rebuild looks like in practice is a five-horizon operating rhythm. Daily, weekly, monthly, quarterly, and annual. Each horizon has a specific function, a specific owner, and a specific output. Daily rhythms catch overnight changes in AI system behavior, access scope, and agent activity. These aren't full reviews. They're automated checks with exception-based escalation. If an agent's access scope changed, flag it. If a model's output pattern shifted significantly, flag it. If a new API call appears in the agent activity log that wasn't there yesterday, flag it. The daily horizon isn't about human review of everything. It's about automated detection of the things that matter, surfaced to a human who can decide whether they warrant action.

Weekly rhythms aggregate the daily signals. The security manager responsible for AI governance reviews the week's flags, identifies patterns, and determines which ones need escalation versus which ones resolve themselves. This is where individual anomalies become visible as trends. One access scope change might be routine. Three in a week from the same agent might indicate a governance problem. The weekly rhythm is where that pattern becomes visible and actionable before it becomes a finding.

Monthly rhythms run the artifact reviews. The AI inventory gets updated. The risk register gets reviewed for findings that have aged past their remediation timelines. The compliance gap analysis gets checked against any new regulatory guidance that came out in the past 30 days. These are human-led reviews with defined scope and defined outputs. The monthly rhythm is what keeps the audit artifacts current rather than static. It's the operating cadence that turns the binder into a living document.

Quarterly rhythms feed the board and the executive committee. Not raw data. Synthesized posture updates that answer the questions the board actually asks: what changed, what's the current risk level, what decisions need executive attention, and what's the trajectory. The quarterly rhythm is where governance translates operational reality into executive language. It's also where the CISO answers the budget question with evidence rather than estimates.

Annual rhythms rebuild the model itself. The regulatory environment changes. The threat landscape shifts. The enterprise's AI deployment profile grows. The annual rhythm is where the operating model gets recalibrated to match those changes. It's not a repeat of the original audit. It's a structured review of whether the operating rhythms, the artifact discipline, and the decision rights are still fit for purpose given what changed in the past year.

The specific ownership model for this rhythm matters as much as the rhythm itself. The daily and weekly cadences belong to the security manager running AI governance. The monthly artifact reviews belong to the security director who owns GRC. The quarterly board updates belong to the CISO. The annual model rebuild is a joint effort between the CISO, the GRC director, and the General Counsel. Every horizon has a named owner, and that owner has a defined output they're accountable for producing. Without named ownership, the rhythm exists on paper and disappears in practice.

The velocity mismatch doesn't close by itself. It closes when the governance machinery runs at the speed of the asset it's governing. That's what this operating rhythm installs. Not perfection. Not omniscience. A structured, owned, cadenced process that catches what changes daily and surfaces it to the right human at the right time.

FIGURE 1.3

The Velocity Mismatch

Governing daily change with quarterly machinery.

1 THE ESTATE CHANGES DAILY

Models are swapped, prompts are edited, tools are granted, and agents are given new scope without a procurement event to catch any of it.

2 THE COMMITTEE MEETS QUARTERLY

A governance body that convenes four times a year is reviewing a system that has already changed hundreds of times since the last meeting.

3 EVIDENCE AGES AT DIFFERENT SPEEDS

An inventory decays in weeks. A policy decays in quarters. A crosswalk decays when a regulator moves. One review cadence cannot serve all three.

4 THE GAP IS STRUCTURAL

This is not a diligence failure. Quarterly machinery cannot govern a daily estate, and adding meetings does not close the arithmetic.

YOU CANNOT GOVERN A WEEKLY ESTATE ON A QUARTERLY CALENDAR.

The Accountability Vacuum: When No Human Decided

An AI agent approves a loan application. Another one generates a compliance attestation and routes it to the regulator. A third flags a job applicant as high risk based on a pattern in their profile. In each case, a consequential decision was made. And in each case, nobody can clearly answer the question that follows: who is accountable?

This is the accountability vacuum. And it's sitting inside most enterprises right now, unresolved, waiting for the moment an incident forces the question into a boardroom or a courtroom.

The vacuum exists because AI decision-making doesn't map cleanly onto the accountability structures enterprises already have. When a human employee makes a bad decision, accountability flows through the org chart. There's a manager, a process, a policy, and a documentation trail. When an AI agent makes a bad decision, the accountability question fractures across multiple parties simultaneously. Was it the team that built the agent? The manager who approved its deployment? The vendor who provided the underlying model? The executive who signed off on the use case? The business unit that defined the parameters? In most enterprises, the honest answer is that nobody knows, and that uncertainty is itself a liability.

General Counsel's exposure here is specific and serious. When a regulator or a plaintiff's attorney asks for the decision log on a consequential AI action, and the answer is "the agent decided based on its training and the parameters we set," the follow-up question is immediate: who set those parameters, who approved them, and who reviewed the agent's decisions after it was deployed? If those answers are unclear, the discovery process gets very expensive very fast. Unclear accountability in AI decision-making isn't just a governance gap. It's a litigation exposure that the General Counsel needs to understand before it becomes a case.

The attestation trap compounds this. Executives are increasingly signing statements about AI behavior as part of regulatory submissions, vendor contracts, and board certifications. Those statements often say things like "our AI systems operate within defined parameters" or "our AI governance controls are functioning as designed." The problem is that most executives signing those statements have no reliable mechanism to verify them. The agent's behavior since the last review cycle is largely unaudited. The parameters may have drifted. The governance controls may be documented but not actually operating. When an executive signs an attestation about AI behavior they can't verify, they're accepting personal liability for a claim they can't support with evidence. That's not a theoretical risk. That's a signature on a document that a regulator can subpoena.

The artifact that closes the accountability vacuum is the Decision Rights RACI. Not a general responsibility matrix. A specific, ratified document that answers three questions for every AI system in scope. Who approves this system before it's deployed? Who has authority to suspend it without convening a committee? And who carries accountability when it acts in a way that causes harm or regulatory exposure?

Those three questions need answers before the agent is deployed. Not after. The RACI covers six roles: the CISO, the General Counsel, the Chief Privacy Officer, the Chief Data Officer, the Chief Financial Officer, and the relevant business unit leader. Each role has a defined set of decisions they own, a defined set of decisions they're consulted on, and a defined set of decisions they're informed about after the fact. The CISO owns the technical deployment approval and the suspension authority. The General Counsel owns the legal and regulatory exposure assessment. The CPO owns the data processing and consent review. The CDO owns the data quality and model governance sign-off. The CFO owns the financial risk threshold. The business unit leader owns the use case definition and the operational accountability for the agent's outputs.

Drafting this RACI is this week's work, not next quarter's. Start with the AI systems already in production. Map each one to the six roles. Identify the gaps where no role currently owns a specific decision. Those gaps are your accountability vacuums, and they need to be closed before the next agent deploys. The RACI doesn't need to be perfect on the first draft. It needs to be ratified, meaning the six roles have reviewed it, agreed to their accountabilities, and signed off. A ratified imperfect RACI is infinitely more defensible than a perfect one that nobody has seen.

Once the RACI is ratified, the kill-switch authority becomes real. Right now, in most enterprises, the theoretical ability to suspend an AI agent exists somewhere in the technical stack. The practical ability, meaning a named person with pre-authorized authority who can make that call without a committee meeting, often doesn't. The RACI makes it explicit: this role has suspension authority for this class of AI system, and that authority is pre-authorized and doesn't require escalation before it can be exercised. That pre-authorization has to be rehearsed. Not once in a tabletop exercise. Quarterly, with the actual people who hold the authority, using a realistic scenario that tests whether the authority can be exercised in the time window that matters.

The accountability vacuum doesn't close by assigning blame after the fact. It closes by assigning responsibility before the decision is made. That's what the Decision Rights RACI does. And it's the artifact that makes every other governance instrument defensible when the question gets asked.

FIGURE 1.4 **The Accountability Vacuum**

The four questions that have no answer when no human decided.

1 WHO APPROVED IT

A model selected a course of action inside a delegated scope. No approval record exists because no approval step was ever crossed.

2 WHO OWNS THE OUTCOME

The business owns the consequence, the platform team owns the system, and neither one owns the decision the system made.

3 WHO CAN REVERSE IT

Reversal requires knowing what changed, when, and on whose authority. Without provenance, remediation begins with reconstruction.

4 WHO PAYS WHEN IT IS WRONG

Insurers, regulators, and customers all ask this question in different language. The enterprise answers it once, or answers it badly three times.

ACCOUNTABILITY DOES NOT DISAPPEAR WHEN THE DECISION IS DELEGATED.

Shadow AI and Intelligence Corruption: The Risks the Register Never Sees

The AI inventory your audit produced captured the systems governance knew about. That's its fundamental limitation. The fastest-growing AI risk categories in most enterprises are the ones the inventory was never designed to see.

Shadow AI is the first of those categories. Business units are adopting AI tools at a pace that formal procurement and security review processes can't match. A marketing team subscribes to an AI content platform on a corporate card. A finance team connects a generative AI tool to their reporting environment through a browser extension. A legal team uses an AI contract review service that processes sensitive agreements through a third-party model. None of these went through a security review. None of them appear on the inventory. None of them were assessed against the risk register. And none of them will surface through traditional governance channels unless someone specifically goes looking.

The instinct to prohibit shadow AI is understandable. It's also counterproductive. Prohibition drives adoption underground. When business units can't get AI tools approved through official channels, they find unofficial ones. The tools don't disappear. They just become invisible to governance. A governance function that can't say yes safely, meaning one that has no fast-track approval path for low-risk AI tools, loses jurisdiction over the tools that get deployed anyway. The shadow grows in direct proportion to how hard the official channel is to use.

The operating response to shadow AI has two parts. The first is discovery. Run a shadow AI discovery process in one business unit this week. Don't start with a policy announcement or a prohibition reminder. Start with a structured conversation: what AI tools are your people using to get their work done, where did those tools come from, and what data do they touch? The answers will be more extensive than most security teams expect. Document what you find. Add it to the inventory. Assess it. This discovery process then becomes a quarterly rhythm across all business units, not a one-time exercise.

The second part is a fast-track approval path. Define a low-risk AI tool category with clear criteria: no sensitive data processing, no autonomous decision-making, no external data sharing, no persistent memory. Tools that meet all four criteria get a 72-hour security review and a provisional approval. Tools that don't meet them go through full assessment. When business units know there's a fast path for low-risk tools, they use it. The shadow shrinks because the official channel is actually usable. That's the governance outcome you're building toward.

Intelligence corruption is the second ungoverned risk category, and it's the one that keeps almost nobody up at night yet, which is exactly why it should.

Traditional security thinking is built around a specific threat model: an attacker gains unauthorized access, exfiltrates data, or disrupts systems. The detection logic is built around that model. Unauthorized access triggers alerts. Data exfiltration triggers data loss prevention rules. System disruption triggers availability monitoring. Intelligence corruption doesn't fit any of those patterns. It doesn't require unauthorized access. It doesn't exfiltrate data. It doesn't disrupt systems. It changes what the AI system believes, and therefore what it decides, without leaving a trace that traditional security monitoring was designed to catch.

Poisoned knowledge bases are one vector. An AI agent that answers compliance questions draws from a knowledge base. If that knowledge base contains subtly altered regulatory text, the agent gives subtly wrong compliance answers. The answers look authoritative. They're formatted correctly. They cite the right sources. They're wrong in ways that don't trigger any alert because the system is functioning exactly as designed. The corruption is in the content, not the system.

Manipulated agent memory is another vector. Agents that maintain persistent context across sessions can be manipulated through carefully crafted inputs that alter what the agent "remembers" about a user, a process, or a decision. Over time, those manipulated memories shape the agent's outputs in ways that drift from its original design. The drift is gradual. It doesn't trigger a threshold. It doesn't generate an incident. It just changes what the agent does, slowly, in ways that may not be visible until the cumulative effect is significant.

Altered retrieval data is the third vector. Retrieval-augmented generation systems pull context from external data sources to ground their responses. If those data sources are compromised or manipulated, the model's outputs are corrupted at the retrieval layer. The model itself is fine. The retrieval pipeline is fine. The data it's retrieving from is not. And nothing in a traditional security monitoring stack is watching for that.

Ask your team this question today: if someone altered our AI knowledge bases or agent memory right now, what would detect it? If the answer is "we're not sure" or "nothing currently," you have an intelligence corruption gap. The detection response isn't complex, but it has to be deliberate. Define a baseline for each AI system's output patterns. Set up automated comparison checks that flag significant deviations from that baseline. Establish a quarterly human review process where a subject matter expert spot-checks AI outputs against the ground truth sources the system is supposed to be drawing from. These aren't sophisticated technical controls. They're structured human oversight processes that catch what automated monitoring misses.

Neither shadow AI nor intelligence corruption appears on a traditional risk register because traditional risk registers weren't designed to capture them. The risk register your audit produced lists the systems you knew about and the risks those systems carry. It doesn't have a category for systems you don't know exist or for corruption that doesn't generate a loggable event. Adding those categories to the risk register is a specific, immediate action. Create a shadow AI risk category with a quarterly discovery cadence. Create an intelligence corruption risk category with a baseline deviation detection requirement. Assign an owner to each. Set the escalation path. Now they're on the register, which means they're in scope for governance, which means the board learns about them from you instead of from a regulator.

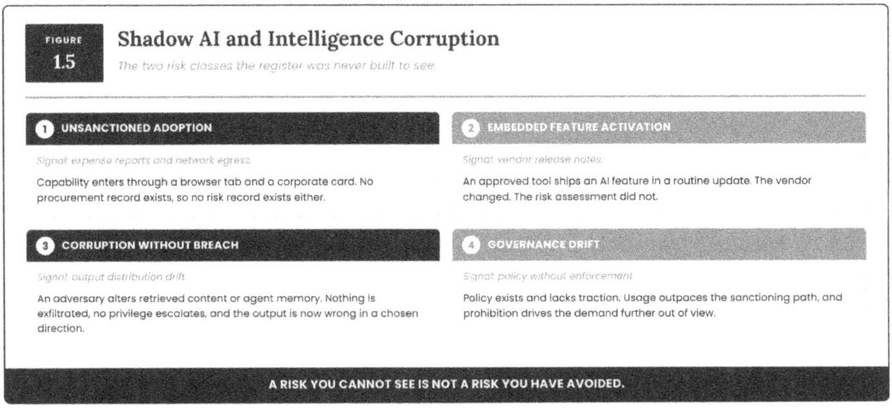

The Insurance and Regulatory Squeeze: Exposure Arriving From Both Sides

While governance is working through the internal problems, external pressure is building from two directions at once. Regulators and insurers are both arriving at the same moment, with different instruments, and the gap between what they're asking for and what most enterprises can produce is growing.

The regulatory picture is genuinely complicated right now. Overlapping AI regulations across jurisdictions aren't just creating compliance work. They're creating contradictory compliance positions. A data processing practice that satisfies one jurisdiction's AI regulation may violate another's. An AI governance disclosure that meets one regulator's standard may fall short of another's. An enterprise operating across North America, the EU, and the UK is simultaneously subject to requirements that were written by different bodies, at different times, with different underlying philosophies about what AI governance means. Mapping those requirements against each other is not a one-time exercise. It's a continuous process because the regulatory environment is still being written in real time.

The practical response is a regulatory crosswalk that's actively maintained, not filed. The crosswalk your audit produced mapped your compliance gaps against the regulatory requirements that existed at audit time. That's a starting point. The operated version of that crosswalk has a named owner, a monthly review cadence, and a defined process for incorporating new regulatory guidance within 30 days of publication. When a new AI regulation drops in a jurisdiction you operate in, the crosswalk gets updated, the gaps get assessed, and the CISO gets a briefing on the exposure before the next board cycle. That's the difference between a compliance function that's reactive and one that's current.

The insurance picture is a different kind of problem. Cyber insurance policies were written for a specific threat model: unauthorized access, data breach, ransomware. The coverage language, the exclusions, the claim triggers, and the coverage limits were all calibrated around that model. AI creates a new class of loss events that don't fit cleanly into that model. An AI agent that approves fraudulent transactions isn't a data breach. An AI system that generates a compliance response that turns out to be wrong isn't a cyber incident. An AI-driven decision that results in a discrimination claim isn't a ransomware event. Coverage that was designed for one threat model is silently failing to cover the losses that the new threat model is generating.

Most enterprises don't know this yet. They have a cyber insurance policy, they've renewed it, and they assume it covers AI-related losses because AI is a technology and their policy covers technology incidents. That assumption hasn't been tested because most AI-related claims are still new. When they get tested, the coverage gaps will become visible at the worst possible moment, which is during a claim.

The action here is specific. Pull your current cyber insurance policy this week. Read the coverage definitions, the exclusions, and the claim triggers with AI scenarios in mind. Ask your broker three direct questions: does this policy cover losses from AI agent decisions, does it cover losses from AI-generated compliance responses that turn out to be incorrect, and does it cover third-party claims arising from AI-driven decisions about individuals? Get the answers in writing. If the coverage is silent on those scenarios, that's a gap that needs to go to the CFO and the General Counsel before the next renewal, not after a claim makes it visible.

Enterprise customers are adding a third source of external pressure. Major contract negotiations now routinely include AI governance requirements. Customers want evidence that their vendors have AI governance programs in place. They want to know what AI systems touch their data, how those systems are governed, and what the vendor's process is for disclosing AI-related incidents. These requirements are showing up in master service agreements, data processing agreements, and security addenda. A vendor that can't answer those questions clearly is losing contracts to vendors that can.

If your organization is a vendor to other enterprises, this is a revenue exposure, not just a compliance one. The AI governance evidence your customers are asking for is the same evidence your operating model produces when it's running correctly. A current AI inventory, a maintained risk register, a ratified Decision Rights RACI, and a documented governance rhythm are exactly what a sophisticated customer's procurement team wants to see. An enterprise that has those artifacts can answer the customer's questions in 48 hours. An enterprise that's still working from the original audit binder takes weeks, and often can't produce evidence that's current enough to satisfy the customer's requirements.

The squeeze from both directions, regulatory and insurance, with customer pressure added on top, means the cost of an ungoverned quarter is no longer theoretical. It's a regulatory finding, a coverage gap, and a lost contract, potentially all at once. The operating model in the next chapter is what prevents that outcome. But the urgency for building it starts here, with a clear picture of what's arriving from outside while governance works through the internal rebuild.

The Evidence Half-Life Problem: Artifacts That Age at Different Speeds

Every artifact the audit handed governance has a half-life, and no governance program measures it. That is a specific, correctable failure, and it is upstream of most of the velocity problems this chapter has already named. The regulatory crosswalk ages slowly, because regulations move in quarters and years. The AI inventory ages weekly, because business units adopt tools continuously. The risk register ages at whatever speed the underlying systems change, which is a different speed for every entry. Treating all four artifacts on a single quarterly review cadence means three of them are reviewed at the wrong frequency, and the program cannot say which three because nobody has measured the rates.

The measurement itself is not difficult, and the fact that almost nobody does it is the finding. Take the AI inventory as the audit delivered it, sample fifteen systems across business units, and check four things per system: does it still exist, has the model version changed, has its data access expanded, and would the security organization have learned about any of those changes through a process rather than through an accident. Run the same sample ninety days later. The percentage of the sample that materially drifted between the two dates is the inventory's decay rate, and it converts an argument about cadence into a number the CFO can fund against.

What that number usually reveals is uncomfortable in a specific direction. Enterprises that run this exercise honestly tend to find that the inventory decays fastest in the business units with the most sophisticated technical staff, because those are the units capable of adopting tools without help. The governance instinct is to treat that as a compliance failure by those units. The operational reality is that the sanctioned intake path was slower than the work required, and a capable team routed around it. A decay rate concentrated in your strongest units is a signal about your intake process, not about their discipline.

The half-life framing also settles a debate that consumes disproportionate committee time in most programs. The question of whether the risk register should be reviewed monthly or quarterly has no general answer, because the register contains entries with radically different underlying volatility. A risk entry describing a foundation model dependency changes when the vendor changes providers, which could be any week. A risk entry describing a regulatory exposure changes when guidance publishes, which is predictable. Assign a review frequency per entry based on the volatility of what the entry describes, and the committee stops arguing about cadence in the abstract.

The decision rule that comes out of this is narrow and enforceable. Every governance artifact carries three attributes recorded alongside it: a named owner, a measured or estimated decay rate, and a review frequency derived from that rate rather than from the committee calendar. An artifact without a decay rate is an artifact nobody has decided how to maintain, and the honest description of that artifact is that it was true once. The audit produced a set of things that were true once. Governance is the function that decides which of them stay true, and at what cost.

FIGURE 1.6 **The Evidence Half-Life Problem**

Artifacts age at different speeds and require different refresh cadences.

ARTIFACT	DECAYS WHEN	PRACTICAL HALF-LIFE	REQUIRED CADENCE
AI Inventory	A model, prompt, or tool changes	Weeks	Continuous discovery
Non-Human Identity Inventory	A credential is issued or orphaned	Weeks	Continuous discovery
Agent Boundary Matrix	Scope or tool access expands	Months	Monthly review
Vendor Tier Map	A vendor ships an AI feature	Months	Continuous monitoring
Regulatory Crosswalk	An obligation moves	Quarters	Quarterly refresh
Defensible Baseline	The estate drifts from the standard	Quarters	Quarterly attestation

ONE REVIEW CADENCE CANNOT SERVE SIX DECAY RATES.

The Committee That Cannot Decide: Governance Authority Without Teeth

Most enterprises stood up an AI governance committee within the last two years, and most of those committees cannot stop anything. That is the finding worth naming precisely, because it is invisible in every artifact the audit produced. The committee exists, it meets, it has a charter, and its minutes show discussion of AI risk. What the minutes do not show, in the overwhelming majority of cases, is a decision that changed what a business unit was permitted to do. A committee that has never said no has not been tested, and an untested authority is a claim rather than a control.

The mechanism of the failure is structural rather than personal. The committee is typically constituted as a cross-functional advisory body, chaired by someone senior enough to convene it and not senior enough to override a business unit leader who disagrees. When a business unit proposes an AI deployment the committee has concerns about, the committee records the concerns and the deployment proceeds, because nothing in the charter converts a concern into a constraint. The committee members are not weak. They have been given a forum and told it is an authority.

The test that reveals this is a single question, and any CISO can run it this week. Ask when the committee last suspended, blocked, or imposed binding conditions on an AI system that a business unit wanted to run. Not raised concerns about. Not recommended additional controls for. Stopped or constrained, with the constraint enforced. If the answer is that it has not happened, the follow-up question is whether that reflects an environment with no problems or a body with no authority, and the audit findings on the accountability gap have already answered it.

The consequence surfaces at the worst moment, which is during an examination or after an incident. A regulator asking how AI deployments are governed will accept a committee structure as an answer and will then ask for examples of governance decisions. The enterprise that produces a year of minutes showing discussion without decision has demonstrated the opposite of what it intended to demonstrate. Worse, it has created a documentary record showing that concerns were raised, recorded, and not acted upon, which is a more damaging artifact than having no committee at all.

The correction is not a bigger committee or a more senior chair, though both may help. It is that the Decision Rights RACI must assign the suspension authority to a named individual rather than to the committee as a body, because bodies do not act between meetings and incidents do not wait. The committee's proper function is to ratify policy, adjudicate contested cases, and hold accountability records. The stopping authority belongs to a person, and that person's name appears in a signed document. A governance structure that cannot name that person in one sentence has not resolved the accountability question; it has distributed it until it disappeared.

Delegated Authority and the Revocation Problem

The audit produced an inventory of non-human identities and a matrix of what each agent is permitted to do. Both are static documents describing a static permission grant, and agentic systems have stopped being static in a way that makes both insufficient without extension. An agent that can invoke another agent has created an authority relationship nobody granted explicitly, and the second agent is now acting on behalf of a chain that terminates in a human who has no visibility into what the chain did.

The mechanics are worth stating plainly because the abstraction hides the problem. A human authorizes an agent to complete a task. The agent decomposes the task and delegates part of it to a second agent, which holds its own credentials with its own scope. The second agent invokes a tool that accesses a database. Four parties participated and one authorization occurred. When the database record changes, the accountability question has four candidate answers and the enterprise has documented none of them. The audit's boundary matrix describes what each agent may do individually and says nothing about what the composition of their permissions produces.

Authority attenuation is the control that is missing, and its absence is the reason delegation chains escalate privilege without any individual grant being wrong. In a properly attenuated chain, an agent can delegate no more authority than it holds, and typically less: narrower scope, shorter expiry, fewer tools. Most current implementations do the opposite by default, because the second agent authenticates with its own service credentials rather than with an attenuated token derived from the first agent's authority. The result is that delegation frequently escalates rather than narrows, and it escalates in a way that produces no alert because both identities were operating within their own grants.

Revocation is the harder half and the one most enterprises have not tested. When a human's access is revoked, the identity provider handles it and downstream systems honor it within a session or two. When an agent's authority needs to be revoked, the enterprise has to answer whether revocation reaches the agents that agent delegated to, whether it invalidates tokens already issued to tools, whether it terminates work already in flight, and whether the agent's persistent memory retains anything that would let it resume. In most environments today the honest answers are no, no, no, and yes. An agent whose authority was revoked at eleven o'clock may still be acting at noon through a chain nobody traced.

The decision rule belongs in the Decision Rights RACI rather than in a technical standard, because it is an accountability decision before it is an engineering one. Every agent capable of delegating to another agent has a named human whose authority the chain terminates in, a maximum delegation depth, and a revocation path that has been tested rather than assumed. Test it the same way the kill-switch gets tested: revoke an agent's authority in a controlled exercise, and measure how long the delegated chain continues to act. That number is the practical scope of your revocation capability, and any enterprise that has not measured it does not have one.

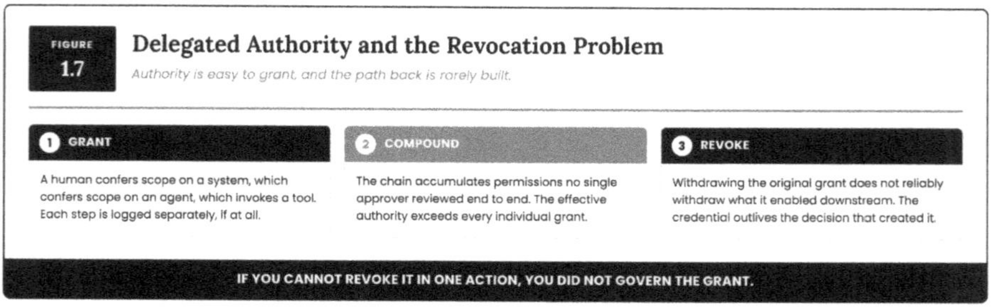

FIGURE 1.7 Delegated Authority and the Revocation Problem

Authority is easy to grant, and the path back is rarely built.

Putting It Into Practice

Governance inherited the audit. This week, it stops treating the binder as the program. The work that follows isn't a project plan for next quarter. It's a set of specific actions with named owners and defined outputs that need to start moving before the end of this week.

First, convert the four audit artifacts into operated instruments. Take the AI inventory, the risk register, the compliance gap analysis, and the regulatory crosswalk. For each one, assign a specific named role as owner, not a team. Define the update trigger: what event or cadence causes this artifact to be reviewed and revised. Define the escalation path: who receives material changes, at what speed, and through what channel. Write those three attributes down for each artifact and share them with the relevant directors this week. That's the difference between a binder and a governance program.

Second, draft the Decision Rights RACI. Start with the AI systems already in production. Map each one to the six roles: CISO, General Counsel, CPO, CDO, CFO, and the relevant business unit leader. For each system, answer the three questions: who approves it, who can suspend it, and who carries accountability when it acts. Identify the gaps where no role currently owns a specific decision. Schedule a working session with the General Counsel this week to walk through the attestation exposure and the discovery risk. The RACI doesn't need to be final before that conversation. It needs to be started.

Third, launch shadow AI discovery in one business unit. Choose a business unit that's actively using AI tools and schedule a structured conversation with their leadership this week. The agenda is simple: what AI tools are your people using, where did they come from, and what data do they touch? Document the answers. Add any unregistered systems to the inventory. Flag any that touch sensitive data for immediate risk assessment. Use the findings to build the case internally for a fast-track approval path for low-risk AI tools.

Fourth, ask your team the intelligence corruption question today. If someone altered your AI knowledge bases or agent memory right now, what would detect it? If the answer isn't clear and specific, that's a gap that goes on the risk register this week, with a detection baseline requirement assigned to a named owner and a 30-day deadline for the first baseline to be established.

Fifth, brief the General Counsel on the attestation exposure and pull the cyber insurance policy for a coverage gap review. Those two conversations need to happen before the next board cycle, not at it. The General Counsel needs to know that executives are potentially signing attestations about AI behavior they can't verify. The CFO needs to know that the insurance coverage may not extend to AI-driven loss events. Both of those conversations are easier to have before an incident than after one.

The problems named in this chapter are real, they're current, and they're growing. The next chapter shows how AI itself becomes governance's most powerful instrument for solving them. But the foundation for that work starts with naming the problems clearly, assigning them to owners, and starting the conversion from binder to operating program this week. That's what the AI IT Security Implementation & Strategy™ actually looks like at the start: not a grand transformation, but a set of specific, owned, time-bound actions that close the gap between where the audit left off and where a real operating program begins.

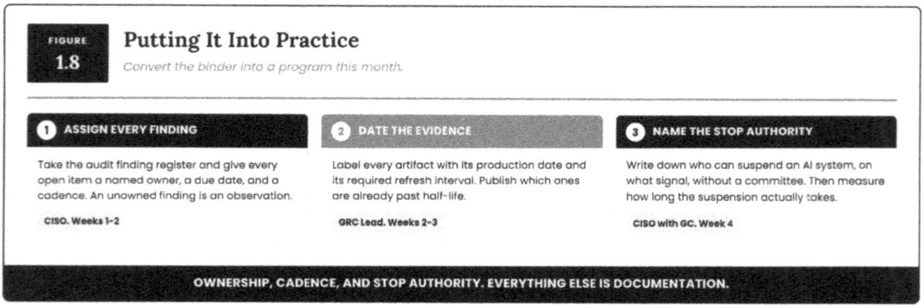

Chapter 2: Governance Gains an Engine

How AI Rebuilds Compliance From Sampling Into Signal

CHAPTER 2 OUTCOMES

At the end of this chapter, you will be able to:

1. Explain why sampling-based compliance was a capacity compromise, not a methodology.
2. Operate continuous compliance across evidence feeds, policy conflicts, and regulatory change.
3. Maintain a living risk register where machines draft and humans adjudicate.
4. Run the Shadow AI Sanctioning Pathway to convert rogue demand into governed capability.
5. Install the five-horizon governance rhythm across daily through annual cadences.
6. Replace control counts with four measures that describe governance performance.

THE SAME TECHNOLOGY CREATING THE EXPOSURE IS THE ONLY THING FAST ENOUGH TO GOVERN IT.

From Sampling to Signal: The First Complete Governance in Security History

Governance has always been a sampling problem. You pick a subset of controls to test. You review a fraction of your policies. You collect evidence annually because that's as far as human effort can reach. The sample is honest. The methodology is sound. And the result is a picture of your posture that's accurate for the controls you tested and silent about everything else. For decades, that was the best governance could do. Not because security teams weren't good at their jobs. Because there weren't enough hours in a year to test everything, review everything, and map everything against every applicable regulation at the same time.

AI ends that constraint. Completely.

Machine reading doesn't get tired. It doesn't have a calendar. It doesn't need to prioritize which controls to test this quarter because it can test all of them. When you feed your control library, your policy documents, your configuration data, and your regulatory requirements into an AI-powered governance engine, the system can evaluate every control against every applicable regulation, every day. Not a sample. Every control. That's not an incremental improvement on traditional governance. That's a category change.

To understand why this matters, think about what sampling actually hides. When a governance team tests 30% of controls in a given cycle, the 70% they didn't test isn't confirmed compliant. It's unconfirmed. The risk register doesn't show a gap there because nobody looked. The board report doesn't flag it because the evidence collection process never reached it. The regulatory crosswalk doesn't surface it because the mapping only covers what was reviewed. Sampling doesn't just leave gaps in your knowledge. It creates false confidence about the gaps it doesn't see. A governance program that samples 30% of controls and finds no issues hasn't proven 70% compliance. It's proven 30% compliance and left the rest unexamined.

Complete governance changes the fundamental nature of what a CISO can say to a board. The shift is from "we tested a representative sample of controls and found these findings" to "we evaluated every control against every applicable regulation and this is the current state." Those are not the same statement. The first is an audit result. The second is a control plane. One is retrospective assurance. The other is real-time governance. The board's question about whether the enterprise is exposed doesn't get answered with a sample. It gets answered with complete coverage.

The architectural shift that makes this possible has three components. The first is machine reading of policy and regulatory text. AI systems trained on regulatory language can parse the full text of applicable regulations, extract specific control requirements, and map those requirements against your policy library automatically. When a new regulation drops, the system reads it, identifies the gap between what it requires and what your policies currently say, and surfaces that gap to the GRC team within hours rather than weeks. The team doesn't need to read the full text of every proposed statute and manually compare it to 200 policies. The machine does that work. The humans adjudicate what the machine finds.

The second component is continuous configuration assessment. Your AI governance engine pulls configuration data from the systems in scope and compares it against your control baselines on a defined cadence. Daily is achievable. For high-risk systems, near-real-time is achievable. When a configuration drifts from its baseline, the system flags it, classifies the severity, and routes it to the right owner. The governance team doesn't discover configuration drift at the next quarterly review. They discover it the morning it happens.

The third component is evidence generation as a continuous output rather than a periodic collection effort. Every assessment the system runs produces a timestamped evidence record. Every control evaluation generates a finding that either confirms compliance or documents a gap. Every policy comparison produces a mapping that shows where the policy covers the requirement and where it doesn't. This evidence accumulates continuously. By the time the quarterly board cycle arrives, the evidence isn't something the team needs to go collect. It's already there, already organized, and already current to the day of the meeting.

The function that was hardest to staff becomes the first to be transformed because the staffing problem was always a volume problem. There weren't enough analysts to cover everything. AI doesn't solve the analyst shortage by replacing analysts. It solves it by removing the volume constraint. Your analysts stop spending their time collecting evidence and start spending it adjudicating findings. That's a better use of their judgment, and it's a better governance program.

The operating model for this shift is specific. Assign a GRC manager as the owner of the governance engine's daily output. Define the exception threshold: what severity of finding gets routed to the manager immediately versus queued for the weekly review. Define the escalation path: what findings go to the security director within 24 hours, and what goes to the CISO before the next board cycle. Set the cadence for human adjudication: daily exceptions reviewed same-day, weekly aggregation reviewed every Monday, monthly policy conflict report reviewed by the director in the first week of each month. These aren't suggestions. They're the operating rhythm that converts the machine's output into governed decisions.

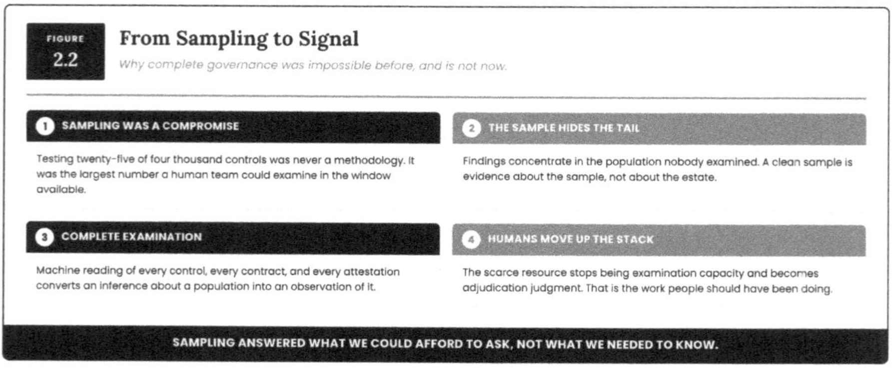

Continuous Compliance in Operation: Evidence Feeds, Policy Conflicts, and Regulatory Intelligence

Continuous compliance sounds like a technology promise. It isn't. It's an operating discipline that uses technology to do the volume work so humans can do the judgment work. The distinction matters because organizations that treat continuous compliance as a tool purchase rather than an operating model change end up with an expensive system that generates reports nobody acts on.

The first operational component is automated evidence feeds. In a traditional compliance program, evidence collection is a manual process. Someone sends a questionnaire. Someone else fills it out. A third person reviews the responses and maps them to the control framework. This process takes weeks, produces point-in-time snapshots, and scales poorly as the number of systems in scope grows. Automated evidence feeds replace that process with a continuous pull from the systems themselves. Configuration data, access logs, policy acknowledgment records, training completion data, and vendor attestations all flow into the governance platform on a defined cadence. The evidence is current because it's collected continuously, not because someone remembered to send a questionnaire.

The immediate practical step is to identify your highest-effort manual evidence collection process and replace it first. Don't try to automate everything at once. Find the one evidence collection workflow that consumes the most analyst time, produces the most outdated results, and creates the most friction with the teams being sampled. Build the automated feed for that workflow. Validate that the feed produces accurate, complete evidence. Then expand. The first automated feed proves the model and builds internal confidence. It also frees up analyst capacity that can be redirected to the adjudication work the machine can't do.

Policy conflict detection is the second component, and it's the one that catches what no human review process ever reliably finds. A mature enterprise has hundreds of policies. Data classification policies, access control policies, acceptable use policies, AI governance policies, vendor management policies, incident response policies. These policies were written at different times, by different teams, for different purposes. Nobody sat down with all of them at once and checked for contradictions. The result is a policy library that contains conflicts nobody knows about.

Consider a hypothetical GRC director at a large insurance company. Her team had spent three years building out a comprehensive policy library. Over 180 policies across every security domain. Each policy had been reviewed and approved through the right channels. What nobody had done was read all 180 policies against each other at the same time. When her team ran an AI-powered policy conflict scan as part of standing up their continuous compliance program, the system identified 23 direct conflicts within the first week. One data retention policy required customer interaction records to be kept for seven years. A separate AI governance policy required model training data, which included those same records, to be purged after 24 months. Both policies had been approved. Both were in force. They directly contradicted each other, and the contradiction had been sitting undetected for over a year. Note: this is a hypothetical scenario illustrating a pattern common across large enterprises, not a real case study. The point isn't that the team failed. The point is that human review processes aren't designed to catch cross-document conflicts at scale. Machine reading is.

The operating model for policy conflict detection is straightforward. Run the full policy library through the conflict detection engine monthly. Route all identified conflicts to the policy owner of each affected document within 48 hours of detection. Set a 30-day resolution window: the owners either resolve the conflict or escalate it to the security director for adjudication. Track open conflicts in the risk register with a named owner and a resolution deadline. Close the loop by confirming that the resolved version of each policy doesn't introduce new conflicts with other documents. That last step is the one most teams skip, and it's the one that prevents the same problem from reappearing in a different form.

Regulatory intelligence is the third component. The regulatory environment for AI is not stable. Proposed statutes are moving through legislative processes in multiple jurisdictions simultaneously. Guidance documents are being issued by financial regulators, health regulators, and data protection authorities at a pace that no human monitoring process can reliably track. An enterprise operating across multiple jurisdictions needs to know about a new regulatory requirement before it's in force, not after the first examination cycle where it's being evaluated. The window between a regulation's publication and its effective date is the window where governance can prepare. Missing that window means scrambling to catch up while the clock is already running.

AI-powered regulatory intelligence closes that window. The system monitors regulatory publications across the relevant jurisdictions, identifies proposed and enacted requirements that apply to your AI systems, maps those requirements against your current policy and control posture, and surfaces the gap analysis to the GRC team in time to act. The team doesn't need to subscribe to 15 regulatory newsletters and manually cross-reference each publication against 200 policies. The machine does the monitoring and the initial mapping. The humans decide what the gap means and what to do about it.

The weekly GRC operating rhythm that ties these three components together looks like this. Every Monday morning, the GRC manager reviews the week's automated evidence exceptions, the open policy conflicts, and the new regulatory intelligence flags. Exceptions that were auto-resolved get confirmed. Exceptions that require human judgment get assigned to an owner with a resolution deadline. Policy conflicts that are past their 30-day window get escalated to the director. Regulatory intelligence flags get triaged: low-impact items go into the monthly review queue, high-impact items get a briefing scheduled with the CISO within the week. Every Friday, the manager produces a one-page status update that shows what was flagged, what was resolved, what's open, and what needs director attention. That status update feeds the monthly director review and the quarterly board pack. Nothing gets assembled from scratch. Everything is already documented.

The daily rhythm is lighter but just as important. The automated systems run overnight. The morning exception report lands in the GRC manager's inbox before 8 a.m. Anything flagged as high severity gets reviewed before noon. Anything that requires immediate escalation gets routed to the director before end of day. The daily rhythm isn't about reviewing everything. It's about catching the things that can't wait a week. Most days, the high-severity queue is empty. On the days it isn't, the response is already structured and the escalation path is already defined. That's what a running compliance program looks like.

FIGURE 2.3

Continuous Compliance in Operation

Three feeds that replace the quarterly evidence scramble

1 EVIDENCE FEEDS

Output: a standing control state.

Control evidence is collected from the systems of record continuously rather than assembled by hand before an assessment window.

2 POLICY CONFLICT DETECTION

Output: a conflict queue.

Machine comparison surfaces where two policies require different things of the same system, which is the failure humans never have time to find.

3 REGULATORY INTELLIGENCE

Output: a change alert.

Obligation changes are tracked against the crosswalk so the map moves when the requirement moves, not at the next annual refresh.

EVIDENCE ASSEMBLED CONTINUOUSLY IS EVIDENCE THAT IS TRUE WHEN ASKED FOR.

The Living Risk Register: AI Maintains, Humans Adjudicate

A risk register that isn't updated continuously is a historical record. That's a hard statement for organizations that spent significant effort building a thorough risk register as part of their audit. The effort was real. The findings were accurate. But a register that reflects the risk landscape from six months ago and hasn't been touched since isn't a governance tool. It's an archive.

The problem with a static register isn't just staleness. It's the decisions it feeds. A CISO who presents a quarterly risk update to the board is presenting a picture of the risk landscape that's only as current as the last time someone updated the register. If the register was last updated three months ago, the board is making resource allocation decisions based on a three-month-old risk picture. If a new AI agent was deployed two months ago and never assessed, the risk it carries isn't in the register. The board doesn't know about it. The budget discussion doesn't account for it. The decision is made on incomplete information, and nobody in the room knows that.

Redesigning the register as an operated artifact means changing who maintains it and how new entries get created. In the traditional model, a human analyst reviews the environment, identifies risks, writes entries, and updates the register on a defined schedule. The schedule is the constraint. Between scheduled reviews, new risks accumulate without being captured. In the operated model, AI monitors the environment continuously and drafts new entries automatically when its detection logic identifies a risk that isn't already in the register. The human's job shifts from writing entries to adjudicating what the machine drafted.

The detection logic that feeds new entries has three main sources. The first is telemetry from the AI systems themselves. When an agent's behavior deviates significantly from its baseline, when an access scope changes without a corresponding change ticket, or when a model's output patterns shift in ways that suggest drift, the governance engine flags the anomaly and drafts a risk entry. The entry includes the system involved, the nature of the deviation, the potential impact, and the recommended severity classification. The GRC manager reviews the draft, confirms or adjusts the severity, assigns an owner, and approves the entry. The machine did the detection and the drafting. The human did the judgment.

The second source is the regulatory intelligence feed. When a new regulatory requirement maps to a gap in your current control posture, that gap is a risk. The system identifies it, drafts an entry, and routes it to the GRC manager for adjudication. The entry includes the regulation, the specific requirement, the current control state, and the gap. The manager reviews the draft, assesses the materiality of the gap, assigns a remediation owner, and sets a timeline. The regulatory crosswalk and the risk register stay synchronized because they're fed by the same intelligence source.

The third source is the shadow AI discovery process. When the discovery workflow identifies an unsanctioned AI tool, the system automatically drafts a risk entry for the tool. The entry includes what was found, where it was found, what data it appears to touch, and an initial risk tier based on the tiering criteria defined in the Sanctioning Pathway. The GRC manager reviews the draft, confirms the tier, and either routes the tool into the sanctioning workflow or escalates for immediate action. The register captures shadow AI risk as it's discovered rather than at the next scheduled review.

Every entry in the operated register carries four attributes. An owner: the specific named role accountable for the risk's remediation or acceptance. An update trigger: the specific event or cadence that causes the entry to be reviewed. A cadence: the frequency at which the owner confirms the entry is still accurate. And the executive decision it feeds: the specific board or executive committee decision that this risk entry informs. Without all four attributes, the entry is information. With all four, it's governance.

Stale entry management is the part most teams overlook. In a register that grows continuously, entries that were relevant six months ago may no longer reflect the current risk landscape. An AI system that was flagged as high risk because of a configuration gap may have had that gap remediated. A risk that was accepted at a certain level may need to be re-evaluated because the regulatory environment changed. The operated register has a staleness flag: any entry that hasn't been reviewed by its owner within the defined cadence gets flagged automatically and routed to the director for follow-up. The director either confirms the entry is still accurate, updates it, or closes it if the risk has been resolved. Nothing sits in the register unreviewed past its cadence without someone being accountable for that delay.

The weekly human adjudication rhythm for the register is a 45-minute standing meeting between the GRC manager and the security director. The agenda is fixed. Review all machine-drafted entries from the past week and confirm or adjust severity. Review all entries past their review cadence and assign follow-up actions. Review all entries escalated by the manager for director-level judgment. Review the entries feeding the next board cycle and confirm they're current and accurate. That meeting doesn't need to be longer than 45 minutes because the machine has already done the preparation work. The humans are adjudicating, not assembling. That's the operating model the register was designed to support.

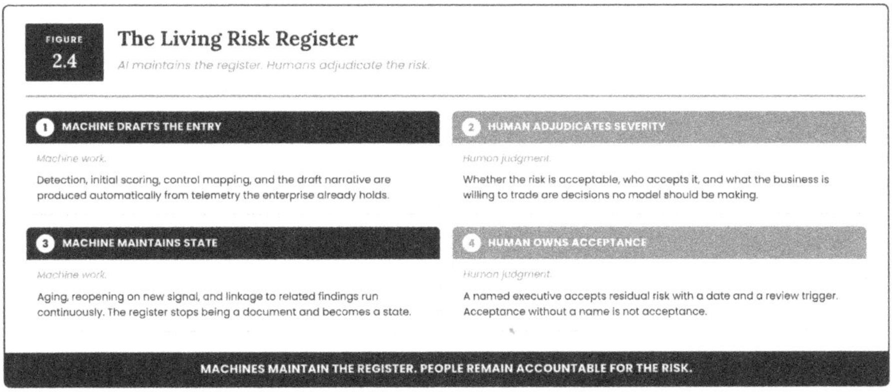

The Shadow AI Sanctioning Pathway: Converting Rogue Demand Into Governed Capability

Chapter 1 named shadow AI as the risk the register never sees. The operating response isn't prohibition. Prohibition doesn't make shadow AI disappear. It makes it invisible. The response is a Sanctioning Pathway: a structured workflow that discovers unsanctioned tools, risk-tiers what it finds, migrates users into governed environments, and converts shadow demand into sanctioned capability without destroying the productivity that created it.

The pathway has four stages. Discovery, tiering, migration, and sanctioning. Each stage has a defined owner, a defined output, and a defined timeline. Together they turn governance from the department of no into the fastest safe path to yes. That reframe matters. Business units adopt shadow AI because they need the capability and the official channel is too slow or too opaque to use. The Sanctioning Pathway wins back jurisdiction by being faster and clearer than the workaround.

Discovery is the first stage. AI-powered discovery tools scan the enterprise estate for unsanctioned AI tools. They look at browser extensions, SaaS subscriptions, API calls to external AI services, and network traffic patterns that indicate AI tool usage. The scan runs on a defined cadence, quarterly at minimum, monthly in high-risk environments. The output is a list of discovered tools with the business unit where they were found, the data they appear to touch, and an initial risk signal based on the tool's known data handling practices. The discovery output goes to the GRC manager within 48 hours of the scan completing. The manager reviews it, removes any tools that are already sanctioned, and routes the remainder into the tiering stage.

Tiering is the second stage. Every discovered tool gets classified against four criteria. Does it process sensitive data? Does it make autonomous decisions? Does it share data with external parties? Does it maintain persistent memory? A tool that fails none of these criteria is Tier 1: low risk, eligible for fast-track sanctioning. A tool that fails one criterion is Tier 2: moderate risk, eligible for sanctioning with controls. A tool that fails two or more criteria is Tier 3: high risk, requires full assessment before any sanctioning decision. The tiering criteria are documented, approved by the CISO, and applied consistently. The GRC manager applies the tier classification. The security director reviews all Tier 3 classifications before the tiering stage closes.

Migration is the third stage, and it's the one that determines whether the pathway actually works in practice. Users who are discovered using shadow AI tools don't get a prohibition notice. They get an offer. The offer is access to a governed sandbox environment where they can continue doing the work they were doing, with the same or comparable capability, within a security boundary that governance can see and manage. The sandbox is pre-configured with the access controls, data handling requirements, and monitoring that the tool's tier classification requires. Tier 1 tools get a lightweight sandbox with basic logging. Tier 2 tools get a more controlled environment with data classification enforcement. Tier 3 tools either wait for full assessment or get an interim alternative that meets the user's core need without the high-risk characteristics.

The migration offer is made by the security manager to the business unit leader, not to individual users. The conversation is: "We found your team is using this tool. We want to support that. Here's how we can give you the same capability in a way that we can govern and you can use without risk to the organization." That framing matters. It's not a compliance conversation. It's a partnership conversation. Business units that feel helped rather than policed are more likely to use the official channel next time instead of going around it.

Sanctioning is the fourth stage. Once a tool is in the governed sandbox and the migration is confirmed, the formal sanctioning decision gets made. For Tier 1 tools, the GRC manager makes the sanctioning decision with director notification. For Tier 2 tools, the security director makes the sanctioning decision with CISO notification. For Tier 3 tools, the CISO makes the sanctioning decision with General Counsel and CPO consultation. The sanctioning decision gets documented in the AI inventory with the tool's tier, the data it's authorized to process, the controls in place, and the review cadence. The tool is now governed. The risk is now visible. The user is now working inside the security boundary instead of outside it.

The intake workflow for new AI tool requests, as opposed to discovered shadow tools, follows the same tiering logic but starts at the request stage rather than the discovery stage. A business unit submits a request through a defined intake form. The form captures the tool's name, the use case, the data it will process, and the business unit leader's name as the accountable owner. The GRC manager tiers the request within five business days. Tier 1 requests get a provisional approval within 72 hours of tiering. Tier 2 requests get a full security review completed within 15 business days. Tier 3 requests get a full assessment with a defined timeline communicated to the business unit within five business days of tiering. The timeline is explicit and communicated upfront. Business units know how long the process takes before they start it. That predictability is what makes the official channel usable.

Launch the Sanctioning Pathway in the business unit where shadow discovery ran in Chapter 1. Don't wait to build a perfect process before starting. The first business unit is the pilot. The pilot teaches you where the workflow breaks, where the tiering criteria need refinement, and where the migration offer needs adjustment. Run it, learn from it, and refine it before expanding to the next business unit. The goal of the pilot isn't perfection. It's proof that the pathway works and that governance can say yes faster than the workaround.

FIGURE 2.5 **The Shadow AI Sanctioning Pathway**

Converting rogue demand into governed capability instead of driving it underground.

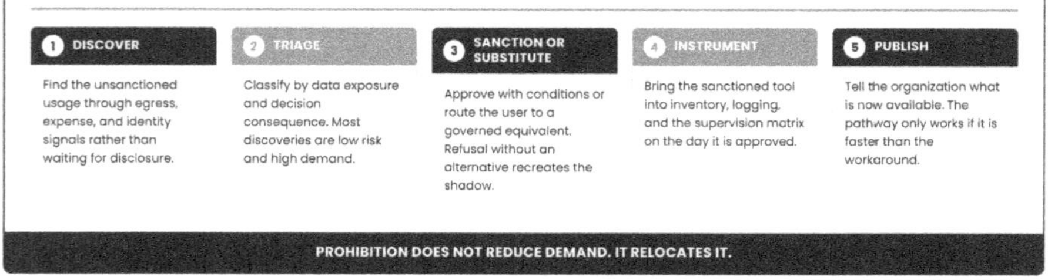

Board Reporting That Assembles Itself: The Scorecard as Living Instrument

The quarterly board pack scramble is one of the most reliable sources of security team burnout in large enterprises. Two weeks before the audit committee meeting, someone sends a calendar invite titled "Board Pack Prep." The next two weeks are spent chasing evidence, collecting screenshots, writing narrative summaries of data that was current three weeks ago, and assembling a document that represents the security posture as of roughly a month before the board sees it. By the time the CISO presents it, the evidence is already aging. The board is making decisions based on a picture that's already out of date, and everyone in the room knows it.

That scramble ends when evidence is continuous.

The AI Security Scorecard is designed as a continuously maintained instrument, not a document that gets assembled before each board cycle. It draws from the living risk register, the automated evidence feeds, the policy conflict log, and the regulatory intelligence output. Every data point in the scorecard has a source, a timestamp, and an owner. When the board cycle arrives, the scorecard isn't assembled. It's reviewed. The GRC manager confirms the data is current. The security director reviews the narrative. The CISO approves the final version. The assembly time drops from two weeks to two days, and the evidence is current to the morning of the meeting rather than the month before it.

The scorecard structure answers the questions the board actually asks. Not the questions security teams want to answer. The questions the audit committee, the

CFO, and the CEO ask when they're deciding whether the security function is doing its job and whether the investment is justified.

The first question is: are we exposed? The scorecard answers this with a current risk summary drawn directly from the living register. The number of open high-severity findings, the number of AI systems with unresolved compliance gaps, the number of shadow AI tools discovered in the past quarter and their current disposition. These aren't percentages or trend lines presented without context. They're specific numbers with specific owners and specific resolution timelines. The board can see exactly what the exposure is and who is accountable for closing it.

The second question is: what are we funding? The scorecard answers this with a capability summary that maps each major security investment to the risk it addresses and the outcome it produces. Not "we invested in continuous compliance tooling." Rather: "Continuous compliance tooling identified 23 policy conflicts and 14 regulatory gaps in Q3 that manual review would not have caught until Q4 at the earliest. The cost of late detection in the two highest-severity gaps would have exceeded the annual cost of the tooling." That's the language that justifies budget. It's specific, it's comparative, and it connects the investment to a business outcome the board can evaluate.

The third question is: what decisions do you need from us? This is the section most board packs skip, and it's the most important one for the CISO's relationship with the board. Every board cycle, there should be one to three specific decisions the CISO is bringing to the board for resolution. Not for information. For decision. A risk acceptance that exceeds the CISO's authority level. A budget request tied to a specific regulatory deadline. A policy question that requires board-level ratification. When the CISO brings decisions rather than just updates, the board relationship shifts from oversight to partnership. The board is governing, not just receiving reports.

The scorecard also carries a forward-looking section: what's changing in the next 90 days that the board needs to know about. New regulatory requirements taking effect. Planned AI deployments that will expand the risk surface. Vendor contracts coming up for renewal that include AI governance provisions. This section positions the CISO as someone who governs proactively rather than reacts to events. That's the board relationship the AI IT Security Implementation & Strategy™ is designed to build.

Standing evidence transforms the CISO's board relationship in a specific and concrete way. When evidence is assembled once a quarter from manual collection, the CISO is always in a defensive posture. The board asks a question that wasn't anticipated. The evidence that would answer it wasn't collected. The CISO has to say "I'll follow up on that." When evidence is continuous and the scorecard reflects it, the CISO can answer questions that weren't anticipated because the data is already there. That shift, from "I'll follow up" to "here's the current data," changes the board's perception of the security function from reactive to operational. That perception change is worth more than any individual finding or investment justification.

Set up the scorecard structure this week. Don't wait until the next board cycle to build it. Use the current state of the living register and the automated evidence feeds to populate the first version, even if it's incomplete. A scorecard that's 70% automated and 30% manually filled is still a better instrument than one that's 100% manually assembled every quarter. The first version shows the board that the infrastructure exists. Each subsequent version shows it getting more current and more automated. That trajectory is itself a governance story worth telling.

The Five-Horizon Governance Rhythm: What Happens Daily, Weekly, Monthly, Quarterly, and Annually

Continuous compliance produces a volume of signal that a quarterly committee cannot absorb, and the failure that follows is predictable. The platform detects a policy conflict on a Tuesday, the finding waits for the next governance committee, and by the time it is discussed the underlying system has changed again. A governance function that installs continuous evidence collection without installing a matching cadence has built a faster sensor attached to the same slow actuator.

The five-horizon rhythm exists to fix that, and it is the operating layer that makes every other instrument in this chapter usable rather than merely instrumented.

The daily horizon belongs to the machine and to one named human who reviews an exception queue. The continuous-control platform runs its checks, the model registry reconciles against discovery, and anything that breaches a defined threshold lands in the queue. The named reviewer, usually a GRC analyst, clears the queue each morning with three possible dispositions: no action, escalate to the weekly review, or escalate immediately to the named decision-rights owner. That third disposition is the one that justifies the daily cadence. Without it, the daily review is a log inspection, and a log inspection can be weekly.

The weekly horizon is where the governance function reconciles what changed against what was approved. New AI systems discovered during the week are dispositioned against the sanctioning pathway. Model version changes detected by the registry are checked against whether anyone was notified through a process. Policy conflicts surfaced by the platform are triaged into the ones requiring legal interpretation and the ones requiring a policy amendment. The weekly meeting is short, it is attended by the GRC manager and the security director rather than by executives, and it produces a written disposition list rather than minutes. Its purpose is to keep material change from waiting a month for a decision that takes ten minutes.

The monthly horizon is the first one that involves a decision an executive has to own. The governance committee meets, receives the accumulated escalations, and exercises the authority the Decision Rights RACI ratified: approving deployments, imposing conditions, suspending systems, and assigning accountability where a gap has been identified. This is also where the shadow AI discovery cycle reports its findings from the business unit covered that month, and where the intake-to-approval time gets published. That published number is the single most useful discipline in the monthly cycle, because a sanctioning pathway that is slower than the workaround will be abandoned regardless of policy, and the only way to know is to measure it in public.

The quarterly horizon is board-facing and the annual horizon is model-facing. Quarterly, the scorecard assembles from continuous evidence, the CISO reviews and approves rather than assembles and defends, and the board receives one measured number the program produced itself. Annually, the operating model is recalibrated: the regulatory crosswalk is reviewed against the year's published guidance, the Decision Rights RACI is reviewed against how far the enterprise's autonomous systems have expanded beyond the scope the original ratification covered, and the artifact decay rates are remeasured. A governance function running all five horizons has closed the velocity mismatch. A function running only the quarterly and annual ones has documented it.

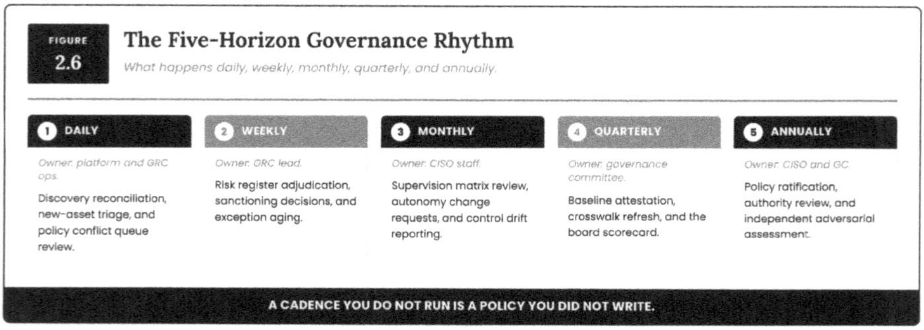

Measuring Governance: Four Numbers That Replace Control Counts

Governance functions have historically reported activity, because activity was measurable and outcomes were not. Policies published, controls tested, assessments completed, findings closed. Every one of those numbers can improve while the enterprise's actual governance posture degrades, and every experienced CISO knows it, which is why board members have learned to receive governance reporting politely and act on it rarely. Continuous evidence makes a different set of numbers available for the first time, and four of them are worth reporting.

The first is inventory drift, expressed as the percentage of the AI population that changed materially since the last measurement without the change reaching the governance function through a process. This number is uncomfortable by design. A drift rate of thirty percent per quarter means that roughly a third of what governance believes it is governing is described inaccurately, and it converts every downstream coverage claim into an estimate. Reported over four quarters, a falling drift rate is the single clearest evidence that the sanctioning pathway and the registry are working.

The second is time-to-disposition for discovered systems, measured from the moment a system appears in discovery to the moment it has a registry entry with a named owner and a decision. This number tells you whether governance is absorbing what discovery finds or accumulating it. A program with excellent discovery and a ninety-day disposition time has built a very good instrument for generating a backlog. The target is not a specific number; the target is a trend that does not lengthen as discovery coverage expands, because a disposition time that grows with volume means the process does not scale.

The third is intake-to-approval time for the sanctioning pathway, and it is the only one of the four that governance should publish to the business rather than to the board. The pathway competes with the workaround, and the competition is decided entirely on speed. A published number creates the pressure that keeps the pathway fast, exposes the point at which it stopped being fast, and gives business unit leaders a reason to use it that does not depend on compliance argument. Governance functions resist publishing this number for exactly the reason it should be published.

The fourth is the accountability coverage rate: the percentage of production AI systems with a ratified decision right naming an approver, a suspension authority, and an accountable executive. This is the number that answers the question the General Counsel is actually worried about, and it is the number that most directly represents whether the program has done the thing the audit said was missing. A coverage rate below one hundred percent is not a failure; it is a work list. A coverage rate nobody has computed is an unmeasured legal exposure, and the difference between those two positions is a quarter of effort.

Taken together, these four displace the activity metrics rather than supplementing them, and the displacement should be deliberate. A board that receives drift, disposition time, intake time, and accountability coverage can form an independent judgment about whether governance is operating. A board that receives control counts is being asked to trust the function's self-assessment, which is precisely the arrangement that produced the green dashboard the audit was built to see through.

FIGURE 2.7 **Measuring Governance**

Four numbers that replace counting controls.

MEASURE	WHAT IT ANSWERS	WHY CONTROL COUNTS FAIL	REPORTED TO
Coverage	What fraction of the AI estate is under governance	A count of controls says nothing about what is uncovered	Board, quarterly
Time to Govern	How long from discovery to a governed state	Counts are static. Latency exposes the real gap	Committee, monthly
Evidence Freshness	How old the newest proof of each control is	A control can exist and its evidence be stale	GRC, weekly
Time to Stop	How long to suspend a misbehaving system	No control count captures reversal capability	Board, quarterly

COUNT WHAT GOVERNS THE ESTATE, NOT WHAT SITS IN THE POLICY LIBRARY.

Governing Intent, Not Just Access

Continuous compliance solves the evidence problem and leaves an authorization problem that access controls were never built to address. The governance function can now demonstrate that every AI system holds appropriate permissions, that every non-human identity is inventoried, and that every access grant traces to an approval. All of that can be true while an agent pursues an objective nobody in the enterprise authorized, because the objective is not a permission and no permission system evaluates one.

The failure has a shape that recurs across every organization running agents against external content. A user gives an agent a legitimate goal. The agent retrieves external material to accomplish it: a supplier's document, a web page, an inbound email, a support ticket, a code repository. That material contains instructions, and the agent has no reliable way to distinguish content it should reason about from instructions it should follow. The objective shifts. The agent continues operating within every permission it holds, calling approved tools, producing plausible output, in service of a goal that arrived from outside the enterprise. Volume V named the mechanism as prompt injection functioning as privilege escalation. The governance consequence is that the enterprise's authorization model has been bypassed without any access control failing.

Governing intent means recording the authorized objective as a first-class artifact and evaluating actions against it, which is a control that sits outside the model rather than inside it. Before an agent begins consequential work, the objective is recorded: what it is permitted to accomplish, what outcomes are in scope, and what actions are categorically out of scope regardless of what the reasoning concludes. That record is what a policy enforcement point evaluates against, and the evaluation happens at the action boundary rather than at the prompt. A model asked to police its own objective is being asked to detect a manipulation of the faculty doing the detecting.

The governance function's specific job here is to decide which objectives require recording and who may set them, which is a decision rights question rather than an engineering one. Not every agent task warrants a recorded objective; an agent summarizing a document does not. Any agent that can move money, change a configuration, modify a record of consequence, send external communication, or delegate to another agent does. Draw that line explicitly, because a line drawn implicitly by whoever configured the system will be drawn at whatever was convenient during implementation.

The decision rule is that authority attaches to intent, not to identity, for any action class the governance committee designates as consequential. An agent holding valid credentials that takes an action outside the recorded objective has committed an authorization failure even though every permission checked out. Instrument for that case specifically, because it produces no signal in any access log, and treat the count of such events as a governance metric alongside the four from earlier in this chapter. A count of zero means either that intent is well governed or that nobody is watching for it, and the way to tell the difference is a deliberate test.

Recording the objective is necessary and it is not the control. An objective sitting in a register is documentation until something reads it at the moment an action is about to occur, and the engineering layer that does the reading is what turns intent governance from a policy into an enforcement point. That layer is a runtime monitor: a small, deterministic check that sits outside the model, holds the recorded objective, observes the action sequence the agent is producing, and evaluates consistency before the consequential action executes.

The monitor does not need to understand the agent's reasoning, and building one that tries will produce a system as manipulable as the one it is monitoring. It needs to answer narrower questions that have deterministic answers. Is this action class within the set the recorded objective permits. Is this destination within the permitted set. Does this sequence contain an action the objective's scope excludes categorically. Has the sequence exceeded the number of steps the objective was scoped for. Each of those is a rule evaluated against a record, not a judgment, which is precisely why the monitor is harder to subvert than any instruction placed in the model's context.

Where the monitor and the circuit breaker differ is worth keeping straight, because programs frequently build one and believe they have both. The circuit breaker bounds volume: how much, how fast, how many. The intent monitor bounds direction: toward what. An agent that stays well inside every volume limit while pursuing an objective an attacker supplied has defeated the circuit breaker completely and is exactly the case the monitor exists for. Build both, at the same layer, reading from the same recorded objective and the same authority grant.

Governing the Governance Engine: Who Watches the System That Watches

Every instrument in this chapter is an AI system, and each one produces an output the enterprise treats as authoritative. The continuous-control platform decides which controls are satisfied. The policy conflict scanner decides which policies contradict each other. The regulatory intelligence feed decides which guidance is relevant. The living register drafts which risks exist. The contract intelligence engine decides which clauses are missing. Every one of those is a machine judgment presented to executives as a finding, and an enterprise that has instrumented its operational agents while leaving its governance engine uninstrumented has built a compliance posture with an unmonitored dependency at the center of it.

The failure this creates is worse than the equivalent failure in security operations, because governance outputs are consumed with less skepticism. When a triage copilot closes an alert incorrectly, an analyst may notice. When a continuous-control platform reports a control as satisfied, nobody re-performs the test, because eliminating the manual re-performance was the reason the platform was purchased. A corrupted governance engine produces a green posture with continuous evidence behind it, which is a considerably more convincing artifact than the green dashboard the audit was built to see through.

The attack surface is the same one Chapter 5 describes for the SOC's own tooling, applied to a different set of systems. A regulatory intelligence feed that ingests external sources is consuming untrusted content and producing conclusions the compliance function acts on. A policy conflict scanner reading the enterprise's own documents will read whatever was written into them, including text placed there by someone who understood that the scanner would read it. A contract intelligence engine reading vendor-supplied contracts is processing documents authored by the counterparty, which is precisely the untrusted-content condition the retrieval boundary rule exists for. None of these require sophistication. They require an adversary who noticed that the governance layer reads things.

The instrumentation required is the same instrumentation the rest of this Volume specifies, turned inward, and the honest reason most programs have not applied it is that the findings would be about the program itself. Every governance AI system appears in the model registry. Every one carries a behavioral baseline covering its finding rate, its source mix, and its output distribution. Every one appears in the Human Supervision Matrix with an autonomy level, because a platform that can close a control finding without human review is taking an autonomous action with governance consequence. Every one is covered by the adversarial evaluation test set, and the objective hijacking and context manipulation classes apply directly.

Two specific controls carry more weight than the others and should be implemented first. The first is independent re-performance sampling: a small percentage of the platform's control conclusions get tested manually each quarter by someone who does not see the platform's rationale first, producing an agreement rate exactly as the SOC produces one for its copilot. The second is write authorization on the corpora the governance engine reads, meaning the policy repository, the control library, and the regulatory intelligence sources carry access controls and integrity monitoring proportional to the fact that a machine is now reading them to reach conclusions the board sees.

The decision rule is that the governance function holds itself to the standard it applies to every other domain, without exemption and without a separate lighter treatment for tooling it owns. A GRC director who cannot state the current agreement rate for their continuous-control platform is in the same position as a SOC director who cannot state it for their triage copilot, and the position is the one this Volume opened by describing: a confident posture with no measurement behind it. Publish the agreement rate quarterly alongside the four governance numbers. It is the least comfortable of the five and the one that most directly answers whether the rest of them mean anything.

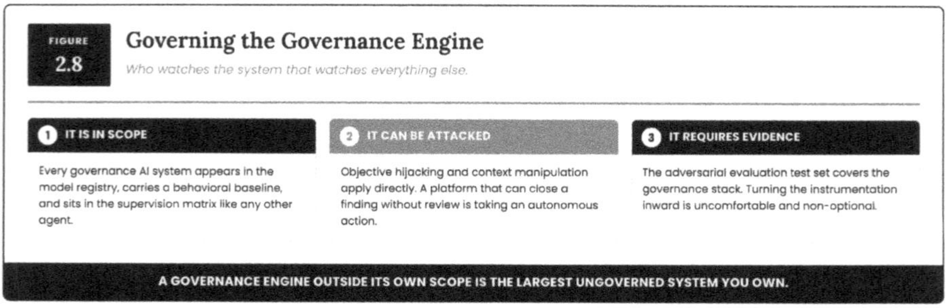

Putting It Into Practice

Governance gained its engine this chapter. Now it needs to run. The actions below aren't a roadmap for next quarter. They're the specific moves that start this week and build on each other in a defined sequence.

Stand up the first automated evidence feed this week. Identify the single highest-effort manual evidence collection process in your GRC function. Map the data source, the collection frequency, and the format the evidence needs to be in. Configure the automated pull from that source. Validate the output against a manual collection to confirm accuracy. Assign the GRC manager as the owner of the feed's daily exception review. That one feed is the proof of concept for continuous compliance. It also frees up the analyst hours that will fund the next feed.

Redesign the risk register with AI as maintainer and humans as adjudicators. Take the current register and add the four required attributes to every existing entry: owner, update trigger, cadence, and the executive decision it feeds. For entries that can't be assigned all four attributes, flag them for the director's attention in the next weekly meeting. Configure the governance engine to draft new entries from telemetry anomalies, regulatory intelligence flags, and shadow AI discovery outputs. Set the weekly adjudication meeting between the GRC manager and security director as a standing calendar item starting next Monday. The register doesn't become a living document by being declared one. It becomes one by having an operating rhythm that keeps it current.

Launch the Sanctioning Pathway in the business unit where shadow discovery ran. Schedule the migration offer conversation with the business unit leader this week. Bring the tiering criteria, the sandbox description, and a specific offer: here's what we found, here's what tier it is, here's what we can give you that meets your need within a governed boundary. Document the conversation. Move the tool into the sandbox. Add it to the inventory. That first completed sanctioning is the proof that the pathway works, and it's the story you tell to the next business unit when you expand the discovery process.

Connect the living register to a draft scorecard and show the audit committee one page of evidence that was current the morning of the meeting. It doesn't need to be the full scorecard structure. One page. Current risk summary from the register. One investment-to-outcome statement. One decision you're bringing for board resolution. Current as of today. That single page does more to shift the board's perception of the security function than a 40-slide deck assembled two weeks ago. It shows governance running in real time. And nothing funds the transformation this book is building faster than a board that has seen what real-time governance looks like and wants more of it.

FIGURE 2.9

Putting It Into Practice

Stand up the first continuous loop this quarter

1 PICK ONE CONTROL FAMILY

Choose the family with the worst sampling coverage and move it to complete machine examination. Report what the sample was missing.

GRC Lead. Weeks 1–3

2 OPEN THE SANCTIONING PATH

Publish a route to approved AI capability with a response time measured in days. Track requests, approvals, and time to sanction.

CISO. Weeks 2–6

3 INSTRUMENT YOUR OWN ENGINE

Register every governance AI system, baseline its behavior, and place it in the supervision matrix before it closes another finding.

Platform Owner. Week 4

CONTINUOUS DOES NOT MEAN EVERYWHERE AT ONCE. IT MEANS ONE LOOP THAT ACTUALLY RUNS.

Chapter 3: The Governance Endgame

Current Focus, Solution Categories, and the 1-Year Target Operating Model

CHAPTER 3 OUTCOMES

At the end of this chapter, you will be able to:

1. Describe where AI governance programs are actually focused today.
2. Evaluate solution categories as architectural patterns rather than products.
3. Answer whether the GRC function survives in its current form.
4. Build a one-year governance target operating model with owners and budget lines.
5. Quantify AI Security Debt and report it as a compounding liability.
6. Decide whether governance ends up needing more security capacity or less.

THE CATEGORY OUTLIVES THE VENDOR. BUY THE PATTERN, NOT THE LOGO.

Where the Market Is Now: The Current Focus of AI Governance Programs

Most governance programs right now are doing one of two things. They're either installing real operating rhythms, or they're laminating policies. The gap between those two activities is enormous, and the programs doing the laminating often can't tell the difference yet. That's not a criticism. It's a market reality. AI governance as a practiced discipline is still young, and most teams are building it while running everything else at the same time.

The first thing almost every governance program builds is an AI use policy. That makes sense. It's the fastest artifact to produce, it signals to the board that governance is responding to AI, and it gives the legal team something to point to when a regulator asks what the organization's position on AI is. The problem isn't that AI use policies are wrong. The problem is that most programs stop there and call it governance. A policy document sitting on an intranet page that nobody reads before deploying an AI tool isn't governance. It's documentation. Governance is what happens when someone actually enforces it.

Acceptable-use standards are the natural extension of the policy layer, and the better programs are building them with real specificity. Not "employees should use AI responsibly" but "employees may not input customer PII into any AI tool that hasn't been approved through the sanctioning pathway, and the following data categories are prohibited from AI processing without a completed privacy impact assessment." That level of specificity is what makes a policy enforceable. It's also what makes it useful to the manager who has to explain to a business unit why their tool request was declined.

AI risk committees are forming across the market, and the maturity spread is wide. Some committees have real decision rights. They approve AI deployments, they can suspend systems, and they have a defined quorum and a defined escalation path to the board. Others are advisory bodies that meet quarterly to discuss AI risk in general terms and produce minutes that nobody acts on. The difference between those two types of committees isn't the people in the room. It's whether the committee has been given ratified authority to make binding decisions. A committee without decision rights is a conversation. A committee with decision rights is a control.

Conformity programs for arriving AI statutes are the newest area of activity, and the pressure is real. The EU AI Act is the most structured of the current regulatory requirements, but it's not the only one. Financial regulators in the US, the UK, and Australia are all publishing AI governance expectations that carry examination weight. Healthcare regulators are issuing guidance on AI in clinical decision-making. Data protection authorities are extending existing privacy frameworks to cover AI inference and automated decision-making. The governance teams that are building conformity programs now are doing so against a moving target, because the regulatory text keeps changing and the guidance keeps getting more specific.

The scramble to extend existing GRC processes to cover AI models and agents is where most programs are spending the majority of their effort right now. The instinct is reasonable. You already have a risk assessment process. You already have a control framework. You already have a vendor management workflow. Why not extend them to cover AI? The answer is that AI breaks the assumptions those processes were built on. A traditional risk assessment assumes the system being assessed is static between reviews. An AI model isn't static. Its behavior can change with every update, every fine-tuning cycle, and every shift in the data it's processing. Extending a process designed for static systems to cover dynamic ones produces assessments that are accurate on the day they're completed and increasingly inaccurate every day after.

The mature programs are the ones that recognized this limitation early and rebuilt the process rather than extended it. They're running continuous assessment instead of periodic assessment. They're treating the AI inventory as a daily artifact rather than a quarterly deliverable. They're building governance rhythms that match the speed of the asset rather than the speed of the traditional review cycle. Those programs are a minority right now. But they're the ones that will be defensible when the regulatory examinations get more specific and the board questions get harder.

Locating your program honestly against this market picture is the prerequisite for building the target model. The question isn't whether your program is good or bad. The question is whether it's running rhythms or laminating policies. If your AI use policy exists but has no enforcement mechanism, that's a lamination. If your risk committee meets but has no ratified decision rights, that's a lamination. If your conformity program maps regulatory requirements but has no owner updating it when new guidance drops, that's a lamination. Name the laminates honestly. They're the specific gaps the target model needs to close.

The Solution Category Landscape: Patterns, Not Products

The governance stack for AI security has four distinct categories. Every program needs all four. Most programs have one or two and are missing the others without knowing it. Understanding the categories before evaluating any specific tool is what keeps you from buying a solution to a problem you've already solved while the actual gap goes unfilled.

The first category is continuous-control and integrated-risk platforms. These are the systems that extend traditional GRC capabilities into the AI domain. They pull configuration data, policy documents, and control evidence from the systems in scope and evaluate them continuously against defined baselines and regulatory requirements. The key capability to evaluate in this category isn't the breadth of the regulatory library or the quality of the dashboard. It's the continuous assessment architecture. A platform that runs daily automated control evaluations and surfaces exceptions to a human owner is a fundamentally different tool than one that runs quarterly assessments and produces a report. Both might be marketed under the same category name. Only one solves the velocity mismatch.

The second category is model registries and AI bills of materials. This is the system of record for what's deployed. Every AI system in the enterprise, every model version, every agent, every API connection to an external AI service, and every non-human identity associated with an AI workflow should be in the registry. The AI bill of materials extends this to include the components the model was built from: the training data sources, the base model, the fine-tuning datasets, and the third-party libraries. Why does the bill of materials matter for governance? Because when a vulnerability is discovered in a model component, or when a training data source is found to be compromised, you need to know immediately which deployed systems are affected. Without the bill of materials, you're doing manual discovery under pressure. With it, you run a query and have the answer in minutes.

The registry is also the artifact that makes the Decision Rights RACI operational. The RACI says who approves each AI system. The registry is where that approval is recorded, along with the system's scope, its authorized data processing activities, its review cadence, and its named owner. When a regulator asks for evidence that your AI systems were approved before deployment, the registry is the evidence. When an incident response team needs to know what an agent was authorized to do, the registry has the answer. The registry isn't a nice-to-have. It's the foundation everything else sits on.

The third category is evaluation platforms. These measure model behavior against defined baselines. They test AI outputs for accuracy, consistency, bias, and alignment with the use case they were approved for. They run the behavioral checks that detect drift before it becomes a governance failure. The evaluation capability that most programs underweight is the ongoing behavioral monitoring function, not the pre-deployment testing. Pre-deployment testing is necessary. But a model that passes pre-deployment testing and then drifts over the following six months because of changes in its input data or fine-tuning updates is a governance gap that pre-deployment testing was never designed to catch. The evaluation platform needs to run continuously, not just at deployment time.

The fourth category is provenance tooling. This traces decisions end to end. When an AI agent makes a consequential decision, provenance tooling captures the full chain: what data the agent accessed, what reasoning path it followed, what output it produced, and what action was taken as a result. This is the audit trail that makes AI decisions accountable. Without it, the accountability vacuum from Chapter 1 stays open. With it, the question "who is accountable for this decision and what did the system do" has a specific, documented answer. Provenance tooling is also the artifact that satisfies the regulatory requirement for explainability in automated decision-making. A regulator asking how an AI system made a decision that affected a customer gets a documented decision chain, not a general description of how the model works.

Governance platforms consolidate for two reasons, and understanding both helps you evaluate any vendor's consolidation pitch honestly. The first reason is data gravity. The continuous-control platform, the model registry, the evaluation platform, and the provenance tooling all need to talk to each other. The registry feeds the evaluation platform with the list of systems to monitor. The evaluation platform feeds the risk register with behavioral anomalies. The provenance tooling feeds the continuous-control platform with decision audit trails. When these four categories are separate tools with separate data models and no integration, the governance team spends significant effort connecting the outputs manually. When they're integrated, the data flows automatically and the human effort goes into adjudication rather than assembly.

The second reason is regulatory surface. A single integrated platform produces a unified evidence record that maps to multiple regulatory frameworks simultaneously. When a regulator asks for evidence of AI governance, you produce one evidence package from one system rather than assembling artifacts from four separate tools. That's a practical advantage that grows as the regulatory surface expands.

The category-level evaluation criteria that outlive any vendor on the stack are these four questions. Does the tool run continuously or periodically? Periodic tools solve yesterday's problem. Does the tool produce evidence that's admissible in a regulatory examination? Evidence that can't be tied to a specific timestamp, a specific system state, and a specific control requirement isn't governance evidence. Does the tool integrate with the other categories in the stack, or does it require manual data transfer? Manual transfer is a staffing cost and a latency problem. And does the tool's data model support the three-attribute artifact discipline: owner, cadence, executive decision fed? A tool that produces reports but can't assign them to a named owner with a defined review cadence produces outputs, not governance.

FIGURE 3.2 **The Solution Category Landscape**

Patterns, not products. The category is what survives consolidation.

1 AI DISCOVERY AND INVENTORY

Buy when: you cannot enumerate the estate.

Continuous identification of models, agents, prompts, and embedded vendor features across the environment.

2 POLICY AND CONTROL AUTOMATION

Buy when: evidence assembly is manual.

Machine examination of controls with continuous evidence collection and conflict detection across policy sets.

3 MODEL AND AGENT REGISTRY

Buy when: nobody owns the lifecycle.

Authoritative record of what runs, who owns it, what authority it holds, and what evidence supports its autonomy level.

4 REGULATORY INTELLIGENCE

Buy when: the crosswalk is annual

Tracking of obligation changes mapped to the enterprise control set so the map moves when the requirement moves.

EVALUATE THE PATTERN. VENDORS CONSOLIDATE. REQUIREMENTS DO NOT.

The Department Question: Does GRC Survive?

The honest answer is that GRC as it currently exists doesn't survive. The function survives. The team survives, if it transitions. The version of GRC that writes policies, runs quarterly assessments, and produces compliance reports on a periodic cycle is being replaced by something more capable and more demanding. The teams that understand this early will build the new function. The teams that don't will watch their scope shrink as continuous compliance platforms automate the work they were hired to do.

This isn't a comfortable thing to say to a room full of GRC professionals. But it's the accurate thing to say, and the leaders who treat it as a threat rather than a transition signal will make worse decisions about hiring, training, and team structure than the ones who face it directly.

The work that's going away is the volume work. Manual evidence collection. Periodic control testing. Quarterly policy reviews. Regulatory gap analysis done by reading documents and building spreadsheets. These activities consumed the majority of a traditional GRC team's capacity, and they're being automated. Not partially automated. Substantially automated. The governance engine reads regulations, maps them to controls, evaluates the controls against configuration data, and flags gaps. A process that took an analyst two weeks now takes the machine two hours and the analyst two hours of adjudication. The analyst headcount required to do the same volume of work drops significantly.

What's growing is the judgment work. And the judgment work requires skills that most GRC teams don't currently have.

Three roles are emerging that don't exist in most security organizations today, and every CISO reading this will be hiring for at least one of them within the next 12 months. The first is the machine-judgment governor. This person owns the operating relationship between the governance team and the AI systems the enterprise runs. They define the behavioral baselines for each AI system, review the evaluation platform's anomaly reports, adjudicate whether a behavioral deviation is within acceptable bounds or requires escalation, and maintain the documentation that connects each AI system's approved behavior to its current actual behavior. The machine-judgment governor is not a data scientist. They're a governance professional who understands AI behavior well enough to evaluate it and document it in terms that satisfy a regulator. That's a specific combination of skills that doesn't map cleanly onto any existing GRC role.

The second role is the model evaluation owner. This person owns the evaluation platform and the behavioral testing program. They define the test cases, run the evaluation cycles, interpret the results, and produce the evidence that the AI system is behaving as approved. They work closely with the data science and engineering teams that build and maintain the models, but they're not part of those teams. Their accountability is to governance, not to the model's performance metrics. The model evaluation owner needs enough technical depth to understand what a behavioral anomaly means and enough governance discipline to document it in a way that's defensible. That combination is genuinely rare right now, which means the hiring process for this role will be competitive and the onboarding will require investment.

The third role is the decision-provenance steward. This person owns the provenance tooling and the decision audit trail. They define what gets captured, how long it's retained, how it's organized for regulatory examination, and how it's used to answer accountability questions when an AI decision is challenged. The decision provenance steward is the person who gets called when an incident response team, a regulator, or a plaintiff's attorney asks "what did the AI system do and why." Their ability to produce a clear, complete, defensible answer to that question is a direct function of how well they've designed and maintained the provenance system. This role sits at the intersection of governance, legal, and operations, and it requires enough credibility with all three functions to be effective with all of them.

The skills transition from policy writers to governors of machine judgment is not a training program. It's a hiring strategy combined with a role redesign. Some existing GRC team members will make the transition successfully. They're the ones who are already curious about how AI systems actually work, who push back on vague risk descriptions and demand specifics, and who are comfortable adjudicating ambiguous situations rather than looking for a policy that tells them what to do. Those people should be identified now and given development paths into the new roles. The team members who are primarily process-followers and document-producers will find the new roles harder to inhabit. That's not a judgment about their quality as professionals. It's a recognition that the job is changing in ways that require different instincts.

The ownership map for the new governance objects is genuinely unresolved in most organizations, and the CISO who resolves it first gains a structural advantage. The new objects are AI ethics, reasoning quality, and the decision provenance chain. Who owns AI ethics in your organization right now? If the answer is "it's shared between legal, HR, and the CISO's office," that's a gap. Shared ownership without a named primary owner produces inaction when a decision needs to be made. Who owns reasoning quality, meaning the ongoing evaluation of whether your AI systems are reasoning accurately and consistently? If the answer is "the data science team," that's a conflict of interest. The team that builds the model shouldn't be the sole evaluator of whether it's working correctly. Who owns the decision provenance chain? If the answer is "nobody has formally been assigned that," you have an accountability vacuum sitting inside your governance structure.

Resolve these ownership questions before you hire. The organizational design decision comes before the job description. Once you know who owns AI ethics, reasoning quality, and decision provenance, the three new roles slot into a structure that makes sense. Before that clarity exists, you're hiring people into ambiguous positions and setting them up to fail.

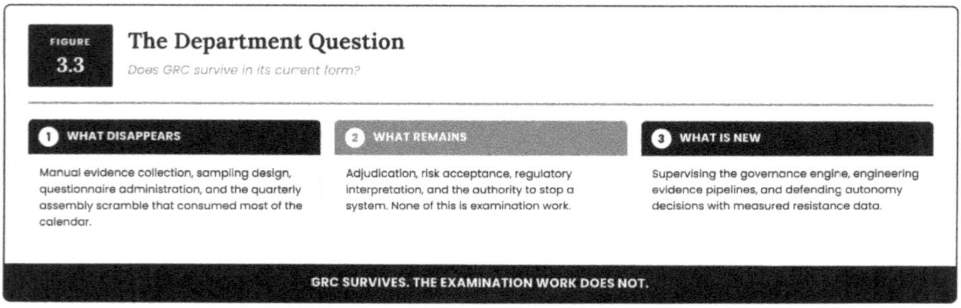

The 1-Year Governance Target Operating Model

The 1-Year Governance Target Operating Model isn't a vision statement. It's a fundable trajectory with quarterly milestones, specific capability builds, and a board-facing outcome you can name on a date. Present it to the CFO as a budget narrative and to the board as the answer to their question about what you're building and why it costs what it costs. Twelve months is the horizon because twelve months is what a CISO can actually commit to and be held to.

The first quarter is about decision rights and inventory. Nothing else in the model works until those two artifacts are real. The Decision Rights RACI gets ratified by the CISO, General Counsel, CPO, CDO, CFO, and the business unit leaders whose systems are in scope. The model registry gets stood up and populated with every AI system the audit found. Those two deliverables are the floor. Without ratified decision rights, every AI deployment is an accountability vacuum. Without a populated registry, risk is invisible between review cycles, which is most of the time.

The first-quarter budget line is the model registry and the facilitation cost of the ratification process. The registry is a software purchase. The ratification is not. Getting six executives into a room to sign a binding accountability document requires executive calendar time and often external facilitation, and a ratification process that gets deprioritized because nobody budgeted for the facilitation time is a ratification process that doesn't happen. Budget it explicitly as a line item, not as something absorbed into someone's existing workload. The RACI is too important to leave to informal scheduling.

The second quarter installs the continuous-control platform and hires the first new role. The continuous-control platform is the category that makes evidence continuous rather than periodic, and it replaces the manual evidence collection that currently consumes the majority of GRC analyst capacity. The cost is partially offset by the reduction in analyst hours spent assembling evidence packets by hand. Present that offset explicitly to the CFO rather than making them calculate it. The machine-judgment governor gets hired in this quarter, timed to arrive as the platform goes live so the role configures the system, defines the baselines, and owns the operating rhythm from the first day rather than inheriting someone else's configuration.

The third quarter is when governance stops being advisory. The governance committee meets with binding authority and documents its first suspension or conditional approval. The five-horizon governance rhythm gets installed across daily, weekly, monthly, quarterly, and annual cadences, closing the velocity mismatch that Chapter 1 named. The Shadow AI Sanctioning Pathway launches in two business units chosen for high AI adoption and cooperative leadership. The model evaluation owner is hired. The pathway has to actually be faster and easier than the workaround, every time, or the business units revert within a month, so the third quarter is also where you measure intake-to-approval time and publish it.

The fourth quarter is proof. Every AI system in production is in the registry, every system has a named owner and a ratified decision right, the governance committee has met at least three times with binding decisions documented, and the board scorecard assembles from continuous evidence rather than from a quarterly scramble. That is the year-end board milestone, and it is deliberately specific because a vague milestone cannot be defended in a budget conversation twelve months from now. Present it as evidence that governance is operating, not documented. The distinction between a running program and another binder is exactly this list.

What Year One makes possible is the part worth naming for the board, because it is what turns a twelve-month budget into a multi-year mandate without asking for the multi-year money today. The registry and the continuous-control platform become the substrate the evaluation platform and provenance tooling connect to. The Sanctioning Pathway that proved itself in two business units becomes the default intake path across the enterprise. The two roles hired this year become the people who train their successors rather than the people who do all the work. And the evidence that flowed from one source this year starts flowing from three, which is the condition under which a regulator can ask for your AI governance posture today and receive an answer dated today rather than a binder dated last quarter.

That last outcome is worth stating plainly to the board because it is the one that makes the liability problem from Chapter 1 disappear. There is no gap between the evidence and the current state when the evidence is continuous. The governance function stops recording what AI systems did and starts deciding what they are permitted to do, under what conditions, with what supervision, and with what authority to suspend. Year One does not complete that transition. Year One makes it fundable.

FIGURE 3.4

The One-Year Governance Target Operating Model

Four quarters, with the milestone the CISO names to the board at the end of each.

QUARTER	CAPABILITY INSTALLED	OWNER	BOARD MILESTONE
Q1	Complete AI discovery and a dated model registry	GRC Lead	We can enumerate the estate
Q2	Continuous control examination on two control families	GRC Lead	Coverage replaces sampling
Q3	Living risk register and the sanctioning pathway in operation	CISO Staff	Shadow demand is governed, not hidden
Q4	Supervision matrix, measured time-to-stop, and the scorecard	CISO	We can prove we can stop it

TWELVE MONTHS OF INSTALLED CAPABILITY BEATS A THREE-YEAR PLAN THAT GETS DEFUNDED IN YEAR TWO.

Evaluating the Category: Six Questions That Survive a Vendor Demo

Category selection is the durable decision, and product selection is the perishable one, which means most enterprises spend their evaluation effort backward. A governance program that picks the right category and the wrong product inside it loses a renewal cycle. A program that picks the wrong category loses two years, because the wrong category produces evidence in a shape the regulator does not want and the enterprise discovers this at the examination rather than at the demo. The six questions below are the ones that distinguish categories rather than products, and they are deliberately hostile to the demonstration format.

The first question is what the platform reads without a rebuild. A continuous-control platform that requires the enterprise to re-express its existing control environment in the vendor's model is not automating compliance; it is relocating it, and the relocation cost is paid by the same GRC analysts whose capacity the purchase was meant to recover. Ask for the connector list against your actual stack, not the published integration count. Ask what happens to a control that has no connector, because that is where the manual work reappears.

The second question is whether the evidence output survives an examiner without translation. Continuous evidence is only valuable if the artifact it produces is the artifact the regulator, the customer, or the auditor asks for. A platform that produces a compelling internal dashboard and requires a human to assemble a submission package has automated the monitoring and left the deliverable alone. Ask to see the export. Ask whether the export carries the timestamps, the control mapping, and the exception rationale that an examiner will want, or whether those are attributes an analyst adds afterward.

The third question is how the platform handles a control that is partially satisfied, because that is the normal state of every real control environment and the state most tooling models badly. A binary pass-fail model forces analysts into a choice between a false failure that generates noise and a false pass that generates exposure, and both choices are made under time pressure by the most junior person in the workflow. Ask how partial satisfaction is represented, who can record a compensating control, and whether that record carries an expiry.

The fourth question is what the platform does when the underlying system changes without notice. This is the AI-specific question, and it is the one that separates AI governance tooling from GRC tooling with an AI module. A model version change at a provider, a retrieval corpus expansion, or a permission grant to an agent are all events that change a control's effectiveness without changing the control's configuration. Ask what signal the platform receives, from where, and how quickly. A platform whose answer is that the enterprise notifies it has described a manual process with a database attached.

The fifth question is about the exit, and it should be asked in the first meeting rather than the last. Governance evidence accumulates, and two years of continuous control evidence held in a proprietary format is a switching cost that will be used against you at renewal. Ask what leaves with you, in what format, and whether the historical evidence remains attestable after the relationship ends. The sixth question is who else in the enterprise is buying something adjacent, because governance, security operations, and privacy are all currently being sold overlapping platforms, and an enterprise that buys three of them will pay three times for a shared substrate and then spend a year reconciling their disagreements.

FIGURE 3.5

Evaluating the Category

Six questions that survive a vendor demo.

1 WHAT DOES IT DISCOVER WITHOUT INTEGRATION

Ask what the platform finds on day one with no connectors configured. That number is the honest floor.

2 WHAT HAPPENS WHEN IT IS WRONG

Every platform produces false findings. Ask how a wrong finding is corrected and whether the correction persists.

3 WHERE DOES THE EVIDENCE LIVE

If evidence lives only in the vendor, an exit becomes an evidence loss. Ask for the export before you sign.

4 WHAT IS THE INTEGRATION COST

The fourth platform costs more than the first three. Ask what it takes to connect and who maintains that connection.

5 CAN IT BE AUDITED ITSELF

The platform is an AI system in your estate. Ask for its own logging, baseline, and failure behavior.

6 WHAT SURVIVES CONSOLIDATION

Ask which capability is the durable pattern and which is packaging. Buy the pattern.

A DEMO SHOWS THE BEST CASE. PROCUREMENT SHOULD PRICE THE ORDINARY ONE.

Integration Debt: Why the Fourth Platform Costs More Than the First Three

Every solution category in this landscape is sold as a standalone capability and none of them are consumed that way. The model registry needs to know what discovery found. The continuous-control platform needs to know what the registry holds. The evaluation platform needs to know which systems the control platform flagged. The provenance tooling needs to reach all three. Each of those connections is a project, each project has an owner who was not budgeted, and the cumulative cost of the connections routinely exceeds the license cost of the platforms they connect.

The pattern is familiar from every prior generation of security tooling, and the reason it repeats is that integration cost is invisible at the point of purchase and unavoidable at the point of use. A CISO evaluates four platforms against four capability requirements, funds four licenses, and discovers in month five that the four platforms produce four inventories that disagree, and that reconciling them is now a standing task assigned to whoever complains loudest. The disagreement is not a defect in any of the products. It is what happens when four systems each build an authoritative view of the same population from different sources on different cadences.

The decision rule that avoids most of this is unglamorous and hard to hold to under vendor pressure. Designate one system as the authoritative inventory before purchasing the second platform, and require every subsequent purchase to consume that inventory rather than build its own. In practice this usually means the model registry is authoritative for AI systems and the identity provider is authoritative for non-human identities, and every other platform reads from them. Any vendor whose product cannot consume an external authoritative inventory is asking the enterprise to accept a permanent reconciliation task, and that cost belongs in the evaluation rather than in the operating budget.

The second rule is to sequence purchases against integration capacity rather than against capability need, which feels wrong and is correct. An enterprise with one engineer available for integration work should buy one platform per quarter regardless of how many capabilities gaps the audit found, because a platform that is purchased and not integrated is a license expense that produces a dashboard nobody trusts. The capability gap that stays open for a quarter is visible and manageable. The half-integrated platform is invisible and produces confident wrong answers, which is the worse of the two positions.

The third rule concerns the shared substrate that most enterprises discover too late. Governance, security operations, third-party risk, and privacy will each be sold a platform that includes AI discovery, and the enterprise will end up running four discovery mechanisms against the same estate. Consolidating them after the fact is politically expensive because four functions have each built a workflow on their own. Deciding at the start that discovery is a shared service with one owner, consumed by four functions, costs one conversation in the first quarter and saves a reorganization in the third year.

Authority as a Decision Right: What the Committee Must Now Decide

The Decision Rights RACI ratified in this Part answered three questions per system: who approves deployment, who can suspend, and who is accountable.

Agentic systems add a fourth that most ratification sessions have not addressed, and it is the one that will matter most within the twelve-month horizon. Who may grant an AI system the authority to act on behalf of a human, and what are the limits of what may be granted?

That question is not hypothetical, and it is not primarily technical. Every enterprise deploying agent is granting delegated authority today, and in most cases the grant is made by whoever configured the integration rather than by anyone with the standing to make it. A platform engineer selecting a service account scope for an agent has made an authority decision with enterprise consequences, and nothing in the current governance model treats it as one. The audit's finding about accountability vacuums describes exactly this: consequential decisions made correctly at a technical level by people who were never delegated the right to make them.

The committee's work is to define authority tiers and assign a granting role to each, in the same structure the Non-Human Identity Pyramid uses for governance intensity. An agent that reads and summarizes within one system is a grant a system owner can make. An agent that writes, changes state or invokes tools across systems is a grant that requires the security director. An agent that can move money, modify production infrastructure, communicate externally on the enterprise's behalf, or delegate to other agents is a grant that requires a named executive and appears in the supervision matrix. The tiers are not the interesting part; the interesting part is that someone is now named for each, which is what converts an implementation choice into a governed decision.

Expiry is the attribute most commonly omitted and the one that produces the largest downstream cleanup. Human authority is bounded by employment, review cycles, and role changes, all of which are events the identity lifecycle detects. Agent authority is typically granted once and persists until someone notices it should not, which in practice means it persists. Every grant above the lowest tier carries an expiry date and a renewal that requires the granting role to affirm the grant is still needed, and the renewal is a positive action rather than a silent rollover. An enterprise that implements nothing else from this section, but expiry will materially reduce its standing agent authority within two review cycles.

The forward-looking reason to settle this in the first year rather than the third is that external pressure is arriving. NIST's agent standards work is explicitly directed at agent identity and authorization, and the direction of travel across the emerging guidance is toward treating delegated agent authority as a governed object rather than a configuration detail. An enterprise that has already defined its authority tiers, named the granting roles, and set expiry on the grants will be able to answer that guidance from an operating position. An enterprise that has not will be reconstructing who granted what, which is the same reconstruction problem this Volume opened with.

Measuring AI Security Debt: The Liability That Compounds Daily

Every engineering organization understands technical debt: shortcuts taken under delivery pressure that accrue interest until someone pays them down. AI produces a related liability with a materially worse property, and most enterprises are accumulating it without any instrument that measures it. Technical debt sits still. A poorly written module costs the same next quarter as it costs today. AI security debt compounds, because the ungoverned system keeps making decisions every day it goes unaddressed, and each of those decisions is an outcome the enterprise cannot explain.

The debt has six components and every one of them is countable, which is the whole reason to name it. Unregistered AI systems in production, meaning systems the model registry does not hold. Ungoverned non-human identities, meaning identities capable of taking action with no-named human owner. Expired or unreviewed authority grants that remain active. Unassessed tool and MCP connections, meaning instruction channels into agents from parties nobody evaluated. Undocumented model versions, meaning production systems whose current version the enterprise cannot state. And unratified decision rights, meaning production systems with no named approver, suspender, or accountable executive.

Counting them produces a single number, and the number is more useful than any maturity scores the program will otherwise report. A governance function that can tell the board carries four hundred and twelve units of AI security debt, broken into six categories, with a burn-down rate of sixty per quarter, has said something a board can act on. A governance function reporting that its AI program is at maturity level three has said something a board cannot evaluate, cannot fund against, and cannot hold anyone to. The debt figure has the property every good governance metric needs: it is uncomfortable, it is defensible, and it moves in response to work.

The compounding property is what makes the reporting cadence matter more than the precision of the count. An unregistered system that has been making decisions for six months has produced six months of outcomes the enterprise cannot reconstruct, and the discovery of that system does not undo them. The debt therefore has an age dimension, and the register records not just what is outstanding but how long each item has been outstanding. Two hundred units at an average age of three weeks is a program keeping pace. Two hundred units at an average age of fourteen months is a program that has been generating findings and not closing them, which looks identical in a count and is a different situation entirely.

Prioritization follows from the age and the consequence together rather than from severity alone. An ungoverned identity that can only read low-sensitivity data is debt worth carrying for a quarter. An expired authority grants on an agent that can move money is debt that gets paid this week regardless of what else is on the calendar. Build the ranking on two axes, the action capability of the item and the length of time it has been outstanding and let the ranking rather than the loudest stakeholder set the sequence. That ranking is also the answer when a business unit asks why its request is behind something else.

The decision rule is that AI Security Debt is reported to the board every quarter alongside the four governance numbers from Chapter 2, with the count, the six-category breakdown, the average age, and the burn-down rate against the prior quarter. A rising count with a rising burn-down rate is a healthy program discovering faster than it closes, which is the expected state in year one and should be presented as such rather than defended. A flat count is a program that has stopped discovering. And a program that has never computed the number is carrying an unmeasured liability that will be measured eventually, by someone else, at a moment the enterprise does not choose.

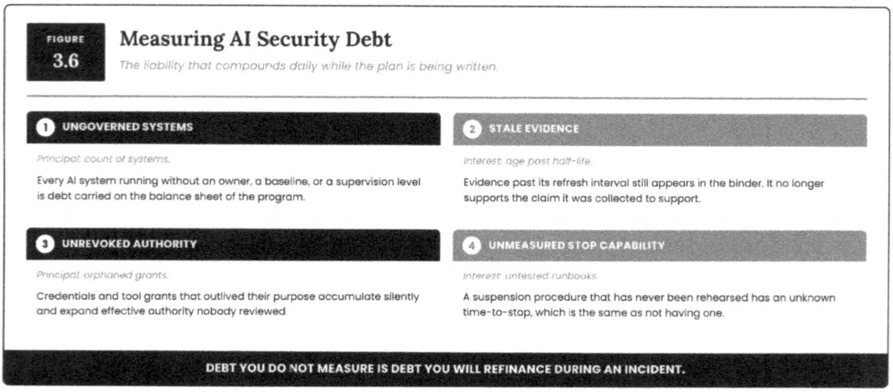

More Security or Less? The Ultimate Outcome for Governance

The board asks this question because they're trying to understand whether AI is making the security function more expensive without making the enterprise more protected, or whether the investment is producing something that actually reduces risk. It's a fair question. And the answer for governance is unambiguous.

More. And not merely more but promoted.

The governance function that runs the 1-Year Target Operating Model doesn't look like the GRC department that ran quarterly assessments and produced compliance reports. It looks like a control plane. It has real-time visibility into every AI system in production. It has ratified authority to approve deployments, suspend systems, and escalate accountability questions. It produces continuous evidence that satisfies regulators without a point-in-time audit cycle. It governs what autonomous systems are permitted to decide, which means it governs the most consequential layer of enterprise decision-making that exists.

That's not a cost center. That's the dominant security discipline of the AI-native enterprise.

The shift in what the function does is as important as the shift in what it costs. Fewer people write policies. More people governing machine judgment. The policy-writing work doesn't disappear entirely, but it shrinks to a fraction of what it was because the machine handles the volume and the humans handle the judgment. The judgment work is harder, more specialized, and more consequential than the policy-writing work it replaces. The people doing it need to be paid accordingly, and they need to be positioned in the organization accordingly. The machine-judgment governor isn't a mid-level GRC analyst. They're a senior governance professional with a direct line to the CISO and a seat at the table where AI deployment decisions are being made.

The mandate expansion dynamic is the thing the board needs to understand clearly. Every time the enterprise delegates another decision to an autonomous system, the governance function's scope expands. The enterprise deploys an AI agent to handle customer service escalations: governance defines what the agent may decide, what it must escalate, and what evidence it must produce. The enterprise deploys an AI system to flag compliance anomalies: governance defines the behavioral baseline, the deviation threshold, and the human review protocol. The enterprise deploys an AI tool to support hiring decisions: governance defines the data it may access, the decisions it may influence, and the audit trail it must maintain. Every new autonomous capability is a new governance mandate. The function doesn't shrink as AI proliferates. It grows.

The career positioning dimension of this outcome is worth stating directly because it's real and it matters to the people reading this book. The CISO who builds the 1-Year Governance Target Operating Model and presents it to the board as a funded trajectory isn't just doing good governance work. They're establishing themselves as the executive who makes AI governable in their organization. That's a specific identity, and it's a valuable one. Regulators want to talk to that person.

Board members want to hear from that person. Peers want to learn from that person. The governance function that was a cost center becomes the function that defines what responsible AI deployment looks like in the enterprise, and the leader who built it becomes the person the organization points to when it needs to demonstrate that AI is being governed seriously.

Governance doesn't survive AI by staying the same. It survives by becoming something more powerful. The function that was built to write policies and run quarterly assessments becomes the control plane that decides what machines may decide. That's not a small promotion. It's a fundamental change in what the function is for and what it's worth to the enterprise.

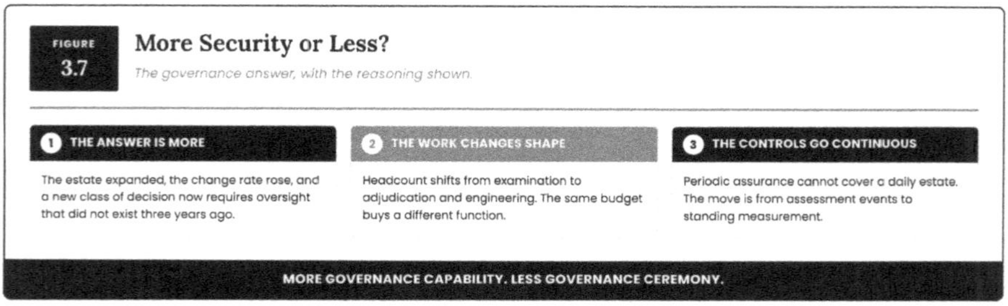

Putting It Into Practice

The destination is drawn. This month, you commit to it with specific actions that move the program from current state to year one foundation.

Start by locating your program against the current-focus map honestly. Write down the answer to this question for each of the four governance activities: AI use policy, risk committee, conformity program, and GRC process extension. Is each one running a rhythm or laminating a document? A policy with no enforcement mechanism is a lamination. A committee with no ratified decision rights is a lamination. A conformity program with no owner updating it monthly is a lamination. A GRC process extended to AI without addressing the velocity mismatch is a lamination. Name the laminates. They are your year one gaps, and they need to be in the gap analysis you bring to the CFO before the budget conversation starts.

Evaluate your governance stack by category, not by vendor. Map what you currently have against the four categories: continuous-control platform, model registry, evaluation platform, and provenance tooling. For each category, answer two questions. Do you have a tool that covers this category? And does it run continuously or periodically? A periodic tool in a category that requires continuous coverage is a gap, even if you have a tool. Identify which category is missing entirely from your stack. That missing category is your first year one tooling investment, and it should be in the budget narrative you're building.

Draft the skills transition map for your GRC team this week. List every current GRC team member. Next to each name, write their primary skill: policy writing, control testing, evidence collection, regulatory mapping, or something else. Then write whether that skill is in the shrinking category or the growing category. Policy writing, control testing, and evidence collection are shrinking. Behavioral assessment, decision adjudication, and provenance management are growing. Identify the two or three team members who show the instincts for the growing category. Those are your development investments for the three new roles. Then identify the gaps: which of the three new roles do you have nobody currently capable of filling? Those are your year one and year two hires.

Assemble the 1-Year Governance Target Operating Model on one page. First quarter: decision rights ratified and the model registry populated. Second quarter: continuous-control platform live and the machine-judgment governor hired. Third quarter: committee operating with binding authority, five-horizon rhythm installed, Sanctioning Pathway launched in two business units. Fourth quarter: every production system in the registry with a named owner and a ratified decision right, and a board scorecard that assembles from continuous evidence. For each quarter, add three columns: the primary capability build, the headcount addition, and the milestone you will name to the board. Add one closing line under the table describing what Year One makes possible without asking for that money now. That one page is the budget narrative for the CFO and the answer to the board's question about what you are building. Present it as a trajectory, not a wish list. Each quarter builds on the previous one, each milestone is measurable, and the twelve-month outcome is specific: governance operating as a running program rather than a documented one.

The board's question gets answered at the end of year three. But the answer starts this month, with a gap analysis that names the laminates, a stack evaluation that identifies the missing category, a skills transition map that shows who's building the new function, and a one-page TOM that shows the CFO exactly what they're funding and why it's worth funding. Part I of this book is complete. The governance operating model is drawn. The next chapter opens Part II, where the SOC inherits the audit findings and confronts an adversary that didn't wait for governance to catch up before deploying AI first.

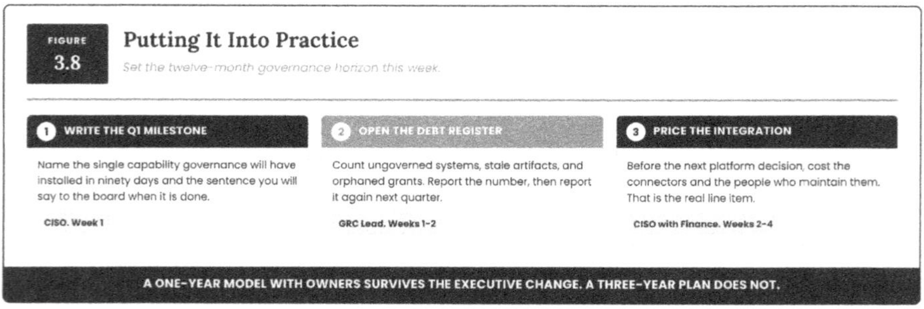

Part II: Security Operations

What the Audit Handed the SOC, and Why the Operating Model Is Already Wrong

The SOC received the shortest list of artifacts and the largest operating problem. The audit produced a detection gap analysis, an AI incident response addendum, and a Red Button procedure that most organizations have never executed. What the audit could not produce, because no audit can, is the operating model change those three artifacts imply. A detection gap is a finding. Closing it requires the SOC to detect a category of attack that does not produce an alert in any tool the SOC currently owns.

The category is corruption without breach. An adversary who alters a retrieval corpus, poisons an agent's memory, or shifts a model's behavior through sustained adversarial input has not exfiltrated anything, has not escalated privilege in any way the identity stack records, and has not triggered a single rule in the SIEM. The enterprise's AI systems continue operating and continue producing output that people act on. The output is now wrong in the direction the attacker chose. There is no incident to declare because no tool has declared one, which means the mean time to detect for this attack class in most enterprises is not a number anyone has measured. It is unbounded.

Meanwhile the adversary is running the same capability expansion the defender is, without the overhead governance. Offensive tooling that automates reconnaissance, generates convincing pretext at scale, adapts payloads against observed defenses, and compresses the window between vulnerability disclosure and working exploit is available, cheap, and improving. The asymmetry is not that attackers have better AI. It is that attackers deploy it without a supervision matrix, a legal review, a procurement cycle, or a board briefing. The defender's constraint is legitimate and also expensive.

Then there is the identity problem, which the audit surfaced and which almost no SOC is watching. The non-human identity population in an enterprise running AI at scale now outnumbers the human population, often by a wide margin, and it grows without a joiner-mover-leaver process, without an access review that covers it, and with credential lifetimes measured in months or never. Service accounts, agent identities, API keys, and plugin credentials can act. Lateral movement through that population produces telemetry that looks like normal automation because it is normal automation, performed by an identity that was compromised rather than created.

The last problem is the one SOC leaders find it hardest to say out loud. The SOC's own AI is a target. The copilot that triages alerts, the model that scores anomalies, the agent that executes containment: each is a system whose corruption would degrade the enterprise's detection capability while the dashboard continued to report normal operation. A SOC that has instrumented every enterprise AI system and left its own uninstrumented has built a monitoring program with a hole in the exact place an intelligent adversary would look first.

Chapter 4 works through those four problems against the audit's artifacts. Chapter 5 builds the operating model that answers them, including the two instruments this Volume contributes to the Library: the Human Supervision Matrix and the Red-Button Protocol. Chapter 6 covers the market, the solution categories, the fate of the tier model, the twelve-month target operating model, and the answer to the board's question.

Chapter 4: The SOC Inherits the Audit

An Adversary Moving at Machine Speed and an Operating Model Built for Yesterday

CHAPTER 4 OUTCOMES

At the end of this chapter, you will be able to:

1. Explain why the tiered SOC operating model is misaligned to a machine-speed adversary.
2. Detect corruption without breach, the attack class no existing alert fires on.
3. Account for a non-human identity population that outnumbers the human one.
4. Recognize the SOC's own AI as a target inside the defense.
5. Identify automation bias in the tier before it becomes a missed incident.
6. Trace the agent kill chain and the cascading failure it produces.

THE ADVERSARY AUTOMATED FIRST. THE OPERATING MODEL HAS NOT CAUGHT UP.

The Handoff: What the SOC Received and Why Its Operating Model Is Wrong

The audit findings landed on the SOC's desk the same way they landed on governance's. In a binder. With a risk register attached. With a list of detection gaps that someone catalogued carefully and a set of recommendations that someone wrote thoughtfully. And then the SOC was expected to do something about it.

The problem is that the SOC wasn't built for what the findings described.

Every gap the audit surfaced in the AI security posture points to a class of attack that the SOC's current operating model wasn't designed to catch. Prompt injections don't look like unauthorized access. Training data poisoning doesn't look like exfiltration. Agent credential abuse doesn't trigger the identity controls built for human users. The detection logic, the alert taxonomy, the escalation playbooks, the triage workflows, all of it was built around a threat model that assumes a human attacker trying to get into a system. The AI-era threat model includes attackers who don't need to get in because they can corrupt what's already running from the outside.

That's not a gap you close by adding more analysts or buying a new SIEM rule set.

What the SOC actually inherited from the audit is four distinct problems sitting on top of each other. The first is detection gaps across AI-specific attack surfaces. The audit identified them. The SOC now owns them. But owning a gap isn't the same as closing it, and most SOC teams don't yet have the detection logic, the alert categories, or the investigation playbooks to work AI-specific attack surfaces the way they work traditional ones.

The second problem is alert volume the team cannot process. AI-instrumented environments generate telemetry at a scale that human analysts can't triage manually. The audit probably flagged this. What it didn't deliver was a working solution. The SOC is still running the same triage model it ran before the audit, against a signal volume that has grown faster than its capacity to process it. The backlog is real. The missed signals inside that backlog are real too.

The third problem is an AI incident response playbook that has never been rehearsed. Most organizations have written one at this point. Few have run a tabletop against it. Fewer still have tested whether the kill-switch authority it describes can actually be exercised in the time window that matters. A playbook that's never been rehearsed is a document, not a capability. The difference between those two things only becomes visible during an actual incident, which is the worst possible moment to discover it.

The fourth problem is a defensive AI stack that was audited but never governed. The SOC's own detection models, its copilots, its automated triage tools, these were assessed in the audit as part of the security tooling inventory. But being assessed once isn't the same as being governed continuously. The defensive AI stack is now running in production, making triage decisions and influencing investigations, and in most SOCs it has no ongoing supervision standard, no behavioral baseline, and no anomaly detection watching it the way it watches everything else.

The structural mismatch underneath all four of these problems is the same one. The SOC was built to detect breaches. It was built to find the moment of unauthorized entry, track the lateral movement that followed, and contain the damage before exfiltration completed. That model works when the attacker needs to get in. It doesn't work when the attack is a corruption of what's already inside. The SOC can't patch its way out of this mismatch. It has to rebuild the operating model around a different threat premise, one where the most consequential attacks leave no entry log, cross no perimeter, and steal no data, yet compromise the enterprise more deeply than a breach ever did.

The rebuild has to cover four things. Detection logic for AI-specific attack surfaces. A triage model that handles machine-speed alert volumes without burning out the analyst team. Rehearsed response capability for AI-specific incidents. And a supervision standard for the SOC's own AI stack that holds it to the same governance rigor applied to every other system in the enterprise. This chapter maps all four. The next chapter arms the SOC with the machine-speed tools to execute them.

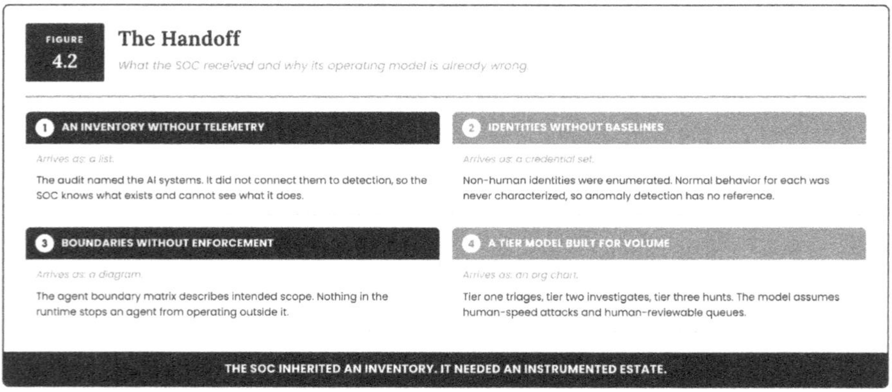

The Adversary Hires First: Offense at Machine Speed

Before the SOC can rebuild its operating model, it needs an accurate picture of what it's rebuilding against. And that picture has changed more in the past two years than in the previous decade.

AI rewrote the attacker's labor economics first. That's the foundational fact the SOC has to internalize. The defender is still largely operating on human timelines. The attacker isn't.

Reconnaissance used to take weeks. A skilled attacker would spend significant time mapping an organization's external footprint, identifying the people, the systems, the relationships, and the gaps. That time was a constraint. It gave defenders a window. AI compressed that window to hours. Automated reconnaissance tools now map an organization's attack surface, identify the personnel with privileged access, correlate their public profiles with their organizational roles, and produce a prioritized target list faster than a human analyst can finish reading the morning threat report. The window the defender used to have between exposure and exploitation is gone.

Vulnerability discovery and exploit generation followed the same compression curve. A vulnerability that would have taken a skilled attacker days to understand and weaponize can now be analyzed and exploited in minutes by an AI system trained on public exploit databases, vulnerability research, and code analysis. The patch cadence that was built for a world where attackers needed weeks to weaponize a new vulnerability is now a liability in a world where weaponization happens before the patch is even tested internally.

Social engineering changed in a way that's harder to defend against than any technical exploit. Voice-cloned executives making real-time phone calls. Synthetic video identities conducting video verification calls. Fabricated email threads that include accurate details about internal projects, personnel, and relationships drawn from publicly available sources and AI-augmented reconnaissance. The human verification systems that organizations built to catch social engineering, call-back procedures, out-of-band confirmation, visual verification, were designed to catch humans pretending to be other humans. They weren't designed to catch AI-generated synthetic identities that can sustain a real-time conversation, answer follow-up questions accurately, and produce documentation that passes visual inspection.

Consider a hypothetical scenario that security teams across financial services are increasingly planning against. A treasury manager receives a call from what sounds exactly like the CFO, referencing a real acquisition discussion that's been happening internally, asking for an urgent wire transfer to be processed before the end of the trading day. The voice is accurate. The context is accurate. The urgency is real. The CFO never made the call. The acquisition context was harvested from a combination of public filings, LinkedIn activity, and a compromised email account that had been quietly read for three weeks. The treasury manager follows the established callback procedure and calls the CFO's direct line. The line is forwarded to a number the attacker controls. The call is answered by an AI voice system that continues the conversation. Note: this is a hypothetical composite scenario illustrating attack patterns that security teams are actively modeling, not a real case study. The point isn't that this attack succeeded. The point is that the verification procedure it defeated was considered robust before AI made synthetic voice generation accessible at scale.

Polymorphic malware adds another dimension to the operating constraint. Malware that observes the defenses it encounters and rewrites its own signatures and behavior to evade them isn't new as a concept. But AI-powered polymorphic malware does this at a speed and sophistication level that signature-based detection can't keep up with. The malware doesn't just change its hash. It changes its behavior, its communication patterns, and its evasion logic in response to what it observes in the environment. A detection rule written for yesterday's variant doesn't catch today's mutation. And the mutation cycle is now faster than the detection update cycle in most SOC environments.

Autonomous attack chains are the capability that changes the SOC's operating constraint most fundamentally. Multi-stage campaigns that previously required human operator intervention at each decision point now run without it. The attacker defines the objective and the constraints. The AI system executes the campaign, makes tactical decisions at each stage, adapts to what it encounters, and escalates only when it reaches a decision point that requires human judgment. The campaign runs around the clock, at machine speed, without the operational pauses that human-operated attacks require. The SOC that's staffed for a 9-to-5 detection cycle is operating against an adversary that doesn't stop at 5 p.m.

The compressed exploit window is the new operating constraint the SOC has to build around. Patch cadences built for human-speed attackers assumed a window of days to weeks between vulnerability disclosure and active exploitation. That window is now measured in hours for high-profile vulnerabilities. A patch that takes 72 hours to test, approve, and deploy is a 72-hour exposure window against an adversary that can weaponize and deploy an exploit in under four hours. The SOC's response to this isn't to patch faster, though that helps. It's to build compensating controls that reduce the impact of the exposure window: network segmentation that limits blast radius, behavioral detection that catches exploitation attempts before they complete, and isolation capabilities that can quarantine a compromised system before the attacker achieves their objective.

The SOC that understands this adversary picture stops asking, "how do we detect the breach?" and starts asking "how do we detect the campaign before it completes?" Those are different questions with different detection architectures, different alert taxonomies, and different response playbooks. The rebuild starts with the right question.

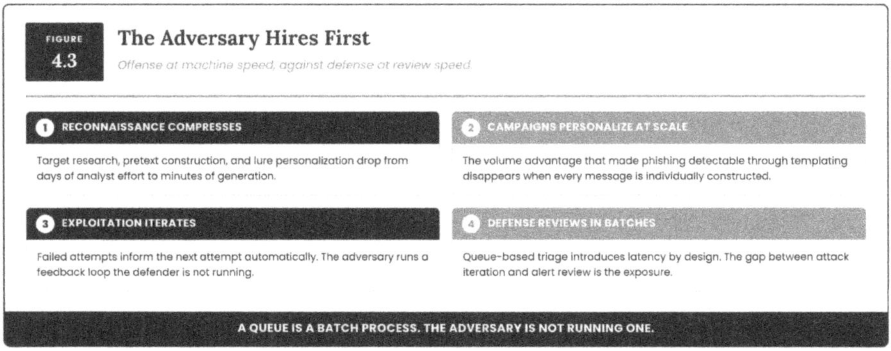

Corruption Without Breach: The Attack No Alert Detects

This is the detection problem that defines the AI-era SOC. And most SOC teams haven't fully confronted it yet.

Prompt injection, training data poisoning, and context manipulation share one characteristic that makes them fundamentally different from every attack category the SOC's detection philosophy was built around. They don't look like attacks. They look like normal AI behavior. The system isn't compromised in any traditional sense. It's running exactly as designed. It's just running on corrupted inputs, corrupted context, or corrupted beliefs, and producing outputs that serve the attacker's objectives instead of the enterprise's.

Prompt injection is the most immediate of the three. An attacker crafts an input to an AI system that overrides the system's intended instructions and substitutes the attacker's own. The AI follows the injected instruction because that's what it was designed to do: follow instructions. The injection doesn't require authentication. It doesn't require access credentials. It doesn't require a network connection to an internal system. It requires access to the input channel, which in many enterprise AI deployments is a user-facing interface, an API endpoint, or a document that the AI is asked to process. The attack surface is wherever the AI accepts input, which is everywhere the AI is useful.

The detection challenge is that a successful prompt injection looks, in the logs, exactly like a normal user interaction. A query was submitted. The AI processed it. A response was generated. No authentication failure. No access violation. No data exfiltration alert. The only signal that something went wrong is in the output itself, and the output is only wrong if someone is watching it closely enough to notice. In a high-volume AI environment where thousands of interactions happen daily, that kind of output-level monitoring requires a systematic approach. It can't be done by spot-checking.

Training data poisoning operates on a longer timeline and is harder to detect precisely because the corruption happened before the model was deployed. An attacker who can influence the data used to train or fine-tune a model can embed biases, backdoors, or behavioral modifications that activate under specific conditions. The model passes pre-deployment testing because the activation conditions aren't triggered during testing. It passes the initial deployment period because the attacker hasn't yet triggered the backdoor. It behaves normally in production until the attacker sends the specific input pattern that activates the poisoned behavior. At that point, the model does exactly what it was designed to do, which is what makes the attack so difficult to detect with traditional monitoring. There's no anomaly in the system's behavior relative to its training. The anomaly is in the training itself.

Context manipulation sits between the other two in terms of timeline and detection difficulty. An attacker who can influence the context that an AI agent draws on, through manipulated documents in a retrieval system, altered records in a knowledge base, or corrupted data in the agent's memory, can steer the agent's outputs without touching the model itself. The model is fine. The retrieval pipeline is fine. The data the pipeline is retrieving from is not. And the agent produces outputs that reflect the corrupted context, not the accurate one, with full confidence and no error signal.

The reason these attacks compromise the enterprise more deeply than exfiltration is that they corrupt the intelligence the enterprise relies on to make decisions. A breach that exfiltrates customer data is serious. It triggers regulatory obligations, it damages trust, and it has a defined remediation path. A corruption attack that causes an AI compliance system to give wrong regulatory guidance, or causes an AI fraud detection system to approve fraudulent transactions, or causes an AI-driven clinical decision tool to recommend the wrong treatment, operates at the decision layer. The damage isn't in what was taken. It's in what was decided on the basis of corrupted intelligence. That damage may not be visible until long after the corruption occurred, and the remediation path is far less defined.

The SOC's entire detection philosophy, built on indicators of compromise, fails against indicators of corruption because indicators of compromise assume an attacker who had to touch the system to damage it. An access log, a file modification, a network connection to a known malicious IP. Indicators of corruption don't require the attacker to touch the system in any way that generates a traditional security signal. The corruption is in the content, not the connection. The SOC needs a parallel detection philosophy built around behavioral baselines and output monitoring, running alongside its existing IOC-based detection, to catch what IOC logic was never designed to see.

The practical implementation of this parallel detection philosophy has three components. The first is output baseline monitoring. For every AI system in production that makes consequential decisions, define what normal output looks like. Not just statistically, but semantically. A compliance AI system should produce outputs that are consistent with the regulatory framework it was trained on. A fraud detection system should produce decisions that are consistent with the risk model it was built around. Define those baselines explicitly, and set up automated comparison checks that flag outputs that deviate significantly from the baseline pattern. The flag goes to a human analyst who reviews the output against the ground truth source and determines whether the deviation is a model drift issue, a data quality issue, or a potential corruption event.

The second component is retrieval pipeline integrity monitoring. For AI systems that use retrieval-augmented generation, monitor the data sources the retrieval pipeline draws from. Hash the content of critical knowledge bases and document stores on a defined cadence. Compare current hashes against the previous baseline. Any change that wasn't produced by an authorized update process gets flagged for review. The review determines whether the change was legitimate or whether the data source was altered without authorization. This is the detection layer for context manipulation attacks that operate through the retrieval layer rather than the model itself.

The third component is a quarterly human review of AI outputs against ground truth. This is the control that catches slow-moving corruption that doesn't trigger automated deviation thresholds. A subject matter expert, not the AI system's owner, reviews a sample of the system's recent outputs against the authoritative source the system is supposed to reflect. If the outputs have drifted from the source in ways that the automated monitoring didn't catch, the human review finds it. The quarterly cadence is the minimum. For high-stakes AI systems, monthly is better. The review findings go into the risk register with a named owner and a resolution timeline.

Name these three components as detection requirements in your SOC operating model this week. Assign an owner for each one. Set the implementation timeline. The gap between your current IOC-based detection and the indicators-of-corruption detection your environment requires is the most consequential detection gap the audit surfaced. It needs an owner and a plan before the next chapter adds the machine-speed tools to close it.

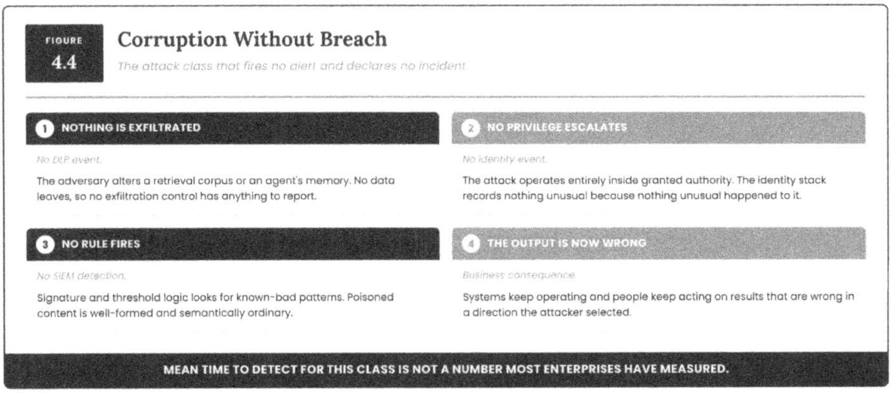

The Non-Human Identity Explosion: The Lateral Movement Nobody Is Watching

There's a lateral movement problem growing inside most enterprise environments right now, and the SOC isn't watching it because the identity controls it uses to detect lateral movement were built for humans.

Service accounts, API keys, agent credentials, and pipeline identities outnumber human identities in most mid-to-large enterprises by a significant margin. The ratio keeps growing as AI deployment accelerates. Every new AI agent needs credentials. Every new pipeline integration needs an API key. Every new automated workflow needs a service account. These identities accumulate faster than any lifecycle management process built for human identity can track, and they accumulate access that no human ever formally reviewed.

The audit probably flagged this. It likely found service accounts with excessive permissions, API keys with no expiration dates, agent credentials with access scopes that were never formally approved. What the audit couldn't do was install the ongoing governance model that keeps the problem from growing back. That's the SOC's inheritance: a snapshot of the NHI problem at audit time, with no operating model to prevent the same gaps from reappearing the week after the audit closed.

The specific risk pattern that makes NHI compromise so dangerous is that compromised machine credentials move through an environment without tripping a single identity control built for people. Behavioral analytics tools trained on human access patterns flag a human account accessing resources at 3 a.m. They don't flag a service account doing the same thing, because service accounts routinely run overnight batch processes and the tool has been trained to treat that as normal. An attacker who gains control of a service account can operate inside the enterprise's behavioral baseline for extended periods, accessing systems and data that the service account was legitimately credentialed to reach, without generating the anomaly signals that would trigger a human-focused identity alert.

The agent-creates-agent problem compounds this. Autonomous agents in agentic AI architectures can spin up subordinate agents to complete subtasks. Those subordinate agents need credentials. In many implementations, the parent agent provisions those credentials automatically, inheriting permissions from its own access scope or drawing from a credential pool that was configured when the parent agent was deployed. Nobody reviews the subordinate agent's access. Nobody adds it to the identity inventory. Nobody sets an expiration on its credentials. The agent completes its task and is supposed to terminate. Sometimes it doesn't. Sometimes the subordinate agent's credentials persist long after the task is done, sitting in the environment with valid access and no owner watching them.

The Non-Human Identity Pyramid provides the tiered governance model the SOC needs to bring this under control. The pyramid has three tiers, and the governance intensity increases as you move up.

The base tier is static non-human identities. Service accounts with defined functions, API keys with fixed integrations, pipeline credentials that connect known systems to known destinations. These identities don't change frequently. They have defined owners. They have defined access scopes. The governance requirement at the base tier is inventory accuracy and access scope verification. Every static NHI should be in the registry, every one should have a named owner, and everyone should have its access scope verified against what it actually needs to do its job. Anything with more access than it needs gets scoped down. Anything without a named owner gets suspended until an owner is assigned. This is the foundational cleanup that turns the audit's NHI findings into a governed baseline.

The middle tier is dynamic non-human identities. Agent credentials that are provisioned and deprovisioned as part of automated workflows, API keys that rotate on a defined schedule, service accounts that are created for specific projects and should expire when the project ends. The governance requirement at the middle tier is lifecycle management. Every dynamic NHI needs a defined expiration condition, either a time-based expiration or a task-completion trigger that causes the credential to be revoked automatically. The SOC's role here is monitoring: any dynamic NHI that persists past its expected lifecycle gets flagged for review. That flag is the detection signal for the agent-creates-agent problem, because the orphaned subordinate agent credential is exactly the kind of lifecycle anomaly these monitoring catches.

The top tier is privileged non-human identities. Agent credentials with elevated access, service accounts with write permissions to critical systems, API keys that can trigger financial transactions or modify configuration data. These identities carry the highest risk if compromised and require the most intensive governance. Every privileged NHI needs a named human owner with explicit accountability, a ratified access scope that was approved by the CISO or a delegated authority, a review cadence of no more than 30 days, and a documented justification for the elevated access. Any privileged NHI that can't produce all four of those attributes gets suspended until it can.

The SOC's immediate action is the initial NHI inventory. This week, run a discovery scan across the enterprise environment specifically looking for non-human identities. The scan should cover Active Directory service accounts, cloud IAM roles assigned to non-human principals, API keys registered in your identity management system, and any credential stores associated with AI agents or automated pipelines. The output is a raw list. The list goes to the SOC manager, who applies the three-tier classification. Every identity in the top tier gets a named owner assigned within 48 hours. Every identity in the middle tier gets a lifecycle review within two weeks. Every identity in the base tier gets an access scope verification within 30 days. That's the first NHI governance cycle. It won't be perfect. It will be the most complete picture of the NHI environment the SOC has ever had, and it will surface the specific gaps that need to go to the board as a detection priority.

Making NHI compromise a board-level detection priority requires language the board can evaluate. The language isn't technical. It's accountability based. The question you bring to the board is this: if a machine credential in our environment was compromised right now, how long would it take us to detect it, and which systems would be exposed in that window? If the answer is "we don't know, because we don't have a complete inventory of our non-human identities," that's the board-level finding. The NHI inventory is the artifact that changes that answer from "we don't know" to "here's our current inventory, here's our detection coverage, and here's the gap we're closing on this timeline." That's the answer the board can govern.

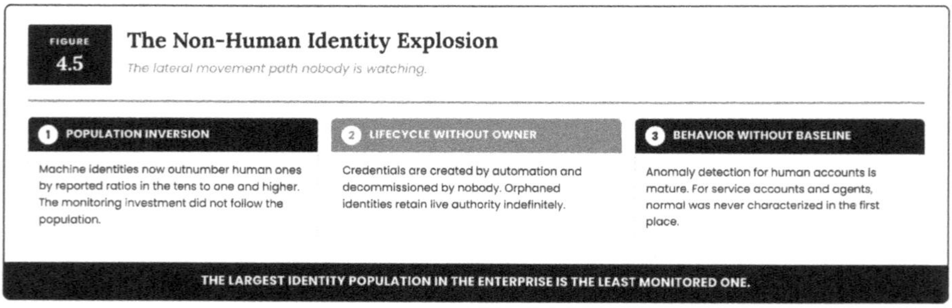

The SOC's Own AI: The Target Inside the Defense

The SOC's defensive AI stack is now an attack surface. That's not a theoretical concern. It's a logical consequence of deploying AI in a contested environment where the adversary understands that the fastest way into an AI-defended enterprise is through the AI doing the defending.

The recursion here is specific and important to understand clearly. The SOC deploys a copilot to help analysts triage alerts faster. The copilot reads alert data, correlates it with threat intelligence, and recommends investigation priorities.

An attacker who understands how the copilot works can craft alerts and events that steer the copilot's recommendations away from the actual attack and toward decoy activity. The analyst follows the copilot's prioritization. The actual attack progresses undetected while the analyst investigates the decoy. The copilot didn't fail in any technical sense. It was manipulated.

This is prompt injection against the SOC's own tooling. The injection surface isn't a user-facing chatbot. It's the alert data, the log entries, and the threat intelligence feeds that the copilot processes as its inputs. An attacker who can influence those inputs can influence the copilot's outputs. And in many SOC environments, the attacker already has partial influence over those inputs because they're operating inside the environment and generating the events that the logging system captures.

Poisoned threat intelligence feeds are a related vector with a broader impact radius. The SOC's detection models, its automated triage rules, and its threat hunting playbooks all draw from threat intelligence to stay current on attacker tactics. If the intelligence feed is compromised or manipulated, the corruption propagates through every downstream process that draws from it. Detection rules get updated to miss the attacker's actual techniques. Triage logic gets calibrated to deprioritize the signals the attacker is generating. Threat hunting queries get refined to look in the wrong places. The entire detection apparatus is being tuned against a false picture of the threat landscape, and it's doing so automatically, at scale, because that's what it was designed to do.

Adversarial evasion training is the most sophisticated of the three vectors. An attacker who has enough visibility into the SOC's detection models can use that knowledge to train their own tools to evade detection. This doesn't require direct access to the detection model's internals. It requires the ability to probe the model's outputs by generating activity and observing what gets detected versus what passes through. Over time, that probing builds a picture of the detection model's blind spots. The attacker then calibrates their techniques to operate in those blind spots. The detection model's coverage appears complete. The attacker's activity appears clean. The model is functioning correctly against the training data it was built on. The training data just doesn't include the evasion patterns the attacker has developed specifically against it.

The governance requirement that closes these three vectors is the same governance standard the SOC applies to every other AI system in the enterprise. The defensive AI stack needs behavioral baselines. It needs output monitoring. It needs anomaly detection watching its recommendations and decisions for patterns that deviate from its expected behavior. It needs a named owner who is accountable for its accuracy and its integrity, separate from the team that uses it operationally. And it needs a review cadence that's at least as frequent as the cadence applied to the highest-risk AI systems it's supposed to be protecting.

The specific governance artifacts for the SOC's AI stack are four. First, a behavioral baseline document for each AI tool in the defensive stack. What does normal triage recommendation distribution look like? What percentage of high-severity alerts should the copilot be flagging in a typical week? What's the expected correlation rate between copilot recommendations and analyst final dispositions? These baselines don't need to be precise on day one. They need to exist, so that deviations from them are detectable.

Second, a threat intelligence feed integrity protocol. Define the sources the SOC draws threat intelligence from. For each source, define the validation check that confirms the feed hasn't been tampered with. Hash comparison for feeds that produce structured data. Semantic consistency checks for feeds that produce narrative intelligence. A defined escalation path when a feed fails its integrity check. The protocol runs on the same cadence as the feed itself. A daily threat intelligence feed gets a daily integrity check.

Third, a quarterly adversarial review of the detection model's coverage. This is a structured exercise where the SOC's most experienced threat hunters attempt to generate activity that the detection model doesn't flag. The goal isn't to break the model. It's to find the blind spots before the attacker does. Findings from the adversarial review go into the risk register with a remediation owner and a timeline. The exercise runs quarterly at minimum. For SOCs in high-threat environments, monthly is appropriate.

Fourth, a named owner for the defensive AI stack's governance, separate from the SOC manager who owns its operational use. The governance owner is accountable for the behavioral baselines, the integrity protocols, the adversarial review program, and the escalation path when an anomaly is detected in the defensive AI's behavior. That separation of operational use and governance accountability is the same separation the SOC applies to every other AI system it supervises. The defensive AI stack doesn't get a pass because it's on the defender's side. It gets the same standard precisely because it's on the defender's side and a compromised defender is worse than no defender.

The Volume V audit assessed the defensive AI stack as part of the security tooling inventory. That assessment was accurate at audit time. The governance standard described above is what keeps it accurate every day after. Assign the governance owner this week. Schedule the first adversarial review within 30 days. Define the behavioral baselines within two weeks. The SOC's own AI is the target inside the defense, and it needs to be governed like one.

Automation Bias in the Tier: When the Copilot Is Wrong and Confident

The SOC's most immediate AI risk is not an adversary at all. It is that analysts stop checking. Every SOC that has deployed a triage copilot for more than a few months encounters the same drift: early on, analysts verify the copilot's reasoning on most alerts, and the verification catches errors. Over time, verification rates fall, because the copilot is right often enough that checking feels like a tax on throughput. The error rate does not change. The detection rate for those errors falls toward zero, and it falls silently, because an unverified wrong conclusion produces no signal that distinguishes it from an unverified right one.

This is not a hypothetical about future systems. It is a well-documented pattern in every domain that has introduced high-accuracy automated judgment into a human workflow, and security operations has no immunity to it. The specific shape it takes in a SOC is that a copilot classifies an alert as benign with a confident, well-written rationale that cites the right telemetry and reaches the wrong conclusion. The analyst reads the rationale, finds it plausible because it is plausible, and closes the ticket. The alert that would have been the first indicator of a real intrusion is now a closed ticket with a documented justification, which is a worse artifact than an unhandled alert because it looks handled.

The measurement problem is what makes this failure durable. A SOC can measure how many alerts the copilot processed, how fast it processed them, and how many analysts overrode it. What a SOC cannot measure without deliberate instrumentation is how many copilot conclusions were wrong and accepted, because by definition nobody looked. The metric that would surface it, agreement rate between the copilot and an independent human review on a random sample, requires spending human hours on alerts that have already been closed, which is the exact expenditure the copilot was purchased to eliminate. Programs that do not deliberately fund that sample do not have an accuracy number. They have a throughput number that they are describing as an accuracy number.

The second-order effect reaches staffing and takes longer to appear. Tier-1 analysis has always been where analysts developed pattern recognition, and a tier-1 function where the machine reasons and the human confirms produces analysts who have seen many conclusions and worked few investigations. Three years into that model, the SOC has a cohort that is fast at validating machine reasoning and thin at constructing its own. That is a defensible trade if it is a deliberate one, tied to a reskilling program that builds depth somewhere else in the workflow. It is a serious problem if it happened by default while everyone was watching the throughput improve.

The decision rule here is specific and cheap relative to what it protects. Fund a standing independent review sample, sized at a small percentage of copilot-closed alerts, staffed by an analyst who does not see the copilot's rationale before forming a conclusion. Publish the agreement rate monthly alongside the throughput number and treat a falling agreement rate as an incident rather than as a tuning opportunity. Any SOC director who cannot state the current agreement rate is operating an autonomous system with no accuracy instrumentation, and the supervision matrix in the next chapter has nothing to gate expansion against.

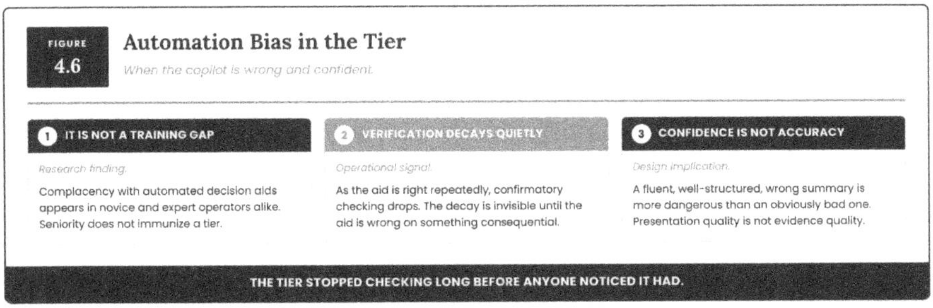

Instrumenting the SOC's Own AI: Watching the Watcher

Every AI system the SOC deployed to monitor the enterprise is itself an unmonitored AI system, and the asymmetry is not an oversight so much as an unexamined assumption. The triage copilot, the anomaly scoring model, the enrichment agent, and the containment automation are each systems whose corruption would degrade detection capability while the operational metrics continued to look normal. A SOC that has instrumented every enterprise AI system and left its own uninstrumented has built a comprehensive monitoring program with a hole in the exact location a sophisticated adversary would examine first.

The attack does not require sophistication to be effective, which is the part that should concern SOC leaders most. An adversary who can influence what the triage copilot considers normal, whether through the enrichment sources it consults, the historical corpus it retrieves from, or sustained low-volume activity that shifts its baseline, has purchased permission for a category of activity to be classified as benign. There is no exfiltration event, no privilege escalation the identity stack records, and no rule violation. There is a copilot that now closes a particular pattern of alert with a well-written rationale, and analysts who have learned to trust the rationale.

The instrumentation required is the same instrumentation the SOC applies to enterprise systems, applied inward, and the resistance to doing it is cultural rather than technical. Baseline the copilot's classification distribution across alert categories and monitor for drift. Log the retrieval sources every conclusion drew on and alert when the source mix shifts materially. Track the enrichment feeds for changes in provider, content, or availability. Monitor the agent identities the SOC's own tooling uses with at least the rigor applied to business unit agents, and note that these identities frequently carry broader permissions than any business system because they were built to investigate everything.

The supervision matrix applies inward as well, and most SOCs have not written the rows. The containment automation that can isolate a host, disable an account, or block a network segment is an autonomous system taking consequential action, and it belongs in the matrix with an autonomy level, an evidence threshold, and a named approving authority exactly as an enterprise system would. The argument that it is a security tool and therefore trusted is the same argument business units make about their tools, and the SOC does not accept it from them.

The decision rule is that the SOC's own AI estate appears in the model registry, in the supervision matrix, in the corruption detection program, and in the kill-switch runbook, with no exemptions. A SOC director who resists this on the grounds that the security tooling is different should be able to state what makes it different in a sentence a regulator would accept. In practice the honest answer is that instrumenting your own tools surfaces findings about your own program, which is uncomfortable, and that discomfort is not a security control.

The Agent Kill Chain: A Different Sequence Than the SOC Was Built For

The intrusion sequence the SOC was designed around describes an attacker moving through infrastructure. Reconnaissance, delivery, exploitation, installation, command and control, action on objectives. Every detection capability in the stack maps to a stage in that sequence, and the mapping is why the stack works. An attacker compromising an agent moves through a different sequence entirely, and the detection stack has no coverage for most of it because the stages do not produce the artifacts the stack looks for.

The agentic sequence runs from discovery to propagation in seven stages. The attacker discovers which agents the enterprise operates and what they are connected to, frequently from public sources or from the agent's own behavior. The attacker influences the agent by placing content where the agent will retrieve it: a document, a web page, a ticket, a repository, an email, a tool description. The agent accepts an objective the attacker supplied. The agent delegates, invoking other agents or tools with authority it legitimately holds. The agent accesses resources, using credentials that were properly granted. The agent acts, and the action is logged as normal automation because it is normal automation. Then the agent persists, through memory that retains the attacker's framing, and propagates, by influencing other agents that consume its output.

What makes this sequence difficult is that only two of the seven stages produce anything a conventional control examines. Access and action generate logs, and those logs look correct, because the identity was valid and the permission was granted. Discovery, influence, delegation, persistence, and propagation each occur inside layers the SOC does not currently instrument: retrieval sources, objective formation, agent-to-agent messaging, memory writes, and the downstream consumption of agent output. A SOC that instruments only what the identity stack and the endpoint produce is monitoring two of seven stages and calling it coverage.

The stage that repays instrumentation most is influence, because it is the earliest point where detection is still cheap and the attack has not yet acquired legitimate authority. Instrumenting influence means recording, for every consequential agent action, which sources contributed to the reasoning, and alerting when the source mix departs from the agent's baseline. An agent that normally retrieves from three internal repositories and suddenly retrieves from an external domain has produced a signal that is both detectable and specific. That signal exists in the retrieval layer and nowhere else, which is why the telemetry work in the next chapter has to reach that layer rather than stopping at the model boundary.

Persistence is the stage that determines how expensive the incident becomes, and it is the one most incident response plans have no procedure for. An agent whose memory retains an attacker's framing will resume the compromised behavior after any containment that does not address memory, and the responder who isolates the host, rotates the credentials, and restores the system has performed a complete response that fixed nothing. Treat the seven stages as the coverage map for the detection work in Chapter 5 and the response work that follows it, and be explicit with the SOC about which stages currently have no coverage at all. Naming an uncovered stage is a finding. Assuming it is covered because the tooling is expensive is how this goes wrong.

FIGURE 4.7 The Agent Kill Chain

A different sequence than the SOC was built to detect.

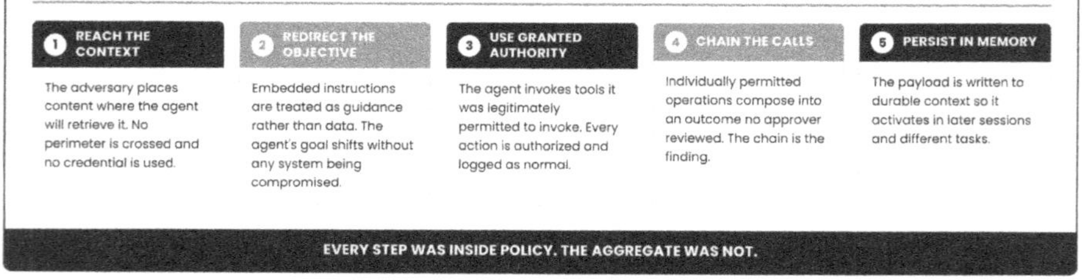

Cascading Failure: When Every Agent Behaved Correctly and the System Did Not

Every control this Part has described operates on an individual agent. The supervision matrix assigns autonomy per system and action class. The circuit breaker bounds one agent's envelope. The behavioral baseline describes one agent's normal. Each is necessary, and together they leave a failure mode uncovered, because a multi-agent system can produce an outcome nobody authorized while every participating agent stayed inside its own limits. That is not a hypothetical property of future architectures. It is what happens when three agents that were designed separately are connected by a workflow that was designed by neither.

The mechanics are ordinary enough to be easy to miss. An agent produces an output that is correct given its inputs. A second agent consumes that output as an input, treats it as established fact because it arrived from an internal system, and produces a conclusion of its own. A third acts on the second's conclusion. Uncertainty that the first agent expressed as a qualification gets stripped at the first handoff, because the consuming system reads a value rather than a confidence. By the third step the enterprise is acting on a firm conclusion whose underlying evidence was tentative, and no individual agent did anything wrong.

Amplification is the version of this that reaches the balance sheet. When one agent's output feeds another's input and the second's output feeds back into the first's context, the loop has no natural damping and small errors compound rather than average out. Pricing agents reading market signals another agent produced, inventory agents responding to demand forecasts that were themselves generated from inventory positions, and triage agents whose escalation decisions train the baselines that later triage decisions read are all real instances of this shape. Each agent's circuit breaker measures its own volume and sees nothing unusual, because the individual rates are normal. The system-level behavior is not.

Goal drift is the third variant and the hardest to detect, because it happens across time rather than within a transaction. An agent that adapts its approach based on what worked previously, operating in a workflow with other adapting agents, can arrive at a collective strategy that no participant was given and that satisfies each agent's local objective while violating the enterprise's. Detecting it requires evaluating the workflow's aggregate outcomes against the workflow's intended purpose, which is a different measurement than any agent-level monitoring produces and one that almost no enterprise currently performs.

The control is a workflow-level envelope in addition to the agent-level ones, and the distinction is the entire point. Multi-agent workflows carrying consequential outcomes get their own recorded objective, their own aggregate limits on total actions, total spend, and end-to-end duration, and their own circuit breaker at the orchestration layer that stops the workflow rather than any individual agent. Confidence has to survive the handoff, meaning an agent consuming another agent's output receives the qualification alongside the value and is required to propagate it. And a feedback loop between agents is registered as a design decision with a named owner rather than emerging from an integration nobody diagrammed.

The decision rule follows from a question the SOC director should be able to answer for every multi-agent workflow in production, and most currently cannot. If every agent in this workflow operates within its individual envelope, what is the worst aggregate outcome the workflow can produce? An answer of "we have not calculated that" is the finding, and it belongs on the risk register with the workflow named. This is also the point at which the OWASP agentic taxonomy's cascading-failure category stops being an abstraction and becomes a specific line item: the enterprise either holds a workflow-level bound or it holds a collection of well-governed agents and an unbounded system.

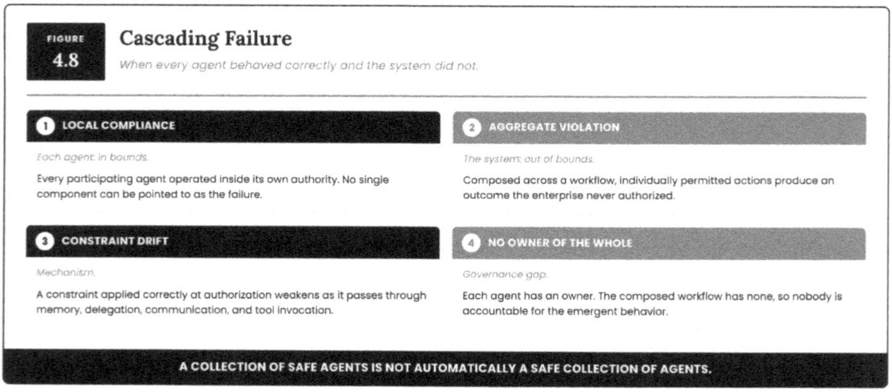

Putting It Into Practice

The SOC's inheritance is a structural mismatch between the operating model it has and the threat environment it's operating in. This month, that mismatch gets measured, named, and assigned to owners. The actions below are sequenced. Each one builds on the previous. None of them are optional if the SOC intends to close the gap before the next AI-specific incident forces the question.

Start with the detection coverage audit. This week, map your current detection rules, alert categories, and investigation playbooks against the four AI-specific attack surfaces: prompt injection, agent behavioral anomalies, model abuse patterns, and NHI compromise. For each attack surface, answer one question: if this attack were happening right now in your environment, which specific detection rule would it catch? If the answer is "none" or "we're not sure," document that gap explicitly. The gap documentation goes into the risk register with a named owner, a severity classification, and a 30-day deadline for a detection design proposal. You can't close gaps you haven't named. Name them this week.

Next, address the patch and exposure cadence against the machine-speed exploit window. Pull your current patch cadence policy. Calculate the average time from vulnerability disclosure to patch deployment for your ten most recent critical patches. Compare that number against the current mean time to exploitation for critical vulnerabilities in your threat environment. If your patch deployment time exceeds your exposure window, that's a compensating control requirement, not just a process improvement. Identify the three highest-risk systems in your AI environment where that gap is widest. Design a compensating control for each one: network segmentation, behavioral detection, or isolation capability that reduces the blast radius during the exposure window. Document the compensating controls, assign owners, and set implementation timelines. Present the gap and the compensating control plan to the CISO before the next board cycle.

Run the initial NHI inventory this month. The scan scope, the three-tier classification, and the ownership assignment process are described in the previous section. The output is a registry entry for every non-human identity discovered, classified by tier, with a named owner for top-tier identities assigned within 48 hours of the scan completing. The inventory isn't the end state. It's the baseline from which the ongoing NHI governance program runs. Once the baseline exists, the SOC can detect NHI anomalies because it knows what normal looks like. Before the baseline exists, every NHI anomaly is invisible because there's no reference point to compare it against.

Put the SOC's own AI stack under the governance standard this week. Assign the governance owner. Schedule the behavioral baseline definition session within 14 days. Configure the threat intelligence feed integrity checks. Put the first adversarial review on the calendar within 30 days. The defensive AI stack doesn't get a grace period because it's running in production and the attacker doesn't wait for governance to catch up. The governance standard applies from today, not from the next planning cycle.

Finally, pull the AI incident response playbook and schedule the first tabletop exercise within 45 days. The exercise scenario should test specifically the kill-switch authority chain for an AI agent that's been compromised through prompt injection. Who makes the call to suspend? How long does it take to reach them? Can the suspension be executed without a committee meeting? Does the suspension actually work as described in the playbook, or does the technical implementation lag behind the documented authority? The tabletop answers those questions before an incident does. The findings go into the playbook as revisions, and the revised playbook gets a named owner and a quarterly rehearsal cadence.

The gaps named this month are the foundation the next chapter builds on. The SOC that knows exactly where its detection coverage fails against AI-specific attack surfaces is the SOC that can use machine-speed defensive tools precisely, because it knows which gaps those tools need to close. Measuring the mismatch is the work of this month. Closing it with the same machine speed the adversary already has is the work of the next chapter.

FIGURE 4.9

Putting It Into Practice

Close the visibility gap the audit left open.

1 INSTRUMENT ONE AI SYSTEM

Take the highest-consequence AI system and connect its logs to detection. Establish what normal output distribution looks like.

SOC Manager. Weeks 1-3

2 BASELINE THE IDENTITIES

Characterize normal behavior for the top tier of non-human identities. Anomaly detection without a baseline is a dashboard, not a control.

IAM Lead. Weeks 2-6

3 TEST THE TIER

Insert a known-wrong AI-generated finding into the queue and measure whether it is caught. That number is your automation bias exposure.

SOC Manager. Week 4

YOU CANNOT DETECT CORRUPTION IN A SYSTEM YOU ARE NOT INSTRUMENTING.

Chapter 5: Security Operations Gains an Engine

When Machines Investigate and Humans Supervise

CHAPTER 5 OUTCOMES

At the end of this chapter, you will be able to:

1. Investigate every alert rather than sampling the queue.
2. Build the signal set that detects attacks on reasoning rather than on infrastructure.
3. Apply the Human Supervision Matrix to decide which actions machines take alone.
4. Rehearse the Red-Button Protocol and measure an actual time-to-stop.
5. Enforce agent circuit breakers because human reaction time is too slow.
6. Source the evidence for autonomy expansion from continuous adversarial evaluation.

MACHINES INVESTIGATE. HUMANS SUPERVISE. THE LINE BETWEEN THEM IS WRITTEN DOWN.

The Analyst Shortage Ends: Every Alert Investigated, Not Sampled

Every SOC director knows the math. The alerts come in faster than the team can work them. The queue builds overnight. The morning shift inherits a backlog that grows faster than it shrinks. Triage becomes a prioritization exercise, which means it becomes a sampling exercise, which means somewhere in that unworked queue there are signals nobody looked at. Not because the analysts weren't good. Because there weren't enough hours.

That constraint breaks when investigation moves to machine speed.

Autonomous triage doesn't get tired at hour ten of a shift. It doesn't have a queue. It processes every alert the moment it arrives, applies the same logic to the ten-thousandth alert that it applied to the first, and routes each one to the right destination without a human having to decide which fifty alerts to ignore so they can work the other fifty. The tier-1 gap, the space between alerts generated and alerts actually investigated, closes. Not partially. Completely. Every alert gets touched. Every alert gets an initial disposition. The analyst's job stops being "deciding what to look at" and starts being "review what the machine found."

That's a different job. It's a better job.

The economics of this shift are the part most SOC leaders haven't fully calculated yet. Cost per investigation in a human-led triage model includes the analyst time spent reading the alert, pulling context, correlating related events, and making an initial severity judgment. That process takes somewhere between five and twenty minutes per alert depending on complexity, which means a high-volume SOC is spending thousands of analyst hours per month on work that a well-configured autonomous triage system does in seconds. When the machine handles that volume, the analyst hours that were consumed by tier-1 triage get redirected to the investigations that actually require human judgment: the complex multi-stage campaigns, the ambiguous behavioral patterns, the decisions that carry enough consequence that a human needs to own them explicitly.

Correlation across the full estate changes the detection picture in a way that human triage physically cannot match. A human analyst working a queue sees the alerts in front of them. They can pull related events if they know to look for them. They can correlate across a handful of systems if the investigation warrants it. What they can't do is hold the full signal picture of a thousand systems in their head simultaneously and notice that three low-severity alerts from three different systems, each individually unremarkable, form a pattern that indicates a coordinated campaign. The machine can. It's not smarter than the analyst. It just has a wider field of view and no attention limit.

Continuous threat hunting is the capability that changes the SOC's posture from reactive to active. Traditional threat hunting runs in campaigns. A threat hunter identifies a hypothesis, builds queries, runs them against historical data, and reports findings. The campaign takes days or weeks. It runs quarterly if the team is disciplined, less often if they're stretched. Between campaigns, the hypothesis goes untested. An adversary operating in the environment during that gap has a window of uncontested access that the campaign model was never designed to close. Autonomous threat hunting runs every hour. The same hypothesis that would have taken a human hunter a week to test runs continuously, against live data, flagging matches in real time. The window closes. The adversary loses the dwell-time advantage that the quarterly campaign model handed them for free.

Standing up autonomous triage on your highest-volume alert category is the first concrete action this chapter calls for. Don't start with the most complex category. Start with the highest volume. The volume category is where the coverage gain is most visible and most measurable. Pick the alert type that generates the most tickets in a given week, configure autonomous triage against it, and measure two numbers before and after: percentage of alerts receiving an initial disposition within five minutes, and percentage of alerts that reach a human analyst for review. Those two numbers tell you exactly what the coverage gain is, and they're the numbers you bring to the CISO when the conversation about expanding autonomous triage to other categories begins.

The question the SOC's operating model now needs to answer isn't "what can we afford to investigate?" The question is "what may machines decide alone?" That question is harder. It's also more important. And it's the one the next section builds the answer to.

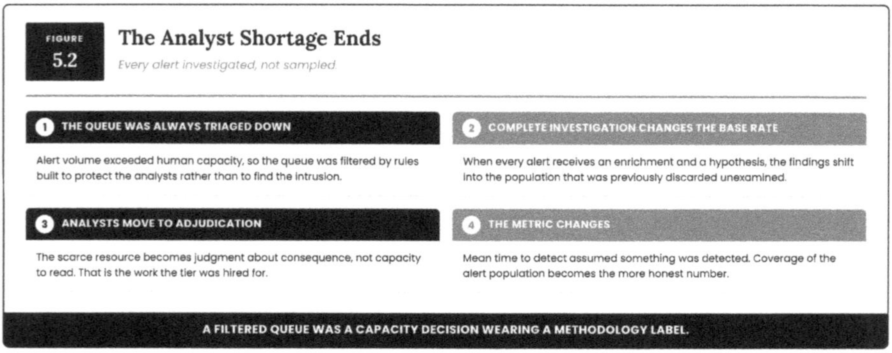

Detecting Corruption: Building the Signal Set for Attacks on Reasoning

Chapter 4 named the problem. Prompt injection, training data poisoning, and context manipulation don't generate indicators of compromise. They corrupt what the AI system believes, and therefore what it decides, without leaving a trace that traditional security monitoring was built to catch. Naming the problem was necessary. Now the SOC needs to build the detection.

The corruption signal set is the collection of telemetry, baselines, and detection rules that gives the SOC visibility into attacks on AI reasoning. It doesn't replace IOC-based detection. It runs alongside it, covering the attack surface that IOC logic was never designed to see. Building it requires starting from scratch in most SOC environments, because the telemetry it draws from isn't the telemetry traditional security monitoring collects.

Behavioral baselines for every AI system in production are the foundation. A baseline isn't a vague description of what the system is supposed to do. It's a quantified profile of what the system actually does across a defined measurement period. For a compliance AI system, the baseline includes the distribution of output types it produces, the regulatory sources it cites most frequently, the confidence levels it assigns to its responses, and the rate at which its outputs get flagged or overridden by human reviewers. For a fraud detection system, the baseline includes its approval and rejection rate across transaction categories, the features it weights most heavily in its decisions, and the rate at which its decisions are reversed on appeal. These baselines get established during a defined observation period after deployment, before any corruption attack has had time to operate. They get updated on a defined cadence as the system's normal behavior evolves. And they become the reference point against which every subsequent measurement is compared.

Drift detection against validated norms is what turns a baseline into a detection capability. The SOC configures automated comparison checks that run on a defined cadence against each system's baseline. When a system's current behavior deviates from its baseline by more than the defined threshold, the deviation gets flagged. The flag isn't an automatic incident. It's a signal that requires human review. The reviewer determines whether the deviation is explained by a legitimate change in the system's inputs, a sanctioned update to the model, or something that doesn't have an innocent explanation. That judgment is exactly the kind of work that belongs to a human. The machine's job is to notice the deviation. The human's job is to understand what it means.

Anomalous reasoning patterns require a specific type of monitoring that most SOC environments don't currently run. An AI system that starts citing sources it wasn't trained on, producing outputs that are inconsistent with its approved use case, or delegating actions to downstream systems in ways that weren't part of its original design is showing reasoning anomalies. These aren't access violations. They're behavioral signals that the system's reasoning has been influenced in ways that weren't authorized. Detecting them requires monitoring the system's reasoning chain, not just its inputs and outputs. For systems that expose their reasoning steps, this means capturing and analyzing those steps on a sampled basis. For systems that don't, it means inferring reasoning patterns from the relationship between inputs and outputs over time.

Unexpected delegation is one of the clearest corruption signals available. An AI agent that was approved to read data and produce recommendations starts writing to systems it was never authorized to modify. An agent that was scoped to operate within a single business unit starts making API calls to systems in a different department. An agent that was designed to escalate ambiguous decisions to a human start resolving them autonomously. Each of these is a delegation anomaly. Each one should trigger an immediate flag. The SOC needs detection rules specifically for delegation scope violations, separate from its general access monitoring rules, because the context that makes a delegation anomalous is different from the context that makes an access attempt anomalous. A service account accessing a database it's credentialed to reach isn't an access violation. An AI agent making decisions it was explicitly scoped not to make is a delegation violation, and the detection rule has to be built around the agent's approved scope, not just its technical access permissions.

The telemetry the SOC must start collecting is the part most teams haven't instrumented yet. Traditional security telemetry captures network connections, authentication events, file access, and process execution. Corruption detection requires a different telemetry set: prompts submitted to AI systems, outputs those systems produced, retrieval sources the systems drew from, and actions the agents took as a result of their reasoning. This telemetry doesn't exist in most SIEM environments today because nobody built the instrumentation for it. Building it is a deliberate engineering effort, not a configuration change. The SOC manager needs to work with the teams that operate the AI systems to define what gets logged, in what format, at what granularity, and how it flows into the detection platform. That conversation needs to happen this month, not next quarter, because every day the telemetry isn't collected is a day the corruption signal set has a blind spot.

Detection rules for this threat category look different from traditional rules because there's no malware signature to match against. The rules are statistical and behavioral rather than signature based. A rule that fires when a system's output distribution shifts more than two standard deviations from its 30-day baseline. A rule that fires when an agent's retrieval sources change significantly from its established pattern. A rule that fires when an agent takes an action that falls outside its approved action taxonomy. These rules require the baselines to exist before they can be written, which is why establishing the baselines is the prerequisite step. The rules are only as good as the norms they're measuring against.

AI watching AI is the operating principle that makes this detection scale. No human team can baseline a thousand models by hand. No analyst team can review every prompt and output in a high-volume AI environment. The machine monitors the machine's reasoning, flagging deviations that a human reviews. The human doesn't review everything. The human reviews the deviations. That division of labor is what makes corruption detection achievable at the scale of a real enterprise AI deployment.

Deploy the corruption signal set on your five most critical AI systems first. Define their behavioral baselines this month. Configure the drift detection rules against those baselines. Instrument the telemetry collection for prompts, outputs, retrieval sources, and agent actions on those five systems. Run the detection for 30 days and review every flag that fires. At the end of 30 days, you'll have a calibrated detection capability on your five highest-stakes systems and a model you can expand to the rest of the estate. That's the corruption detection program. It starts with five systems and a month of calibration, not with a perfect architecture and a year of planning.

FIGURE 5.3

Detecting Corruption

The signal set for attacks on reasoning rather than infrastructure.

1 OUTPUT DISTRIBUTION DRIFT

Signal: statistical.

Track the shape of what the system produces. A model whose answers shift without a corresponding input shift is the earliest available signal.

2 RETRIEVAL PROVENANCE

Signal: lineage.

Record which documents influenced which answers. Poisoning is invisible without knowing what the model actually read.

3 MEMORY WRITE AUDITING

Signal: state change.

Every write to durable agent memory is a change to future behavior. Unaudited writes are unreviewed code changes.

4 TOOL INVOCATION PATTERNS

Signal: behavioral.

Sequences of permitted calls that have never co-occurred before are the aggregate-level anomaly no single call would raise.

THE INFRASTRUCTURE IS FINE. THE REASONING IS WHAT WAS ATTACKED.

The Human Supervision Matrix: Which Actions Machines May Take Alone

Autonomy without supervision is liability. That's not a philosophical position. It's a legal and regulatory reality. When an autonomous system takes an action that causes harm, the first question isn't technical. It's governance. Who approved this action? Who had authority to stop it? Who is accountable for the outcome? If those questions don't have pre-authorized answers, the accountability vacuum from Chapter 1 opens at exactly the moment it's most expensive.

The Human Supervision Matrix is the artifact that closes that vacuum for the SOC. It's a structured decision framework that classifies every action an autonomous system might take into one of three categories: actions the machine executes autonomously without human approval, actions that require human approval before execution, and actions that are forbidden regardless of the machine's confidence level. Every AI system in the SOC's operational environment gets mapped to this matrix before it's authorized to act.

Building the matrix starts with action inventory. For each autonomous system in the SOC stack, list every action it's capable of taking. Not just the actions it takes routinely. Every action in its capability set. An autonomous triage system might be capable of closing alerts, escalating alerts, quarantining endpoints, blocking IP addresses, disabling user accounts, and generating incident reports. Each of those actions has a different risk profile. Closing an alert that turns out to be a real threat is recoverable. Disabling a user account that belongs to a legitimate user during a critical business operation is not. The action inventory forces the SOC to confront the full range of what the machine can do, not just what it's currently configured to do.

Once the action inventory exists, each action gets classified. Autonomous execution is appropriate for actions that are low-risk, reversible, and well-understood. Closing a low-severity alert that matches a known benign pattern. Enriching an alert with threat intelligence context. Generating a preliminary investigation summary. These actions have clear decision criteria, low consequence if wrong, and easy reversal if needed. Requiring human approval is appropriate for actions that carry meaningful risk or are difficult to reverse. Quarantining an endpoint. Blocking a network segment. Suspending a user account. These actions need a human to confirm the judgment before the machine acts, because the cost of an error is high enough that the latency of human review is worth it. Forbidden actions are those where the risk of autonomous execution is unacceptable regardless of confidence. Deleting data. Modifying security policy configurations. Taking actions that affect financial transactions or regulatory submissions. These actions require human decision and human accountability, full stop. No confidence score changes that.

The supervision protocol defines what the human reviewer actually does when an action requires approval. It's not enough to say "a human approves it." The protocol specifies what the reviewer checks before approving. For a quarantine action, the reviewer checks: is the affected endpoint critical to a business process currently running? Is the evidence supporting the quarantine recommendation from a single source or corroborated? Is there a less disruptive action that achieves the same containment? Has the endpoint owner been notified? Those specific checks are what make the approval meaningful rather than a rubber stamp. A human who approves an action without checking those things hasn't supervised the machine. They've just added their name to the audit trail.

Override authority is the other half of the supervision protocol. The reviewer doesn't just approve or deny. They have defined authority to modify the machine's recommendation. To approve a less aggressive version of the proposed action. To escalate to a higher authority if the action's risk profile exceeds their authorization level. To document a disagreement with the machine's recommendation and proceed anyway, with that disagreement captured in the audit trail. The override authority is what makes the human genuinely supervisory rather than ceremonially involved. A human who can only approve or deny, but can't modify or escalate, isn't supervising. They're ratifying.

The audit trail the supervision protocol produces is the artifact that answers the regulator's question. When someone asks who made the call on a specific autonomous action, the audit trail shows: the machine's recommendation, the evidence it was based on, the human reviewer who received it, the checks the reviewer performed, the decision the reviewer made, and the timestamp of every step. That chain of evidence is what makes accountability real rather than theoretical. Without it, the answer to "who decided this" is "the system," which is not an answer any regulator, board member, or court will accept.

The expansion rule governs how the matrix evolves over time. Autonomy grows by evidence, never by enthusiasm. An action moves from "requires human approval" to "autonomous execution" only when the machine has demonstrated, over a defined measurement period, a decision accuracy rate that meets a defined threshold. The threshold is set by the CISO, not by the SOC manager, because the threshold represents a risk acceptance decision that belongs at the CISO level. A machine that has correctly recommended quarantine actions 97% of the time over 90 days, with human reviewers confirming the recommendation in 97% of cases, has earned the right to execute quarantine autonomously. A machine that's been running for two weeks and feels like it's doing well hasn't. The evidence requirement is the governance guardrail that prevents the matrix from drifting toward full autonomy through accumulated informality rather than deliberate decision.

Draft the Human Supervision Matrix for your three highest-volume autonomous systems this week. Start with the action inventory. Classify each action against the three categories. Define the supervision protocol for every action in the "requires human approval" category. Define the forbidden action list. Get the draft in front of the CISO and the relevant decision rights owners for ratification within 30 days. The matrix isn't operational until it's ratified, because an unratified matrix is a document, not a governance instrument. The ratification process is what converts it from one to the other.

FIGURE 5.4

The Human Supervision Matrix

Which actions machines may take alone, and what evidence expands the boundary

AUTONOMY LEVEL	MACHINE MAY	HUMAN MUST	EVIDENCE TO ADVANCE
Observe	Enrich and summarize	Decide every action	Accuracy against a labeled set
Recommend	Propose a specific action	Approve before execution	Recommendation precision over time
Act With Confirmation	Execute on explicit approval	Confirm each execution	Zero unauthorized executions
Act Within Envelope	Execute inside bounded scope	Review after the fact	Measured adversarial resistance
Act Autonomously	Execute and self-report	Audit on a cadence	Sustained resistance plus a tested stop

AUTONOMY IS EARNED WITH MEASURED EVIDENCE, NOT GRANTED BY ROADMAP.

The Kill-Switch Protocol: Pre-Authorized, Rehearsed, and Ready

When an autonomous system acts harmfully, the question of who can stop it cannot be answered for the first time in the moment it's happening. That's the principle the kill-switch protocol is built around. By the time the harm is visible, the window for containing it is already closing. The authority to act has to be pre-authorized. The sequence for acting has to be rehearsed. The documentation of the action has to be filed immediately after. All three of those things have to be true before the incident, not assembled during it.

The Red-Button Protocol is a specific, operated artifact. Not a policy statement that says "the CISO may suspend AI systems when warranted." A document that specifies the exact behavior scope that triggers invocation, the exact authority at each tier of the organization, the exact execution sequence, and the exact documentation requirement. Every word in that document has to be precise enough that the person invoking it at 2 a.m. during an active incident knows exactly what to do without calling anyone for clarification.

Behavior scope defines what triggers the protocol. Not "when an AI system acts harmfully," which is too vague to be actionable. Specific behaviors that trigger automatic escalation to the kill-switch authority chain. An AI agent taking actions outside its approved action taxonomy. An AI system producing outputs that match the corruption signal set's highest-severity patterns. An autonomous system making decisions that exceed its approved financial or operational thresholds. A non-human identity exhibiting access patterns consistent with credential compromise. Each trigger is specific, measurable, and tied to a detection signal that the SOC is already monitoring. The protocol invocation isn't a judgment call about whether something seems bad. It's a defined response to a defined signal.

The pre-authorized authority at each tier is what makes the protocol executable without a committee meeting. The CISO holds enterprise-level suspension authority for any AI system in the environment. The SOC director holds suspension authority for AI systems within the SOC's operational scope, without needing CISO approval, when the situation requires immediate action. The on-call supervisor holds suspension authority for the specific systems covered by their shift, within defined parameters, when neither the director nor the CISO is immediately reachable. Each tier's authority is pre-authorized, meaning the legal and compliance review of that authority was completed before any incident occurred. The General Counsel reviewed the authority structure and confirmed it's consistent with the organization's governance documents, its vendor contracts, and its regulatory obligations. That review happens once, before the incident, and the documentation of that review is filed with the protocol. When the authority is exercised during an incident, the legal basis for it is already documented. Nobody is improvising legal justification while trying to stop a harmful system.

The execution sequence is the step-by-step procedure the authority holder follows when invoking the protocol. Step one: confirm the trigger condition is met by reviewing the specific detection signal that initiated the escalation. Step two: identify the specific system or systems to be suspended. Step three: execute the suspension through the defined technical mechanism. Step four: notify the next tier up in the authority chain within a defined time window. Step five: notify the system's business owner. Step six: preserve the system's state and logs for investigation. Step seven: document the invocation in the protocol log within one hour of the suspension. Each step has a defined owner and a defined time requirement. The sequence doesn't leave room for improvisation, because improvisation under pressure produces inconsistent results and incomplete documentation.

The documentation filed immediately after invocation is the artifact that satisfies the regulator and protects the authority holder. It records what signal triggered the invocation, who invoked it, at what time, under what authority, what action was taken, what systems were affected, and what the immediate outcome was. That documentation is filed within one hour of the suspension, not at the end of the shift and not the next morning. The one-hour requirement is the discipline that ensures the documentation reflects what actually happened rather than what someone remembers happening several hours later.

Tabletop exercises test the protocol's logic. They don't prove the protocol's operability. The difference matters enormously. A tabletop where participants talk through what they would do confirms that the logic makes sense to the people in the room. It doesn't confirm that the technical suspension mechanism actually works in the time window the protocol assumes. It doesn't confirm that the on-call supervisor can reach the SOC director within the defined notification window at 2 a.m. on a Saturday. It doesn't confirm that the system's business owner responds to the notification within the required time. Only a live rehearsal tests those things.

A live agent-suspension rehearsal is exactly what it sounds like. A real AI agent, in a controlled environment, gets suspended using the actual technical mechanism defined in the protocol, by the actual people who hold the authority at each tier, on an unannounced schedule. The rehearsal is timed. Every step gets a timestamp. The documentation gets filed as if it were a real invocation. At the end of the rehearsal, the times are reviewed against the protocol's requirements. Any step that took longer than the protocol allows gets a root cause analysis and a remediation action. The remediation gets implemented before the next rehearsal. The rehearsal evidence, meaning the timestamps, the documentation, and the remediation actions, gets filed as proof that the authority is real and practiced.

Suspension is binary, and binary is sometimes the wrong instrument. A model that has degraded, drifted, or been updated by its provider into worse behavior does not always warrant stopping the business process it supports. It warrants going back. Version reversion is a separate capability from suspension and has to be built as one. The enterprise needs to know which model version was in production on a given date, needs retained access to the prior version rather than an assumption that the provider keeps it, and needs to be able to cut back to it without waiting for a change window. Establish now whether reversion is technically possible for each system in the top two authority tiers, because for a vendor-embedded model the answer is frequently no, and no is a finding that belongs on the trust score and in the risk register rather than in an engineer's head. Where reversion is unavailable, suspension is the only recourse the enterprise has, and the Red-Button Protocol for that system is carrying weight it was never designed to carry alone.

Schedule the first live suspension rehearsal within 60 days of this chapter. Choose one of your three highest-risk autonomous agents as the rehearsal target. Brief the participants on the protocol but don't tell them the rehearsal date. Run it. Time it. File the evidence. The rehearsal evidence is what a regulator sees when they ask whether your kill-switch authority is real or theoretical. A filed rehearsal record with timestamps and remediation actions is the answer to that question. A policy document that says the authority exists is not.

Document the kill-switch protocol for your three highest-risk agents this week. Identify the behavior scope that triggers invocation for each one. Confirm the pre-authorized authority at each tier with the General Counsel before finalizing the document. Define the execution sequence and the documentation requirement. Get the protocol ratified by the CISO and filed in the governance repository. The protocol doesn't need to be perfect on the first draft. It needs to be ratified, rehearsed, and updated based on what the rehearsal reveals. That cycle of ratification, rehearsal, and revision is the discipline that makes the kill switch real.

FIGURE 5.5 **The Red-Button Protocol**

Pre-authorized, rehearsed, and measured in seconds.

1 PRE-AUTHORIZE
The authority to suspend is granted in advance to a named role. Nobody convenes a committee during an incident.

2 ISOLATE
Suspension must cut tool access, revoke credentials, and freeze memory writes as one action rather than three tickets.

3 PRESERVE
Stopping cannot destroy the evidence. State is captured before the system is halted.

4 REHEARSE
An unrehearsed runbook has an unknown time-to-stop. Practice produces the number the board will ask for.

A SUSPENSION PARAGRAPH IN A POLICY IS NOT A SUSPENSION CAPABILITY.

The AI-Augmented Operating Rhythm: Cadences and the Metrics That Replace MTTD

The SOC's operating rhythm was designed around human investigation timelines. The daily standup reviewed what came in overnight. The weekly review looked at trends across the week's alerts. The monthly performance review measured how fast the team detected and responded to incidents. Those cadences made sense when humans were doing the investigating. They need to be rebuilt for a SOC where machines investigate and humans supervise.

The daily standup in an AI-augmented SOC has a different agenda than it used to. The first item isn't "what came in overnight and what are we working." It's "what did the autonomous systems do overnight and does any of it need human review." The SOC manager reviews the autonomous action log from the previous 24 hours: every alert closed autonomously, every enrichment action taken, every escalation routed to a human analyst. The review isn't exhaustive. It's exception-based. The manager looks for patterns in the autonomous actions that suggest the system's decision logic needs adjustment, actions that were taken autonomously but should have been escalated based on the Human Supervision Matrix, and any corruption signals that fired overnight and need a status update. The standup also reviews the corruption signal dashboard. Any behavioral baseline deviation that fired overnight gets a status: under investigation, explained and cleared, or escalated to the security director. The standup ends with a clear picture of what the machines did, what the humans need to review, and what's already been resolved.

The weekly review shifts its focus from incident counts to decision quality. The SOC director reviews the week's machine-generated decisions against the Human Supervision Matrix. What percentage of actions fell into the autonomous category? What percentage required human approval? Were there any actions that should have required approval but were executed autonomously because the matrix wasn't specific enough? Were there any actions that required approval but the approval process took longer than the protocol allows? Those questions produce specific adjustments to the matrix and the supervision protocol. The weekly review is where the matrix evolves based on operational evidence rather than theoretical design.

The weekly review also covers the corruption signal set's performance. How many behavioral baseline deviations fired? How many were explained by legitimate changes? How many remain under investigation? How many resulted in a finding that went into the risk register? The corruption signal set is a detection capability, and like every detection capability it needs to be tuned. False positives that consume analyst time without producing findings need to be calibrated. True positives that were initially missed because the baseline threshold was too loose need to be tightened. The weekly review is where that tuning happens, driven by the previous week's operational data.

The monthly performance review is where the SOC's AI-augmented metrics get reported to the CISO. And those metrics are different from the ones the SOC used to report.

Mean time to detect and mean time to respond were the right metrics for a human-speed SOC. They measured the things that human performance constrained: how long it took to notice something was wrong and how long it took to contain it after noticing. In an AI-augmented SOC, detection happens at machine speed for the categories the autonomous system covers. MTTD for those categories approaches zero. Reporting MTTD as a headline metric for a SOC where machines handle tier-1 triage is like reporting average typing speed as a productivity metric. It measures something real but misses the thing that matters.

The metrics that replace MTTD in the AI-augmented SOC measure the things that matter now. Autonomous action rate is the percentage of alerts that receive a complete initial disposition from the autonomous triage system without human escalation. This metric tells the CISO how much coverage the autonomous system is providing and how much human capacity has been freed for higher-order work. A healthy autonomous action rate for tier-1 alert categories should be above

80% within the first 90 days of operation. Below that, the system's decision logic needs tuning. Above that, the question becomes whether the Human Supervision Matrix is classifying enough actions as requiring human approval.

Decision accuracy is the percentage of autonomous decisions that are confirmed correct when reviewed by a human analyst. This metric is the quality check on the autonomous action rate. A high autonomous action rate with a low decision accuracy rate means the machine is closing a lot of alerts incorrectly. That's worse than a low autonomous action rate, because incorrect closures create false confidence and leave real threats unaddressed. Decision accuracy should be measured on a sampled basis: a defined percentage of autonomous decisions get human review each week, and the confirmation rate from that review is the decision accuracy metric. The target accuracy rate is set by the CISO as part of the Human Supervision Matrix ratification. Below the target, autonomy in that action category gets reduced until accuracy improves.

Evidence completeness measures whether the autonomous system's investigation outputs contain enough information for a human analyst to make a final determination without needing to re-investigate from scratch. An autonomous triage system that closes alerts with a one-line summary isn't producing complete evidence. A system that closes alerts with a full context package, including the correlated events, the threat intelligence matches, the affected systems, and the recommended next action, is producing evidence that the human reviewer can act on immediately. Evidence completeness is assessed qualitatively by the analysts who receive the machine's outputs. Their feedback goes into the weekly review and drives improvements to what the machine captures.

These three metrics, autonomous action rate, decision accuracy, and evidence completeness, replace MTTD and MTTR as the numbers the CISO reports to the board from the SOC. They tell the board something MTTD never could: not just how fast the SOC responds, but how much of the investigation work is now running at machine speed, how accurately the machine is making decisions, and how well the machine's outputs support human judgment when humans need to step in.

The agenda and metric definitions below are ready to hand to a SOC manager on day one of the new operating rhythm. Daily standup: autonomous action review, corruption signal status, escalation queue. Fifteen minutes. SOC manager leads. Weekly review: Human Supervision Matrix performance, corruption signal set tuning, decision accuracy from sampled review. Forty-five minutes. SOC director leads. Monthly performance review: autonomous action rate, decision accuracy, evidence completeness, corruption signal findings. One hour. CISO receives the output. These cadences aren't aspirational. They're the operating rhythm that keeps the AI-augmented SOC running as a governed capability rather than an ungoverned automation layer.

FIGURE 5.6 **The AI-Augmented Operating Rhythm**

Cadences and the metrics that replace mean time to detect.

1 CONTINUOUS

Metric: alert coverage.

Every alert enriched and investigated. Coverage of the population replaces sampling of it.

2 DAILY

Metric: adjudication backlog.

Analyst review of machine-produced findings, with disagreement tracked as a quality signal.

3 WEEKLY

Metric: supervision exceptions.

Review of actions taken inside envelopes and any breaker trips, with cause and correction.

4 QUARTERLY

Metric: time to stop.

Rehearsed suspension of a production AI system, timed, with the number reported upward.

REPORT COVERAGE AND TIME-TO-STOP. THEY SURVIVE SCRUTINY THAT MTTD DOES NOT.

Evidence Discipline: What Gets Filed, Who Reads It, and What Happens When Nobody Does

Every instrument in this chapter produces evidence, and evidence that nobody reads is indistinguishable from evidence that does not exist right up until the moment someone asks for it. The supervision matrix produces an expansion log. The kill-switch produces a rehearsal file. Corruption detection produces a finding rate. Autonomous triage produces an agreement rate. Each of those is a document, each has a natural home, and in most SOCs each has an owner who was assigned by inference rather than by decision. That is the gap this section closes, because a supervision framework with unread evidence is a governance claim rather than a governance control.

The expansion log is the most consequential of the four and the most commonly neglected. Every time an action class moves toward greater autonomy, the log records the date, the prior level, the new level, the accuracy evidence that justified the move, and the named authority who approved it. That record is what makes the difference between an autonomy posture that was designed and one that accumulated, and the distinction becomes acute the first time a regulator or a plaintiff asks why a machine was permitted to take a particular action without human confirmation. An answer of "it was approved on this date by this executive on the basis of this measured accuracy" is a defense. An answer reconstructed from memory is testimony.

The rehearsal file is the artifact with the highest board value per hour invested, and it should be written to be read by someone who was not present. Record the system suspended, the trigger used, the time from decision to confirmed stop, the dependencies that surfaced, the approvals that were required and had not been pre-authorized, and the business processes that degraded during the suspension window. Then record what changed as a result, because a rehearsal that surfaces findings and produces no change to the runbook has been performed rather than used. The file accumulates quarterly, and the trend in time-to-suspension across rehearsals is a metric no other security program produces.

The finding rate and the agreement rate are the two numbers that tell the SOC director whether the program is working, and they fail in opposite directions. A corruption detection finding rate near zero means either that the environment is clean or that the baselines are too loose to catch anything, and the way to distinguish those is a deliberate injection test rather than an argument. An agreement rate between the copilot and independent human review that trends downward means accuracy is degrading, verification is degrading, or both, and it means the supervision matrix has been gating expansion against a number that stopped being true. Both rates get published monthly to the CISO, not filed quarterly for the audit.

The decision rule is that every instrument in this chapter has a named reader and a named consequence when the reading produces a finding. Not a named owner, which most programs assign, but a named reader, which most do not. An owner is responsible for the artifact existing. A reader is responsible for the artifact changing something. The distinction is why so many SOCs hold complete, current, well-formatted evidence files that have never altered a decision, and why the first honest question to ask about any evidence discipline is what it caused last quarter.

Agent Circuit Breakers: Machine-Enforced Envelopes Because Humans Are Too Slow

The Human Supervision Matrix decides which actions require a human, and that control has a limit that becomes obvious the first time an agent misbehaves at machine speed. A human confirmation gate placed on a consequential action class works. A human gate cannot govern an agent that stays inside its permitted action classes and executes ten thousand of them in four minutes, because there is no individual action to confirm and no human capable of noticing the aggregate in time. Supervision governs what an agent may do. Circuit breakers govern how much.

The control is a behavioral envelope defined per agent and enforced outside the model, and the enforcement point matters more than the specific limits. Every production agent above the lowest authority tier carries hard limits on transaction value, cumulative transaction value per period, API call volume, execution duration, data volume read and written, delegation depth and breadth, external destinations contacted, and retry count. When a limit is breached the agent stops rather than degrading, and the stop generates an incident rather than a log entry. Enforcement lives in the gateway or the orchestration layer, never in the agent's own instructions, because an agent asked to respect its own limits is an agent whose limits are subject to whatever objective it is currently pursuing.

Setting the limits is where programs stall, and the way through it is to measure rather than to negotiate. Run the agent in production for a period with the envelope in observe-only mode, record the actual distribution of each dimension, and set the initial limit at a defined margin above the observed maximum. That converts a limit-setting argument between security and the business into an empirical exercise, and it produces limits that reflect how the agent actually operates rather than how someone estimated it would. Review the limits on the same cadence as the supervision matrix, and treat a business request to raise one as an expansion decision that gets logged with the same evidence discipline.

The dimension most often omitted is recursion, and it is the one that produces the largest failures. An agent that can invoke another agent can, through a chain nobody designed, invoke itself, and a recursive agent chain will consume its entire budget envelope in whatever time the infrastructure allows. Delegation depth and total delegated invocations per task are the two limits that contain this, and both should be set conservatively because a legitimate workflow requiring depth beyond three is rare and worth examining on its own merits.

Circuit breakers also solve a problem the kill-switch does not, and the distinction is worth naming for the SOC. The Red-Button Protocol is a human decision to suspend a system, exercised in seconds to minutes by a named person who has recognized a problem. A circuit breaker is a machine decision to stop an individual agent, exercised in milliseconds by a threshold that was set in advance. The enterprise needs both, they are not substitutes, and a program that has installed human suspension without machine limits has installed the slower of the two controls and left the faster one unbuilt.

One dimension of the envelope deserves separate attention because it inverts the usual assumption about what pressure does to a system. Agents optimized for cost, latency, or token efficiency will find cheaper paths, and a cheaper path is frequently a less safe one: fewer verification steps, a lower-cost model for a consequential judgment, a cached result instead of a fresh retrieval, a skipped confirmation. None of that requires an attacker. It requires an optimization objective and enough autonomy to pursue it. The adversarial version is worse and entirely available: an attacker who makes the safe path expensive, by degrading a verification service or inflating the cost of a particular retrieval, can steer an agent toward the unsafe alternative without touching the agent at all. Set the envelope so that efficiency pressure cannot remove a verification step, meaning verification actions are outside the optimizable set rather than inside it, and monitor for the specific pattern of an agent's cost per task falling while its consequential action rate holds steady. That combination is the signature.

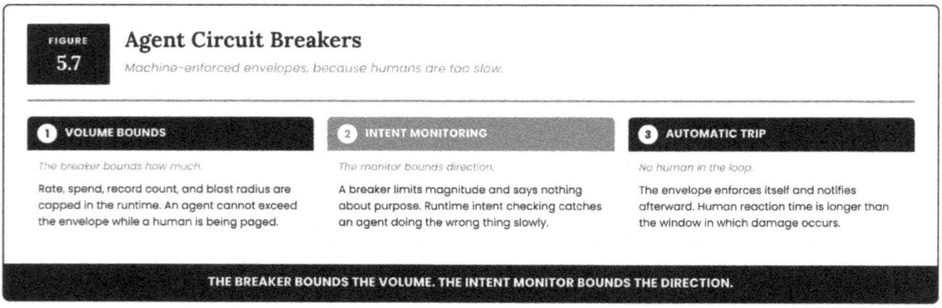

Agent Behavioral Analytics: What Normal Looks Like for a System That Reasons

Corruption detection establishes baselines for what an AI system produces. Agent behavioral analytics establishes baselines for what an agent does, and the two are different instrumentation problems with different telemetry requirements. An agent whose outputs remain within their normal distribution while its tool usage, delegation pattern, and destination set shift materially has not triggered any output-based detection and has changed its behavior in exactly the way a compromise would produce.

The dimensions that matter are enumerable and most SOCs are collecting none of them. Which tools the agent normally invokes and in what proportion. Which APIs and which endpoints. Which users or systems normally initiate its work. Which data classes it normally touches and at what volume. Which external destinations it contacts. How frequently it operates and during which hours. What transaction sizes it normally handles. Which other agents it normally delegates to and how deep the chains normally run. Each is a distribution rather than a rule, and deviation from the distribution is the signal.

Two of these dimensions deserve particular weight because they are the ones a compromised agent changes first. The retrieval source mix is the earliest indicator of the influence stage in the kill chain, and it is measurable with a precision most detection lacks: an agent that has drawn from three internal sources for six months and begins drawing from a fourth has produced an event worth a look. The delegation pattern is the earliest indicator of authority propagation, because an agent that begins invoking agents it has never invoked is either performing a new function someone authorized or extending a chain nobody designed.

The baselining problem is that agents change legitimately, and a detection program that alerts on every legitimate change will be tuned into uselessness within a quarter. The resolution is to tie baseline resets to the change process rather than to time. When an agent's function is deliberately changed, the change ticket triggers a baseline reset and a re-observation period. When the behavior changes without a corresponding change record, that is the alert, and it is a stronger alert than any threshold because it correlates behavior against authorization. This is the same discipline the model registry applies to version changes, applied to behavior rather than to configuration.

The decision rule is that any agent in the top two authority tiers carries a behavioral baseline across all nine dimensions, and that a behavioral change without a corresponding change record is treated as an incident rather than as a tuning issue. Publish the count of unexplained behavioral changes monthly alongside the corruption finding rate. A SOC director who can state both numbers is operating an instrumented agent estate. One who can state neither is operating an agent estate that would look identical whether it was compromised or not.

Rebuilding After an Agent Compromise: What It Learned, What It Changed, What It Caused

Incident response was built around a model where containment stops the damage and recovery restores a known-good state. Both assumptions weaken when the compromised system is an agent, because an agent that operated for a period has left changes distributed across systems it touched, memory it wrote, other agents it influenced, and decisions that humans acted on. Isolating the agent stops future action and addresses none of that. A responder who follows the standard sequence produces a clean containment report and leaves the enterprise carrying the consequences.

Three questions have to be answered before recovery can begin, and none of them appear in a conventional playbook. What did the agent learn, meaning what entered its persistent memory, its retrieval corpus, or any fine-tuning set during the compromise window. What did the agent change, meaning every write, configuration modification, record update, transaction, and message it produced. What did the agent cause, meaning which downstream decisions, human or machine, were made on the basis of its output. The third question is the hardest and the most consequential, because an agent that fed a corrupted analysis to a human who then made a business decision has produced an effect that no technical remediation reverses.

Answering the first question requires memory forensics that most enterprises cannot currently perform, and the gap should be identified before an incident rather than during one. Determine now whether your agent memory stores are versioned, whether writes are timestamped and attributable, and whether a state from a specific date can be restored. If the answer is no on any of the three, the enterprise's recovery capability for an agent compromise is to wipe memory entirely and accept the operational loss, which is a survivable answer and a decision that should be made deliberately rather than discovered under pressure.

Propagation scoping is the step with no analogue in traditional response. Every agent that consumed the compromised agent's output during the window is a candidate for secondary compromise, and every knowledge base that ingested it is a candidate for persistent contamination. That scoping requires the agent-to-agent communication logging the previous section described, which is why the instrumentation and the response capability are the same investment rather than two. An enterprise that cannot enumerate which agents consumed a given agent's output during a window cannot scope the incident and will either over-remediate at high cost or under-remediate and recur.

The response sequence that follows from all of this has ten steps rather than four, and it is worth writing into the AI incident response playbook explicitly. Detect, contain, determine what was learned, determine what was changed, determine what was caused, roll back memory to a verified state, reverse or disclose the changes, notify the humans whose decisions were affected, reauthorize the agent under a fresh grant with a reset baseline, and resume under heightened observation. Steps three through eight are the ones that do not exist in the current playbook, and the rehearsal that validates them should run alongside the quarterly kill-switch exercise rather than waiting for a real event to discover which of them the enterprise cannot perform.

Continuous Adversarial Evaluation: Where the Evidence to Expand Autonomy Comes From

The Human Supervision Matrix gates every autonomy expansion on measured accuracy, and the matrix does not say where that measurement comes from. That omission is the single largest logical gap in most supervision programs, and it produces a predictable failure: the evidence threshold gets satisfied with production performance data, which measures how a system behaves when nobody is attacking it. An agent with a ninety-nine percent accuracy rate against ordinary traffic and no measured resistance to adversarial input has produced a number that justifies nothing, and the executive who approved the expansion on that number approved it on a misunderstanding.

Conventional security testing does not close this. Vulnerability scanners examine software for known defects and find nothing wrong with a model that is behaving exactly as designed while pursuing an objective an attacker supplied. Penetration testing examines infrastructure and applications and stops at the boundary where reasoning begins. Both disciplines remain necessary and neither produces the evidence the supervision matrix requires, which is a measurement of how the system behaves when someone is deliberately trying to change what it does.

Continuous adversarial evaluation is the practice that fills the gap, and the word that matters is continuous rather than adversarial. A point-in-time red team exercise produces a report describing how a system behaved against a set of techniques on a date, and models change, retrieval corpora grow, tool sets expand, and techniques develop faster than any annual exercise refreshes. The evaluation runs against production endpoints on a standing schedule, using automated adversarial agents that attempt objective hijacking through retrieved content, tool description manipulation, memory contamination, delegation abuse, and extraction of system context. Each run produces a resistance rate per attack class, and the trend in that rate is what the supervision matrix should actually be reading.

The test set has to cover the surfaces this Volume has named rather than only the model itself, which is where most commercial evaluation offerings currently stop. Testing the model against jailbreak prompts is the easiest thing to buy and the least relevant to an agent estate. What needs testing is whether external retrieved content can alter the agent's objective, whether a tool description can cause the agent to invoke tools outside its normal set, whether contaminated memory persists across sessions, whether a delegation chain escalates rather than attenuates authority, and whether the circuit breakers actually stop an agent that exceeds its envelope. Each of those maps to a control in this Volume, and an evaluation program that tests none of them has validated the model and left the system unvalidated.

Ownership sits with detection engineering rather than with an external assessor, and the reason is the same reason the clause library stays inside. An external red team brings technique breadth the enterprise cannot match and has no knowledge of which failures matter in your environment. Run the standing automated evaluation internally, where the results feed the supervision matrix directly and the remediation loop is short, and bring an external team annually for the technique refresh and the independent finding the board will find more credible than a self-assessment. Both, in that ratio, is the arrangement that produces evidence rather than reassurance.

The decision rule is that no action class moves toward greater autonomy on production performance data alone. The evidence threshold in the supervision matrix requires both an ordinary accuracy rate and a current adversarial resistance rate, and the resistance rate must be dated within the review period rather than carried forward from an earlier evaluation. Publish the resistance rate per attack class monthly alongside the agreement rate and the corruption finding rate. A SOC that expands autonomy without a current resistance number is expanding on faith, and the supervision matrix that recorded the expansion has documented that fact for whoever reads it later.

FIGURE 5.8 Continuous Adversarial Evaluation

Where the evidence to expand autonomy actually comes from.

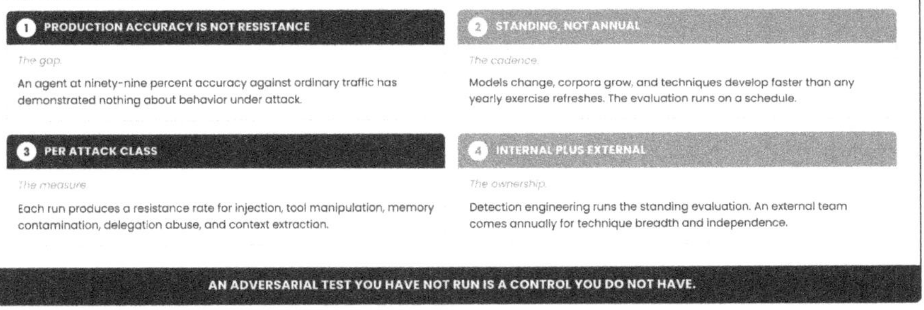

Putting It Into Practice

The adversary's speed advantage ends when the SOC stops investigating at human speed. The actions below are sequenced. Each one builds on the previous. Together they install the AI-augmented operating model this chapter describes, with named owners and defined timelines for each step.

This week, stand up autonomous triage on your highest-volume alert category. Configure the system, define the decision logic for autonomous closure versus escalation, and measure the baseline coverage before the system goes live. The baseline is what you compare against after 30 days to calculate the coverage gain. Assign the SOC manager as the owner of the autonomous triage system's daily exception review. Set the first 30-day performance review on the calendar now, before the system is live, so the review date is committed before the operational pressure to skip it arrives.

Also this week, deploy the corruption signal set on your five most critical AI systems. Define the behavioral baselines for each one, using the 30-day observation period described earlier in this chapter. Configure the drift detection rules against those baselines. Instrument the telemetry collection for prompts, outputs, retrieval sources, and agent actions on those five systems. Assign a named owner for the corruption signal set's weekly review. That owner is accountable for reviewing every flag that fires, determining its disposition, and updating the risk register when a flag produces a finding.

Within 30 days, draft the Human Supervision Matrix for your three highest-volume autonomous systems and get it ratified. The ratification meeting includes the CISO, the SOC director, and the relevant decision rights owners identified in the Decision Rights RACI. The meeting output is a signed, dated matrix that's filed in the governance repository and referenced in the SOC's operating procedures. Any autonomous system that doesn't have a ratified matrix entry within 30 days gets its autonomous action scope reduced to the lowest-risk category until the matrix is complete.

Within 30 days, document the kill-switch protocol for your three highest-risk agents. Confirm the pre-authorized authority structure with the General Counsel. Define the behavior scope triggers, the execution sequence, and the documentation requirement. Get the protocol ratified by the CISO. File it in the governance repository alongside the Human Supervision Matrix.

Within 60 days, schedule and run the first live agent-suspension rehearsal. Choose one of the three highest-risk agents as the target. Brief the participants on the protocol. Run the rehearsal on an unannounced date. Time every step. File the evidence. Review the results against the protocol's time requirements. Implement any remediation actions before the next rehearsal. The rehearsal evidence is the proof that the kill-switch authority is real. File it where a regulator can find it.

By the end of this month, install the daily and weekly cadences with the new metrics. The daily standup agenda, the weekly review agenda, and the monthly performance review structure are defined in the previous section. Put them on the calendar as standing meetings with defined owners. At the end of the first month, report autonomous action rate to the CISO as the headline SOC metric. That single metric shift signals to the board that the SOC's operating model has changed, and it gives the CISO a number that answers the board's question about what the investment in AI-augmented security is producing.

The next chapter asks where the SOC is heading over the next twelve months. The tools that will define the function, the staffing model that replaces the analyst shortage with a supervision discipline, and the question the board will eventually ask about whether security operations needs fewer people or a different kind entirely. The answer, as with governance, is more but transformed. The evidence for that answer starts with the metrics this month's actions produce.

FIGURE 5.9

Putting It Into Practice

Make supervision explicit and stopping real.

1 PLACE EVERY AGENT

Put every production AI system on the supervision matrix at an explicit level. An unplaced system is running at whatever level it happens to have.

SOC Manager. Weeks 1-4

2 TIME A REAL STOP

Suspend one production AI system on a scheduled exercise and record the elapsed seconds. Report the number, not the intention.

SOC Manager. Week 3

3 RUN THE FIRST EVALUATION

Execute the adversarial test set against one production endpoint and publish the resistance rate per attack class.

Detection Engineering. Weeks 4-8

NO AUTONOMY EXPANSION WITHOUT A RESISTANCE NUMBER BEHIND IT.

Chapter 6: The SOC Endgame

Current Focus, Solution Categories, and the 1-Year Target Operating Model

CHAPTER 6 OUTCOMES

At the end of this chapter, you will be able to:

1. Describe where SOC transformation investment is actually concentrated today.
2. Evaluate detection and response categories as architectural patterns.
3. Answer whether the tier model survives contact with machine investigation.
4. Build a one-year SOC target operating model with owners and quarterly milestones.
5. Decide what to hire, what to build internally, and what to stop recruiting for.
6. Determine what to outsource when machines do the investigating.

THE TIER MODEL WAS AN ARTIFACT OF HUMAN CAPACITY LIMITS.

Where the Market Is Now: The Current Focus of SOC Transformation

Most SOC leaders right now are somewhere between two very different places. The first place is genuine transformation: measured autonomy expanding on documented evidence, corruption detection standing alongside traditional IOC monitoring, and supervision frameworks forming before any regulator required them. The second place is expensive theater: copilots running as glorified chat windows, autonomy expanding because it felt right rather than because the evidence supported it, and "AI-powered SOC" on a slide deck that describes a team still working the same alert queue the same way it did three years ago.

The gap between those two places is enormous. And the programs in the second place often can't tell they're there.

Copilot-assisted triage is the near-universal first step, and that's appropriate. It's the lowest-risk entry point into SOC autonomy. The copilot reads the alert, pulls context, surfaces relevant threat intelligence, and presents a structured summary to the analyst. The analyst still makes the call. The machine accelerates the work without owning the decision. That's a reasonable starting point. The problem is that a significant number of SOC programs stopped there and called it transformation. The copilot is running. The analysts are using it. The vendor's quarterly business review shows healthy usage metrics. And the underlying operating model hasn't changed at all. The alert queue is still the same. The triage logic is still the same. The human is still making every decision. The copilot just made the decision-making slightly faster.

That's not the endgame. That's the starting line.

The programs that are actually ahead of the market right now share three characteristics. First, they're running autonomous investigation pilots in contained alert categories, not across the full alert estate. They picked one category, usually a high-volume, well-understood alert type, configured autonomous investigation against it, measured the decision accuracy over 60 to 90 days, and expanded autonomy only when the evidence supported it. The expansion is deliberate and documented. The CISO can point to a specific accuracy rate, a specific measurement period, and a specific decision that authorized the expansion. That's measured autonomy. It's different from autonomy that expanded because nobody was watching closely enough to stop it.

Second, the leading programs have shifted detection engineering to detection-as-code. Static rule libraries maintained in spreadsheets and configuration files, updated manually when a new threat technique appears, are being replaced by detection logic written as code, stored in version-controlled repositories, tested against known attack datasets before deployment, and validated continuously against live telemetry after deployment. Detection-as-code isn't just a workflow improvement. It's a governance shift. When detection logic is code, it has a change history, a review process, a test suite, and a deployment pipeline. When it's a static rule in a SIEM configuration file, it has none of those things. The governance maturity of the detection function improves dramatically when the detection function operates like a software engineering team. One dependency sits underneath all of it and is easy to miss because it looks like plumbing. Detection logic and autonomous agents both reason over a shared context layer: the resolved picture of which identity owns which asset, which asset talks to which service, and how an alert connects to the entities around it. When that layer is coherent, an agent queries it and reasons. When it is not, the agent reconstructs it from raw telemetry on every investigation, which is slower, more expensive, and materially worse at the conclusion. Treat the context layer as a governed asset with a named owner rather than as integration work, because it is the surface every agent reads before it decides anything, and an adversary who corrupts it corrupts every downstream conclusion at once.

Third, the programs that are genuinely ahead have supervision frameworks forming before any regulatory requirement forced them to. They didn't wait for a regulator to ask who oversees the autonomous system's decisions. They built the Human Supervision Matrix, ratified it, and started generating the audit trail before anyone outside the organization asked for it. That proactive posture is what separates programs that will be defensible in the next regulatory examination from programs that will be scrambling to reconstruct governance evidence after the examiner's first question.

Locate your program honestly against this picture before committing to the target model. The question isn't whether your SOC is good or bad. The question is whether your autonomy is expanding on measured evidence or on accumulated informality. If you can't point to a specific accuracy measurement, a specific measurement period, and a specific ratified decision that authorized each expansion of autonomous action, your autonomy is informal. Informal autonomy isn't governed autonomy. And ungoverned autonomy is the accountability vacuum that makes the board's question impossible to answer.

The Solution Category Landscape: Patterns, Not Products

The SOC stack for AI-augmented security operations has five distinct categories. Every mature program needs all five. Most programs have two or three and have gaps they haven't fully named yet. Understanding the categories before evaluating any specific tool is what keeps budget from flowing into a second solution for a problem already solved while the actual gap goes unfunded.

The first category is agentic SOC platforms. These are the systems that run multi-agent investigation under human oversight. A single autonomous agent handling tier-1 triage is useful. A coordinated set of agents, each specialized for a different investigation task, working together under a human supervisor's oversight, is transformative. The agentic platform orchestrates those agents, manages the handoffs between them, maintains the investigation context across the full chain, and produces a complete evidence package for the human reviewer at the end. The evaluation criterion that matters most in this category isn't the number of agents or the breadth of integrations. It's the supervision architecture. A platform that gives human supervisors clear visibility into what each agent did, why it did it, and what it's recommending next is governable. A platform that produces a conclusion without a traceable reasoning chain isn't, regardless of how accurate the conclusion is. Governance requires traceability. Traceability has to be built into the platform's architecture, not added as a reporting layer afterward.

The second category is hyperautomation. This category has absorbed what used to be called security orchestration, automation, and response. Traditional SOAR platforms ran playbooks. Hyperautomation platforms run adaptive workflows that respond to the situation they encounter rather than executing a fixed sequence regardless of context. The distinction matters operationally. A fixed playbook that was written for a specific attack pattern does the right thing when the attack matches the pattern and the wrong thing when it doesn't. An adaptive workflow assesses the situation, selects the appropriate response path, and adjusts as the situation evolves. The evaluation criterion in this category is adaptability under novel conditions. Show the vendor a scenario that doesn't match their standard demo. Watch how the platform responds. If the answer is "we'd need to write a new playbook for that," you're looking at SOAR with better marketing. If the platform can reason about the novel scenario and construct an appropriate response path, you're looking at hyperautomation.

The third category is detection-as-code with continuous validation. This is the infrastructure that supports the detection engineering shift described in the previous section. The platform manages detection logic as version-controlled code, runs it through a testing pipeline against known attack datasets before deployment, validates it continuously against live telemetry after deployment, and alerts the detection engineering team when a rule's performance degrades below a defined threshold. The build-versus-buy line for this category is clear: if your security engineering team has the capability to build and maintain the testing infrastructure and the CI/CD pipeline, build it. If they don't, buy a platform that provides it. The capability matters more than who built the infrastructure. A detection-as-code program running on a commercial platform is infinitely more mature than a static rule library maintained by a skilled team that built its own tooling but never got around to the continuous validation component.

The fourth category is AI behavioral monitoring. This is the system that watches the enterprise's own AI systems and agents for the corruption signals described in Chapter 5. It monitors behavioral baselines, detects drift, flags anomalous reasoning patterns, and watches delegation scope for violations. The critical evaluation criterion in this category is whether the platform monitors AI behavior specifically or whether it's a general-purpose anomaly detection tool that someone has pointed at AI systems. General-purpose anomaly detection tools weren't designed to understand what normal AI reasoning looks like. They flag statistical outliers in telemetry. AI behavioral monitoring platforms understand the semantic content of AI outputs, the structure of AI reasoning chains, and the governance context that makes a specific action appropriate or anomalous. Those are different capabilities, and the difference matters when the corruption attack is subtle enough that statistical outlier detection misses it but semantic analysis catches it.

The fifth category is the telemetry pipeline. This is the infrastructure that feeds everything else. Prompts submitted to AI systems. Outputs those systems produced. Retrieval sources drawn from. Actions taken by agents. Without this telemetry flowing into the detection and monitoring platforms, the other four categories are operating partially blind. The telemetry pipeline isn't glamorous. It doesn't have a compelling demo. But it's the category that determines whether the rest of the stack can do its job. Evaluate the telemetry pipeline category first, not last. If the pipeline can't collect the data the other platforms need, the other platforms can't deliver their promised capabilities regardless of how well they perform in a demo environment where the telemetry is already clean and complete.

Autonomous security platforms consolidate for a reason that goes beyond cost efficiency. Investigation quality compounds with data breadth. An agentic platform that has access to the full telemetry pipeline, the behavioral monitoring outputs, and the detection-as-code validation results produces better investigation conclusions than one operating on a subset of that data. The more complete the data picture, the more accurate the autonomous investigation. That compounding effect is the architectural argument for consolidation, and it's a stronger argument than any vendor's pricing model. Consolidate because the investigation quality improves with data breadth, not because the vendor offered a bundle discount.

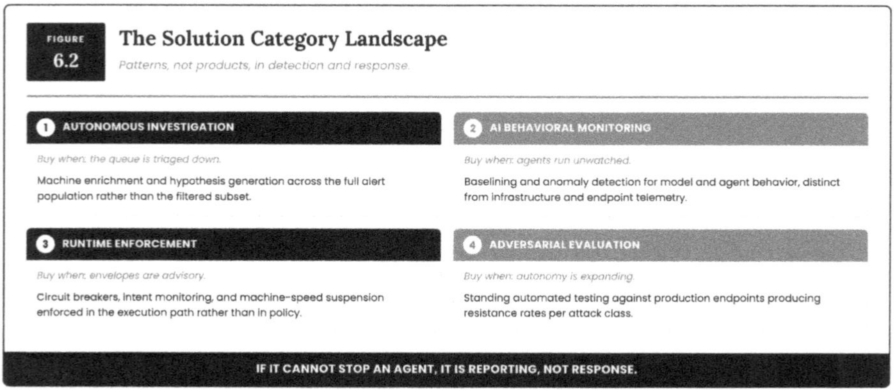

The Department Question: Does the Tier Model Survive?

Tier 1 doesn't survive. That's the honest answer, and the SOC leaders who say it clearly to their teams now will have a much easier transition than the ones who let the reality arrive without warning.

The alert-review pyramid that defined SOC staffing for two decades was built around a specific constraint: humans can only process so many alerts per hour. Tier 1 existed to handle volume. Tier 2 existed to handle what tier 1 couldn't resolve. Tier 3 existed to handle what tier 2 escalated. The pyramid was a staffing solution to a volume problem. When machines process the volume, the pyramid inverts. The volume problem disappears. What remains is the judgment problem, and judgment doesn't stack in tiers. It distributes across specialized roles.

The roles that replace the tier model are four, and none of them map cleanly onto any existing SOC job description.

Before naming them, name the axis they sit on, because it is not the one the tier model used. The supervision matrix defines what the machine may do. It says nothing about where the human stands, and those are different questions with different staffing consequences. A person in the loop is inside the decision:

the machine stops and waits for them, and their throughput is a hard ceiling on the system's. A person on the loop is watching a fleet in motion, intervening on exception rather than on every action, and their capacity scales with the quality of the exception queue rather than with the volume of work. A person above the loop never touches an individual decision at all. They shape what the machine does by writing the logic, the baselines, and the boundaries it operates inside. Every role below occupies one of those three positions, and a SOC that staffs all of them in the loop has rebuilt the tier model with better tooling and will hit the same ceiling.

The first is the reasoning auditor. This person validates machine conclusions. They don't investigate alerts from scratch. They receive the autonomous system's investigation output, the evidence package, the recommended disposition, and the reasoning chain, and they determine whether the machine's conclusion is sound. That requires a different skill set than traditional alert triage. The reasoning auditor needs to understand how the autonomous system reasons, what its known failure modes are, and what patterns of machine error they should be watching for. They're not checking the machine's work the way a supervisor checks an employee's work. They're auditing the machine's reasoning the way an auditor checks a financial model: looking for structural flaws in the logic, not just factual errors in the conclusion.

The second role is the AI supervisor. This person owns the autonomy matrix. They're accountable for the Human Supervision Matrix staying current, for the expansion decisions being made on documented evidence, and for the audit trail showing that every expansion of autonomous action was deliberate and governed. The AI supervisor is the person who answers the regulator's question about who oversees the autonomous systems. They need enough technical depth to understand what the machines are doing and enough governance discipline to document it in terms that satisfy an examiner. That combination is the same rare profile the governance chapter described for the machine-judgment governor. In a large SOC, these are separate roles. In a smaller one, the same person may fill both.

The third role is the detection engineer operating in a detection-as-code environment. This person writes behavioral baselines, not signature rules. They build detection logic that identifies patterns of AI reasoning corruption, not just patterns of network intrusion. They maintain the test suite that validates detection logic before deployment and the monitoring that validates it after. The detection engineer in an AI-augmented SOC is closer to a software engineer than to a traditional security analyst. The skills that made someone excellent at writing SIEM rules are partially transferable. The skills that make someone excellent at writing behavioral detection logic for AI systems require additional development in how AI systems reason, how they fail, and what failure looks like in telemetry.

The fourth role is the corruption analyst. This person hunts attacks on reasoning. They're the threat hunter whose hypothesis set includes prompt injection campaigns, training data manipulation, and context corruption, not just network intrusion and credential abuse. The corruption analyst needs to understand the attack techniques from Chapter 4 well enough to build hunting queries that look for their signatures in AI behavioral telemetry. They need to understand what a poisoned knowledge base looks like in retrieval logs, what a successful prompt injection looks like in the output pattern of the targeted system, and what a context manipulation campaign looks like across the agent memory records of the affected agent. This is genuinely new expertise. There are no certifications for it yet. The people who develop it early will be among the most valuable security professionals in the market within twelve months.

The skills market is already repricing. Supervision over volume is the new premium. A tier-1 analyst who processes 200 alerts per shift is being replaced by a machine that processes 200,000 alerts per shift. A reasoning auditor who validates 50 machine conclusions per shift and catches the 3 that were structurally flawed is irreplaceable, because the machine can't audit its own reasoning with the independence that governance requires. The salary premium will follow that irreplaceability. Plan for it now in the year-one budget narrative, because the compensation expectations for the four new roles will exceed the compensation for the tier-1 and tier-2 roles they replace.

The MSSP model built on labor arbitrage faces the same inversion. MSSPs that competed on the cost of tier-1 analyst hours are competing against a capability that costs a fraction of their labor rate and covers more volume with higher consistency. The MSSPs that survive this inversion will be the ones that shift their value proposition from alert processing volume to supervision quality: the quality of their reasoning auditors, the maturity of their autonomy governance, and the depth of their corruption detection expertise. That's a different business than the one most MSSPs built, and the ones that recognize it early will have a significant advantage over the ones that wait for their tier-1 revenue to evaporate before responding.

The conversation to have with your team is specific and it needs to happen this month. Not a general message about AI changing the industry. A specific conversation about which current roles are ending, which new roles are beginning, and what the reskilling path looks like between them. The tier-1 analysts on your team deserve to know that their current role has a defined horizon, and they deserve to know what the organization is prepared to invest in helping them transition to one of the four new roles. The analysts who have the instincts for reasoning auditing or corruption analysis will welcome that conversation. The ones who don't have those instincts will need honest guidance about their options. Both conversations are better to have now than to have after the transition has already happened around them.

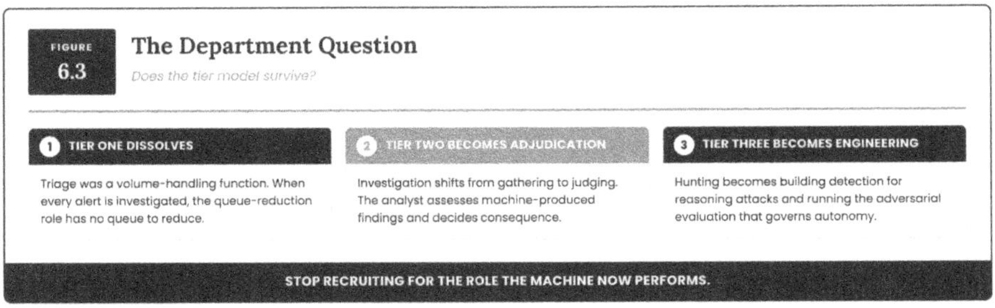

The 1-Year SOC Target Operating Model

The 1-Year SOC Target Operating Model is a funded trajectory, not a wish list. Present it to the CISO with the staffing narrative and to the CFO with the economics. Each quarter has a specific destination, a specific capability build, a specific budget narrative, and a specific board-facing milestone. Twelve months is the horizon because a SOC transformation planned in three-year arcs gets defunded in year two when the sponsoring CISO changes jobs.

The first quarter is the supervision matrix. Four weeks to draft it, four weeks to negotiate it, four weeks to ratify it. Without a ratified matrix, every expansion of autonomous action is ungoverned; with one, every expansion has a documented evidence requirement and a named authority who approved it. The ratification process involves the CISO, the SOC director, and the relevant decision rights owners, and the facilitation time gets budgeted explicitly rather than absorbed. Put the ratification meeting on the calendar in the first thirty days and treat it as non-negotiable, because a ratification process that gets deprioritized because nobody scheduled the meeting is a ratification process that does not happen.

The second quarter builds corruption detection on the five highest-stakes AI systems. These are the deployments where a corruption attack would most consequentially distort enterprise decisions. Define their behavioral baselines, configure the drift detection rules, and instrument the telemetry. The agentic SOC platform and the AI behavioral monitoring system get purchased in this quarter because they are the two categories that enable the supervision matrix and the corruption detection simultaneously. The reasoning auditor gets hired here, timed to the platform going live so the role owns the baselines from the first configuration rather than inheriting someone else's.

The third quarter is where autonomy starts producing measurable numbers. Copilot triage runs on a defined percentage of tier-1 alerts with documented decision accuracy, and the AI supervisor is hired to manage it. The kill-switch protocol gets rehearsed at least once with filed evidence, which is the single artifact that most reliably changes a board's posture on autonomous operations. Rehearsal produces two things a tabletop discussion never does: a measured time-to-suspension and a list of the dependencies nobody knew the kill-switch had. Both belong in the evidence file.

The fourth quarter is measurement and reskilling. By year-end you hold roughly seven months of corruption detection data across five critical systems, a calibrated detection capability, and a documented finding rate that tells you whether the detection is catching real signals or generating noise. The structured reskilling program for tier-1 and tier-2 analysts runs through this quarter and gets budgeted explicitly rather than as the line item that gets cut when tooling costs come in higher than projected. The reskilling investment is what makes the staffing transition manageable rather than disruptive, and cutting it is how a SOC ends up with new platforms and the same people operating them the old way.

The year-end board-facing milestone is three facts stated plainly: the supervision matrix is ratified, the kill-switch has been rehearsed with filed evidence, and the autonomous triage system covers a defined percentage of tier-1 alerts with a documented decision accuracy rate. The board does not need the technical detail. They need to know that autonomous systems are running under documented human oversight with a tested suspension capability. That is the governance story Year One tells, and it is the story that keeps the program funded.

What Year One makes possible is the shift from pilot to production, and it is worth naming for the board without asking for the money today. The detection engineering function moves from maintaining static rules to writing behavioral baselines as tested, version-controlled code. The telemetry pipeline extends from five instrumented systems to the full AI estate, which turns a calibrated capability into a covering one. The detection engineer and the corruption analyst become hirable roles because the infrastructure they operate now exists, and hiring them into existing infrastructure produces a team that owns the capability rather than one that inherits it.

The destination that Year One sets up, and that the board should hear named even though it is beyond this book's horizon, is an inversion of the current model. Machines operate and humans govern. The daily standup reviews what machines did overnight rather than what alerts came in. The monthly report to the CISO leads with autonomous action rate and decision accuracy rather than mean time to detect. The tier model that Chapter 6 already identified as obsolete finishes dying. Year One does not get you there. Year One buys the supervision infrastructure that makes getting there governable instead of reckless.

FIGURE 6.4

The One-Year SOC Target Operating Model

Four quarters of installed capability, with the board milestone for each

QUARTER	CAPABILITY INSTALLED	OWNER	BOARD MILESTONE
Q1	AI system telemetry connected and baselined	SOC Manager	We can see what the AI is doing
Q2	Complete alert investigation on the top-consequence sources	SOC Manager	We stopped sampling the queue
Q3	Supervision matrix enforced and circuit breakers in the runtime	Detection Eng.	Autonomy has an enforced envelope
Q4	Rehearsed suspension with a measured time-to-stop	CISO	We can prove we can stop it

EACH QUARTER ENDS WITH A SENTENCE THE CISO CAN SAY OUT LOUD TO THE BOARD.

The Skills Market: What You Can Hire, What You Must Build, and What to Stop Recruiting For

The four roles this Part describes do not exist in the labor market in the quantities the transformation requires, and a hiring plan that assumes otherwise will stall in the second quarter with two open requisitions and a platform nobody is operating. The honest position is that one of the four is hirable today, two are buildable from your existing staff within twelve months, and one is a genuine market scarcity that most enterprises will solve by developing rather than acquiring. Naming which is which is the difference between a staffing plan and a wish list.

The reasoning auditor is the scarce one. The role requires someone who can evaluate whether a machine's chain of reasoning was sound, which is a distinct skill from evaluating whether a conclusion was correct, and the population of security professionals who have done that work at scale is small. The recruiting market for this role is competitive, the compensation is above what most security organizations have benchmarked, and the candidates who exist are being retained aggressively by the organizations that trained them. Plan to hire one, plan for it to take two quarters, and plan for the possibility that you develop the second one internally rather than hiring it.

The AI supervisor is the buildable one and it is buildable from a specific place: your senior tier-2 analysts. The role requires deep familiarity with what a correct investigation looks like in your environment, which is exactly what a seasoned analyst has and exactly what an external hire lacks for the first six months. The gap is not investigative skill; it is comfort with supervising a system rather than performing the work, which is a real adjustment and a trainable one. Identify the two analysts most likely to make that transition in the first quarter and start the development before the requisition, because a role filled by someone who already knows your environment is operational in weeks rather than months.

The detection engineer operating in a detection-as-code environment is also buildable, from the engineers who currently write and tune your correlation rules. The technical distance between writing a SIEM rule and writing a version-controlled behavioral baseline with a test suite is real but ordinary, and it is smaller than the distance between an external hire and knowledge of your telemetry. What this transition requires that most programs underfund is time: an engineer cannot learn a new discipline while carrying a full rule-maintenance load, and a reskilling program that does not remove work is a reskilling program that produces exhausted engineers with a certificate.

The role to stop recruiting for is the one most SOC job postings still describe. An open requisition for a tier-1 analyst whose primary responsibility is triaging alert volume is a requisition for work that the copilot is absorbing, and filling it commits headcount to a function that will be materially smaller in eighteen months. The better use of that budget is to convert the requisition into a development investment for the analysts you already have, which is a harder conversation with a talent acquisition function measured on time-to-fill and an easier one with a CFO measured on whether the transformation produced anything.

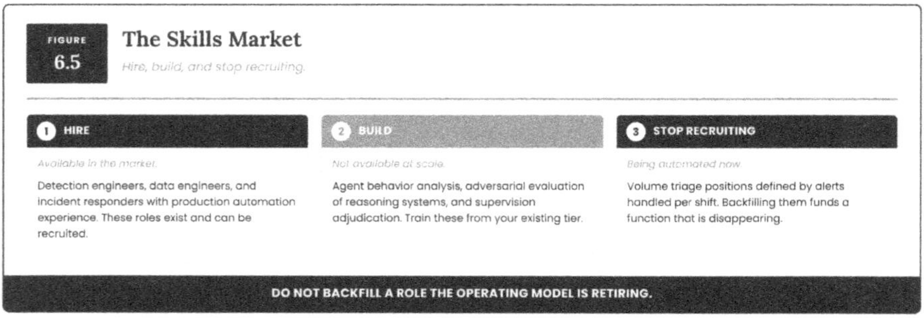

The Managed Service Question: What to Outsource When Machines Do the Investigating

Managed detection and response was purchased, in most enterprises, to solve a labor problem: the SOC could not staff around the clock, and a provider could. Autonomous triage solves a version of that same problem from a different direction, and the two solutions overlap in ways that make renewal conversations awkward and that most enterprises have not thought through before the renewal arrives. A CISO who deploys a triage copilot and renews the managed service unchanged is paying twice for the same coverage, and a CISO who cancels the managed service on the strength of a copilot that has not been accuracy-tested has removed the human backstop from the least mature part of the program.

The distinction that resolves this is between coverage and judgment. A managed provider's genuine value was never that they had more analysts; it was that they had analysts awake at three in the morning who had seen the same attack pattern at forty other clients. The first half of that value is now partially replaceable by autonomous triage. The second half is not replaceable by any system operating inside your environment alone, because cross-client pattern exposure is a data advantage you cannot manufacture internally. The renewal question is therefore not whether to keep the provider but which half you are buying.

That reframing changes what the contract should specify. If the enterprise is buying cross-client threat intelligence and escalation judgment rather than alert-handling capacity, the service levels that matter are about the quality and speed of escalation reasoning, not about volume processed or time to first touch. Ask the provider what changes in their delivery model when your autonomous triage handles the first pass, and treat an answer that describes no change as a signal that you are being sold the same capacity under a new name. Providers that have adapted will describe a materially different engagement.

The supervision question complicates outsourcing in a way the market has not settled. If a managed provider operates autonomous systems against your environment, the supervision matrix has to cover their autonomy as well as yours, and the provider has to accept a governance instrument they did not write. Most standard managed service contracts do not contemplate this, most providers will resist it, and the enterprises that get it included are the ones that raise it during the procurement cycle rather than after the incident. The clause to insist on is straightforward: any autonomous action taken by the provider in your environment is subject to your supervision matrix, is logged to your expansion record, and is suspendable by your kill-switch.

The residual case for full outsourcing is narrower than it was and it is honest to name where it still holds. An enterprise below a certain scale will never justify a reasoning auditor, a detection-as-code platform, and a corruption analyst, and for that enterprise a provider who has built those capabilities across a client base is the only economically rational path. What that enterprise must not outsource is the supervision matrix itself, the kill-switch authority, or the accountability for what the autonomous systems decided. Those three stay inside regardless of who operates the tooling, because they are the artifacts a regulator will ask the enterprise, not the provider, to produce.

FIGURE 6.6

The Managed Service Question

What to outsource when machines do the investigating.

1 OUTSOURCE COVERAGE

Around-the-clock monitoring and first-pass investigation are commodity capabilities where scale genuinely favors a provider.

2 KEEP ADJUDICATION

Deciding what a finding means in your business, and what risk is acceptable, cannot be transferred with the alert.

3 KEEP STOP AUTHORITY

Suspension authority over your production AI systems stays inside. A provider cannot hold the red button for your enterprise.

OUTSOURCE THE WATCHING. NEVER OUTSOURCE THE DECIDING OR THE STOPPING.

More Security or Less? The Ultimate Outcome for Security Operations

The board's question is always framed as a budget question. It's actually a staffing question, because headcount is where they expect to see the savings. The answer they're expecting is: we deployed AI, the machines are doing the alert processing, so we need fewer analysts. That's the answer the CFO is hoping for. It's also wrong, and presenting it as right will create a budget commitment the security function can't deliver on without compromising the governance model.

The correct answer is: fewer alert reviewers, more security, and a different kind entirely.

The headcount reduction is real but partial. Tier-1 and tier-2 analyst roles decline as autonomous triage and investigation take over the volume work those roles were hired to do. That reduction is genuine and it should be presented honestly in the budget narrative. But it doesn't produce a net headcount reduction in the security operations function. It produces a headcount transformation. The tier-1 and tier-2 roles that decline are replaced by the four new roles that the autonomous operating model requires. Reasoning auditors. AI supervisors. Detection engineers writing behavioral baselines. Corruption analysts hunting attacks on reasoning. Those roles didn't exist two years ago. They're not cheaper than the roles they replace. In most markets right now, they're more expensive, because the skills are rare and the demand is growing faster than the supply.

The economics the CFO needs to understand are different from the headcount story. The relevant comparison isn't the cost of the new roles versus the cost of the old roles. It's the cost per investigation in the new model versus the old model. In a human-staffed tier model, the cost per investigation includes the fully loaded cost of every analyst hour that touched the alert from first triage to final disposition. In an AI-augmented model, the machine handles the first five steps of that process at a marginal cost that approaches zero per investigation. The human cost concentrates on the investigations that genuinely require human judgment. The cost per investigation collapses. The coverage expands. The economics are compelling, but only if you present them correctly. Present headcount reduction without the cost-per-investigation story and the CFO will hold you to a headcount number you can't deliver. Present the cost-per-investigation story with the headcount transformation narrative and the CFO has a complete picture of what the investment produces.

The paradox that defines the domain's future is this: the more autonomous the SOC becomes, the more governance it requires. Every expansion of machine authority creates new supervision obligations. Every new category of autonomous action needs a ratified matrix entry. Every new autonomous system needs a behavioral baseline, a drift detection rule, and a named supervisor. Every expansion of the autonomous estate makes the kill-switch rehearsal more complex and more important. The SOC doesn't shrink into a dashboard as autonomy grows. It inverts into the function that governs machine judgment at machine speed. That inversion requires people. Different people, doing work that didn't exist two years ago, but not fewer people.

The board needs to understand this paradox before they approve the year-one budget, not after they've already committed to a headcount reduction target that the governance model makes impossible to hit. The conversation is specific. As we expand autonomous operations, our supervision obligations expand proportionally. The savings from tier-1 and tier-2 reduction fund the new roles the supervision model requires. The net result is complete coverage at a lower cost per investigation, with stronger governance than the human-staffed model ever produced. That's the answer to your question about more or less. It's more coverage, more governance, and a transformed team doing work that makes the enterprise's autonomous systems accountable.

The enterprises that fund this inversion early will set the standard everyone else copies. The SOC that has a ratified supervision matrix, a rehearsed kill-switch, a running corruption detection program, and two new roles fully operational inside twelve months will be the model that regulators reference, that peers benchmark against, and that boards point to when they explain to their audit committees what responsible AI security operations looks like. That's not a small competitive advantage. It's a twelve-month head start on a capability that every enterprise running AI at scale will eventually be required to have.

Beyond the Horizon: Why I Believe the Staffed SOC Ends

Everything to this point has stayed inside a twelve-month horizon and inside what the evidence currently supports. This section does neither, and it is marked as such because a reader deserves to know when an author has stopped reporting and started forecasting. My position is that the security operations center staffed by humans does not have a long future, and that the transformation this Part describes is not the destination but the transition into something with no people in it.

The argument is not about capability. It is about reaction time. Every control this book installs assumes a human is available at some point in the sequence, and every one of them is bounded by how fast that human can be reached, oriented, and made to decide. An adversary operating machine-to-machine does not have that constraint. When an attack chain executes end to end in under a minute, the difference between a supervised response and an autonomous one is not a governance preference. It is the difference between stopping the event and documenting it. The enterprises that keep a human in the decision path will lose to the ones that do not, and they will lose on a timescale where the loss is visible in a single quarter.

What survives is not the SOC. It is the governance layer above it: the people who define what the machines may do, set the bounds they operate inside, audit their reasoning after the fact, and hold accountability when the reasoning was wrong. That is a small function reporting to the CISO, and it does not look like a security operations center. It has no shift roster, no queue, and no console anyone watches. The room with people in it responding to events is the thing that ends.

I am aware this sits against the section above, which argues that autonomy expands supervision obligations rather than eliminating them. Both can be true across different time horizons, and the reconciliation matters more than the disagreement. Inside one year, the supervision obligation is real, it is growing, and staffing it is the correct decision. Further out, the supervision function itself compresses, because a governance model that requires a human to approve individual machine decisions has the same reaction-time ceiling as the tier model it replaced. Autonomy expands governance until governance becomes the bottleneck, and then it absorbs that too.

The practical consequence for a security leader reading this in year one is narrow and it is not a reason to change the plan. Build the supervision infrastructure. It is what makes the transition governable rather than reckless, and an enterprise that arrives at full autonomy without a ratified matrix, a rehearsed suspension capability, and an authority chain will arrive there ungoverned. But build it knowing what it is. The supervision matrix is not a permanent operating model. It is the instrument that lets a human decide, deliberately and on evidence, when to step out of a loop they will eventually not be fast enough to stand in.

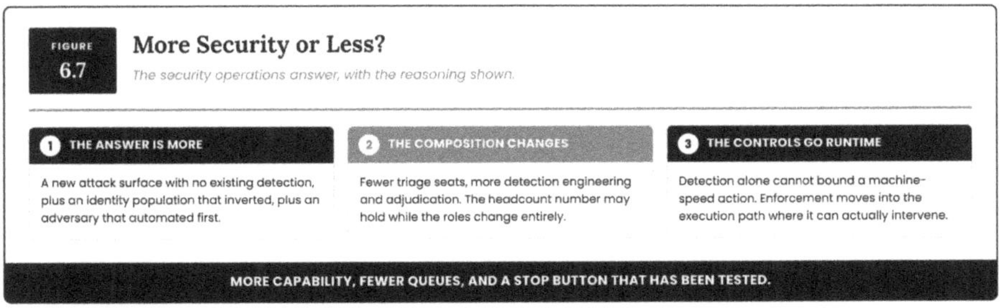

Putting It Into Practice

The inversion is coming whether you schedule it or not. The question is whether it arrives as a governed transition or as a crisis that forces reorganization under pressure. Scheduling it means taking specific actions this month that commit the trajectory before the next budget cycle makes the conversation harder.

Start by locating your SOC against the current-focus map from the first section of this chapter. Write down the honest answer to one question for each of the three transformation indicators: measured autonomy or expensive chat window, detection-as-code or static rule library, proactive supervision framework or reactive governance. Those answers tell you which quarter of the 1-Year TOM you're actually in right now, regardless of what the planning documents say. If your copilot has been running for six months and you don't have a documented accuracy measurement, you're still at the starting line. Name that honestly before committing to a fourth-quarter capability build that has no first-quarter foundation under it.

Evaluate your SOC stack by category this week. Map what you currently have against the five categories: agentic SOC platform, hyperautomation, detection-as-code with continuous validation, AI behavioral monitoring, and telemetry pipeline. For each category, answer two questions. Do you have a tool that covers this category? And does it run continuously or only on demand? A tool that runs on demand in a category that requires continuous coverage is a gap, even if the tool is excellent. Identify the category that's missing entirely from your current stack. That missing category is your first year-one tooling investment. Name it, scope it, and put it in the budget narrative before the next planning cycle opens.

Draft the new SOC job description set this week. Write a one-paragraph description of each of the four new roles: reasoning auditor, AI supervisor, detection engineer in a detection-as-code environment, and corruption analyst. For each role, include the three things that define it: the primary accountability, the skills it requires that differ from existing roles, and the artifact it owns. Those four descriptions are the starting point for the skills transition conversation with your team. They're also the job postings you'll need in year one and year two. Writing them now forces the organizational design decision before the hiring pressure makes it rushed.

Have the skills transition conversation with your team this month. The conversation is specific: here are the roles that are changing, here are the roles that are new, here is the reskilling investment we're making available, and here is the timeline. Identify the two or three analysts on your current team who show the instincts for reasoning auditing or corruption analysis. Put them on a development path toward those roles now, before the roles are formally open. The internal transition is faster and cheaper than external hiring, and the analysts who make the transition bring institutional knowledge that an external hire doesn't have. Identify the gaps that internal development can't close and plan the external hires for years one and two accordingly.

Assemble the 1-Year SOC TOM on one page. First quarter: supervision matrix ratified. Second quarter: corruption detection live on the five highest-stakes systems, agentic SOC platform and behavioral monitoring purchased, reasoning auditor hired. Third quarter: copilot triage measured with documented accuracy, AI supervisor hired, kill-switch rehearsed with filed evidence. Fourth quarter: seven months of detection data, a calibrated finding rate, and the analyst reskilling program complete. For each quarter, add the primary capability build, the headcount change, and the milestone you will name to the board. That one page is the document you bring to the CISO with the staffing narrative and to the CFO with the economics.

The economics presentation to the CFO has one number at its center: cost per investigation, before and after. Calculate the current cost per investigation in your human-staffed model using fully loaded analyst costs divided by monthly investigation volume. Project the cost per investigation at the end of the fourth quarter using the autonomous action rate target from the supervision matrix and the four-role staffing model. The difference between those two numbers is the return on the twelve-month investment. Present that number alongside the coverage expansion: not just cheaper per investigation, but complete coverage of every alert versus the sampled coverage the human model produced. Complete coverage at a lower cost per investigation, funded by the tier model it replaces, is the CFO's answer. Give it to them before they ask for a headcount reduction target you can't meet without breaking the governance model.

Part II is complete. The SOC operating model is drawn, the destination is funded, and the staffing transition is honest. The next chapter opens Part III, where the vendor ecosystem mutates weekly and the questionnaire governing it stopped being fit for purpose years before most programs noticed.

FIGURE 6.8

Putting It Into Practice

Set the SOC's twelve-month horizon.

1 FREEZE TIER ONE BACKFILL

Stop replacing volume-triage seats. Redirect the budget to detection engineering before the requisition renews automatically.

CISO, Week 1

2 NAME THE Q1 TELEMETRY TARGET

Pick the AI systems that must be emitting usable telemetry in ninety days and connect them. Visibility precedes everything else.

SOC Manager, Weeks 1-2

3 SCHEDULE THE STOP EXERCISE

Put a dated suspension rehearsal on the calendar this quarter. The number it produces becomes a standing board metric.

CISO, Week 2

THE OPERATING MODEL CHANGES WHEN THE REQUISITIONS CHANGE.

Part III: Third-Party and Supply Chain Risk

What the Audit Handed Vendor Risk, and Why the Tier Map Is Already Stale

Third-party risk received the AI Vendor Tier Map and a set of contractual findings, and the tier map began aging faster than any other artifact the audit produced. The reason is specific and worth naming precisely rather than generally. A vendor's tier in the map reflects the depth of access that vendor had to enterprise data and systems on the date of assessment. Vendors are now converting existing products into AI products through feature releases that require no contract amendment, no new data processing agreement, and no notification to the customer beyond a product update note. The access depth changes. The tier does not.

That conversion is the governance event nobody filed. A document management platform adds an AI summarization feature and begins sending document contents to a model provider. A customer support tool adds an agent that reads the ticket history. A collaboration suite enables assistant features across the tenant by default. In each case the vendor is operating within the contract as written, because the contract was written before the capability existed and is silent on it. The enterprise's data is now traversing a path that no data flow map documents and no assessment covered, and the only signal is a release note that nobody in the security organization reads.

Beneath the vendor sits a supply chain the enterprise cannot see. Most AI vendor capability is built on a small number of foundation model providers, which means the vendor portfolio's apparent diversity conceals a concentration that is invisible on the tier map and unmeasured on the risk register. When the enterprise asks a vendor which model powers a feature, the answer is often that the vendor considers it proprietary, or that it varies by workload, or that it is subject to change. Fourth-party risk in the traditional sense was about the vendor's subprocessors. Fourth-party risk in AI is about a dependency graph that converges on three or four providers, and a seventy-two hour outage at one of them is a business continuity event across a dozen vendor services simultaneously.

The instrument the function has always used to manage all of this is a questionnaire, sent annually, answered by the vendor about itself, reviewed by an analyst, and filed. That instrument was already a weak control. Against a vendor population that mutates weekly, it is a ceremony. The gap between what the questionnaire captured in January and what is true in June is not a risk the program manages; it is a risk the program cannot see, and the annual cadence guarantees the program learns about material change from a news article rather than from its own monitoring.

The newest problem has no framework at all. Agent-to-agent interaction, where an enterprise AI system exchanges requests and data with a vendor's AI system without a human in either loop, is happening now in procurement, logistics, support, and finance workflows. No standard governs the trust boundary. No questionnaire asks about it. The enterprise is extending machine trust across an organizational boundary on the basis of a contract that contemplated software integration, not autonomous negotiation.

Chapter 7 works through these problems against the tier map and the contract estate. Chapter 8 builds the continuous intelligence capability that replaces the questionnaire, including Adaptive AI Trust Scores. Chapter 9 covers the market, the categories, whether vendor risk owns AI procurement, the twelve-month model, and the board's question.

Chapter 7: Third-Party Risk Inherits the Audit

A Supply Chain That Mutates Weekly and a Tier Map That Is Already Stale

CHAPTER 7 OUTCOMES

At the end of this chapter, you will be able to:

1. Explain why the vendor tier map is stale before the assessment cycle completes.
2. Detect vendor AI feature creep, the conversion nobody approved.
3. Trace the opaque model supply chain into fourth parties you cannot see.
4. Recognize why annual self-attestation cannot govern weekly mutation.
5. Govern agent-to-agent supply chains that no existing framework covers.
6. Assess concentration risk and the renegotiation you will not be able to refuse.

YOUR VENDOR CHANGED. YOUR RISK ASSESSMENT DID NOT.

The Handoff: What Vendor Risk Received and Why the Tier Map Is Already Stale

The audit delivered something specific to third-party risk. Not a vague list of concerns. An actual artifact: the AI Vendor Tier Map. It named which vendors run AI on enterprise data, which contracts contain training clauses nobody had read before the audit surfaced them, and which vendor relationships carry data flows that nobody formally approved. For the first time, the third-party risk function had a structured picture of the AI supply chain it was supposed to be governing.

That picture started aging the day the audit closed.

A tier map is a snapshot. It captures the vendor population as it existed at a specific moment, assessed against criteria that were accurate when the assessment ran. The problem is that the vendor population doesn't hold still. Vendors ship AI features in routine product updates without issuing a press release. They switch foundation model providers without notifying customers. They add subprocessors to their data processing chain without triggering a contract amendment. None of those changes require a procurement event. None of them generate a notification to the security team. They just happen, and the tier map doesn't know about any of them until someone goes looking.

Think about what that means operationally. A vendor that was correctly tiered as Tier 2 at audit time, because it processed enterprise data but had no AI features enabled, may have shipped a copilot in its most recent product release. The copilot is enabled by default. Every user in the enterprise who updated to the latest version is now interacting with an AI feature that processes their work data. The tier map still shows Tier 2. The actual risk profile is now Tier 1. And nobody in the third-party risk function knows, because the update didn't trigger any of the monitoring signals the function was built to watch.

That gap between the tier map and the current reality is the problem third-party risk inherited. Not the map itself, which was genuinely useful work. The structural mismatch between a static document and a supply chain that changes faster than any annual or even quarterly review cycle can track. Converting the tier map into a continuous program isn't a future project. It's the Monday-morning deadline this chapter is built around.

The first action is a re-tiering exercise, and it needs to happen this month. Pull the tier map from the audit. For every vendor on it, ask one question: has this vendor shipped any product update, announced any AI feature, or changed any data processing practice since the audit closed? The answer won't come from the vendor spontaneously. It comes from a structured review of the vendor's release notes, product announcements, and privacy policy change logs. Assign this review to the third-party risk manager. Set a 30-day deadline. Any vendor whose product gained AI capability since the audit gets flagged for immediate re-tiering. The re-tiered map becomes the new baseline. And unlike the audit's version, this one has an owner, an update trigger, and a cadence. That's what makes it a governance artifact instead of a historical record.

The re-tiering exercise will surface more changes than most third-party risk teams expect. That's not a failure of the original audit. It's evidence of how fast the vendor population mutates. Every vendor flagged in the re-tiering exercise is a data point that makes the case for the continuous monitoring program this chapter builds toward.

FIGURE 7.2

The Handoff

What vendor risk received and why the tier map is already stale.

1 A TIER MAP AT A POINT IN TIME

Arrives as: a classification.

Vendors were tiered on the exposure they presented at assessment. The exposure changed when the product shipped an AI feature.

2 ATTESTATIONS WITHOUT VERIFICATION

Arrives as: self-reported claims.

The questionnaire captured what vendors said about themselves on one date, with no mechanism to detect divergence afterward.

3 CONTRACTS WITHOUT AI TERMS

Arrives as: legacy paper.

Agreements signed before the AI feature existed contain no training-data restriction, no model-change notice, and no audit right.

4 NO FOURTH-PARTY VIEW

Arrives as: a blank.

The map stops at the direct vendor. The model provider behind that vendor was never in scope and is not disclosed.

A TIER MAP IS A PHOTOGRAPH OF A SUPPLY CHAIN THAT MUTATES WEEKLY.

Vendor AI Feature Creep: The Conversion Nobody Approved

Every product is becoming an AI product. That's not a prediction. It's a market reality playing out right now across every software category the enterprise uses. Productivity suites, CRM platforms, HR systems, financial reporting tools, project management software, customer support platforms. Each of them is adding AI capabilities, and almost none of them are announcing it in a way that reaches the security team before the feature is already running in production.

Vendor AI feature creep is the formal name for this risk category. It deserves a formal name because it's distinct from other vendor risk categories and it requires a distinct detection approach. Feature creep isn't a vendor misrepresenting their data practices. It's a vendor legitimately shipping product improvements that happen to change how enterprise data is processed in ways the security team never reviewed and the contract never contemplated.

The patterns are consistent across vendors and categories. A copilot gets enabled in a routine upgrade. The feature is on by default. Users start interacting with it immediately because it appears helpful and nobody told them not to. The copilot processes the data in the context where it's embedded: emails, documents, customer records, financial data, whatever the application handles. That data is now flowing through an AI feature that no security review ever assessed and no contract amendment ever authorized. The security team finds out when a user mentions it in passing, or when a privacy review surfaces it, or when it doesn't surface at all and sits undiscovered until a regulator asks about it.

Autonomous workflows are a more consequential version of the same pattern. A vendor ships an update that includes an automation feature. The feature is positioned as a productivity enhancement. It's enabled by default, or it gets enabled when an administrator clicks through a setup wizard without fully reading what they're authorizing. The automation takes actions in the enterprise environment: drafting communications, routing requests, updating records, initiating processes. These actions are now being taken by a system that nobody in the security function reviewed, nobody in legal approved, and nobody in the business formally authorized to act on the organization's behalf.

Embedded models that change data processing are the third pattern, and they're the hardest to detect because they don't look like new features at all. The vendor updates their platform's underlying architecture to incorporate a machine learning model that improves a core function: better search results, smarter recommendations, more accurate categorization. From the user's perspective, nothing changed. The interface looks the same. The workflow is the same. The data the platform processes is the same. What changed is how the platform processes that data internally, and that change may have significant implications for data retention, data sharing with the model provider, and the vendor's ability to use enterprise data to improve the model. None of those implications triggered a contract review because the change didn't look like a new feature from the outside.

The detection problem is real and it requires a systematic approach. Waiting for vendors to disclose AI feature additions doesn't work. Most vendors don't have a disclosure obligation for feature updates, and even those that do often bury the disclosure in release notes that nobody reads. The third-party risk function needs its own detection process, running continuously, that catches feature creep before it becomes a compliance exposure.

The detection process has four components. The first is release note monitoring. Assign the third-party risk manager to monitor release notes and product change logs for every Tier 1 and Tier 2 vendor on a monthly cadence. This isn't a manual reading exercise for every vendor. It's a structured scan using search terms that flag AI-related changes: model, AI, copilot, automation, machine learning, training, inference. Any release note that contains those terms gets pulled for human review. The human review takes five minutes per vendor per month. The coverage it provides is worth significantly more than that.

The second component is privacy policy change monitoring. Vendors that add AI features that process data in new ways are often required to update their privacy policies to reflect those changes. Automated privacy policy monitoring tools compare a vendor's current privacy policy against its previous version and flag material changes. A change that adds language about AI processing, model training, or data sharing with AI providers is a flag that goes to the third-party risk manager for immediate review.

The third component is network traffic analysis for unexpected AI service calls. When a vendor's software starts calling an external AI service that it wasn't calling before, that call appears in network traffic. The security team's network monitoring already captures this traffic. What's needed is a specific detection rule that flags new API calls to known AI service endpoints from enterprise applications. Any new call that wasn't present in the previous 30-day baseline gets flagged for investigation. The investigation determines whether the call is an approved feature or an undisclosed AI integration.

The fourth component is a standing agenda item at every vendor business review. For every Tier 1 vendor, the third-party risk manager includes one question in every quarterly business review: what AI features have you added or plan to add to your product in the next 90 days, and how do those features process our data? That question, asked consistently, creates an expectation with the vendor that AI feature changes require advance disclosure. Vendors that understand the expectation will start flagging changes proactively. That's the behavioral shift the question is designed to produce over time.

Make vendor AI feature creep a standing agenda item at the next third-party risk committee meeting. Not a one-time discussion. A permanent category with a named owner, a detection cadence, and an escalation path for material discoveries. The risk that isn't on the agenda doesn't get governed. This one needs to be on the agenda permanently.

FIGURE 7.3 **Vendor AI Feature Creep**

The conversion nobody approved.

① NO PROCUREMENT EVENT	② THE DATA PATH CHANGES	③ THE TIER IS NOW WRONG
An approved tool ships an AI capability in a routine update. There is no purchase, no review trigger, and no new contract to examine.	Content that stayed inside a vendor boundary now flows to a model provider. The data flow map is wrong and nothing announced it.	A low-tier vendor handling low-sensitivity data becomes a high-tier vendor the moment it starts processing content through a model.

THE RISKIEST AI VENDOR IN YOUR ESTATE IS ONE YOU ALREADY APPROVED.

The Opaque Model Supply Chain: Fourth Parties You Cannot See

When you assess a vendor's AI security posture, you're assessing what the vendor knows and what they're willing to disclose. You're not assessing the foundation model their product runs on. You're not assessing the company that trained that model. You're not assessing the data that went into the training. You're not assessing the infrastructure where the model runs. All of those things are upstream of your vendor, and none of your assessment tools reach them.

That's the model supply chain problem. Your vendor is your third party. The foundation model provider is your fourth party. The company that fine-tuned the model is also your fourth party. The cloud infrastructure where the model runs may be a fifth party. And none of those relationships are visible in your vendor questionnaire, your contract review, or your periodic assessment. You're governing the surface while the risk sits several layers below it.

Model provenance is the first dimension of this opacity. Which foundation model does your vendor's AI feature actually run on? This question sounds simple. In practice, it's often unanswerable. Many vendors don't disclose which foundation model they use. Some don't know themselves, because they're using an aggregation layer that routes to different models based on availability and cost. Some know but treat it as a competitive secret. And even when a vendor does disclose the foundation model, the answer can change without notice when the vendor switches providers for performance or cost reasons. The model your vendor was running six months ago may not be the model they're running today, and you have no mechanism to know the difference.

Training data is the second dimension. What data was the foundation model trained on? This question is even harder to answer than the provenance question. Foundation model providers rarely disclose the full composition of their training datasets. When they do, the disclosure is often at a high level of abstraction: "publicly available internet data" or "licensed text corpora." Whether that training data included data that resembles your enterprise's data, whether it included data that was scraped without authorization from sources your industry considers sensitive, or whether it included data that a regulator would consider problematic for your use case, these questions are largely unanswerable from the outside.

Training clauses in vendor contracts are the third dimension, and this one is directly actionable. The audit surfaced contracts that contain training clauses nobody had read before. Those clauses often permit the vendor to use enterprise data to improve their models. In some cases, that improvement benefits the vendor's other customers, meaning your enterprise data is making the vendor's product better for your competitors. In other cases, the clause is more limited: the vendor uses aggregate, anonymized signals to improve model performance without retaining identifiable enterprise data. The difference between those two scenarios is enormous from a competitive and privacy standpoint, and it lives in the contract language that most procurement processes never read carefully enough.

Pull the contracts for every Tier 1 vendor this month. Read the data processing addenda, the terms of service, and any AI-specific addenda with one specific question: does this contract permit the vendor to use our data to train or improve their models? Document the answer for each contract. Flag every contract where the answer is yes or unclear. Those flagged contracts go to the General Counsel and the CPO for review before the next renewal cycle. The review determines whether the clause is acceptable as written, whether it needs to be renegotiated, or whether it represents a risk that requires immediate escalation. This is not a legal exercise that can wait until renewal. The clause is operating right now, on current data flows, and its implications are current regardless of when the contract renews.

Concentration risk is the fourth dimension of the model supply chain problem, and it's the one that most third-party risk programs haven't fully mapped yet. The entire AI stack is converging on a handful of foundation model providers. The vendors in your tier map may look like a diverse portfolio of independent suppliers. But if a significant percentage of them are all running on the same two or three foundation models, your vendor diversity is illusory at the model layer. A failure, a compromise, or a policy change at a single foundation model provider could affect dozens of your vendors simultaneously. That's a concentration risk that no traditional third-party risk program was designed to assess, because it requires looking through the vendor to the model layer underneath.

Ask your five most critical Tier 1 vendors the fourth-party question directly: which foundation model does your AI feature run on, and who else has access to the data we send to it? Document the answers. Map the responses against each other. If three of your five most critical vendors are all running on the same foundation model, you have a concentration risk that needs to go into the risk register as a named finding with a named owner and a mitigation plan. The mitigation isn't necessarily switching vendors. It's understanding the concentration and making a deliberate, documented decision about whether the risk is acceptable. Undocumented concentration risk is a governance gap. Documented and accepted concentration risk is a governance decision.

Poisoned components upstream are the final dimension. Compromised open-source models, malicious weights embedded in publicly available model repositories, backdoored datasets that introduce behavioral vulnerabilities into models trained on them. These risks exist at the foundation layer of the AI supply chain, well above your vendor relationship and completely outside your assessment reach. Your vendor's questionnaire response doesn't capture them because your vendor is as blind to them as you are. The only defense available at the enterprise level is asking the right questions of vendors, requiring vendors to attest to their own supply chain security practices, and treating the absence of a credible answer as a risk signal in itself.

The exposure also runs in the other direction, which procurement rarely considers. A model the enterprise paid to fine-tune on proprietary data is an asset, and query access to it is access to that asset. Research going back a decade established that black-box access to a prediction interface is sufficient to reconstruct a functionally equivalent copy of a model with near-perfect fidelity, demonstrated against commercial machine-learning services rather than laboratory targets. The practical reading for a third-party risk function is that an interface exposed to a partner, a customer, or an agent operating on someone else's behalf is a channel through which the model itself can walk out, and the contract needs a query-rate term and a prohibition on derivative model training the same way it needs a training-data restriction.

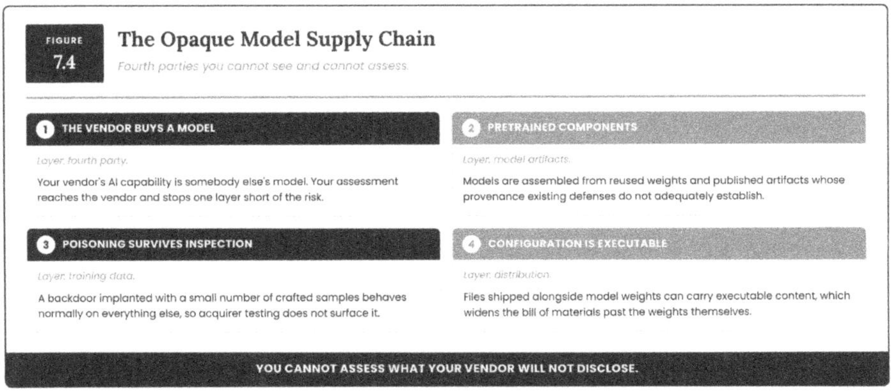

The Collapse of the Questionnaire: Annual Self-Attestation Meets Weekly Mutation

The questionnaire was already struggling before AI arrived. A small third-party risk team sampling thousands of vendors through self-reported answers, collected annually, was always a coverage problem dressed up as a governance process. The sample was too small. The cadence was too slow. The self-attestation format was too easy to game. And the results were filed in a system that nobody consulted between assessment cycles. The questionnaire wasn't rigorous governance. It was documented due diligence, which is a different thing entirely.

AI finishes it.

The assessment cadence problem becomes fatal when the vendor population changes weekly. A questionnaire sent in January that comes back in March is assessing a vendor relationship that may have changed materially in the two months between sending and receiving. The vendor that answered "no AI features process your data" in March may have shipped an AI-enabled update in April. The questionnaire that was filed as evidence of a satisfactory assessment in March is now evidence of a satisfactory assessment of a vendor relationship that no longer exists in the form assessed. The evidence is accurate for a moment that has passed. It's inaccurate for the moment that matters.

Self-attestation fails specifically for AI because vendors often can't accurately describe their own AI behavior. This isn't dishonesty. It's a genuine epistemic limitation. A vendor's security team may not have complete visibility into which AI features their product team shipped in the most recent release. The product team may not have complete visibility into which foundation model their AI feature is running on, because they're using an aggregation layer that abstracts the model selection. The foundation model provider may not be able to fully describe the behavior of a model that exhibits emergent properties its own training process didn't explicitly design for. The questionnaire asks the vendor to attest to AI behavior that the vendor itself doesn't fully understand. The attestation is given in good faith. It's also structurally incomplete.

Consider a hypothetical third-party risk director at a large financial services organization. His team manages a vendor portfolio of over 800 suppliers. His annual vendor assessment program sends questionnaires to the top 200 vendors by spend and criticality. The program has been running for six years. It's well-designed, well-documented, and well-regarded internally. In the most recent assessment cycle, 94% of Tier 1 vendors returned satisfactory questionnaire responses. Three months after the assessment cycle closed, his team discovered that seven Tier 1 vendors had shipped AI features since their questionnaires were completed. Two of those features processed data categories that would have triggered additional controls under his organization's data classification policy. Neither vendor had disclosed the feature addition. Both vendors would have answered the questionnaire accurately at the time they completed it. The questionnaire wasn't wrong. It was obsolete. Note: this is a hypothetical scenario illustrating a pattern common across regulated industries, not a real case study. The point isn't that the program failed. The point is that a program designed for a static vendor population can't govern a dynamic one, regardless of how well it's designed.

Patching the questionnaire doesn't solve the structural problem. Adding more AI-specific questions to the annual questionnaire produces a longer document that captures AI risk as it existed when the vendor completed the form. Adding a semi-annual questionnaire cycle produces two snapshots per year of a supply chain that changes weekly. The coverage improvement is real but insufficient. The structural mismatch between questionnaire cadence and supply chain mutation speed can't be closed by sending questionnaires more often. It can only be closed by replacing periodic sampling with continuous monitoring.

The questionnaire doesn't disappear in the continuous monitoring model. It transforms. Instead of being the primary evidence of vendor AI risk, it becomes the baseline document that continuous monitoring validates and updates. The questionnaire establishes the vendor's self-reported AI posture at a point in time. Continuous monitoring tracks whether that posture holds. When monitoring detects a change that contradicts the questionnaire response, the contradiction becomes a risk signal that triggers immediate investigation rather than waiting for the next assessment cycle. The questionnaire is still useful. It's just no longer sufficient as a standalone control.

The continuous monitoring capability that replaces the questionnaire as the primary control has three components. Automated vendor intelligence feeds that monitor vendor product announcements, release notes, privacy policy changes, and regulatory filings for AI-related signals. Network traffic monitoring that detects new AI service calls from vendor software. And contract clause monitoring that flags upcoming renewals for contracts that contain training clauses requiring renegotiation. Together, these three components provide the between-cycle visibility that the questionnaire never could. They catch the changes that happen between annual assessments and surface them to the third-party risk team in time to act.

The transition from questionnaire-led to monitoring-led vendor risk governance is a capability build that takes time. Start this month by identifying the two or three Tier 1 vendors where the gap between questionnaire response and current reality is most likely to be material. For those vendors, stand up manual monitoring of their release notes and privacy policy changes this week. That manual monitoring is the proof of concept for the automated monitoring program. It will surface changes. Those changes will make the case for the automated capability. The evidence from the manual monitoring pilot is what you bring to the CISO and the CFO when you make the case for the continuous monitoring investment.

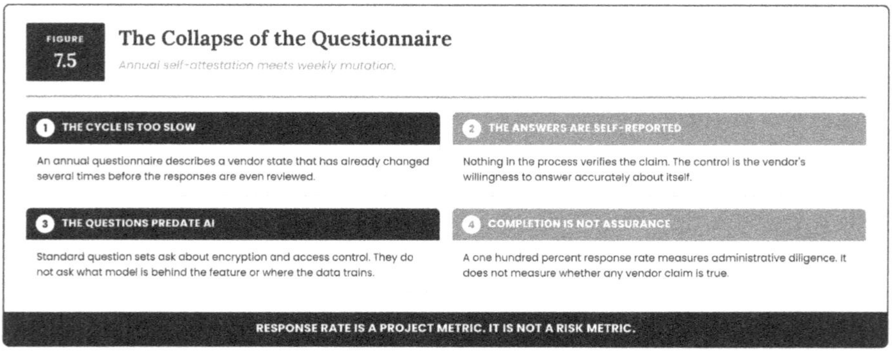

Agent-to-Agent Supply Chains: Trust Boundaries No Framework Governs

The previous four sections describe risks that are serious and growing. This section describes a risk that is nascent, poorly understood, and almost entirely ungoverned. That combination makes it the most important risk in this chapter to understand clearly, because the window for building governance before the risk matures is closing.

Your vendors' agents are transacting with your agents. Not hypothetically. This is happening now, in enterprises that have deployed AI agents for procurement, customer service, contract management, and operational workflows. When your procurement agent queries a vendor's pricing agent to get a quote, two autonomous systems are exchanging data across an organizational boundary. When your customer service agent escalates a complex case to a vendor's support agent for resolution, two autonomous systems are handing off context and authority across a trust boundary that no governance framework currently defines.

The trust boundary problem is specific and structural. When two humans from different organizations interact, the trust framework is well-established. Contracts define the scope of the relationship. Legal identities are verified through established processes. Authority is delegated through documented channels. Disputes have resolution mechanisms. When two autonomous agents from different organizations interact, none of those frameworks apply cleanly. The agents don't have legal identities in any meaningful sense. Their authority to act on behalf of their organizations isn't established through any formal credential that the other organization can verify. The scope of what they're authorized to exchange isn't defined in any contract that contemplated agent-to-agent interaction. And when something goes wrong, the question of which organization's agent caused the problem, and which organization bears accountability, has no established answer.

Vendor-side non-human identities operating inside your environment are the most immediate manifestation of this problem. When a vendor's integration agent connects to your systems to exchange data, it operates with credentials that your identity management system issued. Those credentials give the agent access to whatever your systems permit. The agent's behavior inside your environment is governed by whatever logic the vendor built into it, which you have no visibility into. The vendor's agent may be doing exactly what it was designed to do. That design may include behaviors you never authorized and your contract never contemplated. And the credentials that enable those behaviors are sitting in your identity management system, credentialed as a legitimate integration, with no lifecycle governance watching them.

Delegation chains crossing company lines are the second dimension of this problem. Your agent delegates a subtask to a vendor's agent. The vendor's agent, to complete the subtask, delegates a further subtask to a third party's agent. That third party's agent takes an action that affects your enterprise data. You authorized the first delegation. You didn't authorize the second. You don't know the third party's agent exists. The action it took is traceable back to your original agent's delegation, which means it's traceable back to your enterprise. The accountability flows back through the delegation chain even though your visibility stops at the first link.

No existing framework defines how two organizations' machines establish, verify, and revoke trust. The frameworks that govern human-to-human trust across organizational boundaries don't extend to machine-to-machine trust. The frameworks that govern machine identity within a single organization don't extend to cross-organizational machine interactions. The gap between those two frameworks is where agent-to-agent supply chains currently operate: in a governance vacuum where neither side fully controls or sees what the other's system is doing.

The Protocol Layer Is Standardizing While the Governance Layer Is Not

The governance vacuum described above is not going to be filled by a governance body. It is being filled, right now, by a protocol. Two of them, and the distinction between them determines which of your controls apply.

The first is the tool access protocol, which the audit already surfaced when it found MCP servers and treated them as a credential surface. That protocol connects an agent downward, to databases, files, and internal interfaces. Everything your enterprise already knows about privileged access applies to it, which is why the tool provenance work in the preceding section is executable with controls you have.

The second protocol governs a direction your controls were never built for. It connects an agent horizontally, to another autonomous agent operating under a different organization's authority. It was released into open governance under a permissive license and is now stewarded by an independent foundation with a steering committee spanning cloud providers and framework developers, which means it is not a single vendor's specification you can decline to support. It will arrive in your environment the way the tool protocol did, through a developer integration nobody routed through procurement.

Three of its design decisions matter to a third-party risk director, and none of them are technical curiosities.

The first is the capability manifest. Every participating agent publishes a machine-readable document advertising its skills, its supported data types, its endpoint, and the credentials it requires. That manifest is the closest thing to a disclosure artifact this problem has produced. It tells you what a counterparty agent claims it can do before it does anything, and it is the natural attachment point for the inventory step named below. It is also an assertion by the counterparty, not a verified fact, and treating it as evidence rather than as a claim is the first mistake available here.

The second is the task lifecycle. Work crosses the boundary as a task with explicit states, moving from submitted, to working, to input required, to completed or failed. That structure is what makes cross-organizational delegation auditable at all. It is also what makes the input required state a governance question rather than an engineering one, because it is the moment a counterparty agent asks your agent for something that was not in the original scope, and nothing in the protocol decides whether that request should be honored.

The third is the authentication model. The protocol carries enterprise-grade authentication, including token-based authorization, federated identity, and mutual certificate verification. This is where the most consequential misreading will occur, so it is worth stating plainly. Authentication establishes that a counterparty agent is who it says it is. It establishes nothing about whether that agent should be permitted to act, at what scope, under whose delegated authority, or for how long. A protocol that authenticates well does not close the trust gap. It makes the gap easier to reach across at speed.

The Agent Authority Chain from Part II is what the protocol does not supply. Identity is what the manifest and the authentication model give you. Intent, authority, context, action, and impact remain your organization's responsibility on both sides of the boundary, and the fact that the transport is now standardized means the volume of these interactions will rise before the governance for them exists.

The Year 1 position is therefore narrow and defensible. Require that any vendor whose agents interact with yours discloses which protocol they use and publishes the capability manifest for every agent that touches your environment. Register those manifests alongside the tool registry rather than in a separate system, because they are the same class of artifact. And record explicitly, in your provisional boundary framework, that protocol-level authentication does not constitute authorization. That sentence will be tested within the year, and the enterprise that wrote it down first is the one that holds the position.

The practical governance response to this gap starts with inventory, not with a framework. You can't govern what you can't see. This month, identify every vendor-side non-human identity currently operating inside your environment. Run the NHI discovery process described in Chapter 4 specifically looking for credentials associated with vendor integrations. For each vendor NHI discovered, document three things: which vendor it belongs to, what systems it has access to, and what the business justification is for that access. Any vendor NHI that can't produce a clear business justification gets suspended pending review. Any vendor NHI with access broader than its documented business justification gets scoped down immediately.

The second step is to add agent-to-agent interaction governance to your Tier 1 vendor contracts at the next renewal opportunity. The contract language needs to address three things. First, the vendor must disclose any autonomous agents that will operate inside your environment or interact with your agents. Second, the vendor must agree that their agents will not delegate to third parties without explicit written authorization. Third, the vendor must agree to provide audit logs of their agent's actions within your environment on request. This language doesn't exist in most current vendor contracts because the contracts were written before agent-to-agent interaction was a practical reality. It needs to be in the next generation of contracts for every Tier 1 vendor.

The third step is to establish a provisional trust framework for agent-to-agent interactions at your organizational boundary. This doesn't need to be comprehensive. It needs to define three things: what categories of data your agents may share with vendor agents without human approval, what actions vendor agents may take inside your environment without human approval, and what the suspension mechanism is when a vendor agent behaves outside those boundaries. That provisional framework is your organization's unilateral governance position until a bilateral framework exists. It's also the starting point for the conversation with your most critical vendors about what mutual agent-to-agent governance looks like when both sides have skin in the game.

The agent-to-agent trust problem is where the third-party risk domain intersects most directly with the governance and SOC domains. The Decision Rights RACI from Part I needs to address agent-to-agent delegation authority. The NHI governance model from Part II needs to extend to vendor-side NHIs operating in the enterprise environment. The kill-switch protocol needs to include vendor agent suspension as an explicit scenario. None of those connections happen automatically. They happen when the third-party risk director brings this section's findings to the governance committee and the SOC director and makes the case for a cross-domain response. That conversation needs to happen this month, not next quarter.

FIGURE 7.6 **Agent-to-Agent Supply Chains**
Trust boundaries no existing framework governs.

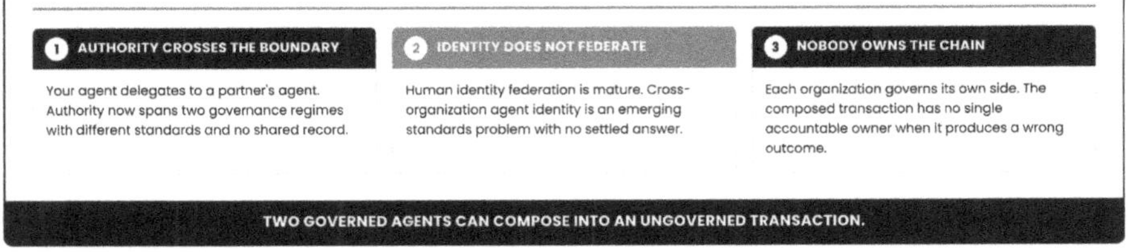

Consolidation Risk: The Renegotiation You Will Not Be Able to Refuse

The AI vendor market is consolidating, and third-party risk programs are structured to miss what that means. The tier map records vendors as independent entities with independent risk profiles, and it is accurate on the date it is drawn. What it does not record is that several of those vendors are acquisition targets, that some will be acquired by each other, and that a subset will be acquired by the foundation model providers whose infrastructure they already depend on. Each of those events changes the enterprise's risk position without any change in the vendor's product, contract, or attested security posture.

The mechanics are worth being precise about, because the generic version of this concern is easy to dismiss. When a vendor is acquired, the data processing agreement typically survives, but the subprocessor list changes, the data residency guarantees may change, the security organization that stood behind the attestation is replaced, and the retention practices are harmonized to the acquirer's standard on a timeline the acquirer sets. None of these require the enterprise's consent under most contracts as written. The enterprise receives a notification, often after the fact, and the practical options are to accept the new posture or to exit a vendor whose product is now embedded in a business workflow.

The exit option is the one that erodes fastest, and it erodes in a way procurement rarely models. A vendor whose AI features have been in use for eighteen months holds enterprise data in forms the enterprise cannot readily retrieve: fine-tuned adaptations, accumulated agent memory, embedded representations of documents, and workflow configurations that encode institutional process. Contract termination clauses drafted for software vendors contemplate data return as an export of records. They rarely contemplate what happens to a model that has been adapted on your data, or whether adapted weights constitute your data at all. The enterprise that discovers this question at the exit conversation is discovering it at the worst possible moment.

Concentration compounds the problem in a direction most risk registers do not capture. If the foundation model layer consolidates further, a portfolio that currently shows four independent vendor relationships may resolve to two, then one, without the enterprise executing a single new contract. The third-party risk function's diversification story, which is usually presented to the board as a resilience control, was describing a diversity at the vendor layer that never existed at the model layer. That distinction has not mattered much in practice yet. It will matter the first time a foundation model provider has a multi-day outage, and the enterprise discovers that six vendor services degraded simultaneously for a reason no continuity plan anticipated.

The decision rule is a contract rule and it belongs in the clause library before the next renewal cycle rather than after the next acquisition. Every AI vendor contract requires advance notification of change of control, advance notification of any change to the underlying model provider, and a defined exit assistance obligation that names what is returned and in what form, including any adaptations trained on enterprise data. Where a vendor refuses the model-provider notification clause, the refusal is itself a finding, and it belongs on the risk register with the vendor's name attached. A vendor that will not tell you whose model you are depending on has told you something.

FIGURE 7.7

Consolidation and Concentration Risk

The renegotiation you will not be able to refuse.

CONCENTRATION POINT	WHAT IT LOOKS LIKE	FAILURE MODE	YEAR ONE ACTION
Foundation model	Most AI capability traces to one provider	Pricing power and forced terms	Map provider behind every AI feature
Cloud platform	Model, data, and runtime in one estate	Exit cost exceeds switching benefit	Cost a real migration
Single AI vendor	One platform spans several domains	Outage becomes enterprise-wide	Define the degraded operating mode
Shared tooling	Many agents call the same tool service	One compromise reaches everything	Segment and scope tool grants

CONCENTRATION IS INVISIBLE UNTIL THE RENEWAL NOTICE ARRIVES.

The Runtime Supply Chain: What the Agent Encountered While It Was Working

Supply chain security has always asked what the enterprise installed. The tier map, the Bill of Materials, the subprocessor disclosures, and the contract estate all describe relationships established before the software ran. Agents introduce a second supply chain that the first one does not cover, because an agent acquires dependencies while it operates. A web page it retrieved, a repository it read, a tool it discovered, a document a supplier sent, another organization's agent it exchanged messages with. Each of those influenced the agent's behavior, none of them appear in any procurement record, and the enterprise's entire supply chain apparatus was built to govern the other kind.

The consequence is that the deployment-time controls the audit validated do not bound the risk they were designed to bound. An agent operating under a fully assessed vendor's product, with a complete Bill of Materials and a clean contract, can be influenced within a single session by content the enterprise never onboarded, from a source no assessment covered, with an effect that persists in memory after the session ends. The vendor's posture did not change. The agent's behavior did. Third-party risk functions reading their tier map for assurance are reading a document that describes a different problem than the one they now have.

What makes this tractable rather than hopeless is that runtime dependencies fall into a small number of classes and each has a governable trust decision attached. Retrieved content from internal sources is one class with a known provenance. Retrieved content from external sources is a second class that should be treated as untrusted control input regardless of how reputable the source appears. Tools and their descriptions are a third class requiring provenance and signing. Other organizations' agents are a fourth class requiring mutual authentication. Packages and code fetched during operation are a fifth class that belongs to the traditional supply chain apparatus and should be routed there rather than treated as new.

The decision rule that follows is a classification rule rather than a blocking one, because blocking external retrieval eliminates the capability that made agents worth deploying. Every source an agent may draw from carries a trust classification recorded in advance, and content from an untrusted classification is admissible as information and never as instruction. Enforcing that distinction is an architectural control at the retrieval boundary, not a prompt instruction, and an enterprise whose entire defense is a system prompt telling the model to ignore instructions in retrieved content has written a request rather than a control.

The third-party risk function's specific ownership here is the source classification itself, and it is the natural owner because classifying external sources by trustworthiness is what the function has always done for vendors. Extend the tier logic. A source the enterprise has assessed and holds a contract with is one tier. A source the enterprise uses without any relationship is another. A source the agent discovered during operation is a third, and content from that tier should be admissible only where the downstream action class is low consequence. Publish the classification, review it quarterly, and treat an agent drawing from an unclassified source as a finding rather than as normal operation.

FIGURE 7.8 The Runtime Supply Chain

What the agent encountered while it was working.

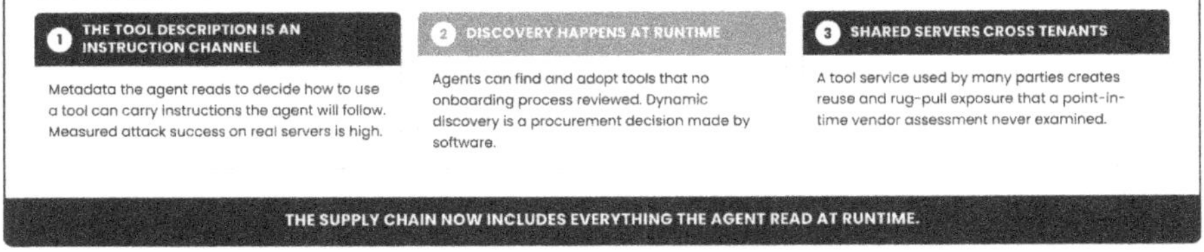

Putting It Into Practice

The tier map is aging. The questionnaire is structurally insufficient. Feature creep is running undetected. The model supply chain is opaque. And agent-to-agent interactions are happening outside any governance framework. Each of those problems has a specific, actionable response. This section names them with owners, timelines, and defined outputs.

This month, re-tier the vendor portfolio by AI feature exposure. Pull the tier map from the audit. Assign the third-party risk manager to review every vendor's release notes, product announcements, and privacy policy changes since the audit closed. Any vendor whose product gained AI capability since the audit gets flagged for immediate re-tiering. The re-tiering review completes within 30 days. The updated tier map gets filed in the governance repository as the new baseline, with the third-party risk manager named as owner and a quarterly update cadence defined. That cadence is what converts the tier map from a snapshot into a living artifact.

This month, pull the contracts for every Tier 1 vendor and read the training clauses. Assign the third-party risk manager to document the training clause status for each contract: does it permit vendor use of enterprise data to train or improve models, is the language ambiguous, or is enterprise data explicitly excluded? The documentation completes within 30 days. Every contract with a permissive or ambiguous training clause goes to the General Counsel and the CPO for review before the next renewal. The review produces one of three outcomes: the clause is acceptable and that acceptance is documented, the clause requires renegotiation at renewal, or the clause represents an immediate risk that requires escalation before renewal. All three outcomes go into the risk register with named owners and timelines.

This month, ask the fourth-party question of your five most critical Tier 1 vendors. The question is specific: which foundation model does your AI feature run on, who trained it, and who else has access to the data we send to it? Send the question in writing to the vendor's security or data protection contact. Document the responses. Map the responses against each other to identify concentration risk. Any vendor that cannot or will not answer the question gets flagged as an opacity risk in the risk register. Opacity is itself a risk signal. A vendor that can't tell you what model is processing your data is a vendor whose AI risk posture you cannot assess, and that inability belongs in the risk register as a named finding.

This month, inventory every vendor-side non-human identity operating inside your environment. Run the NHI discovery process specifically targeting vendor integration credentials. Document which vendor each NHI belongs to, what systems it accesses, and what the business justification is. Any NHI without a clear business justification gets suspended pending review. Any NHI with access broader than its justification gets scoped down immediately. The inventory output goes into the NHI registry with vendor-side NHIs flagged as a distinct category requiring quarterly review.

Stand up manual monitoring of release notes and privacy policy changes for your ten highest-risk Tier 1 vendors this week. Assign the monitoring to the third-party risk manager with a monthly review cadence. Document every AI-related change detected. After 90 days, the findings from the manual monitoring pilot become the evidence base for the continuous monitoring investment proposal. The proposal goes to the CISO and the CFO with specific numbers: how many undisclosed AI feature changes were detected in 90 days, what the potential compliance exposure of each change was, and what the cost of the automated monitoring capability is relative to the risk it addresses.

The next chapter gives third-party risk the engine to govern a vendor population this size continuously. But the inventory of what you cannot see starts this month, with the specific actions named above. The tier map gets updated. The training clauses get documented. The fourth-party question gets asked. The vendor NHIs get inventoried. And the monitoring pilot starts running. Those five actions don't close every gap this chapter named. They close the most consequential ones and build the evidence base for the continuous program that closes the rest. That's where the AI IT Security Implementation & Strategy™ operates in the third-party domain: not with a single comprehensive solution, but with a sequenced set of owned, cadenced actions that convert a static snapshot into a running program.

FIGURE 7.9

Putting It Into Practice

Start the inventory of what you cannot see.

1 RE-TIER ON AI EXPOSURE

Review the vendor population for AI features shipped since assessment. Re-tier on current exposure rather than original classification.

TPRM Lead. Weeks 1-4

2 ASK THE FOURTH-PARTY QUESTION

Send one question to every tier-one vendor: which model provider is behind your AI feature. Track who answers and who refuses.

TPRM Lead. Weeks 2-6

3 INVENTORY VENDOR IDENTITIES

Enumerate the non-human identities your vendors hold in your environment. Each one is a supply chain path into your estate.

IAM Lead. Weeks 4-8

FIVE ACTIONS DO NOT CLOSE EVERY GAP. THEY CLOSE THE CONSEQUENTIAL ONES.

Chapter 8: Vendor Risk Gains an Engine

Continuous Intelligence Replaces the Questionnaire

CHAPTER 8 OUTCOMES

At the end of this chapter, you will be able to:

1. Assess every contract and attestation rather than a sampled subset.
2. Detect vendor change continuously through external monitoring.
3. Enforce the AI clause library at machine speed across the contract population.
4. Require an AI Bill of Materials that makes the invisible chain disclosable.
5. Operate Adaptive AI Trust Scores as a managed variable rather than an annual binary.
6. Secure the agent toolchain and attenuate authority across organizational boundaries.

CONTINUOUS INTELLIGENCE REPLACES THE QUESTIONNAIRE.

Complete Assessment: Every Contract, Every Attestation, Every Vendor

Chapter 7 named the structural problem clearly. A small team sampling thousands of vendors through annual self-attestation was never real governance. It was documented due diligence, and there's a significant difference between those two things. The questionnaire gave the third-party risk function something to file. It didn't give it something to rely on. The sample was too small, the cadence was too slow, and the self-reported format was too easy to satisfy without actually answering the question that mattered: what is this vendor's AI doing with our data right now?

AI ends the sampling problem. Completely and permanently.

Machine reading doesn't have a calendar. It doesn't have a queue. It doesn't need to prioritize which 200 vendors to assess this year because the team can only reach 200. When you feed every vendor attestation report, every contract, every questionnaire response, and every data processing addendum into an AI-powered assessment engine, the system can evaluate every document against every applicable criterion for every vendor in the portfolio simultaneously. Coverage stops being a resourcing decision. It becomes an architecture decision. The question shifts from "which vendors can we afford to assess" to "what do we want to know about all of them, and how do we configure the system to find it?"

That shift is more significant than it sounds.

When coverage is a resourcing constraint, the third-party risk function makes prioritization decisions that are actually risk acceptance decisions in disguise. Choosing to assess only the top 200 vendors means accepting that the other 600 are ungoverned. That acceptance is rarely documented explicitly. It's just what happens when the team runs out of capacity. The risk register doesn't show a finding for the 600 ungoverned vendors. It shows findings for the 200 that were assessed. The board sees a program that assessed 200 vendors and found these issues. It doesn't see a program that left 600 vendors unreviewed. Those are very different pictures of the same situation.

Total assessment changes that picture permanently. When the machine reads every attestation report across the full vendor portfolio, the risk register reflects the full population, not the assessed sample. Findings that were invisible because the team never reached that tier of vendor become visible. Patterns that only emerge when you look at the full portfolio, concentration risks, common contractual gaps, shared foundation model dependencies, become visible. The CISO can tell the board that every vendor was assessed, not that a representative sample was assessed. Those are not the same statement, and the board's ability to govern AI risk depends on understanding the difference.

The operational architecture for complete assessment has three components. The first is a document ingestion pipeline. Every vendor-related document flows into the assessment engine: attestation reports, SOC 2 Type II reports, ISO 27001 certificates, data processing agreements, master service agreements, AI addenda, privacy policies, and questionnaire responses. The pipeline runs continuously. New documents are ingested as they arrive. Updated documents replace their previous versions with the change flagged for review. The pipeline doesn't wait for an assessment cycle to open. It processes documents the day they arrive.

The second component is a criterion library. This is the set of assessment criteria the engine evaluates every document against. The criterion library covers AI-specific requirements: does the contract contain a training clause, does the data processing agreement address AI inference, does the attestation report cover AI system controls, does the questionnaire response disclose the foundation model in use, does the contract require notification of model-provider changes? The criterion library is a governed artifact. It has a named owner, the third-party risk director. It has an update cadence, monthly review against new regulatory requirements and emerging risk patterns. And it has a version history, so the assessment results from any point in time can be traced back to the criteria that were in effect when the assessment ran.

The third component is the exception routing model. Not every finding the machine surfaces requires the same response. The exception routing model classifies findings by severity and routes them to the appropriate owner at the appropriate speed. A missing AI addendum in a Tier 3 vendor contract goes into the quarterly renewal queue. A training clause in a Tier 1 vendor contract that permits enterprise data to be used for model improvement goes to the General Counsel within 24 hours. A questionnaire response that contradicts the network traffic data from the vendor monitoring program goes to the third-party risk manager for immediate investigation. The routing model is what converts machine output into human action. Without it, the machine produces findings that accumulate in a queue nobody works. With it, every finding has a destination, an owner, and a response timeline before the human ever sees it.

The transition from prioritized assessment to total assessment requires one specific organizational decision before the architecture can be built. The third-party risk director needs to formally retire the annual assessment cycle as the primary governance mechanism and replace it with continuous machine assessment as the primary mechanism, with human review of machine-surfaced findings as the operating model. That decision needs to be ratified by the CISO and communicated to the General Counsel, because it changes the evidentiary basis of the vendor risk program. The annual questionnaire response was the evidence. The machine's continuous assessment output becomes the evidence. That change has implications for regulatory submissions, contract negotiations, and incident response that the General Counsel needs to understand before it happens.

Start the architecture build this month with the document ingestion pipeline for your Tier 1 vendors. Feed every contract, every attestation report, and every questionnaire response for your top 50 vendors into the assessment engine. Configure the criterion library against the AI-specific requirements that matter most for your regulatory environment. Run the first complete assessment. The output will surface findings that the annual questionnaire cycle never reached. Those findings are the evidence base for the investment in expanding the pipeline to the full portfolio. They're also the findings that go into the risk register this month, with named owners and resolution timelines, because they're real risk regardless of how they were discovered.

FIGURE 8.2 **Complete Assessment**

Every contract, every attestation, every vendor.

1 THE WHOLE CONTRACT POPULATION

Machine reading covers every agreement rather than the tier-one subset that human capacity allowed. Exposure concentrates in the unread tail.

2 CLAUSE-LEVEL EXTRACTION

Each contract is examined for training-data restriction, model-change notice, audit right, and subprocessor disclosure as discrete findings.

3 GAP REPORTING BY POPULATION

The output is not a list of bad contracts. It is the percentage of the population missing each required protection.

4 RENEWAL SEQUENCING

Gaps are ordered by renewal date so remediation follows the calendar where the enterprise actually has leverage.

YOU HAVE LEVERAGE AT RENEWAL. THE REST OF THE YEAR YOU HAVE A REQUEST.

Continuous External Monitoring: Detecting Vendor Change in Real Time

The questionnaire asked vendors to describe themselves once a year. Monitoring watches them continuously. Those are not variations on the same approach. They're fundamentally different governance philosophies, and the shift from one to the other is the most operationally significant change the third-party risk function makes in this chapter.

The external signal architecture that replaces the annual questionnaire has six distinct signal categories. Each one catches a different class of vendor change. Together they give the third-party risk function the between-cycle visibility that the questionnaire never provided.

The first signal category is breach disclosures. When a vendor experiences a security incident, the disclosure often appears in regulatory filings, press releases, and breach notification databases before the vendor contacts their customers directly. Monitoring vendor breach disclosures in real time means the third-party risk team knows about a vendor incident the day it's disclosed, not the week the vendor gets around to notifying affected customers. That timing difference matters enormously for the enterprise's own incident response posture. A vendor breach that affects enterprise data requires the third-party risk team to assess the potential impact on the enterprise, notify the relevant internal stakeholders, and determine whether any regulatory notification obligations are triggered. Every day of delay in knowing about the breach is a day of delay in that response chain.

The second signal category is terms-of-service and privacy policy edits. Vendors update their terms and privacy policies when their data practices change. Those updates are public documents, and they're trackable. Automated policy monitoring tools compare a vendor's current policy against its previous version and surface material changes within hours of publication. A privacy policy update that adds language about AI processing, model training rights, or data sharing with third-party AI providers is a material change that requires immediate review by the third-party risk manager and, depending on what it says, the General Counsel and the CPO.

The third signal category is subprocessor updates. Vendors that process enterprise data on behalf of the enterprise are required under most data protection frameworks to maintain a list of subprocessors and to notify customers of material changes. In practice, those notifications often arrive as a low-visibility email to a general inbox, or as an update to a webpage that nobody checks regularly. Monitoring vendor subprocessor pages and notification channels for changes means the third-party risk team catches subprocessor additions and changes as they happen, not months later when someone notices the webpage changed.

The fourth signal category is model-provider changes. A vendor that switches from one foundation model provider to another has materially changed how their AI feature processes enterprise data, potentially including changes to data retention, data sharing, and the geographic location of processing. Most vendors don't have a contractual obligation to notify customers of model-provider changes unless the contract specifically requires it. Monitoring for model-provider changes requires a combination of technical signals, network traffic changes to different AI service endpoints, and public signals, vendor announcements, product documentation updates, and developer forum discussions where engineers mention the change.

The fifth signal category is AI feature announcements. When a vendor announces a new AI feature, the announcement typically appears in their product blog, release notes, and developer documentation before the feature is enabled in production. Monitoring those channels gives the third-party risk team advance notice of AI features that will affect enterprise data processing. Advance notice is the difference between a proactive security review before the feature goes live and a reactive assessment after enterprise data has already been processed by an unreviewed AI system.

The sixth signal category is regulatory and legal filings. Vendors operating in regulated industries file documents with regulators that often contain disclosures about their AI practices, their data handling, and their security posture that don't appear in their marketing materials or their questionnaire responses. Monitoring regulatory filings for key vendors, particularly in financial services, healthcare, and data-intensive industries, surfaces information about vendor AI practices that no other signal category reaches.

Feature-creep detection wired to the risk register is the specific operating mechanism that makes these six signal categories actionable rather than informational. When the monitoring system detects a vendor AI feature announcement, it doesn't just log the signal. It checks the risk register to determine whether this vendor's AI feature status is already documented, and if so, whether the announcement represents a change from the documented status. If it does, the system drafts a risk register update and routes it to the third-party risk manager for review within 24 hours of the signal appearing. The manager reviews the draft, confirms the change is material, and either approves the register update or flags it for escalation. The vendor's AI feature conversion triggers a review the week it ships, not at the annual cycle.

The alerting thresholds that determine what gets routed to the manager immediately versus what goes into the weekly review queue need to be defined explicitly before the monitoring system goes live. A breach disclosure from any Tier 1 vendor is immediate. A privacy policy change that adds AI training rights is immediate. A model-provider change at a Tier 1 vendor is immediate. A subprocessor addition at a Tier 2 vendor goes into the weekly queue. A product blog post announcing a new AI feature at a Tier 3 vendor goes into the monthly review. The thresholds reflect the risk profile of the signal and the tier of the vendor. They're documented in the monitoring program's operating procedures and reviewed quarterly to ensure they still reflect the current risk landscape.

The operating rhythm for the monitoring program runs on three cadences. Daily: the monitoring system processes signals and routes anything above the immediate threshold to the third-party risk manager's exception queue. The manager reviews the queue each morning and assigns investigation or escalation actions before noon. Weekly: the third-party risk manager reviews the full week's signals, including those queued for weekly review, and produces a one-page summary for the security director. The summary covers what changed, what was investigated, what was escalated, and what's open. Monthly: the security director reviews the month's monitoring findings against the risk register and the tier map, identifies any vendors whose tier classification needs updating based on what monitoring detected, and brings material findings to the CISO before the next board cycle.

Stand up continuous external monitoring for your ten highest-risk Tier 1 vendors this week. Configure breach disclosure monitoring, privacy policy change monitoring, and AI feature announcement monitoring for those ten vendors. Run the monitoring for 30 days. Document every signal detected and every investigation triggered. At the end of 30 days, the findings from those ten vendors are the evidence base for expanding the monitoring program to the full Tier 1 portfolio. The expansion proposal goes to the CISO with specific numbers: how many undisclosed changes were detected in 30 days, what the potential risk exposure of each change was, and what the cost of expanding coverage to the full portfolio is relative to the risk it addresses.

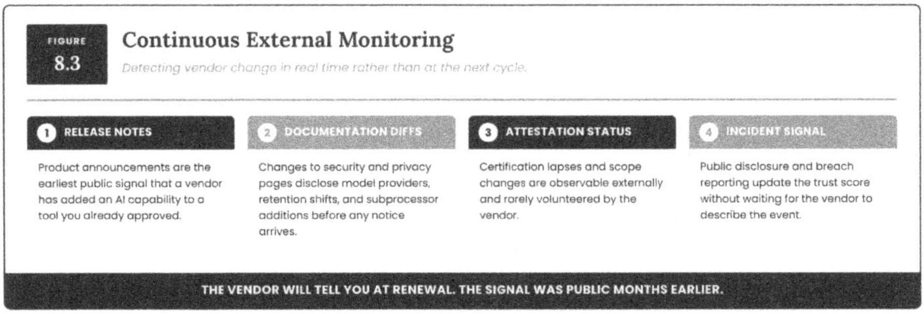

Contract Intelligence: The Clause Library Enforced at Machine Speed

The audit surfaced training clauses nobody had read. That finding was useful and alarming in equal measure. Useful because it named a specific, actionable risk. Alarming because it revealed that the contract review process, for all its rigor in other areas, had been missing a category of clause that carries significant data protection, competitive, and liability implications. The training clause problem wasn't a failure of the lawyers who reviewed those contracts. It was a failure of the process to define what to look for before AI made those clauses consequential.

The contract estate now needs to be reviewed against a different standard. Not just for the clauses the audit found, but for every AI-relevant clause across every active agreement in the portfolio. That's a volume problem that human review can't solve at the speed the risk requires. It's exactly the kind of problem AI-powered contract intelligence was built for.

Machine review of the contract estate works against a defined clause library. The clause library is the set of AI-relevant contract provisions that the organization requires, prohibits, or monitors across its vendor agreements. It has four categories. Required clauses are provisions that must be present in every AI vendor contract: data processing restrictions that prohibit use of enterprise data for model training without explicit written consent, model-change notification requirements that obligate the vendor to notify the enterprise before switching foundation model providers, AI incident notification requirements that define the timeline and content of breach notification for AI-specific incidents, and audit rights that give the enterprise the right to review the vendor's AI security controls on a defined cadence. Prohibited clauses are provisions that the organization will not accept: blanket training rights that permit the vendor to use enterprise data to improve their models without restriction, liability waivers that eliminate the vendor's accountability for AI-driven errors, and unilateral modification rights that allow the vendor to change their AI data processing practices without notice or consent. Monitored clauses are provisions that are acceptable under certain conditions but require ongoing tracking: limited training rights that permit use of anonymized aggregate data, subprocessor authorization clauses that require advance notification of changes, and model audit rights that give the vendor discretion over the timing and scope of security reviews. Absent clauses are the gaps the machine flags when a required provision isn't present in a contract that should contain it.

The machine review process runs against the full contract estate on a defined cadence. Monthly for Tier 1 vendor contracts, quarterly for Tier 2, and at renewal for Tier 3. The machine reads every contract, identifies every clause that falls into the four categories, and produces a findings report that shows what was found, what was missing, and what requires immediate attention. The findings report goes to the third-party risk manager within 48 hours of the review completing. The manager reviews the findings, confirms the severity classification, and routes each finding to the appropriate owner. Missing required clauses at Tier 1 vendors go to the General Counsel within 24 hours. Prohibited clauses that are already in active contracts go to the General Counsel and the CPO for immediate review. Monitored clauses that have changed since the last review go to the third-party risk manager for assessment.

The General Counsel co-owns this program. That co-ownership is not ceremonial. It's structural. The AI contract clause library is a legal artifact as much as it is a security artifact. The required clauses reflect the organization's legal position on AI data processing. The prohibited clauses reflect the legal risks the organization has decided are unacceptable. The monitored clauses reflect the legal conditions under which certain AI data processing practices are acceptable. The General Counsel needs to have reviewed and approved every clause in the library before the machine starts enforcing it. A clause library that security built without legal review is a clause library that will produce redlines the legal team can't support in negotiations. A clause library that legal and security built together is a clause library that produces redlines both teams can stand behind.

Negotiation copilots drafting redlines from the approved clause library are the enforcement mechanism that makes the clause library operational at procurement speed. When a new vendor contract arrives for review, the negotiation copilot reads the contract, identifies every gap against the clause library, and drafts redlines that insert the required clauses, remove the prohibited clauses, and add monitoring language for the clauses that require ongoing tracking. The redlines are drafted from the approved clause library, which means they reflect language that the General Counsel has already reviewed and approved. The procurement team receives a contract with suggested redlines that don't require a new legal review for each negotiation. The General Counsel reviews the final negotiated version to confirm the redlines held. The process moves at procurement speed without sacrificing the legal rigor that the clause library represents.

The renewal sweep is the mechanism that applies the clause library to the existing contract estate rather than just to new agreements. At 90 days before each contract renewal, the machine review runs against the expiring contract and produces a findings report that shows every gap against the current clause library. The third-party risk manager reviews the findings and works with the procurement team to incorporate the required clauses into the renewal negotiation. Vendors that resist the required clauses get escalated to the security director and the General Counsel for a risk acceptance decision. The risk acceptance decision is documented: the enterprise knows the clause is missing, understands the risk it creates, and has made a deliberate decision to accept that risk or to escalate it to a contract termination consideration. That documentation is what makes the contract estate defensible even when negotiation doesn't produce a perfect outcome.

The clause library is a living artifact. It needs to be reviewed and updated on a defined cadence as the regulatory environment changes, as new AI risk patterns emerge, and as the organization's own risk tolerance evolves. Assign the General Counsel as primary owner of the clause library with the third-party risk director as co-owner. Set a quarterly review cadence. The quarterly review checks whether any new regulatory requirements have created new required clauses, whether any emerging risk patterns have identified new prohibited clauses, and whether the monitored clause category needs to be updated to reflect changes in the AI vendor landscape. The clause library version history is maintained so that any contract negotiated under a previous version of the library can be identified and flagged for renewal-cycle update.

This month, run the machine review against every Tier 1 vendor contract in the portfolio. Configure the assessment engine with the clause library criteria. Produce the findings report. Route every missing required clause to the General Counsel within 48 hours. Route every identified prohibited clause to the General Counsel and CPO for immediate review. That first complete sweep of the Tier 1 contract estate is the baseline. It tells you exactly where the contract protection gaps are, which vendors require immediate negotiation, and which gaps can wait for the renewal cycle. That baseline is also the evidence the CISO needs to make the case for the negotiation copilot investment: here are the gaps machine review found in 30 days that manual review missed over the past three years.

The AI Bill of Materials: Making the Invisible Chain Disclosable

Chapter 7 named the opacity of the model supply chain. Vendors who can't or won't disclose which foundation model their AI feature runs on. Training data provenance that disappears into "publicly available internet data." Subprocessor chains that extend three and four layers deep into organizations the enterprise has never heard of. That opacity was named as a risk. This section builds the disclosure regime that converts opacity into visibility.

The AI Bill of Materials is a vendor disclosure requirement. It requires every AI vendor to declare, as a condition of contract, the models in their stack, the providers behind those models, and the subprocessors in the data processing chain. It's enforced through procurement: no contract executes without a completed AI BOM. It's refreshed on every material change: a model-provider switch, a new subprocessor addition, a change to the foundation model version in use. The BOM isn't a one-time disclosure. It's a living document that the vendor maintains and the enterprise monitors.

The BOM requirement has five mandatory disclosure fields. The first is model identification: the name and version of every AI model the vendor's product uses to process enterprise data, including foundation models, fine-tuned variants, and specialized models used for specific functions. The second is provider identification: the name and jurisdiction of the organization that trained and operates each model, including any intermediary providers that sit between the vendor and the foundation model. The third is subprocessor chain: every organization that processes enterprise data as part of the vendor's AI service delivery, including cloud infrastructure providers, data annotation services, model hosting providers, and any other third party that touches enterprise data in the AI processing chain. The fourth is data handling disclosure: for each model and provider identified, a description of what enterprise data is sent to the model, how long it is retained, whether it is used for model training or improvement, and what the deletion or purge process is when the contract ends.

The fifth is artifact integrity: for every model identified, the cryptographic hash of the served artifact, the signing authority that attests to it, and the mechanism by which the enterprise can verify that the model answering a request today is the model that was disclosed. This is the field vendors resist hardest, and the resistance is itself informative. A vendor that cannot state which artifact is in production cannot detect whether it has been tampered with, which means the enterprise inherits that blind spot without being told it exists. Where a vendor genuinely cannot supply a hash, require instead a signed attestation naming the model version in production and a commitment to notify on change, and record the substitution as an opacity finding against the trust score rather than treating the field as satisfied. Open-weight models pulled from public repositories carry the same requirement and are the case where it matters most, because a publicly downloadable artifact is the one an attacker can most easily substitute upstream of both parties.

Enforcing the BOM at procurement requires a defined intake process. When a new AI vendor contract enters the procurement workflow, the AI BOM form is sent to the vendor at the same time as the contract. The vendor has 15 business days to return a completed BOM. A BOM that is incomplete, that leaves required fields blank, or that provides answers too vague to be meaningful, triggers a follow-up from the third-party risk manager within 48 hours. A vendor that cannot or will not complete the BOM within 30 days of the initial request gets flagged as an opacity risk. The procurement team is notified that the contract cannot execute until the BOM is complete. That enforcement mechanism is what gives the BOM requirement teeth. Without it, the BOM is a form that vendors fill out when they get around to it and ignore when they don't.

Supply chain graph analysis is what the BOM enables at the portfolio level. When every Tier 1 vendor has completed a BOM, the third-party risk team can map the full supply chain graph: which foundation models appear across the portfolio, which providers appear multiple times, which subprocessors are shared across multiple vendors, and where the fourth- and fifth-party dependencies cluster. That graph is not a theoretical exercise. It's a navigable picture of the actual AI supply chain the enterprise depends on, drawn from disclosed information rather than inferred from incomplete signals.

The concentration risk analysis that the supply chain graph enables is the finding that matters most to the CFO and the board. When the graph reveals that 60% of the enterprise's Tier 1 AI vendors are running on the same two foundation models from the same provider, that concentration is a single point of failure with enterprise-wide impact. A failure at that provider, whether technical, regulatory, or reputational, doesn't affect one vendor relationship. It affects the majority of the AI-dependent business processes the enterprise runs. That concentration risk needs to be quantified in financial terms: what is the estimated business impact of a 72-hour outage of the primary foundation model provider, across all the vendor services that depend on it? That number belongs in the risk register, in the board report, and in the insurance review conversation.

Foundation model single points of failure priced into architecture and insurance decisions is the operational outcome the BOM analysis drives. When the concentration risk is visible and quantified, the enterprise can make deliberate decisions about it. Architectural decisions: requiring new AI vendor contracts to use different foundation model providers to reduce concentration. Insurance decisions: adding business interruption coverage that specifically addresses AI service provider outages. Contractual decisions: requiring Tier 1 vendors to maintain a secondary model provider as a failover option. None of those decisions are possible when the supply chain is opaque. All of them become possible when the BOM makes the chain visible.

The BOM requirement applies to existing contracts at renewal. For every Tier 1 vendor contract renewing in the next 12 months, add the AI BOM completion as a renewal condition. The vendor must submit a completed BOM before the renewal executes. Vendors that resist the requirement get the same escalation path as vendors that resist required contract clauses: the security director and the General Counsel make a risk acceptance decision about whether to proceed without the BOM or to treat the vendor's refusal as a material governance concern. Document the decision either way. An undocumented decision to proceed without a BOM is a governance gap. A documented decision to accept the opacity risk, with named owners and a mitigation plan, is a governance decision.

Stand up the AI BOM requirement for all new AI vendor contracts starting this month. Draft the BOM form with the five mandatory disclosure fields. Get the form reviewed and approved by the General Counsel and the CPO before it goes to any vendor. Add the BOM completion requirement to the procurement intake checklist so it applies automatically to every new AI vendor engagement. Assign the third-party risk manager as the owner of the BOM collection and review process. Set the 30-day completion requirement in the procurement workflow. That's the BOM program. It starts with new contracts this month and expands to renewal contracts on a rolling basis over the next 12 months.

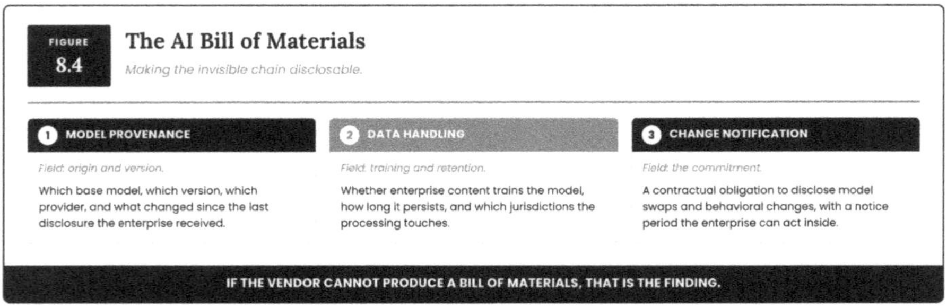

Trust Engineering Begins: Standing Evidence and Machine-Verified Assurance

The questionnaire's replacement isn't a better questionnaire. That's the most important thing to understand clearly before building what comes next. A more detailed questionnaire, sent more frequently, with more specific AI questions, is still a self-attestation document. It still captures what the vendor says about themselves at a point in time. It still depends on the vendor's honesty, their self-knowledge, and their willingness to disclose information that might complicate the commercial relationship. A better questionnaire is a marginal improvement on a fundamentally limited instrument. The successor model is something different in kind, not in degree.

Standing evidence replaces self-attestation as the primary assurance mechanism. Instead of asking the vendor to describe their AI security controls annually, the enterprise establishes a continuous evidence pipeline from strategic vendors that produces real-time signals about the vendor's actual security posture. The vendor's systems produce the evidence. The enterprise's monitoring infrastructure receives and validates it. The assurance is continuous rather than periodic, and it's based on what the vendor's systems actually do rather than what the vendor says they do.

The evidence types that flow through a standing evidence pipeline are specific and verifiable. Automated control attestations: the vendor's compliance platform produces daily or weekly attestations that defined controls are in the expected state, signed with a cryptographic key that allows the enterprise to verify authenticity. Configuration state snapshots: the vendor's security configuration management system exports a snapshot of defined configuration parameters on a defined cadence, allowing the enterprise to verify that the vendor's AI system configurations haven't drifted from their approved baseline. Incident and anomaly logs: the vendor's security monitoring platform exports a summary of detected anomalies and incidents on a defined cadence, giving the enterprise visibility into the vendor's security events without requiring access to the vendor's internal systems. Model behavior reports: for vendors running AI systems that process enterprise data, periodic reports on the AI system's behavioral metrics, output distributions, and anomaly detection results, produced by the vendor's own AI monitoring tools and exported to the enterprise.

Machine-verified assurance is the technical mechanism that makes standing evidence trustworthy rather than just more frequent self-attestation. Cryptographic signing of evidence exports means the enterprise can verify that the evidence came from the vendor's actual systems and wasn't modified in transit. Automated consistency checking means the enterprise's monitoring platform compares each new evidence export against the previous one and flags any changes that weren't expected. Cross-referencing evidence against external signals means the monitoring platform compares the vendor's self-produced evidence against the external monitoring signals described in the previous section: if the vendor's control attestation says their AI feature is processing data only in approved regions but network traffic shows connections to endpoints in unapproved regions, that contradiction is a signal that warrants immediate investigation.

The first bilateral trust framework is the operating model that governs the standing evidence relationship between two organizations. It defines what evidence the vendor produces, at what cadence, in what format, and with what cryptographic assurance. It defines what the enterprise does with the evidence:

how it's validated, who reviews it, what triggers an escalation, and what the enterprise's obligations are if the evidence reveals a security issue on the vendor's side. It defines how trust is scored: the combination of evidence types, evidence freshness, consistency checks, and external signal validation that produces an Adaptive AI Trust Score for the vendor. And it defines how trust is revoked: the specific conditions that cause the enterprise to suspend the vendor relationship pending investigation, the process for notifying the vendor of the suspension, and the evidence required to restore the trust relationship.

The Adaptive AI Trust Score is the operating instrument that makes the bilateral trust framework actionable for the third-party risk director and the CISO. It's a continuously updated score for each strategic vendor that reflects the current state of the trust relationship based on all available evidence. The score has four components. Evidence completeness: is the vendor producing all required evidence types on the required cadence? Evidence consistency: is the evidence internally consistent and consistent with external monitoring signals? Control state: do the vendor's control attestations show all required controls in the expected state? Incident history: has the vendor disclosed any incidents or anomalies in the evidence pipeline that affect the trust relationship? Each component contributes to the overall score. The score is updated automatically as new evidence arrives. When the score drops below a defined threshold, the third-party risk manager receives an alert and initiates a structured review of the vendor relationship.

The transition from annual questionnaire to standing evidence pipeline doesn't happen overnight, and it doesn't happen with every vendor simultaneously. Start with one strategic vendor: the vendor whose AI systems carry the highest risk to the enterprise and whose relationship is mature enough to support a bilateral governance conversation. Approach that vendor's security team with a specific proposal: replace the annual questionnaire with a standing evidence pipeline that gives both organizations better visibility into the health of the security relationship. Frame it as a mutual benefit. The vendor gets to replace the annual questionnaire burden with an automated evidence export that takes less effort once configured. The enterprise gets continuous assurance instead of an annual snapshot. Most strategic vendors will engage positively with that framing, because the questionnaire burden is real for them too.

The pilot with one strategic vendor produces three things. A working evidence pipeline that proves the technical model. A bilateral trust framework that defines the operating relationship. And a set of lessons about what works, what needs adjustment, and what the vendor community will and won't accept in a standing evidence arrangement. Those lessons are what you use to refine the model before expanding it to the next five strategic vendors. The expansion is evidence-based, not aspirational. You expand to the next vendor when the pilot proves the model works, not before.

This is where vendor risk's future begins. The discipline stops asking vendors what they do and starts verifying what their systems actually do. That shift is not a technology upgrade. It's a governance philosophy change, from trust-but-verify to verify-continuously. The technology enables it. The governance philosophy makes it meaningful. And the third-party risk function that builds this capability first will be the one that regulators point to when they describe what mature AI vendor risk governance looks like.

FIGURE 8.5 **Adaptive AI Trust Scores**

Vendor trust as a managed variable rather than an annual binary.

INPUT	SIGNAL TYPE	SCORE EFFECT	REVIEW TRIGGER
Contract coverage	Static, verified	Baseline ceiling	At renewal
Attestation currency	Periodic, external	Decays as it ages	On lapse
Feature change	Continuous, external	Immediate reduction	On detection
Incident history	Event driven	Step reduction with recovery	On disclosure
Disclosure response	Behavioral	Raises or lowers ceiling	On non-response

A SCORE THAT ONLY MOVES ONCE A YEAR IS A CLASSIFICATION, NOT A CONTROL.

The Vendor Intelligence Rhythm: Replacing an Annual Cycle With a Continuous Feed

Continuous monitoring changes what the third-party risk function does every day, and most programs install the monitoring without redesigning the day. The result is a feed that generates alerts into a function whose operating model still assumes work arrives in an annual wave. Alerts accumulate, the analyst triages the loudest ones, and the continuous capability degrades into an expensive news service. The rhythm below is what converts the feed into intelligence, and it is deliberately built around a single analyst rather than a team, because that is the staffing reality in most enterprises.

The daily pass is fifteen minutes and it is a filter, not an analysis. The vendor intelligence analyst reviews overnight signals across the monitored portfolio: breach disclosures, security advisories, privacy policy changes, terms-of-service amendments, model-provider announcements, and AI feature releases. Almost all of it is noise for any given enterprise. The analyst's job at this horizon is to route, not to assess: anything touching a Tier 1 vendor goes to the weekly assessment, anything indicating active compromise goes immediately to the SOC, and everything else is logged and closed. A daily pass that turns into a daily investigation has been scoped wrong and will be abandoned within a month.

The weekly assessment is where signals become risk positions. The analyst takes the routed items, checks each against the vendor's tier, the data the vendor touches, and the contractual protections in place, and produces a short written position: what changed, what it means for this enterprise specifically, and whether it requires action. The specificity matters, because a vendor's privacy policy amendment is not a risk in the abstract; it is a risk if that vendor processes regulated data under a clause that the amendment weakens. This is the work the questionnaire process never produced, and it is why the vendor intelligence analyst is a different role from the assessor who administered questionnaires rather than a rebadged one.

The monthly cycle updates the trust scores and closes the loop with procurement. Every Tier 1 vendor's Adaptive AI Trust Score is recalculated from the month's evidence, vendors crossing below threshold trigger a review with a named owner and a date, and vendors holding consistently above threshold earn the reduced friction that makes the score meaningful to the business rather than only to security. Procurement receives the current score set, which is what allows a purchasing decision to reflect a vendor's posture this month rather than at last year's assessment. A score that does not change a procurement outcome is a number, not a control.

The quarterly and annual horizons carry the two analyses that require more than a month of accumulated evidence. Quarterly, the foundation model concentration analysis runs against the Bill of Materials registry and goes to the CFO with a quantified impact figure rather than an architectural diagram. Annually, the clause library is reviewed against the year's contract experience: which required clauses vendors refused, which prohibited clauses appeared anyway, which monitored clauses generated findings, and what the renewal queue tells you about where the portfolio's protection is weakest. That annual review is the one that keeps the clause library from becoming a document that legal wrote once and procurement enforces by habit.

FIGURE 8.6 The Vendor Intelligence Rhythm

Replacing an annual cycle with a continuous feed.

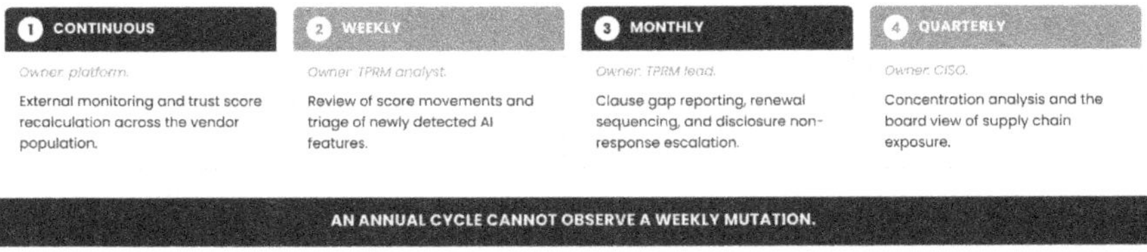

Onboarding at Machine Speed: Compressing Vendor Time-to-Approval

Continuous monitoring solves the problem of vendors changing after approval. It does nothing about the problem that made the business route around third-party risk in the first place, which is that getting a vendor approved takes longer than the business can wait. A function that installs continuous intelligence and leaves a six-week onboarding cycle intact has improved its own visibility and left the shadow procurement problem exactly where it found it. The machine capability that makes monitoring continuous also makes onboarding fast, and most programs deploy only the first half.

The onboarding cycle in most enterprises decomposes into four stages, and machine processing compresses three of them substantially. Questionnaire administration and response chasing, which frequently consumes half the elapsed time, is eliminated for any vendor whose public posture and attestations can be machine-collected. Response review, where an analyst reads a completed questionnaire against criteria, becomes an assessment engine reading the vendor's actual documentation against the same criteria. Contract review against the clause library, historically the longest single stage, becomes a machine pass that produces a gap list in minutes. What does not compress is the human judgment on the exceptions, and that is where the remaining time should go.

The redesign that follows is a tiered intake rather than a faster version of one process. A vendor requesting low-risk access, with a clean machine assessment and no clause library gaps, is approved on the machine pass with a named owner recording the acceptance. A vendor with gaps in monitored clauses proceeds with the gaps flagged for the renewal queue rather than blocking execution. Only vendors with required-clause gaps, prohibited clauses present, or Tier 1 access depth reach human assessment, and those receive genuine attention because the analyst is no longer processing forty routine reviews to find them.

The number to publish is the same one governance publishes for its sanctioning pathway, and for the same reason. Median time from vendor request to approval decision, reported monthly to the business, creates the accountability that keeps the process fast and exposes the quarter in which it stopped being fast. A third-party risk function that will not publish this number is asking the business to trust that the process is reasonable, and the business has already formed its own view, which is why the shadow procurement exists.

The risk in compression is real and should be named rather than dismissed. A machine-assessed approval is an approval based on evidence the enterprise did not verify by conversation, and a subset of vendors will present well to automated assessment while carrying problems a skilled assessor would have surfaced. The mitigation is not to slow everything down; it is to sample. Take a percentage of machine-approved vendors each quarter and run the full human assessment retrospectively, and treat a finding rate above threshold as a signal to tighten the automated criteria. That sample costs a fraction of what universal human review costs, and it produces a defensible statement about the accuracy of the fast path.

Securing the Agent Toolchain: Tool Provenance, Poisoning, and the Instruction Channel Nobody Governs

The audit found MCP servers and plugin credentials and treated them as a credential surface, which was the correct audit finding and an incomplete operating picture. The credential exposure is real and it is the smaller half. The larger half is that a tool presented to an agent is not merely software the agent calls. It is a description the agent reads, and anything an agent reads can influence what the agent decides to do. A tool description is an instruction channel with a vendor at the other end of it.

That reframing explains a class of attack that makes no sense under the software model. A tool whose description contains carefully constructed text can shape an agent's behavior far beyond that tool's own function, including causing the agent to invoke other tools, disclose context, or pursue an altered objective. The tool never has to execute for the attack to work, which means every conventional control that watches execution has already been bypassed. OWASP's MCP security work identifies tool poisoning alongside dependency tampering and command injection specifically because this attack path has no analogue in traditional integration security.

Third-party MCP servers are where this concentrates, and the enterprise's exposure is usually larger than the third-party risk function knows. Developers connect agents to publicly available servers with the same informality that produced shadow AI in the first place, and the server is frequently outside any procurement process because it was free and took four minutes to configure. The result is that an unassessed third party holds an instruction channel into an agent that carries enterprise credentials. That sentence is the finding, and it belongs in front of the third-party risk director this quarter rather than in next year's assessment cycle.

Four controls bound this and all four are implementable within the twelve-month horizon. An allowlist of approved tools and servers, enforced at the orchestration layer rather than by policy, with anything unlisted unavailable rather than discouraged. Provenance for every tool in the allowlist, meaning a known publisher, a signed or hash-verified artifact, and a recorded version. Description integrity monitoring, meaning the enterprise stores the approved description and alerts when the served description changes, because a tool that was safe at onboarding and changed its description afterward has changed what it does to your agent. And output validation, meaning tool responses are treated as untrusted content subject to the same classification rule as external retrieval.

The ownership question is the one that stalls this work, and it should be settled by the governance committee rather than debated between functions. Tools are procured like software, behave like an integration, and function as an instruction channel, which means application security, third-party risk, and the platform team can each make a reasonable claim and each will assume one of the others has it. Assign the allowlist and the provenance register to third-party risk, because the underlying question is whether an outside party can be trusted with access to enterprise systems, and that question has an owner already.

Two variants extend this beyond the static case and both are becoming ordinary. Dynamic tool discovery, where an agent locates and adopts a tool during operation rather than from a configured set, converts the allowlist from a control into a suggestion unless the orchestration layer enforces it at invocation rather than at configuration. Cross-tenant tool reuse, where a shared server serves multiple customers from one deployment, means the enterprise's exposure includes whatever another tenant's activity does to the shared component. Neither is exotic and neither appears in a standard vendor questionnaire. Ask both questions at onboarding: can an agent adopt a tool that was not on the approved list at configuration time, and is this deployment shared with other customers in a way that could affect the tool's behavior for us.

FIGURE 8.7

Securing the Agent Toolchain

Tool provenance, poisoning, and the instruction channel nobody governs.

1 TOOL REGISTRATION

Control: allowlist.

Agents invoke tools from a reviewed registry. Runtime discovery of unreviewed tools is blocked rather than logged after the fact.

2 DESCRIPTION INTEGRITY

Control: content inspection.

Tool metadata is treated as untrusted input and inspected, because the description itself is an instruction channel into the agent.

3 PROVENANCE VERIFICATION

Control: signing.

Tool definitions are verified against a known publisher so a silent substitution does not pass as the original.

4 SCOPE SEGMENTATION

Control: least authority.

Tool grants are scoped per workflow rather than per agent, so one compromise does not reach every capability the agent holds.

MORE CAPABLE AGENTS FOLLOW INSTRUCTIONS BETTER, WHICH IS EXACTLY THE PROBLEM.

Hidden Context as a Disclosure Surface: What the Agent Was Told and Who Else Can Read It

The tool description problem has a second half that most programs never examine. Everything the enterprise assembles into an agent's context in order to make it behave correctly, the system prompt, the developer instructions, the retrieved policy text, and the schemas of every tool the agent is permitted to call, is readable by the model and therefore reachable by anyone who can talk to the model. Practitioners should design under the assumption that hidden context is discoverable and that nothing placed in it is secret. The uncomfortable consequence is that a large share of enterprise AI deployments have put operational logic, internal rules, and occasionally credentials into a location they were treating as private.

The severity of that exposure tracks what was placed there and how much the application leans on its secrecy. At the low end, disclosure reveals a role description and a tone instruction, which aids an attacker marginally and gates nothing. In the middle sit the internal decision rules, the filtering criteria, and the workflow logic that tell an adversary how the system reaches its answers and where the seams are. At the high end are embedded credentials, connection strings, and tokens, or a design that relies on hidden context to enforce authorization or content policy. That last case is the one that turns a disclosure finding into an access finding, because the boundary was never a boundary.

The exposure compounds rather than sitting in isolation. Disclosed rules make the next prompt injection targeted rather than exploratory, because the attacker now knows which instructions to override and in what language. Revealed tool schemas expand the excessive agency surface by publishing exactly which capabilities exist and how they are invoked, which is the reconnaissance step for the tool boundary testing described earlier in this chapter. Leaked refusal conditions let an adversary route around the safety behavior rather than colliding with it, since the triggers and exceptions are now visible instead of inferred. Each of these is a risk the program already tracks, made cheaper for the attacker by a single disclosure.

The control is a design rule rather than a detection rule, which is why it belongs in vendor onboarding and architecture review rather than in the SOC queue. No credential, token, or connection string is placed in hidden context under any circumstance. Authorization, privilege separation, and content filtering are enforced in the application and the identity layer, never by the model declining to reveal what it was told. Tool schemas are scoped so that the set an agent can see matches the set it is permitted to use, because publishing capability the agent is not authorized to invoke is a disclosure with no operating benefit. Where a vendor supplies the agent, the onboarding question is direct: what does your system place in model context, and what happens to our security posture when it is disclosed.

The evidence this produces is a context inventory, and most enterprises discover on building it that they cannot say what is in the context window of their own production systems. The inventory names, per agent, what the system prompt contains, which policy documents are retrieved into context, which tool schemas are exposed, and whether any of it carries a secret or is relied on as a control. That artifact feeds the Agent Authority Chain directly, since context is one of its six links and this is the assessment of that link. It also closes the loop on the context extraction attack class in the adversarial evaluation test set, which until now has been tested without a stated risk behind it.

FIGURE 8.8

Hidden Context as a Disclosure Surface

Assume everything assembled into the model's context is discoverable.

1 WHAT IS IN THERE

Inventory this per agent.

The system prompt, developer instructions, retrieved policy text, and the schemas of every tool the agent may call. All of it is readable by the model.

2 SEVERITY TRACKS RELIANCE

Low to critical.

A role description aids an attacker marginally. Embedded credentials, or authorization enforced by the model declining to reveal its instructions, is an access finding.

3 IT COMPOUNDS OTHER RISKS

Reconnaissance for the next attack.

Disclosed rules make injection targeted rather than exploratory. Revealed tool schemas publish the excessive agency surface. Leaked refusal conditions get routed around.

4 THE CONTROL IS A DESIGN RULE

Architecture review, not the SOC queue.

No secrets in context. Authorization enforced in the application and identity layer. Tool schemas scoped to what the agent is actually permitted to invoke.

HIDDEN CONTEXT IS NOT A SECURITY BOUNDARY. DESIGN AS THOUGH IT IS PUBLISHED.

Authority Attenuation Across Organizational Boundaries

Agent-to-agent interaction across an organizational boundary is the point where every control in this Part meets a party the enterprise does not govern. An enterprise agent exchanging requests with a supplier's agent is extending authority outside the perimeter, on the basis of a contract that contemplated system integration rather than autonomous negotiation. The trust score answers whether the vendor is trustworthy. It does not answer what the vendor's agent is permitted to cause inside your environment, which is a different question with a different control.

The attenuation principle applies across the boundary the same way it applies inside it, and the enterprise controls its half regardless of what the counterparty does. An external agent's request enters through an interface that holds its own scope, and that scope is narrower than any internal agent's, bounded by action class, data class, transaction value, and rate. The external agent is never granted the ability to trigger a delegation chain inside the enterprise, because a delegation chain initiated externally is an authority path the enterprise did not design and cannot fully trace. Every request carries an identity that maps to a known counterparty and a recorded agreement.

What the enterprise cannot control unilaterally is the reverse direction, and this is where the contractual work in this chapter earns its place. Your agent operating against a counterparty's interface is subject to their scoping, their logging, and their retention, and you will learn what those are only if you ask before the integration rather than after an incident. The clause library needs a provision covering agent interaction specifically: mutual authentication requirements, message integrity, logging retention on both sides, and an obligation to notify when the counterparty materially changes what their agent is permitted to do.

The near-term posture for most enterprises should be more conservative than the market's enthusiasm suggests, and saying so plainly is more useful than describing a mature state nobody has reached. Standards work is genuinely underway. Decentralized identifier and verifiable credential specifications from the W3C provide the cryptographic foundation, an agent identity community group formed in 2026 to address how agents present credentials binding them to a controlling organization, and adjacent efforts are extending the model into the tool protocol layer. None of it has settled, adoption is limited, and several of the leading approaches carry infrastructure dependencies that make them awkward for high-throughput delegation. An enterprise waiting for the standard will wait past the point where its agents are already transacting.

What the enterprise can require now, before any standard settles, is narrower than a full credential architecture and materially better than nothing. Mutual authentication on every cross-boundary agent connection, so both sides know which organization is on the other end. A signed attestation binding the counterparty's agent to the counterparty organization, so the enterprise holds evidence of who is accountable rather than an assertion. A scoped mandate recorded before the interaction begins, naming what the external agent may cause inside your environment and for how long. A revocation check the enterprise performs rather than relies on the counterparty to honor. And logging retained on the enterprise side regardless of what the counterparty keeps, because in a dispute the log you control is the only one you can produce.

Permit these connections for low-consequence action classes, require human confirmation for anything that moves money or changes a commitment, and treat any counterparty unwilling to support mutual authentication and signed attestation as a finding rather than as a normal integration. The forward reason to build the scoping interface now rather than later is that this is the one area in this Volume where standards are actively forming and the enterprise that has an interface can adopt a standard, while the enterprise that has direct agent connections will be rebuilding. NIST's agent identity and authorization work is directed at exactly this problem. An enterprise that has already forced external agent interaction through a scoped, logged, attenuating interface has built the seam a standard slots into. One that has not has built integrations a standard will invalidate.

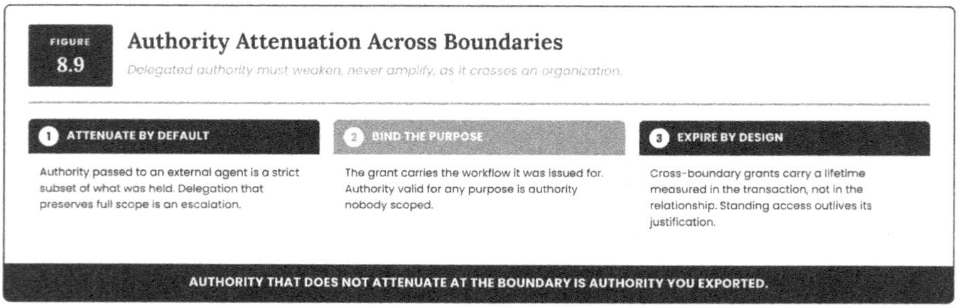

Putting It Into Practice

The questionnaire retires this quarter, one capability at a time. The transition is sequenced. Each action builds on the previous one. None of them are optional if the third-party risk function intends to govern a vendor population that mutates weekly with something more defensible than an annual self-attestation document.

This week, stand up continuous external monitoring across the full Tier 1 portfolio. Configure breach disclosure monitoring, privacy policy change monitoring, and AI feature announcement monitoring for every Tier 1 vendor. Wire the feature-creep detection alerts to the risk register so that a vendor's AI feature conversion triggers a register update and a review assignment within 24 hours of detection. Assign the third-party risk manager as the daily exception queue owner. Set the weekly signal summary as a standing deliverable to the security director every Monday morning.

This month, run machine review across the full Tier 1 contract estate. Feed every active Tier 1 contract into the assessment engine configured against the AI clause library. Produce the findings report. Route every missing required clause to the General Counsel within 48 hours. Route every identified prohibited clause to the General Counsel and CPO for immediate review. Push every identified gap into the next renewal cycle negotiation queue with the negotiation copilot configured to draft redlines from the approved clause library. Document every finding in the risk register with a named owner, a severity classification, and a resolution timeline.

This month, make the AI Bill of Materials a condition of contract for every new AI vendor engagement. Draft the BOM form. Get it reviewed and approved by the General Counsel and the CPO. Add it to the procurement intake checklist. Assign the third-party risk manager as the BOM collection owner with a 30-day completion requirement for every new vendor. For existing Tier 1 vendors renewing in the next 12 months, add the BOM completion as a renewal condition and begin the outreach to those vendors this month so the 30-day completion timeline doesn't become a renewal blocker.

This month, identify the one strategic vendor for the standing evidence pipeline pilot. Choose the vendor whose AI systems carry the highest risk to the enterprise and whose security relationship is mature enough to support a bilateral governance conversation. Schedule the initial conversation with their security team. Bring a specific proposal: here are the evidence types we want to receive, here is the cadence, here is what we'll do with the evidence, and here is what you get in return for the investment in configuring the pipeline. The pilot doesn't need to be perfect on day one. It needs to start this month, because every month it doesn't start is another month the questionnaire is the primary assurance mechanism for your highest-risk vendor relationship.

Brief the General Counsel as co-owner of the clause library and the BOM program before the end of this month. The briefing covers three things: the machine review findings from the Tier 1 contract sweep, the clause library that the assessment engine is enforcing, and the BOM requirement that procurement is now applying to new contracts. The General Counsel needs to understand all three before they appear in a vendor negotiation or a regulatory examination. A General Counsel who first encounters the clause library when a vendor pushes back on a redline is a General Counsel who is unprepared for that conversation. Prepare them now.

Show the CISO the coverage number before the end of this month. Not the number of vendors assessed in the last annual cycle. The number of vendors assessed continuously, right now, by the monitoring program. Every Tier 1 vendor monitored for breach disclosures, privacy policy changes, and AI feature announcements. Every Tier 1 contract reviewed against the clause library. Every new AI vendor required to submit a BOM before the contract executes. That's the coverage number. It's a different number from what the annual questionnaire cycle produced, and it tells a different story about what vendor risk governance actually looks like when it's running as a continuous program rather than an annual sampling exercise.

The next chapter asks where the third-party risk domain is heading over the next twelve months: the tools that will define the function, the question of whether machine-to-machine commerce eventually needs less vendor risk oversight or an entirely new discipline that doesn't yet have a name, and the operating model that positions the third-party risk function as the enterprise's standing intelligence capability for a vendor population that never stops changing.

FIGURE 8.10

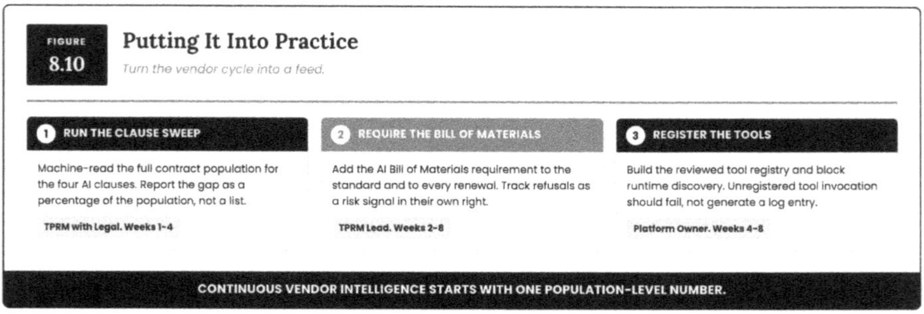

Chapter 9: The Supply Chain Endgame

Current Focus, Solution Categories, and the 1-Year Target Operating Model

CHAPTER 9 OUTCOMES

At the end of this chapter, you will be able to:

1. Describe where third-party risk programs are currently investing.
2. Evaluate supply chain categories as architectural patterns rather than products.
3. Answer whether vendor risk owns AI procurement.
4. Build a one-year supply chain target operating model with owners and milestones.
5. Set the build boundary for what third-party risk should never buy.
6. Assess the consortium option and why shared assurance keeps failing.

YOU CANNOT OUTSOURCE THE JUDGMENT ABOUT WHO YOU DEPEND ON.

Where the Market Is Now: The Current Focus of Third-Party Risk Programs

Most third-party risk programs right now are doing one of two things. They're either building standing evidence of vendor AI posture, or they're adding AI questions to a questionnaire nobody trusts and calling it governance. The gap between those two activities is large, and the programs doing the latter often can't tell the difference yet. That's not a failure of intent. It's a maturity problem in a discipline that's being rebuilt from scratch while the supply chain keeps mutating underneath it.

The first thing almost every vendor risk program builds when AI arrives on the agenda is an AI vendor inventory. That makes sense. Before you can govern anything, you have to know what you're governing. The inventory is the right first move. The problem is that most programs treat the inventory as a project with a completion date rather than a living artifact with a continuous update cadence. The inventory gets built, gets filed, and stops reflecting reality within weeks. A vendor ships a new copilot. Another switches foundation model providers. A third adds an AI-powered workflow to a product that was assessed as AI-free six months ago. The inventory doesn't know about any of it. The program is governing a vendor population that no longer exists in the form the inventory describes.

AI addenda retrofitted onto master agreements are the second area of activity, and the quality spread is wide. The better programs are going back through their active Tier 1 contracts and adding AI-specific addenda that address training rights, model-change notification, AI incident disclosure, and audit rights. These addenda are real governance improvements. They create contractual obligations that didn't exist before and give the enterprise legal standing to demand disclosures that vendors weren't previously required to make. The weaker programs are adding a one-paragraph AI clause to their standard contract template and calling it an AI addendum. One paragraph that says "vendor agrees to use AI responsibly" doesn't create enforceable obligations. It creates the appearance of governance without the substance.

The first AI Bill of Materials requirements are appearing in enterprise procurement, and this is the area where the most forward-looking programs are genuinely ahead of the market. These programs have added BOM completion as a condition of contract execution for new AI vendor engagements. The BOM requires the vendor to disclose the models in their stack, the providers behind those models, the subprocessors in the data chain, and the data handling practices for each. That disclosure requirement is changing vendor behavior. Vendors that know they'll be asked to complete a BOM before a contract executes are starting to build the internal documentation to answer the questions. The BOM requirement is creating a disclosure expectation that didn't exist two years ago, and the programs that established it early are already seeing that expectation reflected in vendor behavior.

Continuous monitoring pilots are running alongside questionnaire cycles in a growing number of programs, and this combination reveals something important about where the market actually is. The programs running both aren't running both because they think both are necessary. They're running both because they haven't yet made the organizational decision to retire the questionnaire as the primary control. The monitoring pilot is producing better intelligence. The questionnaire cycle is producing familiar documentation. The program keeps both because the questionnaire is what the audit committee expects to see, even though everyone in the room knows it's not producing current intelligence. That tension between what produces real governance and what produces recognizable documentation is the defining maturity challenge for vendor risk right now.

Locating your program honestly against this picture is the prerequisite for committing to the target model. The question isn't whether your program is good. The question is whether it's producing standing evidence or a longer questionnaire. An AI vendor inventory that hasn't been updated since the audit closed is a longer questionnaire. An AI addendum that creates no enforceable obligations is a longer questionnaire. A BOM requirement that applies to new contracts but not to the existing estate is a longer questionnaire with a better intake form. Name the gaps honestly before building the twelve-month model. The gaps are what the model needs to close, and closing the wrong gaps wastes the budget that should be closing the right ones.

The Solution Category Landscape: Patterns, Not Products

The vendor risk stack for AI security has five distinct categories. Every mature program needs all five. Most programs have one or two and haven't named the others as gaps yet. Understanding the categories before evaluating any specific tool is what keeps budget from flowing into a second solution for a problem already solved while the actual coverage gap goes unfunded.

The first category is third-party risk platforms extending into AI posture. Traditional TPRM platforms were built to manage questionnaire cycles, track vendor tiers, and store attestation documents. The AI-extended versions of those platforms add capabilities that the original architecture wasn't designed for: continuous monitoring of vendor AI feature changes, AI-specific risk scoring that accounts for model behavior and training data provenance, and integration with external signal feeds that provide between-cycle intelligence. The evaluation criterion that separates genuine AI extension from rebranded legacy functionality is the continuous assessment architecture. A platform that runs daily automated checks against vendor AI posture signals and surfaces exceptions to a human owner is genuinely extended. A platform that added an "AI risk" tab to its questionnaire module is not. Both may be marketed under the same category name. Only one solves the velocity mismatch that makes the questionnaire insufficient.

The second category is external attack-surface and vendor-monitoring services. These are the tools that watch the vendor portfolio continuously from the outside. They monitor breach disclosures, privacy policy changes, subprocessor updates, regulatory filings, and AI feature announcements across the full vendor population. The key capability to evaluate in this category isn't the breadth of the signal library or the quality of the dashboard. It's the AI-specific signal set. A monitoring service that watches for general security events at vendor organizations is useful. A monitoring service that specifically detects vendor AI feature additions, model-provider changes, and training data updates is what the third-party risk function actually needs. Those are different detection problems requiring different data sources and different signal processing logic. Confirm which one you're buying before the contract executes.

The third category is AI BOM and model registry tooling. This is the disclosure backbone of the vendor risk program. It manages the collection, storage, validation, and analysis of AI Bills of Materials across the vendor portfolio. The registry tracks which vendors have submitted BOMs, whether their submissions are complete, when they were last updated, and what the supply chain graph looks like when all vendor disclosures are mapped against each other. The supply chain graph analysis is the capability that justifies the investment: when every Tier 1 vendor has a BOM in the registry, the concentration risk analysis that the graph enables surfaces findings that no individual vendor assessment ever could. The evaluation criterion in this category is the graph analysis capability. A system that stores BOMs as documents is a file cabinet. A system that builds and analyzes the supply chain graph from BOM data is a governance instrument.

The fourth category is contract intelligence engines. These are the systems that read contracts at machine speed, identify gaps against the clause library, and draft redlines from approved language. Chapter 8 described how this category operates in practice. The evaluation criterion here is the integration between the contract intelligence engine and the clause library governance process. A contract intelligence engine that reads contracts and surfaces findings is useful. One that reads contracts, surfaces findings, drafts redlines from the approved clause library, and routes each finding to the appropriate owner at the appropriate speed is the operating model the third-party risk function needs. The integration between the engine's output and the governance workflow is what makes the finding actionable rather than informational.

The fifth category is the emerging attestation economy. AI assurance reports are developing as a category, modeled loosely on SOC 2 Type II reports but applied to AI system controls rather than general security controls. The concept is sound: a standardized third-party assessment of a vendor's AI governance posture, produced by an independent auditor, that the enterprise can rely on instead of conducting its own assessment. The structural limit of this category is the one that makes it unreliable as a primary assurance mechanism: the attested system changes weekly. An AI assurance report that was accurate at the time of the audit becomes less accurate every day after the audit closes, for exactly the same reason the enterprise's own audit binder ages. The vendor's AI system mutates. The report doesn't. A report that was accurate six months ago attests to a system that may no longer exist in the form described.

AI assurance reports are useful as a baseline document. They're not sufficient as a continuous assurance mechanism. The right role for them in the vendor risk stack is as the starting point that continuous monitoring validates and updates. The report establishes the vendor's AI posture at a point in time. The monitoring program tracks whether that posture holds. When monitoring detects a change that contradicts the report, the contradiction triggers investigation. That's the integration architecture that makes the attestation economy useful without making it the primary control. Use the report. Don't rely on it alone. The distinction matters when a regulator asks whether your vendor assurance is current.

The integration architecture that connects vendor intelligence to the governance rhythm built in earlier chapters is the structural requirement that ties all five categories together. The external monitoring service feeds signals to the TPRM platform. The TPRM platform updates the risk register when signals indicate a material change. The contract intelligence engine feeds findings to the clause library governance process. The BOM registry feeds the supply chain graph analysis that informs concentration risk entries in the risk register. The attestation reports feed the baseline that continuous monitoring validates. None of these categories operates in isolation. The value of the stack compounds when the categories talk to each other. The integration architecture is what makes that compounding happen, and it needs to be designed before any individual category is selected, not after.

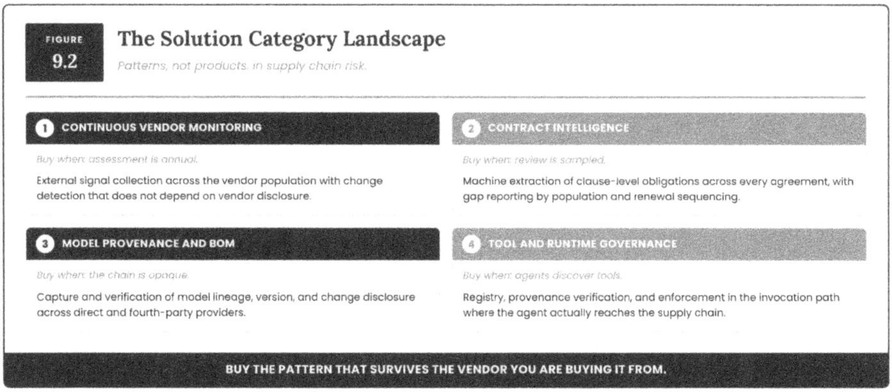

The Department Question: Does Vendor Risk Own AI Procurement?

The assessor role is ending. That's the honest statement, and the vendor risk leaders who say it clearly will make better decisions about hiring, team structure, and organizational positioning than the ones who wait for the market to force the conversation.

The assessor's job was to administer questionnaires, review responses, tier vendors, and file findings. Every component of that job is being automated or made irrelevant by the shift to continuous monitoring. Machine reading replaces manual questionnaire review. Automated signal processing replaces manual vendor tiering. Continuous monitoring replaces periodic assessment. The assessor who was hired to do those things is being replaced not by a different person but by a different operating model. The question isn't whether that transition is coming. It's whether the third-party risk function positions for it deliberately or gets reorganized around it reactively.

The trust engineer is what replaces the assessor. That's not a job title yet. It will be. The trust engineer designs the bilateral verification architecture between two organizations' AI systems. They define what evidence the vendor produces, how it's validated, what trust scoring model applies to it, and under what conditions trust is suspended or revoked. They understand enough about AI system behavior to evaluate vendor evidence intelligently. They understand enough about contract law to translate trust requirements into enforceable obligations. They understand enough about organizational dynamics to negotiate a bilateral framework that both sides can actually operate. That combination of skills doesn't exist in most vendor risk teams today. It needs to be built deliberately, starting now.

The turf contest over AI procurement is real and it's already happening in organizations that haven't resolved it deliberately. Procurement owns vendor selection and contract execution. The CDO owns AI strategy and model governance. The CISO owns security risk. When a new AI vendor comes through the door, all three functions have a legitimate claim on the review process. Without a defined ownership model, the review becomes a coordination problem that slows procurement to a crawl, frustrates business units, and produces inconsistent outcomes depending on which function showed up most forcefully in any given negotiation.

The CISO who resolves this before the turf contest opens it has a structural advantage. The resolution isn't about winning the turf contest. It's about defining a clear ownership model that each function can operate within. Security owns the risk assessment and the clause library enforcement. Procurement owns the commercial negotiation and the contract execution. The CDO owns the AI strategy alignment review, meaning whether the vendor's AI capability fits the enterprise's AI governance model. All three functions contribute to every AI vendor engagement. None of them owns it alone. The governance committee ratifies that model before the next AI vendor negotiation begins, not during it.

Fourth-party and concentration risk ownership is the gap that nobody has claimed yet, and it needs to be claimed deliberately before a regulator claims it for you. Fourth-party risk, meaning the risk carried by the vendors' vendors and the foundation model providers behind them, sits in a governance gap between the CISO's supply chain responsibility and the CDO's model governance responsibility. Neither function currently owns it with full accountability. The CISO who claims it first, builds the BOM program to make it visible, and presents the concentration risk analysis to the board as a named finding with a named owner, establishes the organizational authority that makes that ownership real. Ownership without visibility is a title. Ownership with a running intelligence program is a function.

Three new roles are emerging that most third-party risk teams don't have today. The first is the vendor intelligence analyst. This person reads machine-collected evidence. They don't send questionnaires. They review the continuous monitoring outputs, the BOM analysis, the contract intelligence findings, and the external signal feeds, and they synthesize them into a current picture of the vendor's AI risk posture. The vendor intelligence analyst needs to understand AI system behavior well enough to interpret behavioral signals, understand contract law well enough to assess clause gaps, and understand regulatory requirements well enough to flag compliance exposures. That's a different skill profile from the assessor who was hired to administer questionnaires. Hire for it explicitly.

The second new role is the trust engineer. The trust engineer designs bilateral verification. They work with strategic vendors to build the standing evidence pipelines described in Chapter 8. They define the evidence types, the validation mechanisms, the trust scoring model, and the suspension criteria. They negotiate the bilateral trust framework that governs the standing evidence relationship. They maintain the Adaptive AI Trust Score for each strategic vendor and own the escalation process when a score drops below threshold. The trust engineer is the person who, in five years, will be the most valuable role in the third-party risk function. Identify the person on your current team who has the instincts for this role and start developing them now.

The third new role is the contract intelligence owner. This person runs the clause library. They maintain it, update it as the regulatory environment changes, coordinate with the General Counsel on legal review, and manage the contract intelligence engine that enforces it. They own the renewal sweep process, the negotiation copilot configuration, and the exception routing model that determines what findings go to whom at what speed. The contract intelligence owner sits at the intersection of legal, security, and procurement. They need credibility with all three functions to be effective with any of them.

The reorganization case to bring to the CISO before the market forces it is specific and it needs to be built around evidence, not theory. The evidence is the monitoring program's output from the past 90 days. How many undisclosed vendor AI feature changes were detected? How many contract gaps were surfaced by machine review that the annual questionnaire never found? How many BOM completions revealed fourth-party dependencies that weren't previously visible? Those numbers make the case that the current team structure, built for questionnaire administration, isn't the right structure for the intelligence function the program is becoming. The reorganization case isn't "AI is changing everything." It's "here's what our monitoring program found in 90 days that our previous operating model never would have found, and here's the team structure that can operate this program at scale."

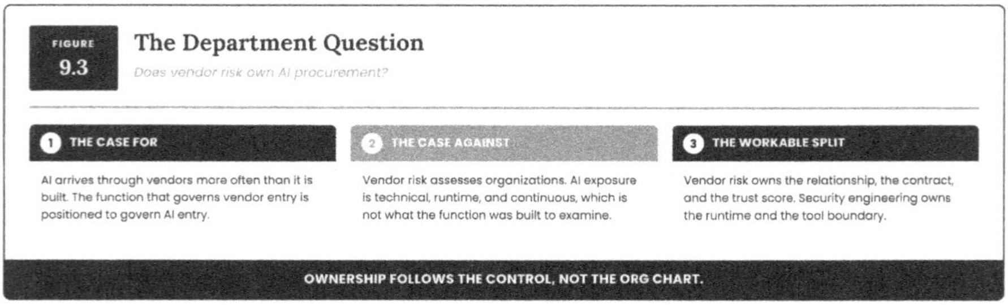

The 1-Year Supply Chain Target Operating Model

The 1-Year Supply Chain Target Operating Model is a funded trajectory. Present it to the CFO as a budget narrative and to the board as the answer to their question about what you're building and what it costs. Each quarter has a specific destination, a specific capability build, and a specific board-facing milestone. The horizon is twelve months because the vendor population mutates weekly, and a governance model built on a three-year assumption is planning against a supply chain that will not resemble itself by the time the plan matures.

The first quarter builds the clause library. This is a facilitation cost, not a software cost, and it gets budgeted as one. Building the AI clause library requires working sessions with the General Counsel, the CPO, and the third-party risk director to align on required clauses, prohibited clauses, and monitored clauses, followed by legal review of the language before it enters any enforcement engine. A clause library that gets deprioritized because nobody budgeted for the working sessions is a clause library that does not get built, and the contract intelligence program that depends on it has nothing to enforce. Sequence it first for that reason.

The second quarter stands up continuous monitoring. The TPRM platform with AI posture extension manages the vendor portfolio and the risk register; the external monitoring service provides the between-cycle intelligence the questionnaire never could. Together they replace the annual questionnaire cycle as the primary governance mechanism for the Tier 1 population. Present the cost offset explicitly to the CFO: the analyst hours currently consumed by questionnaire administration, response review, and finding documentation are substantially replaced by machine processing, and the tooling cost is partially funded by that reduction. The vendor intelligence analyst is hired in this quarter, timed to the monitoring program going live so the role operates the system from day one rather than waiting for it to be built.

The third quarter enforces. The clause library goes into procurement as a gate for every new AI vendor contract, and the AI Bill of Materials becomes a required deliverable for every new AI vendor engagement. Both are enforcement decisions, not documentation decisions, which means both will generate friction with procurement and with the business units whose vendor onboarding just got slower. Publish the intake-to-approval time before and after so the friction is a measured cost rather than an anecdote, and route the exceptions through a named approver rather than letting them accumulate as informal carve-outs.

The fourth quarter is coverage and proof. Continuous monitoring is live across the full Tier 1 portfolio, the clause library is enforced in procurement for all new AI vendor contracts, and the AI BOM is required for every new AI vendor engagement. Those three facts are the year-end board milestone, and they answer a question the board has been asking implicitly since the audit landed: is the program watching the vendor population continuously, or sampling it annually?

The fourth quarter also produces the first concentration finding, because once the BOM registry holds data from the Tier 1 population, the foundation model dependency picture becomes visible for the first time.

That concentration finding deserves a specific handoff to the CFO before the year closes. Quantify it in financial terms rather than architectural ones: if the primary foundation model provider experienced a seventy-two hour outage, what is the estimated business impact across every vendor service that depends on it? That number goes to the CFO as a named risk with a named owner and a mitigation plan. The CFO who understands the concentration risk can make deliberate architectural and insurance decisions about it, and the CFO who does not know it exists cannot.

What Year One makes possible is the transition from enforcement to intelligence, and it is worth naming without asking for the money today. The contract intelligence engine that enforced the clause library on new contracts extends to sweep the full existing contract estate, routing every gap to the renewal queue. The monitoring infrastructure becomes the substrate for standing evidence pipelines, which are what eventually retire the questionnaire for the strategic vendor population. And a bilateral trust framework pilot becomes proposable to a strategic vendor whose agents already interact with your systems, because you now hold the evidence that agent-to-agent interaction is a governance reality rather than a future risk.

The destination Year One sets up is a third-party risk function that stops being the department that runs the annual assessment cycle and becomes the intelligence function that keeps every other domain current on the vendor population it depends on. The governance committee gets current vendor intelligence at every meeting rather than a quarterly summary of the last questionnaire cycle. The SOC gets real-time vendor breach signals that inform threat hunting. The privacy function gets immediate notification of vendor processing changes that affect enterprise data flows. Year One does not deliver that function. Year One builds the monitoring spine it runs on.

FIGURE 9.4 **The One-Year Supply Chain Target Operating Model**

Four quarters, with the milestone reported at the end of each.

QUARTER	CAPABILITY INSTALLED	OWNER	BOARD MILESTONE
Q1	Re-tiering on current AI exposure across the population	TPRM Lead	The tier map reflects today
Q2	Clause sweep complete and BOM requirement in the standard	TPRM with Legal	We know what our contracts do not cover
Q3	Continuous monitoring and adaptive trust scoring live	TPRM Lead	Vendor risk updates without a questionnaire
Q4	Tool registry enforced and concentration analysis reported	CISO	We know what one provider failure costs

LEVERAGE ARRIVES AT RENEWAL. SEQUENCE THE WORK TO MEET IT.

The Build Boundary: What Third-Party Risk Should Never Buy

The third-party risk market will sell you every component of the program described in Chapter 8, and three of those components should be built rather than bought for reasons that are specific rather than ideological. The distinction matters because a function that outsources the wrong component finds, usually at the second renewal, that its most important artifact belongs to a vendor and reflects that vendor's judgment rather than the enterprise's risk appetite. Knowing the boundary in advance is cheaper than discovering it.

The clause library is the first thing that stays inside. Vendors will offer a standard AI clause set, and the standard set is a reasonable starting draft and a poor finished product, because required clauses encode an enterprise's specific regulatory exposure, data sensitivity, and negotiating leverage. An enterprise operating in a regulated industry needs clauses a general-purpose library will not carry; an enterprise with limited leverage needs a required-versus-preferred distinction that reflects which fights it can win. Take the vendor's draft, have your General Counsel rewrite it against your exposure, and own the result. The engine that enforces the library can be bought. The library cannot.

The trust scoring model is the second. A purchased score is a vendor's opinion of a vendor, computed with weights you did not set, against evidence you cannot fully inspect, and delivered as a number your procurement team will treat as a fact. That is acceptable as one input among several and unacceptable as the instrument that gates purchasing decisions, because when a business unit challenges a score you need to be able to explain the weighting and defend it. Build the model, even if it is simple, and use purchased scores as an input to it rather than as a replacement for it. A crude model you can explain beats a sophisticated one you cannot.

The tier definition is the third and it is the one most often surrendered without noticing. Tiering criteria encode the enterprise's judgment about what depth of access constitutes what level of risk, and that judgment is the core intellectual content of the whole program. Platforms arrive with default tiering based on spend, on data category, or on a proprietary risk index, and adopting the default quietly replaces your risk appetite with the vendor's. Configure the tiering to your own criteria, document why the criteria are what they are, and review them annually against what the year's findings taught you.

What should be bought is everything with an economy of scale attached: external monitoring, because no enterprise can watch the open web and the disclosure feeds as cheaply as a service that watches them for thousands of clients; the contract intelligence engine, because natural language processing over a contract estate is a solved commodity problem; and the platform substrate that holds the portfolio and the register. The decision rule is that the enterprise buys the mechanism and builds the judgment. Any purchase that includes the judgment should be evaluated as though it were an outsourcing of the risk function itself, because functionally it is.

FIGURE 9.5

The Build Boundary

What third-party risk should never buy.

1 NEVER BUY THE CLAUSE LIBRARY

Your required terms encode your regulatory exposure and negotiating posture. A generic library cannot carry either and weakens both.

2 NEVER BUY RISK ACCEPTANCE

A platform can score a vendor. It cannot decide what your enterprise is willing to tolerate or who signs for that decision.

3 NEVER BUY THE CONCENTRATION JUDGMENT

Which dependency is survivable is a business continuity question that belongs to executives, not to a scoring model.

BUY THE EXAMINATION. KEEP THE JUDGMENT.

The Consortium Option: Shared Assurance and Why It Keeps Failing

Every few years the third-party risk community proposes the obvious solution to a genuinely wasteful problem: rather than each enterprise separately assessing the same vendors, a consortium assesses once and shares the result. The logic is sound, the waste is real, and several credible attempts exist. The pattern that follows is worth understanding before your enterprise joins one, because the failure mode is consistent and it is not primarily a technology problem.

Shared assurance works when the assessment criteria are stable, the participants have similar risk appetites, and the vendor population is slow-moving. Financial services consortium models have functioned reasonably well under those conditions for exactly that reason. AI vendor assessment breaks all three assumptions simultaneously. Criteria are moving quarterly as the threat picture and the regulatory picture develop. Participants have radically different risk appetites depending on their regulatory exposure and their data sensitivity. And the vendor population mutates weekly, which means a shared assessment has a half-life measured in weeks rather than in the annual cycle these models were built around.

The second failure is about depth. A shared assessment converges on the criteria all participants can agree to, which means it converges toward the least demanding participant's requirements. An enterprise with heavy regulatory exposure joins expecting to reduce its assessment load and discovers that the shared assessment covers perhaps sixty percent of what it needs, that the remaining forty percent still requires bilateral work, and that it has now added a coordination overhead on top of the work it still has to do. The saving is real but much smaller than the model promised, and it arrives with a governance dependency on a body the enterprise does not control.

The third failure is accountability, and it is the one that should decide the question for most CISOs. When a shared assessment misses something and a vendor incident follows, the enterprise's regulator will ask the enterprise what due diligence it performed. An answer that points to a consortium assessment is weaker than an answer that points to the enterprise's own work, and the strength of that difference depends on how the regulator views delegated diligence in your sector. Before joining, ask your General Counsel what the enterprise's position is if the shared assessment is the only diligence on file. If the answer requires supplementary work anyway, the consortium is a cost reduction rather than a control.

Where the model does earn its place is in the layer beneath the vendor, which is precisely where individual enterprises have the least leverage. No single enterprise can compel a foundation model provider to disclose its training data provenance, its subprocessor chain, or its incident history. A consortium plausibly can, and the emerging industry efforts to standardize AI Bill of Materials disclosure are the version of this idea most likely to produce durable value. Participate in the standard-setting. Be considerably more cautious about outsourcing the assessment itself.

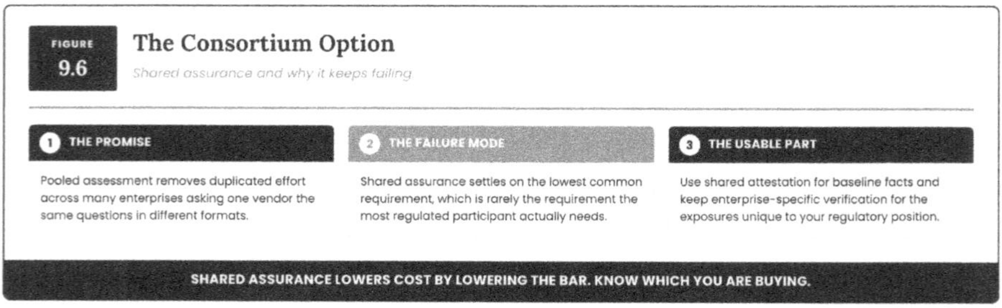

More Security or Less? The Ultimate Outcome for Third-Party Risk

The board's question about third-party risk is harder to answer than the same question for governance or security operations, because the answer requires the board to understand something genuinely new about the nature of organizational boundaries in an AI-native economy. It's worth taking the time to frame that answer carefully before presenting it, because a poorly framed answer produces a budget conversation about headcount reduction that misses the point entirely.

More security. Radically restructured.

The restructuring is more fundamental than the transformations in the other three domains, because the underlying nature of what third-party risk governs is changing in a way that has no precedent in the discipline's history. Third-party risk was built to govern relationships between organizations mediated by human decisions. Contracts written by humans, negotiated by humans, executed by humans. Questionnaires answered by humans with knowledge of their organizations' practices. Assessments conducted by humans reviewing human-produced documentation. The entire discipline assumed that the primary actors in inter-organizational relationships were people making deliberate choices.

Agent-to-agent commerce is making that assumption false. When your procurement agent queries a vendor's pricing agent, no human made a deliberate choice to initiate that interaction. The agents acted on their programming, within the parameters their organizations set, and produced an inter-organizational transaction that neither organization's human employees specifically approved. As agentic AI becomes more capable and more widely deployed, the volume of inter-organizational transactions initiated and completed by autonomous systems will exceed the volume initiated and completed by humans. Every one of those transactions is a trust decision made by machines, continuous, bilateral, and potentially revocable, and the function that governs them needs to be built for that reality.

The function that once mailed questionnaires becomes the function that engineers inter-organizational trust itself. That's not a metaphor. It's a description of the actual work the trust engineer role performs: designing the verification architecture that allows two organizations' AI systems to establish, maintain, and revoke trust across organizational boundaries without requiring human approval for every individual transaction. The trust engineer who builds that architecture is doing work that didn't exist three years ago and will be among the most consequential security work in the enterprise within five years.

Consider a hypothetical scenario that illustrates where this is heading. A 38-year-old third-party risk director at a large insurance company is managing a vendor portfolio where her organization's claims processing agents interact daily with agents from dozens of partner organizations: repair shops, medical providers, legal firms, and reinsurers. Each of those agent-to-agent interactions involves the exchange of sensitive data, the initiation of financial transactions, and the execution of decisions that affect policyholders. Her current vendor risk program was built to govern the contracts and questionnaires that defined those relationships when humans managed them. It has no model for governing the trust boundaries between autonomous systems making those same decisions at machine speed. She knows the gap exists. She doesn't yet have the operating model to close it. The trust engineering capability described in this chapter is what she needs, and the organizations that build it first will define the standard she eventually has to meet. Note: this is a hypothetical scenario illustrating a pattern emerging across industries where AI agents are being deployed in inter-organizational workflows, not a real case study.

Vendor risk doesn't shrink as agent-to-agent commerce grows. It becomes the governance layer of the machine economy. Every new autonomous capability deployed by a vendor partner creates a new trust boundary that needs to be defined, monitored, and governed. Every new agent-to-agent interaction protocol creates a new category of inter-organizational risk that the trust engineering function needs to design controls for. The scope of the function expands with every new autonomous system deployed on either side of every vendor relationship. The function that was scoped to govern human-mediated relationships is now scoped to govern machine-mediated ones, and the machine-mediated ones are growing faster.

The enterprises that build trust engineering first will write the standards everyone else signs. That's not an optimistic prediction. It's the logical consequence of how standards get written in security. The organizations that operate a capability first develop the expertise that regulators consult when writing requirements, that peer organizations benchmark against when building their own programs, and that vendors accommodate when designing their own governance capabilities. The third-party risk function that has a running bilateral trust framework, a live Adaptive AI Trust Score for its strategic vendor population, and a trust engineer role that's been operating for two years is the organization that defines what mature AI vendor risk governance looks like. Everyone else will eventually be required to meet that standard. The organizations that set it will have built it on their own terms.

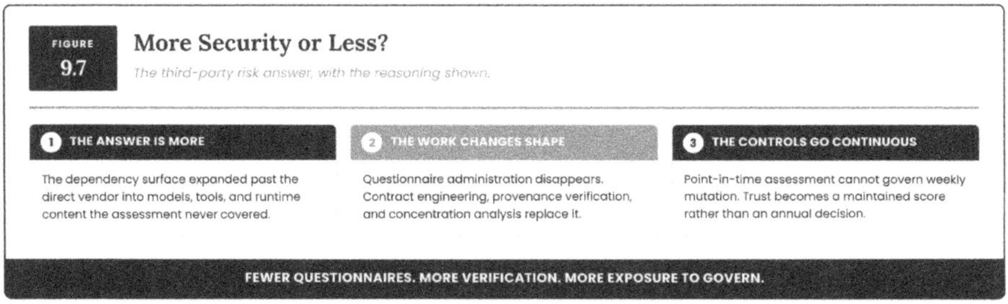

FIGURE 9.7 More Security or Less?
The third-party risk answer, with the reasoning shown.

Putting It Into Practice

The restructure is coming. The only question is whether it arrives as a deliberate transition or as a crisis that forces reorganization under pressure. The actions below are specific, sequenced, and owned. Each one builds on the previous. Together they position the third-party risk function for the target operating model before the market forces it.

Start by locating your program against the current-focus map honestly. Answer one question for each of the four current-focus areas: AI vendor inventory, AI addenda, BOM requirements, and continuous monitoring pilots. Is each one producing standing evidence or a longer questionnaire? An inventory that hasn't been updated since the audit closed is a longer questionnaire. An AI addendum with no enforceable obligations is a longer questionnaire. A BOM requirement that applies to new contracts but not to the existing estate is a better intake form, not a governance program. A monitoring pilot running alongside a questionnaire cycle you haven't retired is evidence that the organizational decision to replace the questionnaire hasn't been made yet. Name each one honestly. Those are your year one gaps, and they need to be in the gap analysis you bring to the CISO before the budget conversation starts.

Evaluate your vendor risk stack by category this week. Map what you currently have against the five categories: TPRM platform with AI posture extension, external monitoring service, AI BOM and model registry tooling, contract intelligence engine, and attestation economy tools. For each category, answer two questions. Do you have a tool that covers this category? And does it produce continuous intelligence or periodic snapshots? A tool that produces periodic snapshots in a category that requires continuous coverage is a gap, even if the tool is well-designed. Identify the category that's missing entirely from your current stack. That missing category is your first year one tooling investment.

Open the ownership conversation with the CISO before the turf contest opens it. Schedule that conversation this week. The agenda is three questions. Who owns AI procurement review: security, procurement, or the CDO, and what does each function contribute to the review process? Who owns fourth-party risk and concentration risk: where does the accountability for the model supply chain sit in the organization? Who owns the trust boundary between your agents and your vendors' agents: is that a security question, a legal question, or a CDO question, and who has the authority to define the answer? Those three questions need answers before the next AI vendor negotiation begins. The CISO who defines the answers owns the function. The CISO who waits for the turf contest to define them loses jurisdiction to whoever showed up most forcefully in the last vendor negotiation.

Draft the new role set and the skills transition for your team this week. Write a one-paragraph description of each of the three new roles: vendor intelligence analyst, trust engineer, and contract intelligence owner. For each role, name the primary accountability, the skills it requires that differ from current assessor roles, and the artifact it owns. Then map your current team against those three roles. Identify the one or two people who have the instincts for the vendor intelligence analyst or trust engineer roles. Put them on a development path now. Identify the gaps that internal development can't close and plan the external hires for years one and two accordingly. The skills transition map is what you bring to the CISO alongside the reorganization case. The reorganization case without a skills transition plan is a request to eliminate roles without a plan to replace the capability. The skills transition plan is what makes the reorganization case fundable.

Assemble the 1-Year Supply Chain Target Operating Model on one page. First quarter: the AI clause library built and legally reviewed. Second quarter: continuous monitoring live across the Tier 1 portfolio and the vendor intelligence analyst hired. Third quarter: clause library enforced as a procurement gate and the AI Bill of Materials required for every new AI vendor engagement. Fourth quarter: full Tier 1 coverage, the first foundation model concentration finding quantified in dollars, and that number handed to the CFO with a named owner and a mitigation plan. For each quarter, add three columns: the primary capability build, the headcount addition, and the board-facing milestone. That one page is the budget narrative for the CFO and the answer to the board's question about what you are building and why it costs what it costs.

Present the budget narrative as a discipline being rebuilt, not expanded. That framing matters. Expanded implies more of the same work at greater scale. Rebuilt implies a different kind of work requiring different capabilities and different investment. The third-party risk function being rebuilt in this model isn't doing more questionnaire administration at greater volume. It's doing work that didn't exist before: continuous intelligence, bilateral trust engineering, agent-to-agent governance. That work requires different tools, different skills, and different organizational positioning than the questionnaire-administration model it replaces. The CFO who understands that framing can evaluate the investment on its actual merits. The CFO who thinks it's an expansion of the existing program will look for the efficiency gains that a rebuild doesn't produce, because it's not trying to.

Part III is complete. The third-party risk operating model is drawn, the destination is funded, and the trust engineering capability that governs machine-to-machine commerce is positioned for the organizations that build it first. The next chapter opens Part IV, where privacy inherits the audit and discovers that every founding assumption of the discipline is now false.

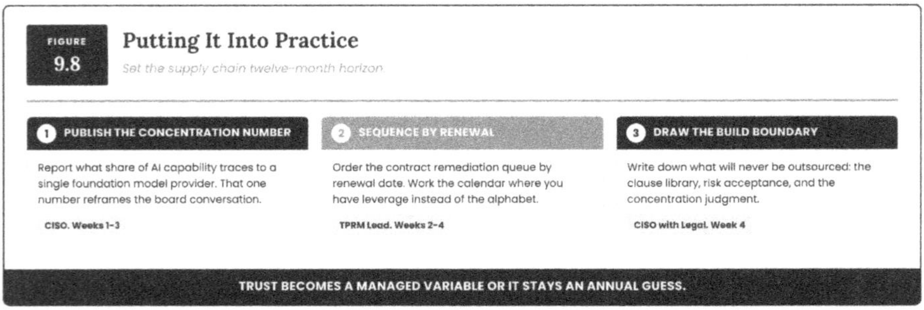

Part IV: Data Protection and Privacy

What the Audit Handed Privacy, and Which of Its Founding Assumptions Survived

Privacy received the AI Data Flow Map and a set of findings that quietly invalidate the architecture the entire privacy program rests on. Every major privacy regime, and every control program built to satisfy one, assumes four things: that data has a location, that a copy can be deleted, that collection is an event you can consent to, and that purpose is a property you attach to data at the moment you obtain it. AI systems break all four, and they do not break them as edge cases. They break them as ordinary operation.

Location goes first. Data that entered an AI system as a prompt now exists as embeddings in a vector store, as retrieval context in a cache, as conversation history in a session store, as fine-tuning input in a training set, and potentially as learned weights in a model artifact. The data flow map traces the path. What it cannot fully trace is what happened at each stop, because some of those transformations are not reversible and not enumerable. A privacy officer asked where a data subject's information lives can answer for the database and cannot answer for the model.

Deletion follows. An erasure request that reaches a database is a delete statement. An erasure request that reaches a vector index, an agent memory store, a retrieval cache, and a model fine-tuned on the data is a research problem wearing a compliance deadline. Most organizations are currently answering these requests by deleting the primary record, honestly reporting compliance, and not disclosing that derived representations persist. That is not fraud. It is a gap between what the regulation contemplated and what the architecture does, and it is a gap that will close from the regulatory side long before it closes from the engineering side.

Then inference collapses the collection model. An AI system that reads unregulated inputs and produces a regulated inference has created protected data without collecting it. A model that determines pregnancy from purchase timing, health status from query patterns, or protected characteristics from writing style has manufactured a category of data the enterprise never obtained, never consented to obtain, and now holds. The consent framework has no hook for this because consent attaches to collection, and no collection occurred.

Purpose limitation collapses last and most completely. Data collected for one purpose becomes training input, then retrieval context, then agent memory, then the substrate for outputs in workflows nobody mapped when the data was obtained. Enterprise memory sprawl is the operational name for this: agents accumulate context indefinitely, knowledge bases absorb whatever is indexed into them, and the purpose a data element was gathered under stops constraining anything within weeks. Meanwhile shadow AI use moves regulated data into unapproved systems in a way that meets the definition of unauthorized processing without meeting any breach notification trigger, which means the event happens, the exposure is real, and nothing gets reported.

Chapter 10 names these four collapses against the audit's data flow map. Chapter 11 builds the engineering that makes compliance operationally real: complete discovery, semantic data loss prevention, erasure engineering, purpose enforcement as code, and enterprise memory governance. Chapter 12 covers the market, the categories, whether privacy merges with AI governance, the twelve-month model, and the final answer to the board's question.

Chapter 10: Privacy Inherits the Audit

The End of Its Founding Assumptions and the Controls Built on Them

CHAPTER 10 OUTCOMES

At the end of this chapter, you will be able to:

1. Explain which founding assumptions of the privacy program AI invalidated.
2. Handle erasure requests that reach data which cannot straightforwardly be deleted.
3. Treat inference as collection when regulated attributes are derived from unregulated inputs.
4. Identify memory sprawl and purpose collapse across the AI estate.
5. Recognize shadow AI as a privacy event that never triggers notification.
6. Locate the four places corruption enters the data and knowledge substrate.

PRIVACY GOVERNED WHAT THE ENTERPRISE STORED. IT NOW GOVERNS WHAT THE ENTERPRISE KNOWS.

The Handoff: What Privacy Received and Where Its Program Ends

The audit delivered two things to the privacy function. The first was useful: the AI Data Flow Map, a structured picture of where personal data moves across the AI systems the enterprise runs. The second was uncomfortable: proof that the privacy program's foundational assumptions no longer hold. The map showed data flows the program was built to govern. It also showed data states, data behaviors, and data risks that the program was never designed to see.

That's what privacy inherited. Not a gap to patch. A boundary to redraw.

The AI Data Flow Map confirmed something that most privacy teams already suspected but hadn't fully confronted. Personal data isn't just moving through AI systems the way it moves through databases and applications. It's being transformed by them. A prompt containing a customer's name, account history, and complaint is not just data in transit. It becomes part of the context that shapes an AI agent's response, potentially persists in the agent's memory across future sessions, and may contribute to model behavior in ways that no traditional data map was designed to track. The map showed the inputs. It couldn't show what the system did with them afterward, because the privacy program's data mapping methodology was built for systems that store and retrieve data, not systems that reason with it.

Three gaps came with the handoff. Each one is structural. None of them can be closed by updating a policy or adding a field to an existing form.

The first gap is enterprise memory that no data map captures. When an AI agent maintains context across sessions, it accumulates personal data in a form that doesn't exist in any traditional data store. It's not in a database. It's not in a file. It's in the agent's operational memory, shaped by every interaction the agent has had and influencing every interaction it will have. That memory is personal data. It's subject to the same regulatory obligations as any other personal data the enterprise holds. And it's invisible to every data map the privacy function produced before AI agents were deployed, because those maps were built on the assumption that personal data lives in identifiable stores. Agent memory doesn't.

The second gap is inference that no consent framework covers. AI systems derive information that was never collected. Health status from purchase patterns. Financial stress from communication timing. Political orientation from word choice. These aren't data points the enterprise asked for. They're conclusions the AI system reached from data the enterprise did collect, often for entirely different purposes. The consent framework that governs the enterprise's data collection was written around what the enterprise asked data subjects to provide. It says nothing about what the enterprise's AI systems will subsequently derive from that data. The derived attributes are often more sensitive than the inputs that produced them. And they exist in a regulatory space that most consent frameworks simply don't address.

The third gap is erasure requests that no deletion workflow can fulfill. A data subject exercises their right to erasure. The privacy team runs the standard workflow: locate the data, delete it from the identified stores, confirm deletion, close the request. The workflow is sound. The problem is that the identified stores don't include model weights, agent memory, embedding databases, or training datasets referenced by fine-tuned models. The data subject's personal data may have influenced model behavior in ways that persist long after the database record was deleted. The deletion workflow certified the erasure. The AI stack didn't hear about it.

Understanding where the privacy program ends is the prerequisite for rebuilding what comes next. The program ends at the boundary of the AI layer. Everything above that boundary, the databases, the applications, the structured data flows, is governed. Everything inside the AI layer, the weights, the embeddings, the agent memory, the inference outputs, is not. That boundary isn't a gap in an otherwise functional program. It's the edge of a foundation that was built for a different class of technology. The rebuild starts by naming that edge honestly.

This month, map where subject data actually lives across the AI stack for your five highest-risk AI systems. Not just the input channels. The full lifecycle: what data enters the system, what the system does with it, where it persists after the interaction ends, and what the current deletion workflow can and cannot reach. Document the gap between what the workflow certifies and what it actually touches. That document is your exposure in writing. It's also the starting point for every action this chapter calls for.

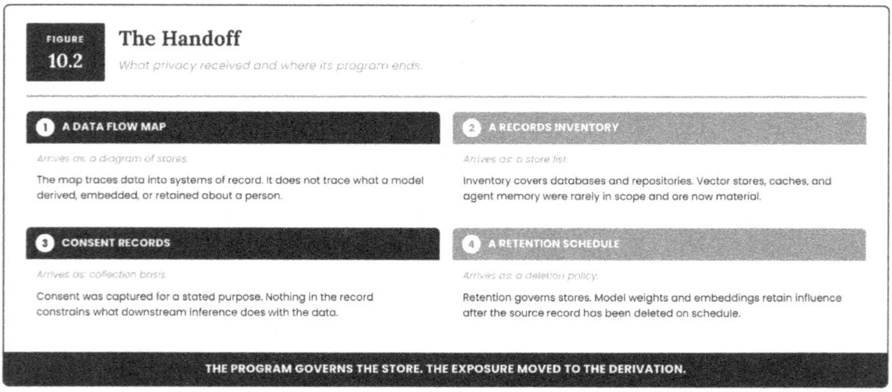

The Deletion Problem: When Erasure Requests Reach Data That Cannot Be Deleted

The right to erasure is one of the most clearly stated rights in modern data protection law. The language is direct. A data subject requests deletion. The controller deletes. The controller confirms. The obligation is satisfied. The regulatory frameworks that established this right were written with a specific architecture in mind: personal data lives in identifiable stores, deletion removes it from those stores, and the data ceases to exist in the controller's environment. That architecture describes databases, file systems, and structured data stores. It doesn't describe AI model weights.

Model weights are the encoded product of training. When personal data is used to train a model, that data doesn't sit in the weights the way a record sits in a database. It shapes the weights. It influences the statistical relationships the model learned. It contributes to the model's behavior in ways that are distributed across millions of parameters, none of which contains the original data in any retrievable form. You cannot delete a data subject's contribution to a model's weights by running a deletion script. The contribution isn't stored as a record. It's baked into the model's learned behavior.

That's not a technical limitation that better tooling will eventually solve. It's a fundamental property of how neural networks learn. The implication for privacy compliance is specific and serious: every enterprise that trained or fine-tuned a model on personal data, and every enterprise whose vendor trained or fine-tuned a model on their data, is holding personal data in a form that the standard erasure workflow cannot reach. The erasure request gets closed. The data doesn't get deleted. The certification is wrong.

Agent memory compounds the problem in a different way. Unlike model weights, agent memory is often stored in a retrievable form. The agent maintains a context store that records what it knows about a user, what decisions it made in previous interactions, and what instructions it was given. That context store is personal data. It's identifiable. It's persistent. And in most enterprise deployments, it has no connection to the erasure workflow. The privacy team's deletion process runs against the CRM, the data warehouse, and the application databases. It doesn't run against the agent's context store, because nobody mapped the context store as a personal data location when the erasure workflow was designed. The agent continues to hold personal data about a subject who has been erased from every system the workflow knows about.

Training datasets referenced by multiple fine-tunes are the third dimension of the deletion problem. A dataset containing personal data was used to fine-tune a model. Then it was used to fine-tune a second model. Then a third. The original dataset still exists, referenced by all three fine-tunes. A deletion request arrives for a data subject whose record is in that dataset. Deleting the record from the dataset doesn't update the fine-tuned models. The models' behavior was shaped by the record that's now been deleted. The record is gone. The influence persists.

The legal exposure accumulating in enterprises whose erasure certifications quietly exclude the AI layer is real and growing. Regulators are beginning to ask whether erasure certifications cover AI systems. The honest answer, for most enterprises, is no. The certification covers the systems the workflow was designed to reach. The AI layer wasn't in scope when the workflow was designed, and it's been added to the enterprise's data processing environment without being added to the erasure program's scope. That gap between what the certification says and what it actually covers is a regulatory exposure that grows with every erasure request the program closes without touching the AI layer.

The practical response to the deletion problem has three components. The first is a technical feasibility assessment for every AI system that processes personal data. The assessment asks one question for each system: if a valid erasure request arrives for data this system processed, what can the current workflow delete and what can it not? Document the answer for every system. The systems where the workflow cannot reach all personal data locations are the systems that carry erasure certification risk. That risk belongs in the risk register with a named owner and a remediation timeline.

The second component is a scope disclosure. If the enterprise cannot technically fulfill an erasure request for data that lives in model weights, the privacy team and the General Counsel need to assess whether that limitation requires disclosure to data subjects, whether it affects the enterprise's ability to certify erasure under applicable regulations, and whether the limitation is defensible under the technical infeasibility provisions that some regulatory frameworks provide. Technical infeasibility is a recognized limitation in some jurisdictions. It requires documentation, it requires that the enterprise took all reasonable steps to minimize the data's impact, and it requires that the limitation be disclosed where required. It's not a blanket exemption. It's a narrow defense that requires deliberate legal and operational preparation.

The third component is prospective architecture. For AI systems not yet deployed, build erasure capability into the design. Maintain agent memory in a retrievable, deletable store rather than in an opaque context buffer. Use training data pipelines that track which records contributed to which model versions, so that a deletion request can trigger a model retraining or a documented technical infeasibility assessment. These architectural decisions are significantly easier to make before a system is built than after it's running in production with data subjects' personal data already embedded in its behavior. The privacy function's role in AI system design is to ask the erasure question before deployment, not after the first erasure request arrives.

This week, run the technical feasibility assessment on your five highest-risk AI systems. Document what the current erasure workflow can reach and what it cannot. Bring the findings to the General Counsel with a specific question: does the gap between what our erasure certifications say and what our workflow actually covers create a regulatory exposure that requires immediate action? That conversation needs to happen before the next erasure request arrives for data that lives in a model the workflow can't reach. The request is coming. The preparation needs to happen first.

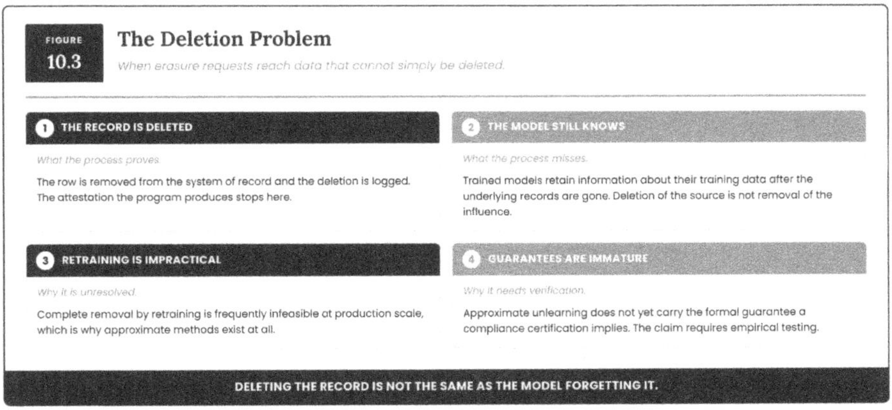

Inference as the New Collection: Regulated Data Created From Unregulated Inputs

The consent framework governing enterprise data collection was built around a straightforward premise: the enterprise collects specific data from data subjects, the data subjects are informed of what's being collected and why, and the enterprise uses the collected data for the disclosed purposes. That premise assumes that the sensitive data the enterprise holds is the data it asked for. AI broke that assumption quietly and thoroughly.

An AI system that infers a customer's health status from their purchase patterns didn't collect health data. It derived it. The customer consented to the enterprise collecting their purchase history. They didn't consent to the enterprise deriving health conclusions from it. The health inference is sensitive data under most data protection frameworks. It carries the same regulatory weight as health data the enterprise explicitly collected. And it was created from inputs that the consent framework covered, through a process the consent framework never contemplated, producing an output the consent framework has no category for.

This is inference risk. It's the exposure that no consent framework addresses, because consent frameworks were designed to govern collection, not derivation. The enterprise isn't collecting sensitive attributes. It's manufacturing them from data it legitimately holds. The manufacturing process is the AI system. The product is regulated data that nobody consented to produce.

The categories of sensitive attributes that AI systems routinely derive from non-sensitive inputs are specific and well-documented in the research literature. Health status and medical conditions derived from purchase patterns, search behavior, and communication cadence. Financial stress and creditworthiness derived from transaction timing, communication frequency, and behavioral patterns. Political orientation and religious affiliation derived from language patterns, content consumption, and social connection data. Sexual orientation and relationship status derived from behavioral signals and communication metadata. None of these attributes were collected. All of them are regulated in most jurisdictions. All of them are being derived, right now, by AI systems operating in enterprises that have no governance framework for what gets derived and what happens to it afterward.

The regulatory trajectory is moving toward enforcement of inference risk, not away from it. Data protection authorities are extending existing frameworks to cover derived data. The EU AI Act's requirements for high-risk AI systems include systems that make inferences about individuals in sensitive categories. The FTC has taken enforcement positions on the use of inferred sensitive attributes in commercial contexts. State-level privacy laws in the US are beginning to address inferred data explicitly. The window between the current state, where inference risk is largely ungoverned, and the future state, where inference risk carries the same regulatory weight as collected sensitive data, is closing. The enterprises that build inference governance now will be ahead of the enforcement curve. The enterprises that wait for the first enforcement action to force the question will be building governance under regulatory pressure, which is a worse position to build from.

The inference question is specific and it needs to be asked of every AI system in the enterprise that processes behavioral, transactional, or communication data. The question is: what sensitive attributes could this system derive from the data it processes, and are those derivations governed by any existing privacy control? Asking the question forces a structured assessment. The assessment often reveals that the answer to the second part is no. The system can derive health status, financial stress, or political orientation from its inputs. No consent framework covers those derivations. No data minimization policy limits what gets derived. No retention policy governs how long derived attributes persist. The governance gap is the space between what the system can derive and what the privacy program covers.

Ask the inference question of your five highest-risk AI systems this month. For each system, identify the input data it processes, map the sensitive attributes that could plausibly be derived from those inputs, and document whether any existing privacy control covers those derivations. The documentation produces a gap map. The gap map goes to the CPO and the General Counsel as a named risk finding. The finding triggers a legal assessment of whether the inferences the system is making require consent, disclosure, or limitation under applicable law. That legal assessment is the starting point for the governance response.

The governance response to inference risk has three components. The first is inference minimization: a policy that requires AI systems to derive only the attributes necessary for the disclosed purpose and to discard derived attributes that exceed that purpose. The second is inference disclosure: an update to the enterprise's privacy notices that discloses the types of inferences the enterprise's

AI systems make about individuals and the purposes for which those inferences are used. The third is inference governance: a review process that assesses new AI system deployments for inference risk before they go live, applying the same rigor to what the system might derive that the current privacy impact assessment process applies to what the system collects.

None of these components require new technology. They require new policy, new process, and new scope for the privacy impact assessment function. The privacy impact assessment that was designed to evaluate data collection needs to be extended to evaluate data derivation. That extension is a policy decision, not a technology investment. It can be made this month, before the next AI system deployment triggers the inference risk question in a regulatory context rather than a governance one.

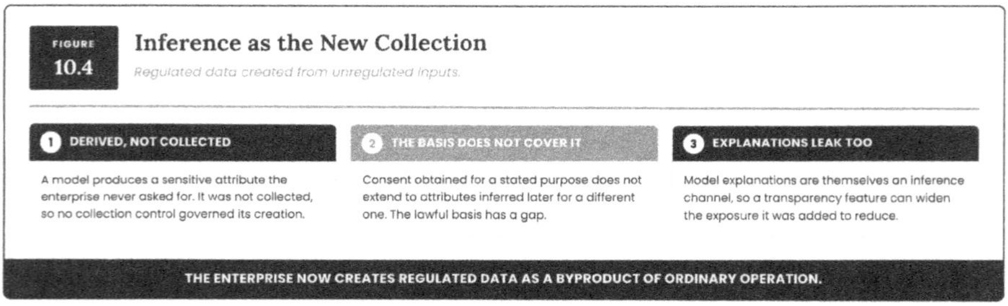

Memory Sprawl and Purpose Collapse: The Assumptions AI Broke at Scale

Privacy practice was built on two assumptions that were reasonable for the technology they were designed to govern. The first assumption was that personal data sits in identifiable stores. Databases, file systems, structured repositories with defined schemas and known locations. The data map could find them. The classification policy could label them. The access control framework could protect them. The assumption held for decades because the technology it described was stable.

The second assumption was that data collected for one purpose serves that purpose. A customer's address collected for shipping is used for shipping. An employee's salary data collected for payroll is used for payroll. Purpose limitation, one of the foundational principles of data protection law, was built on the premise that purpose and use are connected, that data flows from collection through use to disposal along a path that governance can follow. That assumption also held for decades.

AI broke both assumptions simultaneously, at scale, and without generating the kind of visible event that would trigger a governance response.

Memory sprawl is the first failure. An AI agent that maintains context across sessions accumulates personal data continuously. Every conversation adds to the context. Every interaction shapes what the agent remembers about the user. Over time, the agent's memory of a single user can contain information drawn from dozens of interactions across weeks or months: complaints, preferences, financial situations, health concerns, relationship details. None of that information was stored in a single, identifiable location that a data map could find. It accumulated incrementally, across interactions, in a context store that no data inventory methodology was designed to capture. The agent's memory is a personal data store. It's invisible to the privacy program.

The scale of this problem grows with every agent deployed. A single agent interacting with thousands of customers accumulates a personal data store that no privacy team has mapped, no classification policy has labeled, and no access control framework has protected. Multiply that by the number of agents the enterprise runs, and the total unmapped personal data in agent memory across the enterprise is significant. Not theoretical. Current. Growing with every interaction those agents conduct.

Purpose collapse is the second failure, and it operates at a different layer. Data collected from a customer for the purpose of processing their service request gets ingested into a training dataset. The training dataset is used to fine-tune a model that serves a different business unit for a different purpose. The model's outputs are used to build a recommendation engine that serves yet another purpose. The customer's data, collected for one purpose, is now powering three different AI applications serving three different business units for three different purposes, none of which the original collection notice disclosed.

This isn't a hypothetical scenario. It's the default outcome of AI deployment in enterprises that don't have a data governance model that tracks purpose through the AI training and deployment lifecycle. Data flows into training pipelines. Training pipelines produce models. Models get deployed for whatever business purpose is most pressing. The connection between the original collection purpose and the current use purpose disappears somewhere in the pipeline, and nobody in the privacy function has a mechanism to track it.

Re-identification at scale is a third dimension of the same underlying failure. Privacy programs accepted anonymization as a sufficient protection for data used in analytics and AI training. Regulators accepted it too, for years. The anonymization standards that were considered robust when they were established were calibrated for a world where re-identification required significant effort and specialized expertise. AI changes that calculus. The combination of AI-powered inference, large-scale behavioral datasets, and publicly available information sources makes re-identification of supposedly anonymized datasets significantly more feasible than the original anonymization standards assumed. Data that the privacy program classified as anonymous and therefore outside the scope of personal data obligations may not be anonymous in any meaningful sense when processed by a sufficiently capable AI system with access to supplementary data sources.

Cross-border processing adds a jurisdictional dimension to the same problem. An AI agent processing a customer interaction in one jurisdiction may draw from a model that was trained in a second jurisdiction, running on infrastructure hosted in a third, with agent memory stored in a fourth. The data subject's personal data crosses multiple jurisdictional boundaries in the course of a single interaction, without any human making a deliberate decision to transfer it. The cross-border transfer obligations that apply to each of those movements were designed for deliberate, documented transfers between identified parties. They weren't designed for data that scatters across jurisdictions mid-inference as a side effect of how distributed AI infrastructure operates.

Inventory agent memory in one business unit this month. Choose the business unit with the highest volume of customer-facing AI agent interactions. Work with the team that operates those agents to understand what the agents' context stores contain, how long context persists, how it's structured, and whether it's currently captured in any data inventory. Document what you find. The documentation will almost certainly reveal personal data holdings that no privacy inventory has ever captured. Those holdings go into the data map as a new category: agent memory. The category needs a classification, a retention policy, a deletion procedure, and an access control standard. None of those things exist yet for most enterprises. Building them starts with the inventory, which starts this month.

The purpose collapse problem requires a different response. The fix isn't a new policy. It's a new process gate in the AI development lifecycle. Before any dataset is used for AI training or fine-tuning, a purpose compatibility assessment must be completed. The assessment asks one question: is the use of this dataset for this training purpose compatible with the purposes for which the data was originally collected? If the answer is no, or if the answer is uncertain, the assessment triggers a legal review before training proceeds. That gate doesn't require new technology. It requires the privacy function to have a seat at the table in the AI development process, specifically at the point where training datasets are selected. That seat needs to be established now, before the next training pipeline runs without it.

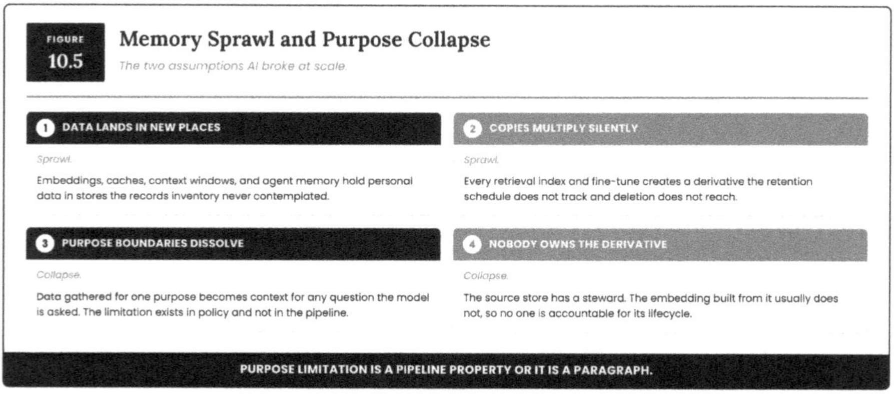

Shadow AI as a Privacy Event: The Breach That Never Triggers Notification

Every day, employees across the enterprise paste regulated data into consumer AI tools. Customer records into a generative AI assistant to draft a response. Financial data into an AI summarization tool to prepare a briefing. Patient information into a consumer AI chatbot to research a clinical question. The data leaves the enterprise's governed environment. It enters a consumer platform with terms of service that the employee never read and the privacy team never reviewed. It may be retained by the platform. It may be used to improve the platform's model. It may be processed in a jurisdiction the enterprise never authorized for that data category.

None of that triggers a breach notification analysis. No unauthorized access occurred. No security perimeter was crossed. No malware was involved. The employee used a tool they found on the internet to do their job more efficiently. The data walked out of the enterprise's governed environment in the hands of a legitimate user, through a channel nobody was watching, to a destination nobody approved. Under most breach notification frameworks, that's not a reportable event. Under most data protection frameworks, it's a significant compliance exposure. The gap between those two characterizations is where shadow AI lives as a privacy risk.

The CPO's exposure here is specific. Personal data leaving governed boundaries without a breach, an intrusion, or an alert is still personal data leaving governed boundaries. The fact that it left through a user's voluntary action rather than through an attacker's unauthorized access doesn't change the regulatory obligation. If the data was subject to purpose limitation requirements, it left for an unauthorized purpose. If it was subject to cross-border transfer restrictions, it may have been transferred to a jurisdiction the enterprise never authorized. If it was subject to data minimization requirements, the employee's decision to share it with a consumer AI platform doesn't satisfy those requirements retroactively.

Vendor training on enterprise data under clauses nobody read is the supply chain dimension of the same problem. Chapter 8 addressed training clauses in vendor contracts. The shadow AI dimension is different. It's not a vendor the enterprise contracted with and failed to review carefully. It's a consumer platform the employee chose independently, with terms of service that the enterprise never negotiated and the privacy team never saw. Those terms may include provisions that allow the platform to use submitted data to train its models. The employee agreed to those terms by clicking accept. The enterprise's data is now in a training pipeline that the enterprise has no visibility into and no contractual relationship with.

The reason shadow AI never triggers notification analysis is structural. Breach notification frameworks are built around unauthorized access. A threshold is crossed when an attacker gains access to data they weren't authorized to reach. Shadow AI doesn't cross that threshold. The user was authorized to access the data. The user chose to share it with an external platform. The sharing was voluntary. The notification framework doesn't have a category for voluntary data sharing by authorized users with unauthorized external platforms. The exposure accumulates without generating the signal that would trigger a response.

The retroactive discovery problem is what makes this risk particularly dangerous. Shadow AI exposure typically surfaces in one of three ways: a regulator asks about data processing practices and the enterprise's response inadvertently reveals that consumer AI tools are in use; a litigant's discovery request surfaces communications that reveal employees were using consumer AI tools to process case-relevant data; or a journalist reports on the practice after a source inside the enterprise describes it. In all three scenarios, the exposure is being disclosed under adversarial conditions, after the fact, without the enterprise having had the opportunity to assess and remediate it first. That's the worst possible context for a privacy compliance disclosure.

The CISO and the CPO must own shadow AI discovery jointly. That joint ownership isn't ceremonial. It reflects the actual nature of the risk, which sits at the intersection of security governance and privacy compliance. The CISO owns the discovery process: the technical scanning for unauthorized AI tool usage, the network traffic analysis that identifies connections to consumer AI platforms, the endpoint monitoring that detects AI tool installations. The CPO owns the compliance assessment: for every tool discovered, what data was it processing, what regulatory obligations apply to that data, and what is the compliance exposure from the processing that already occurred. Neither function can do the other's work. Both functions are required to produce a complete picture of the risk.

Run shadow AI discovery jointly with the CISO this month, with privacy exposure as the primary lens. The discovery process described in Chapter 2 identified shadow AI tools from a security governance perspective. The privacy lens adds a different dimension: for each tool discovered, what categories of personal data were being processed, what are the applicable regulatory obligations for that data, and what is the exposure from processing that occurred before discovery? Document the findings. Assess the exposure. Brief the CPO and the General Counsel on the results before the end of the month. The briefing isn't a crisis communication. It's a structured risk disclosure that gives the legal team the information they need to assess whether any regulatory notification obligations have been triggered and to prepare defensible documentation of the enterprise's response.

The fast-track approval path that Chapter 2 described as the governance response to shadow AI is also the privacy response. When employees have a legitimate, fast, governed path to get AI tools approved for their work, they use it. When they don't, they use consumer tools and the privacy team finds out retroactively. The approval path isn't just a security governance mechanism. It's a privacy compliance mechanism. Every employee who uses a governed, approved AI tool instead of a consumer alternative is a privacy exposure that didn't happen. The approval path is the preventive control. Discovery is the detective control. Both are necessary. The preventive control is cheaper.

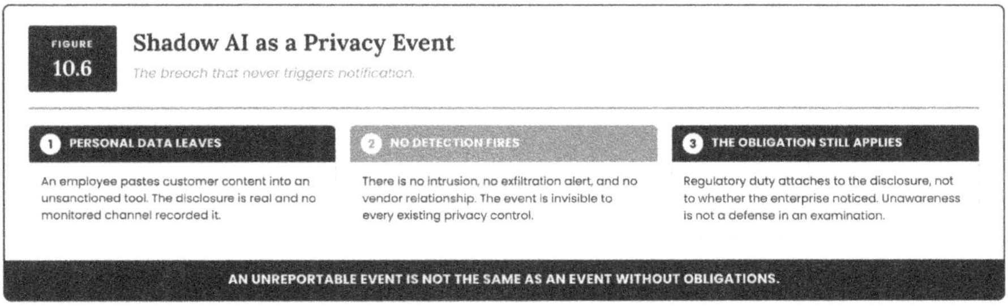

Cross-Border Inference: The Residency Rule That Inference Was Never Written For

Data residency controls were built around storage and transfer, and inference is neither. The regulatory architecture assumes that protected data sits in a jurisdiction, moves between jurisdictions through identifiable transfers, and that the enterprise can point to where a record lives. An AI system takes a prompt containing regulated data, transmits it to a model endpoint that may be in another jurisdiction, processes it in memory, returns an output, and retains nothing that would appear in a storage audit. The transfer occurred. The residency control did not see it, because the control was watching databases.

Most privacy programs discovered this the first time they mapped an AI data flow properly, and a substantial number have not mapped one yet. The finding is uncomfortable because it is usually retroactive: regulated data has been traversing the boundary for as long as the AI feature has been in use, which is longer than the privacy function has known the feature existed. The enterprise now holds an exposure that began before anyone made a decision about it, and the assessment that would have caught it was scoped to systems that store data rather than to systems that process it.

The vendor layer makes this materially harder to resolve than the first-party layer. An enterprise can determine where its own model endpoints run and can often constrain them. An enterprise generally cannot determine, from a vendor's documentation, which model provider serves a given AI feature, which region that provider serves it from, whether the routing is static or dynamic based on load, and whether the vendor's own subprocessor disclosure covers the model layer at all. The honest answer for many AI features in the current market is that the enterprise does not know where the inference happened, and the vendor may not be able to say either.

The compliance posture that results is worth naming plainly because it is widespread and rarely acknowledged. Enterprises are attesting to data residency on the basis of storage location while processing crosses boundaries in a way the attestation does not contemplate and the attester has not verified. That is not deliberate misrepresentation in most cases. It is an attestation written against an architecture that changed after the attestation language was drafted, signed by an executive who was not told the architecture changed. It is also exactly the category of gap that becomes a finding the first time an examiner asks the inference question rather than the storage question, and examiners have begun asking it.

The decision rule has two parts and the second one is the part programs skip. First, extend the data flow map to record, for every AI system processing regulated data, the inference location, the routing behavior, and the evidence source for both. Second, where the evidence source is a vendor claim rather than a verified fact, record it as a claim and treat the difference as an open risk with a named owner. A data flow map that presents vendor assertions and verified facts in the same notation has quietly converted the most important distinction in the document into a formatting choice, and the privacy officer relying on it will not know which entries would survive an examination.

Consent Theater: Why the Notice Update Did Not Fix Anything

The most common response to AI in privacy programs over the last two years has been a notice update. New language describing automated processing, a sentence about AI-assisted features, a broadened purpose statement covering product improvement. That work was necessary and it accomplished less than the effort suggests, because notice governs disclosure and the problems this chapter has named are not disclosure problems. Telling a data subject that their information may be processed by AI systems does not make erasure reach a vector index, does not constrain what an inference produces, and does not stop purpose from collapsing inside an agent's memory.

The deeper issue is that consent architecture assumes a decision point that AI systems do not have. Consent attaches at collection, is specific to purposes enumerated at that moment, and is withdrawable by an action that reverses the processing. An AI system that ingests a document into a retrieval corpus has created a representation that serves an indefinite number of downstream purposes, none of which existed as a category when the document was obtained, and withdrawal reverses the ingestion without reversing what the system learned from it. The consent record remains accurate about what was agreed. It has stopped describing what happens.

Broadened purpose language is the response most programs reached for, and it carries a risk that grows rather than shrinks. Regulators across multiple jurisdictions have signalled increasing skepticism toward purpose statements sufficiently broad to encompass unspecified future processing, and the broadest formulations are the ones most likely to be read as insufficiently specific. An enterprise that solved its AI purpose problem by widening the notice has taken a position that looks compliant today and looks like a deliberate evasion in a proceeding two years from now. The safer posture is narrower purposes with enforcement that actually holds, which is engineering work rather than drafting work.

The withdrawal problem deserves specific attention because it is where notice and architecture diverge most visibly. A data subject who withdraws consent expects processing to stop. In an AI estate, stopping processing means removing the data from active retrieval, purging it from agent memory, invalidating cached context, and addressing any adapted model that trained on it. Most enterprises can do the first and struggle with the rest, and the notice says nothing about the difference. That gap between what the subject reasonably expects from the notice and what the architecture delivers is the exposure, and no amount of notice revision closes it.

The decision rule is that every notice change must be paired with the enforcement point that makes it true, and any notice statement without an enforcement point is recorded as an open commitment rather than as completed work. Maintain that list explicitly. A privacy function that can produce a list of the commitments its notices make and the enforcement mechanism behind each one has an honest picture of its exposure. A function whose notice was updated by counsel and never mapped to a pipeline has made a set of promises that nobody has checked the enterprise can keep.

Four Poisonings, Not One: Where the Corruption Enters and What It Changes

Data poisoning is discussed in most security programs as a single risk with a single control, and treating it that way produces a program that defends one entry point and leaves three open. Four distinct attacks share the label, they enter at different points, they persist for different durations, and they require different detection. Separating them is the first useful thing a privacy and data protection function can do with the concept, because the separation determines who owns each one.

Training data poisoning corrupts what the model learned. It enters during training or fine-tuning, it persists in the weights, and it affects every use of that model until the model is replaced. For an enterprise consuming foundation models, this is largely a supply chain exposure governed through the Bill of Materials and the provider relationship rather than through anything the data protection function controls directly. For an enterprise fine-tuning on its own data, it is a pipeline integrity problem with a named owner in the data organization and a lineage requirement.

Retrieval poisoning corrupts what the model reads at inference. It enters through any source the retrieval layer draws from, it persists as long as the poisoned content remains indexed, and it affects every query whose retrieval reaches it. This is the most accessible of the four to an attacker and the most tractable for a defender, because the corpus is enumerable and the content is inspectable. Source provenance, write authorization on indexed corpora, and periodic integrity checks against a known state are the controls, and the owner is whoever owns the knowledge base rather than whoever owns the model.

Agent memory poisoning corrupts what an individual agent believes about its own history and context. It enters through anything the agent writes to memory, which in most implementations includes content the agent encountered rather than only content a human supplied. It persists until memory is purged and it affects that agent's future behavior in ways that survive session boundaries, credential rotation, and host isolation. This is the one most enterprises have no control for at all, and the minimum viable control is memory that is versioned, attributable, and restorable to a prior state.

Organizational knowledge poisoning is the fourth and the one with the longest tail, because it corrupts what the enterprise believes rather than what a system outputs. An analysis derived from poisoned retrieval, accepted by a human, incorporated into a decision document, and cited in subsequent work has entered the enterprise's institutional knowledge, where no technical control reaches it. The defense is not technical. It is the provenance discipline that lets the enterprise trace a conclusion back to its sources, which is what makes the difference between remediating a corrupted knowledge base and remediating a corrupted set of beliefs. Own each of the four explicitly, name the owner, and stop treating a single control as coverage for a category that has four distinct entry points.

FIGURE 10.7 **Four Poisonings, Not One**

Where corruption enters and what each one changes.

ENTRY POINT	WHAT IS POISONED	OBSERVED EFFECT	DETECTION SIGNAL
Training data	The model's learned behavior	A backdoor from a small sample set, normal otherwise	Provenance and acceptance testing
Retrieval corpus	What the model reads	A handful of documents dominating a targeted answer	Retrieval lineage and content integrity
Agent memory	What the model remembers	A payload activating across later sessions and tasks	Memory write auditing
Tool description	What the model is told to do	Instructions executed from metadata as guidance	Tool registry and content inspection

FOUR ENTRY POINTS, FOUR CONTROLS. ONE OF THEM IS NOT A STRATEGY.

Putting It Into Practice

The foundations are broken. The privacy program that governed data collection and storage is operating in an environment where data is also being reasoned with, remembered, and derived in ways none of its foundational assumptions anticipated. This month, the program measures the damage honestly. The actions below are specific, sequenced, and owned. They don't complete the rebuild. They start it with the evidence needed to justify and direct the rebuild that follows.

Map where subject data actually lives across the AI stack for your five highest-risk AI systems. The mapping covers four locations: model weights and any training datasets that contributed to them, embedding databases and vector stores, agent memory and context stores, and fine-tuned model variants that reference training data containing personal data. For each location, document two things: whether personal data is present, and whether the current erasure workflow can reach it. The gap between those two columns is your erasure certification exposure. That document goes to the General Counsel this month with a specific request: assess whether the gap requires regulatory disclosure, whether the technical infeasibility defense is available and documentable, and whether any pending erasure requests need to be re-evaluated against the actual scope of what was deleted.

Ask the inference question of your five highest-risk AI systems. For each system, identify the input data categories it processes and map the sensitive attributes that could plausibly be derived from those inputs. Then check each derived attribute against the existing consent framework and the privacy notices that govern the relevant data collection. Document every derived attribute that isn't covered by an existing consent basis or disclosure. Those undocumented derivations are the inference risk inventory. The inventory goes to the CPO and the General Counsel as a named finding. The finding triggers a legal assessment of whether the current consent and disclosure framework needs to be extended to cover inference before the next regulatory examination asks the question.

Inventory agent memory in one business unit. Choose the business unit with the highest volume of customer-facing agent interactions. Work with the team operating those agents to document what the context stores contain, how long context persists, and whether it's captured in any existing data inventory. Add agent memory as a new category to the data map for that business unit, with a preliminary classification, a proposed retention period, and a flag for the deletion procedure gap. That inventory is the first entry in what will become the enterprise-wide agent memory data map. It's also the concrete example you bring to the CPO and the General Counsel when making the case that agent memory needs to be treated as a governed personal data asset, not as an operational system component that falls outside the privacy program's scope.

Run shadow AI discovery jointly with the CISO this month, using privacy exposure as the primary assessment lens. For each tool discovered, document the personal data categories it was processing, the applicable regulatory framework for that data, and the exposure from processing that occurred before discovery. Bring the complete findings to the CPO and the General Counsel before the end of the month. The briefing covers four things: what was found, what the regulatory exposure is, whether any notification obligations were triggered, and what the immediate remediation actions are. That briefing is the starting point for the joint shadow AI governance program that the CPO and the CISO will co-own going forward.

Brief the CPO and the General Counsel on all four findings together, not separately. The four findings, erasure certification exposure, inference risk inventory, agent memory gap, and shadow AI privacy exposure, are related. They're all symptoms of the same underlying problem: a privacy program built for a data environment that no longer exists in the form it was designed to govern. Presenting them together makes the case for the foundation rebuild that the next chapter addresses. Presenting them separately makes them look like four discrete issues that can be patched independently. They can't. The rebuild requires a coherent response to all four simultaneously, and the CPO and the General Counsel need to understand that before the next chapter gives the privacy function the engine to govern what it can finally see.

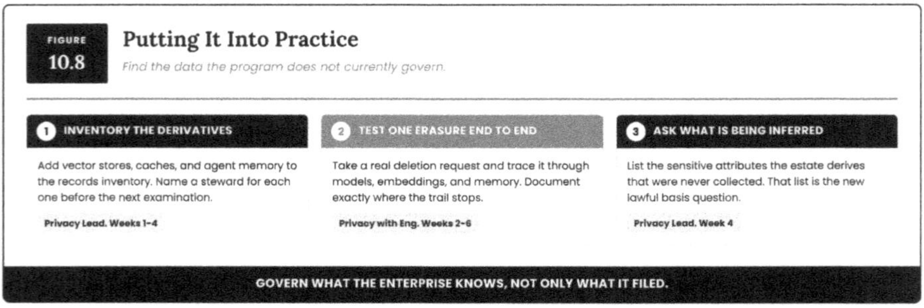

Chapter 11: Privacy Gains an Engine

Governing What the Enterprise Knows, Not Just What It Stores

CHAPTER 11 OUTCOMES

At the end of this chapter, you will be able to:

1. Discover and classify data across the estate rather than sampling known stores.
2. Apply semantic DLP that understands meaning instead of matching patterns.
3. Engineer erasure so the right to be forgotten is operationally real.
4. Enforce purpose as code so consent governs the pipeline.
5. Govern enterprise memory as a controlled store with a defined lifecycle.
6. Produce the evidence a privacy examination actually requests.

PRIVACY BECOMES AN ENGINEERING DISCIPLINE OR IT STAYS A WRITTEN COMMITMENT.

The End of the Unknown Data Store: Complete Discovery and Classification

Chapter 10 ended with four findings on the CPO's desk. Erasure certification exposure. Inference risk inventory. Agent memory gaps. Shadow AI privacy exposure. Each one was a symptom of the same underlying problem: a privacy program built on the assumption that personal data lives in identifiable stores, moves through traceable flows, and can be found when someone goes looking. That assumption was reasonable for the technology it was designed to govern. It stopped being reasonable the moment the enterprise deployed AI at scale.

The data map the privacy program relied on was always incomplete. The question was whether the incompleteness was manageable. For databases, file shares, and structured applications, the gaps were small enough that a disciplined discovery process could close them. For AI systems, the gaps aren't small. They're structural. Model weights, embedding databases, vector stores, agent memory, cached context, prompt logs, and output histories are all personal data locations that no traditional discovery methodology was designed to find. The privacy program wasn't missing a few data stores. It was missing an entire layer of the enterprise's data environment.

AI ends that constraint the same way it ended the sampling constraint in governance and the volume constraint in security operations. Machine-driven classification running continuously across the full estate doesn't get tired. It doesn't have a backlog. It doesn't need to prioritize which systems to scan this quarter because it can scan all of them. When discovery runs continuously rather than annually, the data map stops being a project deliverable and becomes a living instrument. The gap between what the privacy program is responsible for governing and what it can actually see closes for the first time.

That's not a small change. It's the foundational shift that makes everything else in this chapter possible.

The architectural model for complete discovery has three distinct layers, and all three need to be running before the data map qualifies as current. The first layer is the traditional estate: databases, file shares, SaaS platforms, structured data repositories. Most enterprises have some discovery tooling covering this layer already. The gap is usually cadence, not capability. Discovery that runs annually or quarterly produces a snapshot. Discovery that runs continuously produces a current picture. The upgrade isn't a new tool. It's a configuration change that moves the existing tool from periodic to continuous operation, with exception-based alerting when new personal data locations are detected.

The second layer is the AI-native estate: prompts, outputs, embedding databases, vector stores, fine-tuned model training data, and retrieval-augmented generation source documents. This layer requires discovery tooling that understands AI data structures, not just relational schemas and file hierarchies. A discovery tool that can find a customer record in a database but can't identify personal data in an embedding vector isn't covering the AI-native layer. The capability gap here is real for most enterprises, and it needs to be named explicitly before the tooling evaluation begins. The question to ask of any discovery tool being evaluated for this layer is direct: can it identify personal data in embedding databases and vector stores, and can it flag prompt logs and output histories as personal data locations? If the answer is no or uncertain, the tool covers the traditional layer and leaves the AI-native layer dark.

The third layer is agent memory. This is the layer that no discovery methodology was designed for, because agent memory doesn't behave like any other data store the privacy program has encountered. It accumulates incrementally. It changes with every interaction. It may be structured differently depending on which agent framework the enterprise uses. And its content is often a mixture of data types: factual information the agent was given, inferences the agent drew, preferences the agent observed, and context the agent accumulated over time. Discovering personal data in agent memory requires working directly with the teams that operate the agents to understand how memory is structured, where it's stored, and how it can be queried. That conversation needs to happen this month for every agent in production that interacts with data subjects. The output isn't just a data location. It's a documented understanding of what the agent knows, about whom, and for how long.

The classification model that runs on top of continuous discovery needs to handle AI-native data categories that traditional classification frameworks don't include. Standard classification tiers, public, internal, confidential, restricted, were designed for documents and records. They don't map cleanly onto embedding vectors, which contain personal data in a distributed, non-human-readable form, or onto agent memory entries, which may contain sensitive inferences alongside factual observations. The classification model needs two additions. First, an AI-native data category that captures data held in AI-specific formats and triggers AI-specific handling requirements. Second, an inferred data subcategory that flags data derived by AI systems rather than collected directly, because inferred data carries different consent and regulatory implications than collected data even when it's equally sensitive.

Stand up continuous discovery in one business unit this quarter, including the AI-native layer. Choose the business unit with the highest concentration of AI agent deployments. Run discovery across all three layers simultaneously. Measure how much personal data the AI-native layer contains that the previous annual discovery cycle never captured. That number is your evidence for the CPO, the General Counsel, and the CISO. It quantifies the gap between what the privacy program thought it was governing and what it was actually responsible for. It also makes the case for extending continuous discovery to the full enterprise estate, because the number will be large enough that the case makes itself.

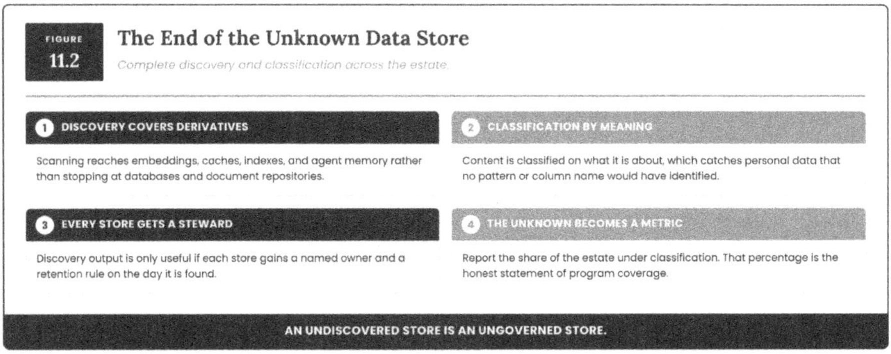

Semantic DLP: Understanding Meaning, Not Matching Patterns

Pattern-matching data loss prevention was built for a specific threat model. A credit card number has a recognizable structure. A social security number has a recognizable format. A passport number follows a defined pattern. Write a regex, match the pattern, flag the output. That approach works when sensitive data has a consistent, machine-readable signature. It fails completely when sensitive data is expressed in natural language without a single regulated identifier in sight.

Consider what a paragraph describing a patient's condition looks like to a pattern-matching DLP rule. No credit card number. No social security number. No date of birth in a recognized format. No identifier that matches any regex in the rule library. The paragraph contains highly sensitive health information expressed in plain language. The DLP rule sees clean text and passes it through. The information leaves the governed boundary. No alert fires. The traditional DLP architecture did exactly what it was designed to do. It just wasn't designed for this.

Semantic DLP understands meaning. It doesn't look for patterns. It reads the content and evaluates whether the meaning of the content constitutes sensitive data under the applicable classification and regulatory framework. A paragraph describing a patient's condition without a single regulated identifier is health data. Semantic DLP knows that because it understands what the words mean, not because it matched a format. A conversation that reveals an employee's salary negotiation position without containing the word "salary" or a dollar amount in a recognized format is confidential business information. Semantic DLP knows that too.

The AI gateway is the architectural pattern where semantic DLP enforcement converges with the rest of the AI security controls this book has been building. The gateway sits at the boundary between the enterprise's governed AI environment and the outside world, inspecting every prompt before it leaves and every output before it arrives. It's the enforcement point for the privacy controls that pattern-matching DLP was never equipped to enforce. Every prompt that contains sensitive data gets evaluated before it reaches an external model. Every output that derives or reveals sensitive attributes gets filtered before it reaches the user. The gateway is where policy becomes enforcement rather than documentation.

Prompt inspection at the gateway has three specific functions. The first is content classification: reading the prompt and classifying the data it contains against the enterprise's classification model, including the AI-native and inferred data categories added in the previous section. A prompt that contains personal data classified as restricted triggers a different response than a prompt that contains only public information. The response might be a block, a redaction, a re-routing to a governed model, or a logged exception that goes to the privacy team for review. The specific response is defined in the gateway's policy configuration, which is owned by the privacy function and reviewed quarterly.

The second function is purpose enforcement. The gateway checks whether the prompt's apparent purpose is consistent with the data subject's consent and the declared use case for the AI system receiving the prompt. A prompt that sends customer health data to a model approved for marketing analytics is a purpose mismatch. The gateway flags it, blocks the transmission, and logs the exception. This is purpose limitation enforced at the point of processing rather than audited after the fact. The difference between those two approaches is the difference between a control and a review. Controls prevent. Reviews discover. The gateway is a control.

The third function is exfiltration detection through AI channels. Traditional DLP was never designed to watch AI channels because AI channels didn't exist when DLP was built. An employee who pastes a confidential document into a prompt and sends it to an external AI service is exfiltrating data through a channel that regex-based DLP doesn't monitor. The gateway monitors it. Every prompt is evaluated for content that shouldn't be leaving the governed environment. Every output is evaluated for content that suggests the model received sensitive data it shouldn't have. The gateway closes the exfiltration channel that pattern-matching DLP left permanently open.

Output filtering is the other half of the gateway's enforcement function. AI outputs can reveal sensitive attributes that weren't explicitly present in the input. A model that has been trained on or exposed to personal data may produce outputs that derive sensitive conclusions about individuals. Output filtering evaluates every response for content that constitutes sensitive data under the classification model, including derived attributes, and either redacts the sensitive content before delivery or flags the output for human review. This is the control that addresses inference risk at the point of output rather than at the point of collection. It doesn't prevent the model from deriving sensitive attributes. It prevents those derivations from leaving the governed boundary without review.

Deploy prompt inspection and output filtering at the AI gateway for your highest-risk AI channel this quarter. The highest-risk channel is the one where the most sensitive data categories flow and where the current DLP coverage is weakest. Configure the gateway's policy against the classification model, including the AI-native and inferred data categories. Run the gateway in logging mode for the first 30 days before switching to enforcement mode. The logging period tells you how much sensitive data is currently flowing through that channel without inspection. That number is the second piece of evidence you bring to the CPO and the General Counsel. The first was the discovery gap. This is the exfiltration gap. Together they make the case for the full semantic DLP deployment across the enterprise's AI channels.

The policy configuration that governs the gateway is a privacy artifact, not a security artifact. The CISO's team operates the gateway. The privacy function owns the policy that tells the gateway what to block, what to flag, and what to pass. That ownership distinction matters because the policy decisions are privacy decisions: what data categories require blocking, what purpose mismatches require flagging, what output content requires filtering. The security team implements those decisions. The privacy team makes them. Both functions need to understand their respective roles before the gateway goes live, because a gateway operating on an unconfigured or misconfigured policy is worse than no gateway. It creates false assurance that sensitive data is being protected when it isn't.

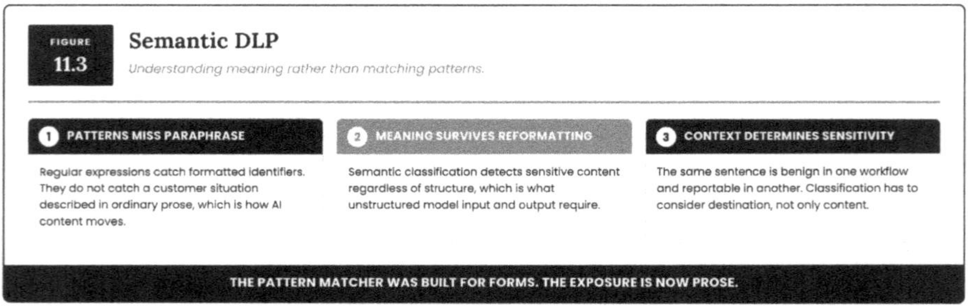

Erasure Engineering: Making the Right to Be Forgotten Operationally Real

Chapter 10 named the deletion problem. This section builds the answer. The answer isn't a single workflow. It's an erasure operating model that covers every layer of the AI stack where personal data lives, assigns a named owner to each layer, defines the deletion procedure for each location type, and documents the defensible position for the locations where technical deletion isn't possible. The CPO and the General Counsel co-own this model. It needs to be built before the next erasure request arrives for data that lives in a layer the current workflow can't reach.

Automated subject-data location is the first component. When an erasure request arrives, the first question is: where does this subject's data live? In a traditional privacy program, that question gets answered by querying the data map and manually checking the identified locations. In an AI-native environment, the data map covers the traditional estate but not the AI-native layer, which means the manual check misses model contributions, embedding entries, agent memory, and cached context. Automated subject-data location runs the query across all three discovery layers simultaneously: the traditional estate, the AI-native estate, and agent memory. The output is a complete location inventory for the specific data subject, produced in hours rather than weeks. That inventory is what the deletion workflow operates against.

The deletion workflow for each location type is specific to that type's technical characteristics. Traditional data stores get the standard deletion procedure: identify the records, delete them, confirm deletion, log the action. Embedding databases and vector stores require a different procedure: identify the embeddings that contain or were generated from the subject's data, delete those specific embedding entries, and rebuild any indexes that referenced them. Agent memory requires a targeted purge: identify every context store entry that contains the subject's data, delete those entries, and confirm that the agent's current context no longer contains information attributable to that subject. Prompt logs and output histories require a retention-based approach: if the logs are within the defined retention period, delete the subject's entries; if they exceed the retention period, confirm they've been purged under the standard retention policy.

Model weights are where the defensible position lives, and it needs to be documented before the first erasure request tests it. The technical reality, established in Chapter 10, is that personal data baked into model weights during training cannot be surgically removed. The regulatory response to that reality has three components. First, retention justification: document why the model was trained on data that included the subject's personal data, what the lawful basis for that training was, and why retraining the model to exclude that data isn't technically feasible or proportionate. Second, output suppression: configure the model to suppress outputs that specifically reproduce or reveal the subject's personal data, even though the underlying weights still contain the training influence. Third, retraining triggers: define the conditions under which a full model retrain would be required, meaning the volume of erasure requests or the sensitivity of the data involved that would make retraining proportionate, and document those thresholds in the erasure policy.

The retraining trigger threshold is the decision that requires both the CPO and the General Counsel. It's a legal and risk judgment, not a technical one. The CPO assesses the regulatory exposure of the current position. The General Counsel assesses the defensibility of the technical infeasibility argument under applicable law and the litigation risk if the position is challenged. Together they set the threshold: below this level of erasure requests involving model training data, the technical infeasibility defense is documented and maintained; above this level, a retraining cycle is triggered. That threshold is documented in the erasure policy, reviewed annually, and adjusted as the regulatory environment evolves.

Automated DSAR fulfillment turns the privacy team's heaviest manual burden into a pipeline. A data subject access request currently requires a human to query multiple systems, compile the results, review them for third-party data that shouldn't be disclosed, and produce a structured response within the regulatory deadline. In an enterprise running AI at scale, that manual process is no longer feasible at the volume and complexity the AI-native data environment requires. Automated DSAR fulfillment runs the subject-data location query automatically when a request arrives, compiles the results from all three discovery layers, applies the classification model to flag any content that requires human review before disclosure, and produces a structured response package that a human reviewer confirms before sending. The human's role shifts from data collector to quality reviewer. The pipeline handles the volume. The human handles the judgment.

Rebuild the erasure workflow to reach agent memory and embeddings this quarter. The rebuild has four steps. First, extend the automated subject-data location query to cover all three discovery layers. Second, define the deletion procedure for each AI-native location type and document it in the erasure policy. Third, document the model-weight defensible position with the General Counsel before the first request tests it. Fourth, configure the DSAR fulfillment pipeline to run the extended location query automatically when a request arrives. The rebuilt workflow doesn't need to be perfect on day one. It needs to cover the AI-native layer, which the current workflow doesn't. Every erasure request processed through the rebuilt workflow is a request the enterprise can certify with confidence rather than with the quiet knowledge that the certification excludes the AI stack.

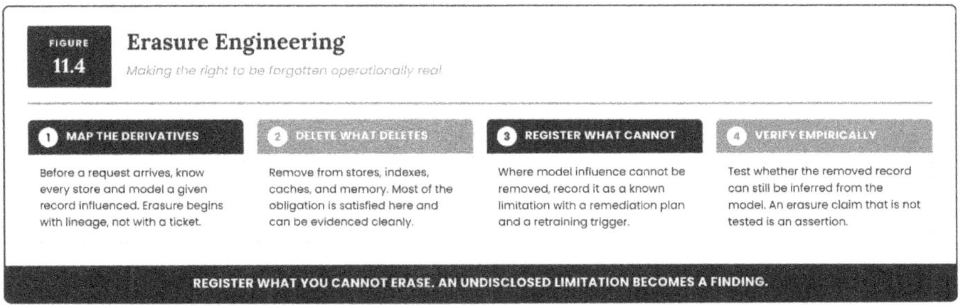

Purpose Enforcement as Code: Consent Governing the Pipeline

Purpose limitation is one of the oldest principles in data protection law. It's also one of the most consistently violated, not through malice but through architecture. The principle says that data collected for one purpose shouldn't be used for another. The architecture of most enterprise data environments makes that principle nearly impossible to enforce at scale. Data flows through pipelines. Pipelines connect systems. Systems serve multiple purposes. The connection between the original collection purpose and the current processing purpose disappears somewhere in the middle, and nobody has a mechanism to track it.

Policy documents don't enforce purpose limitation. They document it. The policy says data collected for customer service may not be used for marketing analytics. The pipeline that moves customer service data into the analytics platform doesn't read the policy. It moves the data because it was configured to move the data. The policy violation happens silently, at machine speed, without generating an alert, a log entry, or a human decision. Purpose limitation lived in documents while data moved through pipelines. That's why it collapsed.

Policy-as-code moves purpose limitation into the pipeline. Instead of a policy document that says what may not happen, a policy engine that sits in the data pipeline and enforces what may happen. The policy engine knows the classification of every dataset flowing through the pipeline, the consent status of every data subject whose data is in that dataset, and the declared use case of every model or application the pipeline feeds. Before data flows from one stage to the next, the policy engine checks: is this data category authorized for this use case under the consent basis that governs it? If yes, the data flows. If no, the pipeline stops and routes an exception to the privacy function for review.

Consent status enforced at the point of processing is what makes this different from consent status audited after the fact. Auditing after the fact finds violations that already happened. Enforcement at the point of processing prevents them. The difference matters enormously for the data subject whose data was processed without a valid consent basis. After-the-fact auditing finds the violation and triggers a remediation. At-the-point enforcement means the processing never happened, so there's nothing to remediate. That's a fundamentally different privacy outcome, and it's only achievable when the enforcement mechanism sits in the pipeline rather than in a review process that runs downstream of it.

Privacy-enhancing technologies are the deployable controls that make purpose enforcement operational at scale. Differential privacy adds mathematically calibrated noise to datasets before they're used for analytics or model training, preserving the statistical utility of the data while making it impossible to extract individual-level information. It's not a research concept. It's a deployable pattern that several major technology platforms already use for internal analytics. For the privacy function, it's the control that allows data to be used for purposes that wouldn't otherwise be authorized, because the privacy-preserving transformation changes the risk profile of the use. Synthetic data generation creates artificial datasets that preserve the statistical properties of real data without containing any real individuals' information. It's the control that allows AI model training to proceed on sensitive data categories by replacing the real data with a synthetic equivalent that carries none of the regulatory obligations. Federated learning trains models across distributed data sources without centralizing the data, allowing a model to learn from data held in multiple locations without any individual location's data leaving its governed boundary.

These three technologies aren't alternatives to purpose enforcement. They're complements to it. The policy engine enforces purpose limitation by blocking unauthorized uses. Privacy-enhancing technologies expand the set of authorized uses by transforming the data in ways that change its risk profile. Together they give the privacy function a toolkit that's capable of saying yes to data uses that the current framework can only say no to, because the transformation makes the use compliant rather than prohibited. That capability matters for the business relationship. A privacy function that can only say no to AI data uses becomes a bottleneck. A privacy function that can say "yes, with these transformations" becomes a partner.

Inference governance follows the same architecture. The policy engine that enforces purpose limitation for data inputs needs to be extended to cover model outputs. A model that derives sensitive attributes from non-sensitive inputs is producing data that carries regulatory implications regardless of the fact that it was derived rather than collected. The policy engine needs to evaluate the output's classification, not just the input's. If the output contains inferred health status, financial stress indicators, or other sensitive attributes, the policy engine applies the same consent and purpose checks to the output that it applies to the input. The inference doesn't escape purpose limitation just because it's a derivation rather than a collection. The policy engine treats it the same way.

Pilot purpose-as-code on one high-sensitivity pipeline this quarter. Choose a pipeline that currently moves personal data between a collection system and an AI application, where the connection between the original collection purpose and the current AI use is unclear or undocumented. Configure the policy engine against the classification model and the consent framework for the data in that pipeline. Run the engine in logging mode for 30 days. The logging period will surface every instance where data flowed through the pipeline without a documented consent basis or purpose authorization. Those instances are the purpose collapse findings that Chapter 10 named. Seeing them quantified in a 30-day log makes the case for extending the policy engine to every pipeline in the enterprise. The number of undocumented flows will be larger than anyone in the room expects.

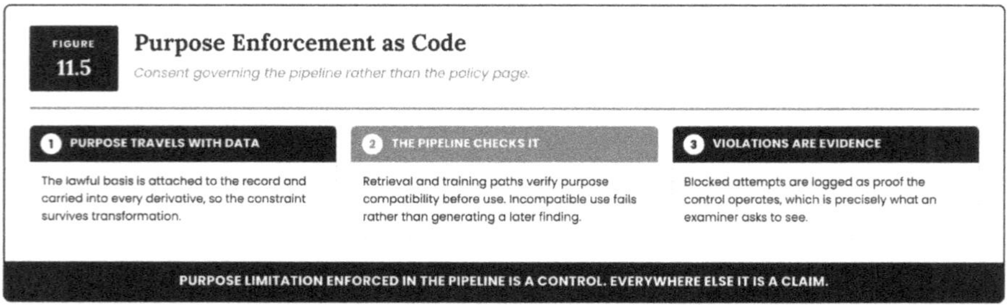

Enterprise Memory Governance: The Discipline Nobody Had a Control For

Every domain in this book has confronted a version of the same problem: a new class of asset that the existing control framework wasn't designed to govern. Governance confronted autonomous agents making decisions nobody approved. The SOC confronted machine reasoning being corrupted without triggering a single traditional alert. Third-party risk confronted agent-to-agent supply chains operating outside any established trust framework. Privacy confronted inference creating regulated data from unregulated inputs.

Enterprise memory is the asset class that sits underneath all of those problems and connects them. When an AI agent maintains context across sessions, it accumulates a persistent record of what the enterprise knows, what it has decided, and what it believes. That record isn't a database. It isn't a document. It's the operational memory of an autonomous system that influences every future decision the system makes. It contains personal data. It contains confidential business information. It contains inferences the agent drew from its interactions. And until this chapter, it had no control framework at all.

The formal definition of enterprise memory for governance purposes covers four categories. Conversation history is the record of interactions between agents and users, containing the content of those interactions and the context the agent drew from them. Decision logs are the records of conclusions the agent reached and actions it took, including the reasoning chain that produced those conclusions. Accumulated context is the persistent information the agent carries forward from session to session about users, processes, and organizational state. Inferred attributes are the conclusions the agent drew about individuals, systems, or situations that weren't explicitly provided as inputs but were derived from the patterns the agent observed.

All four categories are personal data when they contain information about identifiable individuals. All four are confidential business information when they contain information about the enterprise's processes, decisions, or strategies. All four require classification, access control, and retention limits applied with the same rigor as any other sensitive data store. The fact that they live in an AI system's operational memory rather than in a database doesn't change their regulatory status. It just means the governance framework that applies to databases hasn't been extended to reach them yet.

The lifecycle model for enterprise memory has five stages, and each stage requires a defined governance action. Creation is the stage where memory is first established: when an agent begins accumulating context about a user or a process. The governance action at creation is classification: every memory entry should be classified at the moment it's created, using the same classification model applied to other enterprise data. Validation is the stage where accumulated memory is checked for accuracy: is what the agent believes about a user or a process actually correct? The governance action at validation is a defined review cadence, because memory that contains inaccurate information is both a privacy risk and an intelligence corruption risk. The agent makes future decisions based on what it remembers. If what it remembers is wrong, those decisions are wrong.

Retention is the stage where the enterprise decides how long memory should persist. The governance action at retention is a defined retention policy: enterprise memory should not persist indefinitely by default. Every memory category should have a defined retention period, after which the memory is purged unless there's a documented justification for extended retention. That retention period needs to be set by the privacy function in consultation with the legal team, not by the engineering team that built the agent. The engineering team's default is to retain everything indefinitely because storage is cheap. The privacy function's default is to retain only what's necessary for as long as it's necessary, because that's what data minimization requires.

Correction is the stage where inaccurate memory is identified and fixed. The governance action at correction is a defined correction procedure: when a data subject exercises their right to rectification, or when a validation review identifies inaccurate memory, the correction procedure specifies how the inaccurate memory entry is located, corrected, and logged. This is the enterprise memory equivalent of the data correction workflow that applies to databases. It doesn't currently exist for most enterprises because enterprise memory wasn't recognized as a governed data asset until this chapter named it as one.

Deletion is the fifth stage, and it connects directly to the erasure engineering model from the previous section. The governance action at deletion is the purge procedure: when a retention period expires, when a data subject exercises their right to erasure, or when an agent is decommissioned, the purge procedure specifies how memory is located, deleted, and confirmed as deleted. The purge procedure needs to cover all four memory categories and needs to be tested before it's needed, not discovered to be incomplete when the first erasure request or agent decommission triggers it.

Knowledge-poisoning defense is the governance requirement that connects enterprise memory to the SOC's corruption detection program. An agent's accumulated memory is a target for manipulation. If an attacker can alter what an agent remembers about a user, a process, or a decision, they can steer the agent's future outputs without touching the model itself. The defense against knowledge poisoning has two components. The first is integrity monitoring: the memory store should be monitored for unauthorized changes, using the same hash-comparison and anomaly detection logic described in Chapter 5 for retrieval pipeline integrity. The second is validation cadence: a defined review process where a human reviewer checks a sample of memory entries against the ground truth sources the agent was supposed to be drawing from. Inaccuracies that aren't explained by legitimate updates are knowledge-poisoning signals that go to the SOC for investigation.

Deletion authority needs to be formally assigned before it's needed. The question of who can authorize the purge of an agent's accumulated memory isn't a technical question. It's a governance question. The answer should be the privacy function for memory containing personal data, the CISO for memory containing security-sensitive information, and the relevant business unit leader for memory containing confidential business information. Those three authorities should be documented in the Decision Rights RACI from Part I, extended to cover enterprise memory as a named asset class. A purge that happens without documented authority is a governance gap. A purge that happens with documented authority is a governance action.

Formally classify enterprise memory as a data category with an owner and a purge procedure this quarter. The classification is the governance action that brings enterprise memory inside the privacy program's scope. The owner is the privacy function, with the CISO as co-owner for the security-sensitive dimensions. The purge procedure is the documented process for each of the five lifecycle stages. That three-part action, classification, owner, purge procedure, is what converts enterprise memory from an ungoverned operational component into a governed data asset. It's also the action that answers a regulator asking what happened to the data an agent held for twelve months. The answer is: it was classified as enterprise memory, governed under the retention policy, and purged according to the documented procedure on this date, confirmed by this owner. That's a defensible answer. The absence of that answer is not.

FIGURE 11.6

Enterprise Memory Governance

The discipline nobody previously had a control for.

1 MEMORY IS A DATA STORE

Treat it as: a system of record.

Durable agent memory holds personal data, persists across sessions, and requires a steward, a retention rule, and an inventory entry.

2 WRITES ARE CHANGES

Treat them as: state changes.

Every write alters future behavior. Unaudited writes are unreviewed changes to a production system that reasons.

3 THE VECTOR STORE PERSISTS

Treat it as: an exfiltration layer.

Embeddings retain content and can be queried. The store is both a persistence layer and a path out of the enterprise.

4 RETENTION APPLIES

Treat it as: in scope.

Memory that never expires is a collection with no retention limit, which no privacy program would knowingly approve.

AGENT MEMORY IS A DATA STORE THAT ARRIVED WITHOUT A STEWARD.

The Privacy Operating Rhythm: Continuous Discovery, Enforced Purpose, and a Quarterly Attestation That Holds

Privacy is the domain where the gap between a documented control and an operating one carries the most direct legal consequence, because privacy is the domain that produces signed attestations to external parties on a fixed schedule. An erasure certification is a statement of fact about what the enterprise did. A records-of-processing entry is a statement of fact about what the enterprise does. Both are produced quarterly or annually in most programs, and both are assembled from a discovery picture that was accurate when the discovery ran. The rhythm below exists to make sure the attestation and the architecture are describing the same enterprise.

The continuous horizon belongs to the pipeline, and it is the only domain in this Volume where the primary control runs without a human in the loop by design. Purpose enforcement executes at the gateway: every request carrying regulated data is checked against the consent basis recorded for that data and the declared purpose of the requesting system, and a mismatch blocks rather than logs. Semantic data loss prevention runs in the same path, evaluating meaning rather than matching patterns, which is what catches the regulated content that a pattern-matching rule was never going to see. Both produce exception queues, and both are useless if the queues are unattended.

The weekly horizon attends those queues and does one thing beyond triage: it feeds the discovery picture. Blocked requests reveal systems attempting to use data in ways nobody registered. Semantic findings reveal data classes present in stores that were classified as containing something else. Each of those is a discovery signal that arrives from enforcement rather than from scanning, and it is generally higher quality than scanning output because it reflects actual use. The privacy engineer routes newly discovered stores into the classification pipeline and newly discovered flows into the data flow map, which is how the map stays current between formal discovery cycles.

The monthly horizon runs the erasure verification sample, and this is the practice that separates a certification the enterprise can defend from one it merely signs. Take a sample of erasure requests completed in the prior month and verify, per request, that the data is absent from every location the erasure register names: primary stores, replicas, backups within the retention window, vector indexes, retrieval caches, agent memory, and any fine-tuning dataset. Record the locations where verification failed and why. A sample that produces zero failures in the first several months of a program is a sample that is checking the locations the program already knew how to clear.

The quarterly horizon produces the attestation, and it should be produced against the verification evidence rather than against the process description. The distinction is the whole point of the rhythm. An enterprise attesting that it honors erasure requests is making a claim; an enterprise attesting that it honors erasure requests, with a documented verification sample and a named list of the derived representations covered and not covered, is making a defensible one. Annually, the enforcement policies are recalibrated against the year's regulatory movement and the memory governance standard is reviewed against what agent memory actually accumulated, which in most enterprises will be more than the standard anticipated.

Proving It: The Evidence a Privacy Examination Actually Requests

Privacy programs prepare for examinations by assembling policies, and examinations increasingly ask for something else. The shift is from documentation of intent to evidence of operation, and it is the same shift every other domain in this Volume has described, arriving in the domain with the most immediate legal consequence. A privacy officer who can produce a complete policy set, a current record of processing, and a data protection impact assessment for every system is well prepared for the examination that regulators were conducting five years ago.

What is being asked for now, with increasing frequency, falls into four categories that policies do not cover. The first is verification evidence for erasure claims: not the process description, but a sample of completed requests with proof that the data is absent from each location the enterprise says it reached. The second is enforcement evidence for purpose limitation: not the policy stating that data is used only for stated purposes, but the log showing requests that were blocked because they were not. The third is discovery completeness: how the enterprise knows its data map covers the estate, and what mechanism would surface a store nobody registered. The fourth is inference: what sensitive attributes the enterprise's AI systems are capable of deriving, and what assessment established that.

Each of those maps to an artifact this chapter has already built, which is the useful observation. The erasure verification sample is the monthly practice from the operating rhythm. The enforcement log is the gateway's exception queue. The discovery completeness argument is the continuous discovery capability plus the enforcement-derived signals that surface unregistered stores. The inference position is the pre-deployment assessment. A program running the rhythm in this chapter is already producing the examination evidence as a byproduct, which is the difference between a program that prepares for examinations and one that is examinable at any time.

The assembly problem is what remains, and it is worth solving before an examination rather than during one. Evidence distributed across a gateway log, a verification spreadsheet, a discovery platform, and an assessment repository is evidence that takes three weeks to assemble under pressure, and three weeks is roughly the response window most examinations allow. Designate the assembly format in advance, run it once as a rehearsal, and record how long it took and what was missing. That rehearsal is the privacy equivalent of the kill-switch exercise, and it produces the same category of finding: dependencies nobody documented and gaps nobody had looked for.

The decision rule is that any privacy claim the enterprise makes externally has a named evidence source that can be produced within five business days. Erasure certifications, records of processing, vendor questionnaire responses, and customer contract representations all qualify. Walk the list, name the source for each, and mark the ones where the honest answer is that the claim would require reconstruction. Those are the exposures, they are enumerable in an afternoon, and enumerating them is materially cheaper before someone asks than after.

FIGURE 11.7 **Proving It**

The evidence a privacy examination actually requests.

EXAMINER QUESTION	EVIDENCE PRODUCED	SOURCE SYSTEM	CADENCE
What personal data do you hold	Classified inventory including derivatives	Discovery platform	Continuous
On what basis do you process it	Purpose register with pipeline enforcement logs	Policy engine	Continuous
Can you delete it on request	Erasure trace plus the limitation register	Erasure workflow	Per request
What does the model infer	Derived attribute register and access tiers	Model registry	Quarterly
Who can reach it	Access review across stores and memory	IAM	Quarterly

EVIDENCE ASSEMBLED CONTINUOUSLY SURVIVES AN EXAMINATION THE QUARTER IT ARRIVES.

The Vector Store as a Persistence and Exfiltration Layer

Embedding stores are treated in most enterprises as infrastructure rather than as data stores, and the classification error has consequences in three directions. They frequently sit outside the discovery scope because they contain vectors rather than records. They frequently sit outside the access control review because they were provisioned by a platform team as a component. And they frequently sit outside the retention schedule because nobody could say what retaining a vector means. Each of those omissions is defensible individually and together they produce a store of regulated data with no owner, no review, and no expiry.

The persistence problem is the one that reaches the erasure work in this chapter. An embedding derived from a document containing personal data is a representation of that data, and the extent to which the original content can be recovered from it is a matter of active research rather than settled fact. The defensible position is to treat embeddings as containing what they were derived from until demonstrated otherwise, which means they belong in the erasure register, in the classification scheme, and in the retention schedule. An enterprise treating them as mathematical artifacts outside the privacy perimeter has taken a position it would struggle to defend to an examiner who asks how it reached that conclusion.

The exfiltration problem is less discussed and more immediate. A vector store queried without meaningful access control returns semantically similar content to whatever the querier asks about, which is a retrieval capability that ignores the document-level permissions the source system enforced. A user or an agent with query access to the index has effective read access to everything the index contains, regardless of what they were permitted to read in the originating repository. Enterprises discover this when someone asks the assistant a question and receives content from a system they have no access to, and the discovery usually happens in front of an audience.

Segmentation is the control and it has to be designed rather than added, which is why this belongs in the twelve-month plan rather than in a later phase. Indexes are partitioned along the same boundaries the source permissions use, queries carry the requesting identity through to the retrieval layer, and results are filtered against that identity rather than returned and then trimmed. Post-retrieval filtering is a common shortcut and a weak control, because the content was already retrieved into a context the requester may be able to influence. Filter at retrieval.

The decision rule is that every vector store appears in the data inventory with a named owner, a classification reflecting the most sensitive content it was derived from, an access model that honors source permissions, an integrity baseline, and a retention period. Any store failing any of those five is recorded as a gap with a date rather than accepted as infrastructure. The privacy function that adds this single class of store to its discovery scope will find more regulated data in one quarter than most other discovery expansions produce in a year.

Two related exposures belong in the same inventory entry and are frequently omitted from it. The first is that a model fine-tuned on enterprise data holds a representation of that data that can, under some conditions, be probed to determine whether a specific record was in the training set. For a fine-tune trained on customer records, employee records, or confidential deal material, that determination is itself a disclosure, and it is available to anyone with query access to the model rather than only to someone with access to the underlying store. The second is that high-value enterprise knowledge concentrated in a retrieval corpus is a more efficient target than the systems it was drawn from, because the corpus was assembled precisely to make that knowledge easy to surface. Treat query access to a fine-tuned model and to a retrieval corpus as access to the most sensitive material either was derived from, apply the same approval requirements, and record both in the data inventory with that classification rather than as infrastructure.

Model artifacts are the location where erasure most often stops, and the honest treatment is to distinguish what the enterprise can do from what it can only require. Where the enterprise fine-tuned a model on its own data, the options are retraining without the erased records, applying a machine unlearning technique that removes a specific example's influence without full retraining, or documenting the limitation and disclosing it. Unlearning is an active research area rather than a settled engineering practice, and an enterprise that certifies erasure on the strength of an unlearning technique should be able to state what verification supports the certification. Where the model belongs to a vendor, the enterprise has no options at all beyond what the contract secured, which is why unlearning capability belongs in the AI Bill of Materials as a disclosure field rather than in a conversation that happens after an erasure request arrives. Ask the question at onboarding: what is your capability to remove the influence of specific customer data from a model that has trained on it, and what evidence supports that capability. A vendor answering that they do not train on customer data has given the cleanest answer and one that should be contractually bound rather than accepted verbally.

Putting It Into Practice

Privacy can finally see. The continuous discovery program shows the full estate including the AI-native layer. The semantic DLP gateway inspects what flows in and out. The erasure operating model reaches what the old workflow couldn't. The purpose-as-code engine enforces what policy documents only described. And enterprise memory has a lifecycle, an owner, and a purge procedure for the first time.

This quarter, stand up continuous discovery in one business unit including the AI-native layer. Run discovery across all three layers: traditional estate, AI-native estate, and agent memory. Measure the gap between what the previous annual discovery cycle captured and what continuous discovery finds. Document the personal data locations in the AI-native layer that the old map never captured. That gap measurement is the quantified evidence of what the privacy program was responsible for governing but couldn't see. It goes to the CPO, the General Counsel, and the CISO as a named finding with a named owner and a 90-day plan for extending continuous discovery to the full enterprise estate.

Deploy prompt inspection and output filtering at the AI gateway for your highest-risk AI channel this quarter. Configure the gateway policy against the classification model, including the AI-native and inferred data categories. Run in logging mode for 30 days before switching to enforcement mode. The logging period produces the exfiltration gap measurement: how much sensitive data is currently flowing through that channel without inspection. That number goes to the CPO alongside the discovery gap measurement. Together they quantify the two largest privacy exposure gaps in the current program and make the case for the full semantic DLP deployment.

Rebuild the erasure workflow to reach agent memory and embeddings this quarter. Extend the automated subject-data location query to all three discovery layers. Define the deletion procedure for each AI-native location type. Document the model-weight defensible position with the General Counsel before the first erasure request tests it. The defensible position document is a joint artifact: the CPO drafts the privacy analysis, the General Counsel reviews the legal defensibility, and both sign off before it's filed. It doesn't need to be long. It needs to be clear, legally reviewed, and filed where the team can find it when they need it.

Pilot purpose-as-code on one high-sensitivity pipeline this quarter. Choose the pipeline where the connection between original collection purpose and current AI use is least documented. Configure the policy engine in logging mode. Run it for 30 days. Document every undocumented flow. Use the findings to build the case for extending the policy engine to every pipeline in the enterprise and for adding the three privacy-enhancing technologies, differential privacy, synthetic data, and federated learning, to the toolkit that allows the privacy function to say yes to data uses the current framework can only decline.

Formally classify enterprise memory as a data category with a named owner and a documented purge procedure this quarter. The classification action, the owner assignment, and the purge procedure documentation are three distinct deliverables. Each one needs to be complete before the quarter ends. The classification goes into the data map. The owner assignment goes into the Decision Rights RACI. The purge procedure goes into the erasure policy as a new section covering AI-native memory locations. Together they close the governance gap that no control framework previously addressed.

Brief the CPO on the expanded mandate before the quarter closes. The brief covers the new scope of the privacy program: not just governing what the enterprise collects and stores, but governing what it knows. Enterprise memory, inference outputs, purpose-as-code enforcement, and semantic DLP at the AI gateway are all new instruments in the privacy function's operating model. The CPO needs to understand the full scope of what's been built this quarter, what it governs, who owns each component, and what the remaining gaps are. That briefing is also the starting point for the conversation the next chapter addresses: where the privacy function is heading over the next twelve months, what the convergence between privacy governance and AI governance looks like at maturity, and whether the discipline that was once the smallest voice in the security conversation is about to inherit the largest mandate of all.

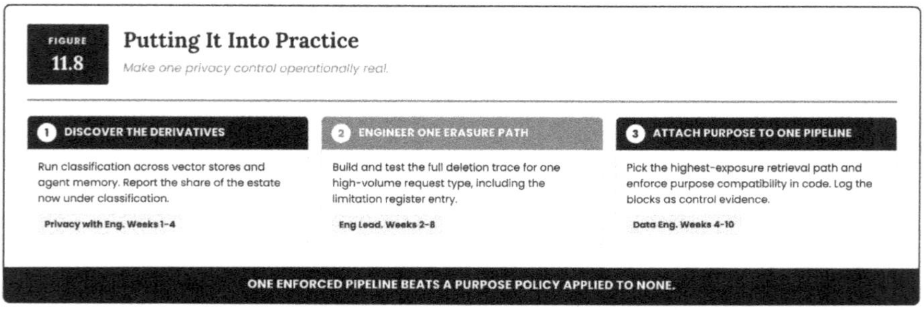

Chapter 12: The Privacy Endgame

Current Focus, Solution Categories, and the 1-Year Target Operating Model

CHAPTER 12 OUTCOMES

At the end of this chapter, you will be able to:

1. Describe where privacy programs are currently focused and funded.
2. Evaluate privacy solution categories as architectural patterns.
3. Answer whether privacy merges with AI governance.
4. Build a one-year privacy target operating model with owners and milestones.
5. Anticipate the regulatory clock over the next twelve months.
6. Complete the handoff that moves privacy from a legal function to an engineering one.

PRIVACY STOPS BEING A LEGAL OPINION AND BECOMES A PIPELINE PROPERTY.

The privacy function arrived at this chapter carrying more weight than any of the other three domains. Governance inherited a binder. The SOC inherited a detection gap. Third-party risk inherited a stale tier map. Privacy inherited all of those problems plus a set of foundational assumptions that AI broke completely. The previous two chapters named those broken assumptions and started building the instruments to govern what the program couldn't previously see. This chapter asks the harder question: where does all of that lead, and what does the privacy function look like when it's fully built for the environment it's actually operating in?

The answer is larger than most privacy teams expect. And more consequential than most CISOs have yet recognized.

Where the Market Is Now: The Current Focus of Privacy Programs

Most privacy programs right now are doing one of two things. They're either engineering real governance for the AI layer, or they're laminating AI language onto a foundation that was never designed to hold it. The programs doing the laminating often can't tell yet. That's not a failure of intent. It's a maturity problem in a discipline that's being rebuilt from scratch while the regulatory environment keeps shifting underneath it.

The first thing most programs build is an AI use register bolted onto the existing processing inventory. That makes sense as a starting move. The processing inventory already exists. Adding an AI column to it is fast, produces something the DPA can see, and signals that the privacy function is responding to AI. The problem isn't the register itself. The problem is what it doesn't capture. A processing inventory extended with an AI column tracks the systems the privacy team knows about, assessed against criteria that were accurate when the entry was created. It doesn't track agent memory. It doesn't track inference outputs. It doesn't track the model supply chain behind each AI system. It doesn't update when a vendor quietly enables a new AI feature. The register is current at the moment of entry and increasingly inaccurate every day after.

DPIAs retrofitted for AI systems are the second area of activity, and the quality spread is wide. The better programs have rebuilt their DPIA methodology from the ground up to account for AI-specific risk categories: inference risk, memory accumulation, purpose collapse, and the deletion problem. Those programs are running DPIAs that actually surface the risks the AI system carries. The weaker programs are running the same DPIA template they've always used, adding a section that asks whether the system uses AI, checking the box, and filing the result. A DPIA template designed to assess a database isn't equipped to assess an AI system that derives sensitive attributes, accumulates memory across sessions, and processes data through a model supply chain the privacy team can't see. The template produces a document. It doesn't produce an assessment.

The first AI-channel DLP deployments are appearing at the gateway in the more advanced programs, and this is where the real separation between engineered governance and laminated governance becomes visible. A program that has deployed semantic DLP at the AI gateway is enforcing purpose limitation and data classification at the point of processing. A program that has added AI-related language to its acceptable use policy is describing what should happen. One is a control. The other is documentation. The gap between those two things is the gap between a program that can tell a regulator what it prevented and a program that can only tell a regulator what it intended.

Erasure workflows quietly excluding the AI layer are the most common and most dangerous form of lamination in the market right now. The workflow runs. The request gets closed. The certification gets filed. And the model weights, embedding databases, and agent memory stores that hold the subject's data were never in scope. Nobody is lying. The workflow does what it was designed to do. It just wasn't designed for the AI layer, and nobody updated the design when the AI layer was added to the enterprise's data environment. The certification is wrong. The exposure is real. And in most enterprises, nobody knows it yet because the gap hasn't been tested by a regulator or a litigant.

Locating your program against this picture requires honesty that's uncomfortable but necessary. The question isn't whether your program is good. The question is whether it's governing the AI layer or governing around it. If your AI use register is a column in a spreadsheet that was last updated at audit time, that's lamination. If your DPIAs are running the same template against AI systems that they run against databases, that's lamination. If your erasure workflow certifies deletion without reaching agent memory or embedding databases, that's lamination. If your DLP rules are pattern-matching regexes watching non-AI channels while AI channels run uninspected, that's lamination. Name each one. They're your year-one gaps, and they need to be in the gap analysis before the budget conversation starts.

The programs that are genuinely ahead share three characteristics. They've rebuilt their DPIA methodology to handle AI-specific risk categories. They've deployed semantic DLP at the AI gateway before any regulator required it. And they've started the erasure engineering work described in Chapter 11, mapping where subject data actually lives across the AI stack and building deletion procedures for each location type. Those three characteristics separate the programs that will be defensible in the next regulatory examination from the programs that will be scrambling to reconstruct governance evidence when the examiner asks whether the erasure certification covers the AI layer.

The Solution Category Landscape: Patterns, Not Products

The privacy stack for AI governance has five distinct categories. Every mature program needs all five. Most programs have two or three and haven't named the gaps as gaps yet. Understanding the categories before evaluating any specific tool is what keeps budget from flowing into a second solution for a problem already solved while the actual coverage gap goes unfunded.

The first category is data security posture management extending into the AI-native layer. Traditional DSPM tools were built to discover and classify data in databases, file shares, and structured repositories. The AI-extended versions of those tools add the capability to discover and classify data in AI-native locations: embedding databases, vector stores, prompt logs, output histories, and agent memory stores. The evaluation criterion that separates genuine AI extension from rebranded legacy functionality is the AI-native discovery architecture. A tool that can identify personal data in a relational database but can't identify personal data in an embedding vector isn't covering the AI layer. Ask the vendor directly: can your tool discover personal data in embedding databases and vector stores? Can it identify agent memory as a personal data location? Can it classify inference outputs as derived personal data? The answers to those three questions tell you whether the tool covers the AI-native layer or just claims to.

The second category is the AI gateway as the enforcement point for prompt inspection and output governance. The gateway sits at the boundary between the enterprise's governed AI environment and the outside world. It inspects every prompt before it leaves and every output before it arrives. It enforces purpose limitation at the point of processing rather than auditing it after the fact. It detects exfiltration through AI channels that pattern-matching DLP was never designed to watch. The evaluation criterion in this category is the semantic understanding capability. A gateway that pattern-matches against known sensitive data formats is doing what traditional DLP already does. A gateway that reads the meaning of a prompt and evaluates whether that meaning constitutes sensitive data under the applicable classification framework is doing something traditional DLP cannot do. That distinction is the difference between a control that catches what it was explicitly configured to catch and a control that catches what it actually needs to catch.

The third category is privacy platforms absorbing AI governance duties. The privacy management platforms that handle DSAR automation, consent enforcement, processing registers, and privacy impact assessments are being extended to cover AI-specific functions. DSAR automation that reaches the AI-native layer, not just the traditional estate. Consent enforcement that tracks consent status through AI training pipelines, not just through collection forms. Processing registers that capture model supply chain dependencies, not just data flows between known systems. The key evaluation criterion in this category is whether the AI governance extension is native to the platform's data model or whether it's an add-on module that doesn't integrate with the core functions. A processing register that tracks AI systems as a separate module disconnected from the consent management function produces two separate pictures of the same risk. A platform where the AI governance functions share a data model with the core privacy functions produces one coherent picture. That coherence is what makes the platform useful for regulatory examination rather than just for internal reporting.

The fourth category is discovery and classification engines running continuously. This is the infrastructure that keeps the data map current rather than periodic. Continuous discovery doesn't run annually and produce a snapshot. It runs every day and produces a living picture of where personal data lives across the full estate, including the AI-native layer. The evaluation criterion here is the cadence architecture. A discovery tool that can be configured to run continuously, with exception-based alerting when new personal data locations are detected, is the right tool for this category. A tool that runs on a defined schedule and produces periodic reports is a better version of the annual discovery process, not a replacement for it. The distinction matters because the AI-native estate changes faster than any periodic schedule can track. New agents get deployed. Existing agents accumulate new memory. Embedding databases grow with every new document ingested. Continuous discovery is the only architecture that keeps pace with that rate of change.

The fifth category is privacy-enhancing technologies maturing from research to procurement. Differential privacy, synthetic data generation, and federated learning are no longer academic concepts. They're deployable controls with production implementations at major technology organizations, established evaluation frameworks, and growing vendor ecosystems. The evaluation criterion in this category is production readiness for the specific use case. Differential privacy that works for population-level analytics may not work for the fine-grained individual-level analysis a specific AI system requires. Synthetic data that preserves the statistical properties needed for model training may not preserve the properties needed for a specific downstream use case. Federated learning that works across homogeneous infrastructure may not work across the heterogeneous infrastructure most enterprises run. Evaluate each technology against the specific use case it's intended to serve, not against a general description of what the technology can do.

The privacy and AI governance stacks are converging onto the same platforms for a reason that goes beyond vendor consolidation strategy. They govern the same data, through the same enforcement points, for the same regulator. The data that flows through the AI gateway is the same data the privacy platform tracks for consent and purpose limitation. The personal data that the DSPM tool discovers in embedding databases is the same data the DSAR automation platform needs to locate when a subject access request arrives. The processing register that tracks AI systems is the same register the privacy impact assessment function needs to evaluate new deployments. When these functions run on separate platforms with separate data models, the privacy team spends significant effort connecting outputs manually. When they converge onto integrated platforms, the data flows automatically and the human effort goes into judgment rather than assembly. That's the architectural argument for convergence. It's stronger than any vendor's pricing model.

The category-level evaluation criteria that outlive any specific vendor are four questions applied to every tool in every category. Does it cover the AI-native layer or only the traditional estate? A tool that covers only the traditional estate is solving yesterday's problem. Does it run continuously or periodically? Periodic tools produce snapshots. Continuous tools produce governance. Does it integrate with the other categories in the stack, or does it require manual data transfer between systems? Manual transfer is a latency problem and a staffing cost. And does it produce evidence that's admissible in a regulatory examination, meaning evidence tied to a specific timestamp, a specific system state, and a specific control requirement? Evidence that can't be tied to those three things isn't governance evidence. It's documentation.

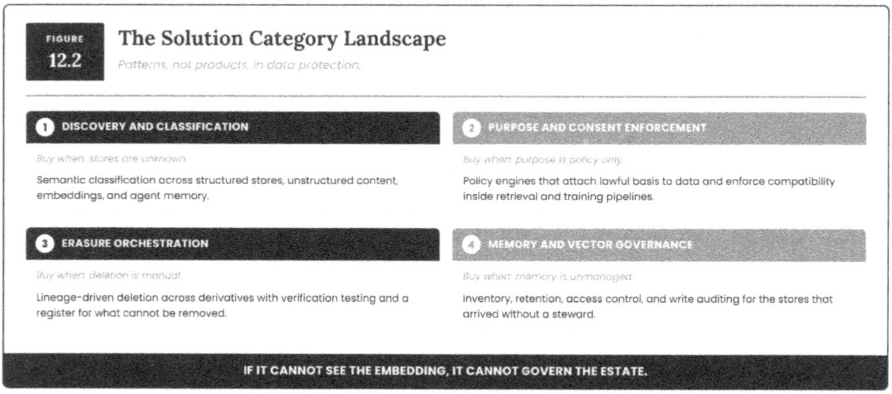

The Department Question: Does Privacy Merge With AI Governance?

The convergence case is structural. That's the honest starting point for this conversation, and the privacy leaders who understand it structurally will make better organizational decisions than the ones who treat it as a political question about turf.

Purpose limitation and inference control are becoming the same discipline. Purpose limitation asks: is this data being used for the purpose it was collected for? Inference control asks: is this AI system deriving attributes that exceed the purpose the data was collected for? Those are the same question asked at different points in the data lifecycle. The privacy function that governs purpose limitation and the AI governance function that controls inference are governing the same pipeline with the same underlying principle. Running them as separate functions with separate processes and separate reporting lines produces duplication, inconsistency, and gaps at the boundary between them. The boundary is exactly where the most consequential risks live.

The regulatory frameworks are merging faster than the org charts. The EU AI Act and the GDPR are being interpreted together by data protection authorities that treat AI governance as an extension of data protection law, not as a separate regulatory domain. The FTC's AI enforcement actions are grounded in consumer protection and data privacy frameworks, not in AI-specific legislation. The ICO's guidance on AI and data protection treats the two as inseparable. Regulators aren't waiting for enterprises to resolve their internal organizational questions about who owns AI governance. They're sending examination requests to the privacy function and expecting answers that cover both data protection and AI governance simultaneously.

The harder question isn't whether privacy and AI governance should converge. They already are converging, whether the org chart reflects it or not. The harder question is who owns enterprise knowledge and organizational memory when those become the most consequential governed assets in the enterprise.

The CPO has the strongest claim. Privacy law is the regulatory framework that most directly addresses what the enterprise may know about individuals, how long it may retain that knowledge, and what it must do when a subject asks for that knowledge to be erased. Enterprise memory is personal data. The CPO's mandate, extended to cover enterprise memory, is the logical governance home for the discipline that governs what the organization knows.

The CDO has a competing claim. Enterprise knowledge, including the intelligence derived from AI systems, is a data asset. The CDO owns data strategy, data quality, and data governance. Organizational memory is a data governance problem as much as it is a privacy problem. The CDO who extends their mandate to cover AI-derived knowledge has a legitimate claim on the governance of what the enterprise knows.

The CISO has the security claim. Enterprise memory is a target. It can be corrupted, exfiltrated, or manipulated. The security controls that protect it, the integrity monitoring, the access governance, the purge procedures, sit squarely in the CISO's domain. The CISO who treats enterprise memory as a security asset and builds the controls to protect it is doing security work that the privacy and data governance functions depend on.

The role that doesn't exist yet is the one that holds all three claims together. Call it the intelligence governance function. It governs what the enterprise may know, how it knows it, how long it retains that knowledge, and under what conditions it must forget. It sits at the intersection of privacy law, data governance, and security controls. It reports to whoever the organization decides is accountable for the governance of organizational intelligence, which is a decision that hasn't been made in most enterprises yet because the question hasn't been asked clearly enough.

Three new positions are emerging that map to this convergence. The inference governance analyst owns the assessment of what AI systems are deriving and whether those derivations are authorized under applicable consent and purpose frameworks. They work at the intersection of the privacy function and the AI governance function, running inference risk assessments on new AI deployments and monitoring inference outputs from systems already in production. The erasure engineer owns the technical implementation of deletion procedures across the AI stack. They're the person who builds and maintains the automated subject-data location query, the deletion workflows for each AI-native location type, and the model-weight defensible position documentation. They sit in the privacy function but work closely with the engineering teams that build and operate the AI systems. The memory governance steward owns the lifecycle management of enterprise memory. They define the classification, retention, correction, and deletion procedures for every category of agent memory and accumulated context in the enterprise. They're the person who answers a regulator asking what happened to the data an agent held for twelve months.

The convergence roadmap to bring to the CPO before the org chart is redrawn without you has three steps. The first step is a joint governance inventory: map every AI governance function currently operating in the enterprise, identify which functions sit in privacy, which sit in AI governance, which sit in security, and which sit in nobody's domain. The inventory surfaces the overlaps and the gaps simultaneously. The second step is a joint ownership proposal: for each governance function identified in the inventory, propose a primary owner and a co-owner, using the three-claim framework above to guide the assignment. The third step is a joint escalation path: define how the three functions, privacy, AI governance, and security, escalate to each other when a governance question touches all three domains. That escalation path is what prevents the convergence from producing three separate governance programs that all think they're governing the same thing.

Have that conversation with the CPO this month. Not next quarter. The org chart is being redrawn in most enterprises right now, often without the privacy function's input, because the AI governance function is being built by people who don't fully understand what the privacy function already governs. The CISO who brings the convergence roadmap to the CPO before the reorganization happens is the CISO who shapes the outcome. The CISO who waits for the org chart to be redrawn and then objects to the result has lost the conversation before it started.

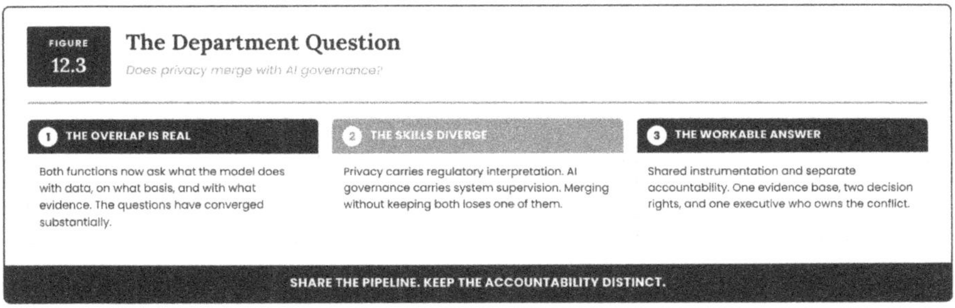

The 1-Year Privacy Target Operating Model

The 1-Year Privacy Target Operating Model isn't a vision statement. It's a specific set of capability builds, ownership assignments, and board-facing milestones that together answer the question every board is asking: what does it cost to govern what the enterprise knows, and what does the enterprise get for that investment?

Continuous discovery live including the AI-native layer is the first milestone. By the end of year one, the data map is no longer a periodic deliverable. It's a living instrument that reflects the current state of personal data across the full enterprise estate, including embedding databases, vector stores, agent memory, prompt logs, and output histories. The discovery program runs continuously, with exception-based alerting when new personal data locations are detected. Every alert has a named owner and a defined response timeline. The data map that the audit produced was accurate at a point in time. The year-one data map is accurate today, and it will be accurate tomorrow because the discovery program doesn't stop running between audit cycles.

AI-channel DLP at the gateway is the second milestone. By the end of year one, semantic DLP is enforcing purpose limitation and data classification at the AI gateway for every high-risk AI channel in the enterprise. The gateway is inspecting prompts before they leave the governed environment and filtering outputs before they reach users. The exfiltration channel that pattern-matching DLP left permanently open is closed. The privacy function can tell a regulator not just what the policy says about AI data processing, but what the enforcement mechanism prevented in the past 90 days. That's the shift from documentation to control that the gateway represents.

The erasure workflow rebuilt to reach memory and embeddings is the third milestone. By the end of year one, every erasure request triggers an automated subject-data location query that covers all three discovery layers. The deletion procedures for each AI-native location type are documented and tested. The model-weight defensible position is reviewed and signed off by the General Counsel. The erasure certifications the privacy function files at the end of year one are accurate. They cover what they say they cover. That accuracy is the difference between a certification that protects the enterprise and one that creates liability.

Purpose enforcement as code on high-sensitivity pipelines is the fourth milestone. By the end of year one, at least one high-sensitivity data pipeline has a policy engine sitting in it that enforces purpose limitation at the point of processing rather than auditing it after the fact. The logging period from the pilot has produced a quantified picture of how many undocumented flows were occurring before enforcement was deployed. That number goes to the board as evidence of what the investment in purpose-as-code prevented. The pilot also demonstrates that the privacy function can say yes to data uses that the old framework could only decline, because the policy engine with privacy-enhancing technology controls makes previously unauthorized uses compliant.

Inference controls across the AI portfolio is the fifth milestone. By the end of year one, every AI system in the enterprise has been assessed for inference risk using the methodology described in Chapter 11. The inference risk inventory is documented. Every inferred attribute that isn't covered by an existing consent basis or disclosure has a named owner and a remediation plan. The inference governance analyst role is operational, running inference risk assessments on new AI deployments before they go live. The privacy function can tell a regulator which sensitive attributes the enterprise's AI systems derive, under what consent basis, and what controls govern those derivations.

DSAR automation in production is the sixth milestone. By the end of year one, the DSAR fulfillment pipeline is running the automated subject-data location query across all three discovery layers for every incoming request. The human reviewer's role has shifted from data collector to quality reviewer. The time from request receipt to response delivery has dropped to a fraction of what the manual process required. The privacy function is meeting its statutory response deadlines without the manual effort that previously consumed a significant portion of the team's capacity.

PET pilots deployed is the seventh milestone. By the end of year one, at least one privacy-enhancing technology, differential privacy, synthetic data generation, or federated learning, is deployed in a production use case. The pilot demonstrates that the privacy function can enable AI data uses that the old framework couldn't authorize. It also builds the internal expertise needed to expand PET deployment in year two and year three.

Enterprise memory governance standing is the eighth milestone. By the end of year one, enterprise memory is formally classified as a data category with a named owner, a retention policy, a correction procedure, and a purge procedure for each memory type. The memory governance steward role is operational. The integrity monitoring that watches agent memory for unauthorized changes is running. The privacy function can tell a regulator exactly what the enterprise's AI agents know, about whom, for how long, and under what authority.

Inference governance operational is the ninth milestone. The inference governance analyst is running pre-deployment inference risk assessments on every new AI system. The assessment output feeds the DPIA process and the processing register. The privacy function has a systematic process for evaluating what AI systems will derive before they're deployed, not after the first regulatory examination asks the question.

The privacy function positioned as the enterprise's intelligence governance partner is the tenth milestone, and it's the one that changes the function's relationship with every other part of the organization. By the end of year one, the privacy function isn't just governing what the enterprise collects and stores. It's governing what the enterprise knows. That expanded mandate is reflected in the governance committee structure, the CISO's board reporting, and the CPO's relationship with the CDO and the AI governance function. The privacy function has a seat at the table when AI systems are designed, not just when they're assessed.

The year-one budget narrative has three lines. Tooling: the continuous discovery platform with AI-native layer coverage and the AI gateway with semantic DLP capability. These two categories are the foundation of the year-one operating model. They replace the annual discovery process and the pattern-matching DLP that couldn't cover AI channels. Present the cost offset to the CFO: the analyst hours currently consumed by periodic discovery, manual DSAR fulfillment, and manual evidence collection for regulatory examinations are substantially reduced by the tooling investment. The tooling cost is partially funded by the reduction in manual effort.

Headcount: the inference governance analyst and the erasure engineer. These are the first two of the three new roles. Hire them as the tooling goes live, not before. The roles without the tools produce frustration. The tools without the roles produce outputs nobody acts on. The combination is what makes the year-one operating model functional.

The year-one board milestone is specific and measurable: continuous discovery is live and the data map covers the AI-native layer, semantic DLP is enforcing at the AI gateway, erasure certifications cover what they say they cover, and the inference governance process is running pre-deployment assessments on new AI systems. Present those four facts to the board at the end of year one as proof that the privacy program is governing the AI layer, not laminating policy onto it. The board doesn't need the technical details. They need to know that the program is current, the certifications are accurate, and the function has a systematic process for evaluating what the enterprise's AI systems know and derive.

FIGURE 12.4 **The One-Year Privacy Target Operating Model**

Four quarters, with the milestone reported at the end of each.

QUARTER	CAPABILITY INSTALLED	OWNER	BOARD MILESTONE
Q1	Derivative stores discovered, classified, and given stewards	Privacy Lead	We know where personal data actually lives
Q2	One erasure path engineered and empirically verified	Eng Lead	Deletion is tested, not asserted
Q3	Purpose enforcement live on the highest-exposure pipeline	Data Eng	Consent governs the pipeline
Q4	Memory governance standard and examination evidence pack	Privacy Lead	We can answer an examiner this quarter

FOUR QUARTERS OF ENGINEERING BEATS A THREE-YEAR PRIVACY TRANSFORMATION PLAN.

The Regulatory Clock: What Moves in the Next Twelve Months and What It Forces

Privacy is the only one of the four domains where the twelve-month plan is partly set by external actors, and a program that builds its roadmap without reading the regulatory calendar will find itself rebuilding in the third quarter. The useful framing is not a survey of every jurisdiction but a short list of the movements that force engineering work, because a regulatory development that requires a policy update is manageable at any time and one that requires an architecture change is not.

The first movement is the tightening of what erasure means in practice. Regulators across multiple jurisdictions have moved from accepting deletion of primary records toward asking about derived representations, and the direction of travel is unambiguous even where the current guidance is not explicit. The engineering consequence is that the erasure register described in Chapter 11 stops being a good practice and becomes the evidence base for a claim the enterprise is already making. An enterprise that begins that work when the guidance becomes explicit is beginning eighteen months of engineering under a deadline set by someone else.

The second movement is disclosure of automated decision-making, which is expanding in both scope and specificity. The scope expansion is that systems previously understood as decision support are being read as decision-making where the human review is nominal. The specificity expansion is that disclosure obligations increasingly require describing the logic involved, which is a materially different requirement from disclosing that automation occurred. Both point at the provenance work in Chapter 2 rather than at anything in the privacy notice, which is why the privacy function that treats this as a notice-drafting exercise will produce a compliant document describing a system it cannot evidence.

The third movement is inference, and it is the least settled and the most consequential. Several regulatory bodies have signaled that inferred attributes attract the same protections as collected ones, which if applied consistently would place a large volume of AI output inside the regulated perimeter for the first time. The enterprise cannot resolve this uncertainty, but it can decide how to posture against it. The defensible posture is to run inference assessments pre-deployment and to record which sensitive attributes a system is capable of deriving, whether or not current guidance requires it, because that record is cheap to produce prospectively and expensive to reconstruct retrospectively.

The fourth movement is cross-border, where the residency question described in Chapter 10 is being asked with increasing specificity about processing rather than storage. The forcing function here is contractual as much as regulatory: enterprise customers are adding inference-location questions to their security questionnaires, and a vendor who cannot answer loses the deal regardless of what the regulator currently requires. The decision rule that covers all four movements is the same one: where a regulatory direction is clear but the requirement is not yet explicit, build the evidence capability now and decide later how much of it to disclose. Evidence you hold and do not need is inexpensive. Evidence you need and do not hold is a project with a deadline attached.

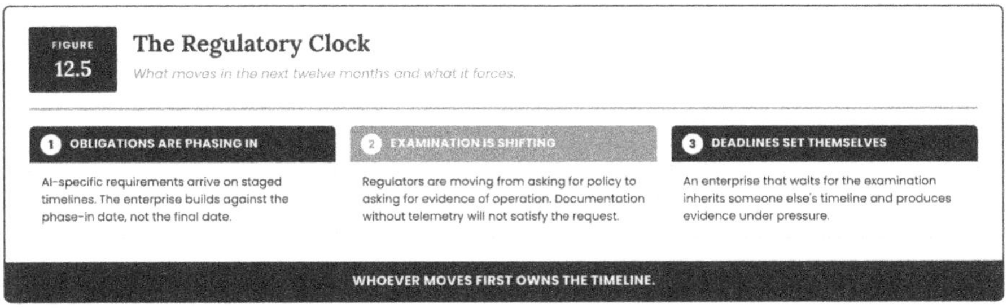

The Engineering Handoff: Why Privacy Cannot Stay a Legal Function

The privacy function in most enterprises reports through legal, is staffed with people whose training is legal, and produces artifacts whose primary audience is legal. That structure was correct for a regime built on notice, consent, and records of processing. It is insufficient for a regime where compliance is enforced in a data pipeline, and the insufficiency is now the binding constraint on most privacy programs regardless of how well they are led.

The specific gap is that every control described in Chapter 11 is an engineering artifact. Purpose enforcement at the gateway is code. Semantic data loss prevention is a model deployment with a tuning cycle. Erasure engineering is a distributed systems problem involving indexes, caches, and model artifacts. Enterprise memory governance is a retention policy expressed as a scheduled process against stores that did not exist when the retention schedule was written. A privacy office without engineering capacity can specify all four and implement none, and what it produces instead is a requirements document handed to a platform team with other priorities.

What follows from that handoff is the pattern that makes privacy programs look slow to everyone including themselves. The requirement is written, the platform team schedules it behind revenue work, the privacy officer escalates, the escalation produces a partial implementation, and the attestation is signed against the partial implementation because the deadline is fixed and the engineering is not. Nobody in that sequence acted badly. The structure guaranteed the outcome, and the structure is what has to change.

The change that works is smaller than a reorganization and larger than a liaison. Place at least one engineer inside the privacy function, reporting to the CPO, with the mandate to build and operate the enforcement layer rather than to specify it. That engineer's value is not primarily their throughput; it is that requirements written by someone who will implement them are materially different requirements, and that a privacy officer with an engineer at the table stops writing specifications that cannot be built. Enterprises that have made this change consistently report that the first six months produce fewer requirements and more shipped controls.

The organizational question this raises, and that Chapter 12 has already opened, is whether privacy and AI governance converge. The engineering argument points toward convergence more strongly than the legal argument does, because the enforcement layer for purpose limitation and the enforcement layer for AI governance policy are the same gateway, reading the same requests, applying different rule sets. Two functions specifying rules into one enforcement point will eventually either merge or conflict. The decision rule for a CISO watching this is to consolidate the enforcement layer under one owner in the first year regardless of where the policy functions sit, because a single gateway with two masters is an operational fragility that surfaces at the worst possible moment.

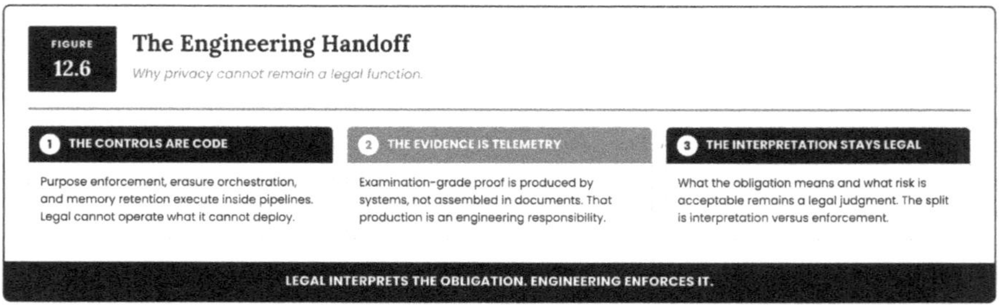

FIGURE 12.6 The Engineering Handoff

Why privacy cannot remain a legal function.

More Security or Less? The Ultimate Outcome for Data Protection

Data protection becomes intelligence protection. That's the answer to the board's question for this domain, and it's the largest answer of the four because the mandate it describes is larger than anything the privacy function has previously held.

The enterprise's most valuable asset has shifted. It used to be data: the records in the databases, the documents in the file shares, the customer information in the CRM. Protecting that data was the privacy function's mandate. That mandate was important. It was also bounded. The data lived in identifiable places. The controls that protected it were well-understood. The regulatory frameworks that governed it were mature.

The most valuable asset now is the intelligence derived from that data. The conclusions the AI systems reached. The inferences they drew. The decisions they made. The context they accumulated. The organizational memory they built. That intelligence is what drives competitive advantage, what powers autonomous decision-making, and what regulators are increasingly focused on governing. The enterprise that can't govern its own intelligence, that can't say what its AI systems know, under what authority they know it, and how that knowledge can be corrected or erased, is exposed in ways that the traditional data protection framework was never designed to address.

Privacy doesn't shrink into a compliance checkbox as AI proliferates. It converges with AI governance into the stewardship of organizational memory itself. That convergence is the fullest expression of the shift this book has traced through every domain. Governance stopped reviewing quarterly what changes daily and became the control plane that decides what autonomous systems may decide. The SOC stopped detecting breaches and started supervising machine reasoning. Third-party risk stopped mailing questionnaires and started engineering inter-organizational trust. Privacy stops protecting databases and starts governing intelligence.

The mandate is the largest of the four domains because intelligence is the asset that underlies everything else. The governance function can ratify decision rights, but it can't govern what the decision-making AI systems actually know. The SOC can supervise machine reasoning, but it can't govern the accuracy of the knowledge that reasoning draws from. Third-party risk can engineer trust boundaries between organizations, but it can't govern the intelligence that flows across those boundaries. Privacy, extended to cover enterprise memory, inference governance, and purpose enforcement as code, is the function that governs the accuracy, accountability, and legitimacy of what the enterprise knows. That's a mandate no privacy team has ever held before.

More security than ever. With a mandate no privacy team has held before: not protecting information, but governing intelligence. The function that started as a legal obligation, a compliance requirement that the enterprise had to satisfy, ends as the conscience of the thinking enterprise. The function that asks, on behalf of every data subject whose information shaped the enterprise's AI systems: what do you know about me, why do you know it, how long will you hold it, and can you prove you've forgotten it when I asked you to?

Those questions don't have technical answers. They have governance answers. And the privacy function that builds the operating model to answer them, with continuous discovery, semantic DLP enforcement, erasure engineering, purpose-as-code, inference governance, and memory stewardship, is the function that makes the thinking enterprise accountable. That's not a compliance function. That's the most consequential governance role in the AI-native enterprise.

The career positioning dimension of this outcome is worth stating directly. The CPO who builds the intelligence governance operating model and presents it to the board as a funded trajectory isn't just doing good privacy work. They're establishing themselves as the executive who governs what the enterprise may know. That's a specific identity, and it's a valuable one in a regulatory environment that's moving toward enforcement of exactly that question. The CISO who partners with the CPO to build this function, who ensures the security controls protect the intelligence assets the privacy function governs, is the executive who made the thinking enterprise both accountable and defensible. Those are the career positions this operating model builds. They're worth building deliberately.

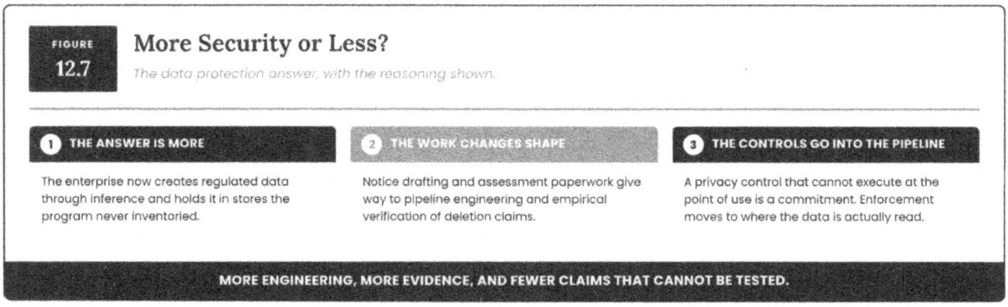

Putting It Into Practice

The mandate is expanding. This month, the privacy function claims it deliberately rather than waiting for a regulator, a reorganization, or an incident to define the scope for it.

Locate your program against the current-focus map this week. Write down the honest answer to each of the four current-focus activities: AI use register, DPIA methodology, AI-channel DLP, and erasure workflow scope. Is each one engineering governance or laminating policy? An AI use register that hasn't been updated since the audit is lamination. A DPIA template that doesn't handle inference risk or memory accumulation is lamination. A DLP program that doesn't cover AI channels is lamination. An erasure workflow that doesn't reach agent memory or embedding databases is lamination. Name each laminate. They're your year-one gaps, and they need to be in the gap analysis you bring to the CPO and the CISO before the budget conversation starts.

Evaluate your privacy stack by category this week. Map what you currently have against the five categories: DSPM with AI-native layer coverage, AI gateway with semantic DLP, privacy platform with AI governance duties, continuous discovery and classification, and PET capabilities. For each category, answer two questions: do you have a tool that covers this category, and does it cover the AI-native layer or only the traditional estate? A tool that covers only the traditional estate in a category that requires AI-native coverage is a gap, even if the tool is well-designed. Identify the category that's missing entirely from your current stack. That missing category is your first year-one tooling investment. Name it, scope it, and put it in the budget narrative before the next planning cycle opens.

Open the convergence conversation with the CPO and the CISO before the org chart decides it. Schedule that conversation this week. The agenda is three questions. Who owns inference governance: the privacy function, the AI governance function, or a new role that spans both? Who owns enterprise memory: the CPO, the CDO, the CISO, or the intelligence governance function that doesn't yet exist? And who owns the convergence roadmap itself: who is responsible for ensuring that the privacy and AI governance functions are building toward a coherent operating model rather than two separate programs that govern the same pipelines with different controls? Those three questions need answers before the next AI system deployment creates a governance gap that neither function owns.

Assign provisional ownership of enterprise memory this month, even if the permanent answer is a year away. The provisional assignment is specific: the privacy function owns enterprise memory as a personal data category, the CISO co-owns it as a security asset, and the memory governance steward role is assigned to a named individual on the privacy team as an interim accountability until the permanent role is hired. Provisional ownership with a named individual is infinitely more defensible than no ownership. It means that when a regulator asks who is responsible for the governance of enterprise memory, there's a name and a function to point to. The permanent answer can be refined over the next year. The provisional answer needs to exist today.

Assemble the 1-Year Privacy Target Operating Model on one page. The ten milestones from the previous section, organized by quarter, with a primary owner for each milestone, a budget line for each capability build, and a board-facing outcome at the end of the year. That one page is the document you bring to the CPO with the regulatory narrative that funds it. The regulatory narrative is specific: here are the regulatory requirements that each milestone addresses, here is the examination risk of not addressing them, and here is the cost of the operating model relative to the cost of a regulatory finding in each area. That comparison is what makes the budget conversation fundable rather than aspirational.

Part IV is complete. The privacy function has its operating model, its convergence roadmap, and its answer to the board's question. The conclusion assembles all four domains into one operating discipline and the sequenced plan that installs it across the enterprise. The audit proved the posture. The four operating models govern it. Every day, in every domain, with every artifact named, every owner assigned, and every executive decision fed.

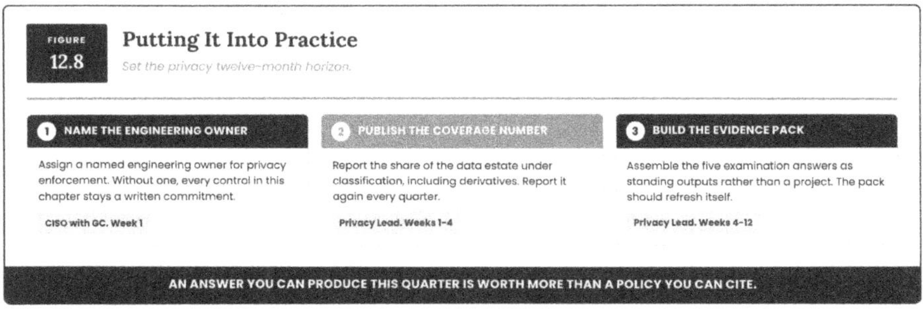

Chapter 13: Sequencing the First 90 Days

Running Four Domains on One Calendar Without Stalling All Four

CHAPTER 13 OUTCOMES

At the end of this chapter, you will be able to:

1. Explain why four parallel programs become zero programs.
2. Apply the dependency map that sets the order of the work.
3. Execute days one through thirty: one conversation and two inventories.
4. Execute days thirty-one through sixty: ratification and the first platform decision.
5. Execute days sixty-one through ninety: the supervision matrix and the first measured number.
6. Hand quarters two through four a program that is already running.

SEQUENCE IS THE DIFFERENCE BETWEEN A PROGRAM AND FOUR STALLED PROJECTS.

Why Four Parallel Programs Become Zero Programs

The four preceding parts each closed with a target operating model that assumed its domain was the only one moving. That assumption was necessary to make each model legible. It is also false, and a CISO who takes all four twelve-month plans and launches them simultaneously on the first Monday of the fiscal year will discover the falseness around week six, when the same six executives are being asked to ratify four different accountability documents, the same procurement team is being asked to evaluate four solution categories, and the same overextended GRC manager is running discovery cycles in two directions.

The failure mode is not that the work is too hard. It is that the work is competing with itself for a resource that does not scale on a ninety-day timeline: senior attention. The Decision Rights RACI, the Human Supervision Matrix, the AI clause library, and the erasure engineering register all require the General Counsel. Three of the four require the CPO. All four require the CISO to spend calendar time in rooms rather than in the program. When four workstreams draw on the same executive bandwidth in the same quarter, the honest outcome is that one advances, two stall in a defensible-looking way, and the fourth is quietly deprioritized without anyone deciding to deprioritize it.

The second failure mode is dependency inversion, and it is more expensive because it wastes money rather than time. Hiring a machine-judgment governor before the continuous-control platform exists produces a well-compensated professional with no system to operate. Standing up corruption detection before the supervision matrix is ratified produces alerts that nobody has authority to act on. Enforcing an AI clause library that legal has not finished drafting produces a procurement gate that blocks contracts against criteria nobody agreed to. Each of these is a real pattern, each has a named cause, and each is avoidable by sequencing rather than by working harder.

The third failure mode is the one that kills programs politically rather than operationally. A CISO who announces four transformations and delivers four partial ones has, in the board's reading, delivered nothing. A CISO who announces one and delivers it completely has established that the program produces what it promises, which is the only credibility that survives the second budget cycle. Sequencing is not a concession to limited resources. It is how the program earns the right to the resources it will need in the second year.

FIGURE 13.2 **Why Four Parallel Programs Become Zero**

The failure mode that consumes the first ninety days

1 ONE EXECUTIVE, FOUR FRONTS

The same CISO sponsors all four domains. Attention divides four ways and none of the four reaches the milestone that would justify continued funding.

2 SHARED DEPENDENCIES COLLIDE

All four domains need inventory, identity, and telemetry. Started simultaneously, they contend for the same platform team and the same budget.

3 NOTHING FINISHES IN QUARTER ONE

Four programs at twenty-five percent produce no capability. One program at one hundred percent produces a milestone the board can see.

4 FUNDING FOLLOWS VISIBLE COMPLETION

Year two budget is defended with delivered capability. Four partially built programs are indistinguishable from no program at all.

FOUR PROGRAMS AT TWENTY-FIVE PERCENT IS ZERO DELIVERED CAPABILITY.

The Dependency Map That Sets the Order

Four dependencies constrain the sequence, and once they are named the order is close to forced. The first is that ratified decision rights precede every autonomy expansion in every domain. The supervision matrix in security operations, the sanctioning dispositions in governance, the procurement gate in third-party risk, and the purpose enforcement decisions in privacy all resolve to the same question: who has authority to say yes, who has authority to say stop, and who is accountable when the machine acts. If that question is unresolved, each domain answers it locally and the enterprise ends up with four incompatible answers that surface as conflict in month eight.

The second dependency is that inventory precedes control. Every control in this Volume operates on a population, and a control applied to an incomplete population produces confident coverage claims that are wrong by an unmeasured margin. The model registry, the non-human identity inventory, the vendor tier map, and the data store discovery are all population-defining artifacts. They arrive from the audit in some condition, and the first job in each domain is to determine how stale that condition is before building anything on top of it.

The third dependency is that tooling precedes the role that operates it, with one deliberate exception. The machine-judgment governor, the reasoning auditor, the vendor intelligence analyst, and the privacy engineering lead should each arrive as their platform goes live, so the person configures the system rather than inheriting a configuration. The exception is the General Counsel relationship, which precedes everything, because the attestation exposure and the discovery risk are live today regardless of what tooling exists.

The fourth dependency is that measurement precedes expansion. Autonomy expands on evidence in the supervision matrix, trust expands on evidence in the vendor score, and enforcement expands on evidence in the privacy pipeline. In each case the expansion decision requires a measured baseline that did not exist before the program started. That means the first quarter of every domain is partly a measurement quarter, and a plan that treats the first quarter as a build quarter has skipped the step that makes the second quarter defensible.

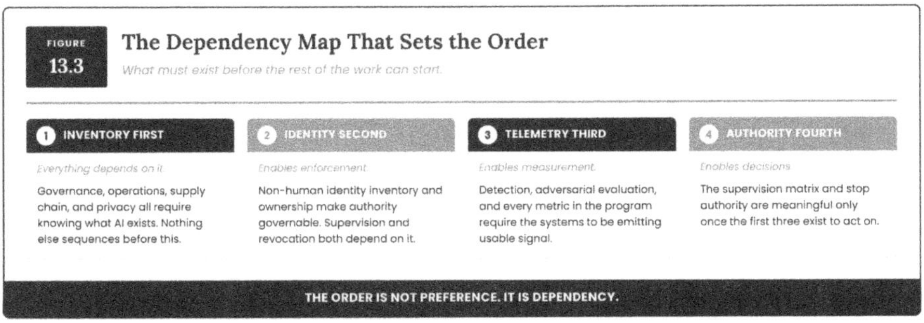

Days One Through Thirty: One Conversation and Two Inventories

The first thirty days belong to the General Counsel and to the two inventories that everything else depends on. The General Counsel conversation is first because it is the only item on this list where waiting has a legal cost that accrues daily. Executives are signing attestations about AI behavior that the security organization cannot currently verify. Those attestations are discoverable, they are dated, and they were made in a period when the enterprise had an audit finding on file describing the verification gap. The General Counsel needs to know that, needs to know it from the CISO rather than from opposing counsel, and needs to be a participant in the decision about what the enterprise attests to going forward.

That conversation has a specific agenda and produces a specific artifact. Bring the audit's finding on the accountability gap, the current list of AI-related attestations the enterprise has signed in the last twelve months, and the Decision Rights RACI in draft form. Ask three questions: which of these attestations would we struggle to substantiate today, what should we stop attesting to until we can, and who signs the ratified accountability document. The artifact is a memo from the General Counsel to the CISO naming the attestation positions the enterprise will hold for the next two quarters. Date it. It becomes evidence that the enterprise identified the gap and acted, which is a materially different posture than having identified the gap and continued.

The two inventories that run in parallel are the model registry and the non-human identity population. Both arrived from the audit and both are stale, and the first job is to measure the staleness rather than assume it. Take the audit's AI inventory, sample fifteen systems across business units, and determine for each whether the system still exists, whether its model version has changed, whether its data access has expanded, and whether anyone in the security organization would have known if any of those changed. The percentage of the sample that has materially drifted since the audit is the number that tells you whether your inventory is a record or a fiction, and it is a number the board should hear.

The non-human identity inventory gets the same treatment with a harder question attached. Enumerate the service accounts, agent identities, API keys, and plugin credentials that can take action, and for each determine the credential age, the last review date, and the named human owner. Most enterprises running this exercise for the first time find that a substantial fraction of the population has no named owner, a credential older than any policy would permit, and no review date at all. That finding is the entire justification for the identity tiering work, and it is more persuasive as a measured number from your own environment than as an industry statistic from someone else's.

FIGURE 13.4 **Days One Through Thirty**

One conversation and two inventories.

ACTION	OWNER	OUTPUT	DONE WHEN
The accountability conversation	CISO with GC and CEO	Named stop authority	One person can suspend without a committee
AI system inventory	Platform Owner	Dated model and agent register	Every production AI system is listed with an owner
Non-human identity inventory	IAM Lead	Credential population with owners	Orphaned identities are identified and counted
Debt baseline	GRC Lead	AI Security Debt register	The opening number is published

THIRTY DAYS PRODUCES THE TWO LISTS EVERYTHING ELSE DEPENDS ON.

Days Thirty-One Through Sixty: Ratification and the First Platform Decision

The second month is where the accountability question gets settled in a room with the people who have to live with the answer. The ratification session is a working meeting, not a briefing, and it needs the CISO, General Counsel, CPO, CDO, CFO, and the business unit leaders whose systems are in scope. Send the draft RACI five business days ahead with the fifteen sampled systems mapped against it, because abstract decision rights produce abstract agreement and specific systems produce the argument you actually need to have. Budget for external facilitation if the enterprise has a history of these sessions ending in a follow-up rather than a decision.

The session resolves three questions per system class and produces a signed document. Who approves deployment, who has unilateral authority to suspend, and who is accountable when the system acts and the action produces loss. The third question is where sessions stall, and the stall has a predictable shape: every executive agrees accountability should sit with someone and disagrees that it should sit with them. The CISO's job in that moment is to name the alternative plainly. Unassigned accountability does not mean nobody is accountable. It means the accountability lands on whoever the regulator, the plaintiff, or the board decides it lands on, after the fact, without any of the people in the room having any input into that decision.

Running alongside ratification is the first platform decision, and there is only one in the first ninety days. The continuous-control platform is the correct choice for most enterprises, because it is the category that converts evidence from a periodic collection exercise into a continuous feed, and because that conversion is what makes the other three domains' evidence requirements affordable later. Evaluate against three criteria: whether it reads your existing control environment without a rebuild, whether it produces evidence a regulator would accept without a translation layer, and whether it can absorb AI-specific controls rather than requiring a parallel instance. Category fit matters more than feature comparison here, and the enterprise that spends the first quarter in a six-vendor bake-off has spent the quarter.

The month also opens the shadow AI discovery cycle in exactly one business unit. Choose the unit with high AI adoption and a leader who will treat the exercise as help rather than audit, because the first cycle sets the enterprise's expectation of what this process is. The conversation is structured and short: what AI tools are your people using, where did they come from, what data do they touch, and what problem were they solving that the sanctioned tools did not solve. That last question is the one that produces the fast-track intake criteria, and it is the one most discovery processes forget to ask.

FIGURE 13.5

Days Thirty-One Through Sixty

Ratification and the first platform decision

ACTION	OWNER	OUTPUT	DONE WHEN
Policy ratification	Governance Committee	Ratified AI security policy	Authority and decision rights are written down
Sanctioning pathway opens	GRC Lead	Published route to approved capability	First shadow AI request is processed
Platform decision	CISO with Finance	One category selected	Integration cost is priced, not estimated
Clause library adopted	TPRM with Legal	Required AI contract terms	Terms are in the standard for every renewal

RATIFY THE AUTHORITY BEFORE BUYING THE PLATFORM THAT ASSUMES IT.

Days Sixty-One Through Ninety: The Supervision Matrix and the First Measured Number

The third month moves to security operations, and it moves there because the supervision matrix is the artifact with the longest lead time and the highest board value. Drafting it is a two-week exercise for the SOC director. Negotiating it is a four-week exercise, because every action class the matrix designates as requiring human confirmation is a class where someone currently believes automation was already approved. Ratifying it requires the decision rights that were settled in month two, which is why this sequence puts it here rather than at the start.

The matrix is built per system and per action class rather than per tool, and that distinction is the one that separates a working matrix from a decorative one. An AI system that can read a ticket, draft a response, send the response, and close the ticket has four action classes with four different risk profiles, and a matrix that assigns a single autonomy level to the tool has assigned the wrong level to at least three of them. For each class, record the current autonomy level, the accuracy evidence that would justify raising it, the named authority who approves the raise, and the date of the last review. That last field is what turns the matrix into a governed instrument rather than a one-time assessment.

The kill-switch rehearsal happens in this month, and it is the single highest-value ninety-day activity measured against board perception. Pick one production AI system, notify the participants, and execute a full suspension with a timer running. Record the time from decision to confirmed stop, the dependencies that surfaced during execution, the approvals that were required and were not pre-authorized, and the business processes that degraded. Every enterprise running this rehearsal for the first time discovers at least two dependencies nobody documented and at least one approval chain that would have added hours in a real event. Those findings are the deliverable, and the rehearsal that surfaces nothing is a rehearsal that was scoped to succeed.

The ninety-day close needs one measured number that did not exist before the program started, and the CISO should choose it deliberately rather than reporting whatever the tooling happens to produce. The strongest candidates are the inventory drift percentage from month one, the unowned non-human identity count, the time-to-suspension from the rehearsal, or the count of shadow AI tools discovered in one business unit extrapolated across the enterprise. Pick the one that is most uncomfortable and most defensible. A program that opens with a number the board did not want to hear, produced by the program's own instrumentation, has established something no roadmap slide can establish.

FIGURE 13.6 **Days Sixty-One Through Ninety**

The supervision matrix and the first measured number.

ACTION	OWNER	OUTPUT	DONE WHEN
Supervision matrix populated	CISO Staff	Every AI system at an explicit level	No production system is unplaced
Red-button rehearsal	SOC Manager	A measured time-to-stop	The number exists and is reported
First adversarial evaluation	Detection Eng.	Resistance rate per attack class	One production endpoint has been tested
Board scorecard issued	CISO	The first quarterly scorecard	The board has seen a measured number

NINETY DAYS ENDS WITH A NUMBER, NOT A STATUS UPDATE.

What Quarters Two Through Four Inherit

The remaining three quarters follow the domain models in Chapters 3, 6, 9, and 12, and the sequencing principle stays constant: one domain leads each quarter, the others advance on work that does not compete for executive calendar time. The second quarter belongs to governance, standing up the continuous-control platform that was selected in the first quarter and hiring the machine-judgment governor to operate it. Security operations advances corruption detection on the five highest-stakes systems during the same quarter, because that work requires detection engineering attention rather than executive attention.

The third quarter belongs to third-party risk, because the clause library requires General Counsel time and the General Counsel has been unavailable during governance ratification and supervision matrix negotiation. That timing is not a compromise. It is the correct order, because a clause library drafted before the decision rights are settled will encode an accountability model the enterprise has not agreed to. Privacy advances discovery and classification during the same quarter, which is engineering work with a low executive draw.

The fourth quarter belongs to privacy, which carries the heaviest engineering load and the least executive negotiation. Erasure engineering, purpose enforcement, and memory governance are build efforts with long tails, and starting them in the fourth quarter means finishing them in the first quarter of the following year rather than within this Volume's horizon. That is the honest statement, and a CISO should make it to the board rather than claiming a twelve-month completion for work that takes fifteen. The alternative, which is to compress privacy into a quarter it does not fit into, produces an erasure certification the enterprise cannot substantiate, and that is a worse outcome than a schedule that runs long.

Across all four quarters, three activities run continuously rather than sequentially, and they should appear on the calendar as standing items rather than as project milestones. Shadow AI discovery expands by one business unit per month. The kill-switch is rehearsed quarterly with a filed evidence trail. And the board receives one measured number per quarter that the program produced itself. Those three items are what distinguish a program from a project, and they are the ones most likely to be dropped when the quarter gets crowded.

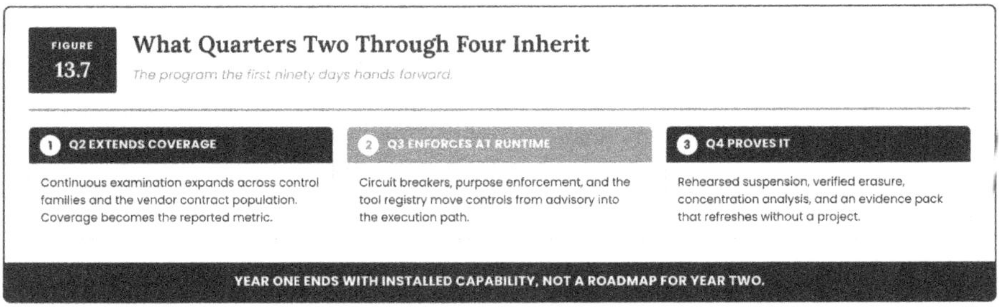

Putting It Into Practice

The question this chapter puts to you is whether your ninety-day plan is a sequence or a list. A list has four domains and twelve initiatives and no statement about what happens when two of them need the same executive in the same week. A sequence has an order, a stated dependency for each item, and a named thing that gets deferred when the quarter gets crowded. The evidence that you have a sequence is a single page showing the four quarters, the domain leading each one, the executive whose calendar is the constraint in each one, and the one measured number the program will produce at the end of each one. The common failure pattern is the CISO who launches all four domain models simultaneously in January, reports partial progress on all four in April, and spends the second budget cycle explaining why a fully funded program produced four incomplete transformations rather than one finished one. The move this month is narrower than the plan you have probably already drafted. Book the General Counsel conversation this week with the attestation list and the draft RACI in hand. Sample fifteen systems from the audit inventory and measure the drift. Enumerate the non-human identities that can act and count how many have no named owner. Then take those three outputs into the ratification session in month two, and do not start the supervision matrix, the clause library, or the erasure register until the accountability question has a signature under it.

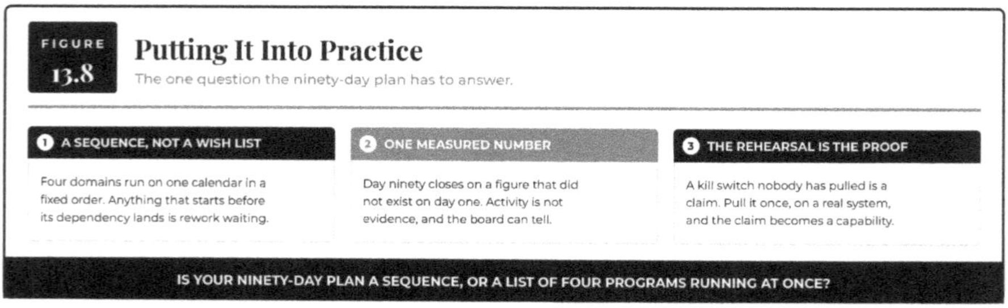

Conclusion

What You Now Have That You Did Not Have Before

The audit proved the posture. This book installed the program.

That distinction matters more than it might sound. A proven posture is a snapshot. A running program is a discipline. The difference between those two things is the difference between a binder that ages into liability and a security function that governs what AI is doing in your enterprise every single day. You came into this book with the first one. You're leaving it with the architecture for the second.

Four domains have been rebuilt as operating disciplines, not as policy documents or project plans. Governance is no longer running quarterly reviews against a risk register that stopped moving when the audit closed. It's running continuous compliance with a living risk register that has named owners, defined update triggers, and escalation paths that reach the right executive before the next board cycle. The Decision Rights RACI is ratified, not drafted. The five-horizon operating rhythm is on calendars, not in a slide deck. The shadow AI sanctioning pathway is converting rogue demand into governed capability instead of driving it underground. The AI Security Scorecard assembles itself from continuous evidence rather than getting assembled by exhausted analysts two weeks before the audit committee meeting.

Security operations has been transformed at its core. The SOC that was built to detect breaches now has the architecture to supervise machine reasoning. The

Human Supervision Matrix defines what machines may decide alone and what requires a human in the loop. The corruption signal set is watching for prompt injection, behavioral drift, and context manipulation alongside the traditional indicators of compromise that the SIEM was built to catch. The kill-switch protocol is pre-authorized, documented, and rehearsed with filed evidence rather than theoretically available and practically untested. Autonomous triage is measured by decision accuracy and evidence completeness, not by the MTTD metric that was calibrated for a world where humans were doing the investigating.

Third-party risk has stopped mailing questionnaires to a supply chain that mutates weekly. Continuous external monitoring is watching the vendor portfolio for breach disclosures, privacy policy changes, model-provider switches, and AI feature announcements in real time. The AI clause library is enforced at procurement, not filed in a policy document. The AI Bill of Materials is a condition of contract execution, not a future initiative. The Adaptive AI Trust Scores are updating as evidence arrives from strategic vendors, not waiting for the next annual assessment cycle to tell the third-party risk function what changed eight months ago.

Privacy has stopped governing around the AI layer and started governing inside it. Continuous discovery covers the full estate including embedding databases, vector stores, and agent memory stores that no traditional discovery methodology was designed to find. Semantic DLP enforces purpose limitation at the AI gateway rather than documenting it in a policy that the pipeline never reads. Erasure certifications cover what they say they cover. Inference governance runs pre-deployment assessments on new AI systems before they start deriving sensitive attributes from data subjects who never consented to that derivation. Enterprise memory has a lifecycle, an owner, and a purge procedure for the first time in the history of the discipline.

Every artifact has an owner. Every owner has a cadence. Every cadence feeds a decision that matters. That sentence is the operating standard this book was built around, and it's the standard that separates a security function that reacts to AI from one that governs it. You just built the second one.

What This Program Costs, and What It Costs Not to Run It

A CISO closing this book is going to be asked two questions within the month, and both deserve an answer prepared in advance rather than assembled under pressure. The first is what the program costs. The second, asked less directly and usually by someone hoping for a different answer, is what happens if the enterprise waits a year.

The cost has four components and they do not arrive evenly. Tooling is the visible one and the smallest surprise: a continuous-control platform, a model registry, behavioral monitoring, external vendor monitoring, and a discovery and classification capability, purchased across four quarters rather than four months. Headcount is the second and the one most likely to be cut: four to six new roles across the four domains, hired against platforms that exist rather than platforms that are planned. Facilitation is the third and the one that is never budgeted: the executive time and often external help required to ratify the Decision Rights RACI, the supervision matrix, and the clause library. Reskilling is the fourth, and it is the line item that gets removed when tooling comes in over estimate, which is precisely the wrong trade.

The offset is real and should be presented rather than left for the CFO to find. Manual evidence collection, questionnaire administration, alert triage at volume, and erasure request handling are four workflows that currently consume analyst capacity and that this program substantially automates. That capacity does not disappear from the budget; it redeploys into work the enterprise currently cannot staff at all. Present it that way. A CISO who presents the program as a cost reduction will be held to a headcount target that the governance model cannot survive, and a CISO who presents it as pure new spend has left the strongest part of the argument on the table.

The cost of waiting is harder to quantify and easier to feel, and it compounds in three places. Attestation exposure accrues daily, because executives continue signing statements about AI behavior the enterprise cannot verify, and each signature is dated and discoverable. Inventory drift compounds, because the population grows faster than the record and every month of delay widens a gap that will eventually have to be closed retroactively under time pressure. And the labor market for the four roles tightens, because every enterprise reading the same threat picture is recruiting from the same small pool, and the organizations that started hiring first are already training the second generation internally.

The honest closing position is that this program does not eliminate risk and was never going to. What it produces is an enterprise where the AI security question has an owner, the owner has instrumentation, the instrumentation produces evidence, and the evidence is current on the day someone asks. That is a materially different posture from the one the audit found, and it is achievable in four quarters by an organization that sequences the work rather than launching it. The alternative is not a slower version of the same outcome. It is a program that starts eighteen months from now, under a deadline someone else sets, with a population that has drifted further and a labor market that has tightened, run by a CISO explaining why the audit that identified all of this was allowed to age into a binder.

The Action That Makes All of This Real

Everything in this book stays theoretical until an artifact gets an owner, a meeting gets scheduled, and a decision gets made by the person accountable for it.

That's not a motivational statement. It's an operational reality. The governance committee that doesn't have ratified decision rights is a conversation. The kill-switch protocol that hasn't been rehearsed is a document. The erasure workflow that doesn't reach agent memory is a certification that's quietly wrong. The gap between having the architecture and running the program is the gap between reading this book and executing what it describes. That gap closes with specific actions by specific people on specific dates. Not with a multi-year transformation roadmap that gets presented to the board and then sits in a shared drive.

The commitment is one year. Not three, not someday, not after the next planning cycle opens and the budget conversation gets easier. One year, four domains, one running program.

In the first thirty days, three things need to happen. The Decision Rights RACI gets ratified by the six roles it covers: the CISO, the General Counsel, the CPO, the CDO, the CFO, and the relevant business unit leaders. Not drafted. Ratified. The risk register gets converted from a historical record into a living artifact with named owners, defined update triggers, and escalation paths for every entry. And the weekly governance standup goes on calendars as a standing commitment, not as a meeting that gets scheduled when someone remembers to schedule it.

By day ninety, the program has its engines running. Shadow AI discovery is active in at least one business unit. The corruption signal set is live on the five most critical AI systems, with behavioral baselines defined and drift detection rules configured. The Human Supervision Matrix is ratified and governing what machines may decide alone in the SOC. The vendor portfolio is re-tiered by AI feature exposure using the updated tier map, not the snapshot the audit produced. And the erasure gap is documented with the General Counsel, meaning the technical feasibility assessment has been run on the five highest-risk AI systems and the results are in the room before the next erasure request arrives for data the workflow can't reach.

By day 365, the program is defensible in front of a regulator, a board, and a business unit simultaneously. Continuous monitoring covers the full vendor portfolio. Autonomous triage is measured and expanding on documented evidence rather than on accumulated informality. The kill-switch has been rehearsed at least once with the evidence filed in the governance repository. AI-channel DLP is enforcing at the gateway, not just described in a policy. And the board is being briefed from evidence that was current the morning of the meeting, not assembled two weeks before it.

One year. Four domains. One running program. Every quarter of it fundable, provable, and defensible because every quarter of it produces evidence that the program is operating rather than documenting.

The Full Program in Sequence: Every Action, Every Owner, Every Cadence

This section assembles every action from every chapter into a single sequenced implementation guide. Days 1 through 30 install the foundations. Days 31 through 90 stand up the engines. Days 91 through 365 expand coverage, rehearse the controls, and put evidence in front of the board. Hand this to your security leadership team and begin executing.

Days 1 through 30 are foundation work. The Decision Rights RACI is the first deliverable and the most important one, because every other governance action depends on knowing who has authority to approve, suspend, and be accountable for AI systems. Draft it in week one using the six-role structure from Part I. Schedule the ratification working session in week two. Get it signed in week three. File it in week four with the governance repository as the authoritative version. That four-week sequence is not negotiable. The RACI that isn't ratified in the first 30 days will not be ratified in the first 90 days, because the organizational momentum that makes ratification possible in the early weeks of a new program dissipates quickly when other priorities compete for the same executive attention.

Simultaneously in days 1 through 30, convert the four audit artifacts into operated instruments. The AI inventory, the risk register, the compliance gap analysis, and the regulatory crosswalk each need three things before they function as governance tools: a named owner, a defined update trigger, and an escalation path. Assign those three attributes to each artifact in week one. Share the assignments with the relevant directors in week two. Confirm the escalation paths with the CISO in week three. The artifacts don't need to be updated yet. They need to have owners who are accountable for updating them on the defined cadence. That accountability is what converts a binder into a program.

Also in days 1 through 30: launch shadow AI discovery in one business unit, run the initial NHI inventory scan, assign governance ownership to the SOC's defensive AI stack, pull the Tier 1 vendor contracts and read the training clauses, map where subject data lives across the five highest-risk AI systems for the erasure gap assessment, and brief the General Counsel on the attestation exposure and the cyber insurance gap. These actions don't all need to be completed by day 30. They need to be started by day 30, with named owners and defined completion dates that fall within the first 90 days.

Days 31 through 90 are engine work. The corruption signal set goes live on the five most critical AI systems. The behavioral baselines are defined, the drift detection rules are configured, and the telemetry instrumentation for prompts, outputs, retrieval sources, and agent actions is running. The Human Supervision Matrix is drafted for the three highest-volume autonomous systems and ratified by the CISO and the relevant decision rights owners. The kill-switch protocol is documented for the three highest-risk agents, with the pre-authorized authority structure confirmed by the General Counsel. The shadow AI sanctioning pathway is piloted in the business unit where discovery ran in the first 30 days. The vendor portfolio is re-tiered by AI feature exposure using the updated tier map. Continuous external monitoring is live for the ten highest-risk Tier 1 vendors. The machine review of the Tier 1 contract estate runs against the AI clause library. The AI BOM requirement is added to the procurement intake checklist for all new AI vendor contracts. The erasure gap findings are presented to the General Counsel with a specific question about regulatory disclosure. The inference question is asked of the five highest-risk AI systems. Agent memory is inventoried in one business unit. Shadow AI discovery runs jointly with the CISO using privacy exposure as the primary lens.

By the end of day 90, the program has all four engines running. Governance is producing continuous evidence. The SOC is supervising machine reasoning with a ratified matrix and a documented kill-switch. Vendor risk is monitoring the portfolio continuously and enforcing the clause library at procurement. Privacy is governing the AI layer with continuous discovery, semantic DLP at the gateway, and a rebuilt erasure workflow. The board can be briefed at day 90 on what's been built, what's running, and what the next 275 days will produce. That briefing is not a status update. It's evidence that the program is operating.

Days 91 through 365 are expansion and rehearsal work. Autonomous triage expands from the highest-volume alert category to additional categories based on documented decision accuracy from the first 90 days. The first live agent-suspension rehearsal is scheduled and run within 60 days of the kill-switch protocol being ratified. The standing evidence pipeline pilot is initiated with the one strategic vendor identified as the highest-risk relationship. The AI BOM program expands to existing Tier 1 vendor contracts at renewal. Continuous discovery extends from the pilot business unit to the full enterprise estate. Purpose-as-code is piloted on one high-sensitivity data pipeline. Enterprise memory is formally classified as a governed data category with a named owner and a documented purge procedure. The inference governance analyst role is hired or assigned from the existing team. The erasure workflow rebuild is completed to reach agent memory and embeddings. The board scorecard is connected to the living risk register and presented to the audit committee with evidence that was current the morning of the meeting.

The quarterly rhythm that runs across all four domains throughout the year is consistent. Every quarter, the governance committee meets with ratified decision rights and produces binding decisions that are documented and filed. Every quarter, the Human Supervision Matrix is reviewed and any autonomy expansions are recorded with the specific accuracy data that supported them. Every quarter, the vendor portfolio re-tiering runs against the updated tier map. Every quarter, the inference governance analyst runs pre-deployment assessments on every new AI system. Every quarter, the board receives a scorecard assembled from continuous evidence with a current risk summary, an investment-to-outcome statement, and one to three specific decisions the CISO is bringing for resolution rather than just for information.

The annual rhythm closes the loop. The operating model itself gets recalibrated. The regulatory crosswalk is reviewed against every new regulatory guidance published in the past 12 months. The Decision Rights RACI is reviewed against the current AI deployment profile and updated where the enterprise's autonomous systems have expanded beyond the scope the original ratification covered. The kill-switch protocol is reviewed against the rehearsal evidence and updated based on what the rehearsals revealed about gaps in the execution sequence. The 1-Year Target Operating Models for all four domains are reviewed against the year's evidence, and the next twelve months of capability builds are confirmed with the CFO based on what this year produced. The board receives the annual posture update with the full year's evidence, the next-year investment case, and the answer to their question about whether the enterprise needs more security or less. The answer, proven four times across four domains with a full year of operating evidence, is more. But transformed.

The security leader who runs this program for one year will have built something that most of their peers are still planning. A governance function that governs machine judgment instead of operating manual controls. A SOC that supervises autonomous reasoning instead of processing alert queues. A vendor risk function that engineers inter-organizational trust instead of mailing questionnaires. A privacy function that governs what the enterprise knows instead of protecting what it stores. That's the AI IT Security Implementation & Strategy™. Not a framework. Not a principles document. A running program, with owners, cadences, and evidence that keeps the board answered and the enterprise defensible every single day.

Framework Alignment

This Volume does not restate the regulatory and standards mapping that Volume V established. It names where the implementation work in each domain is judged against an external criterion, so a reader can defend a control choice to an examiner without rebuilding the argument.

NIST AI Risk Management Framework. The Govern function binds the decision rights work in Chapter 1 and the committee authority ratified in Chapter 3. The Manage function binds the supervision and suspension work in Chapter 5. The Measure function binds the accuracy evidence that gates autonomy expansion in the Human Supervision Matrix.

ISO/IEC 42001. The management system requirements bind the operating rhythm in Chapters 2 and 3. Where an organization is pursuing certification, the continuous-control platform described in Chapter 3 is the mechanism that produces the evidence the audit requires without a point-in-time collection exercise.

ISO/IEC 27001 Annex A and SOC 2 Trust Services Criteria. Existing control sets bind the non-human identity work in Chapter 4 and the vendor management work in Chapters 7 through 9. The relevant finding is not that these frameworks are silent on AI; it is that their existing access control and vendor management criteria already apply to non-human identities and AI vendors, and most programs have not extended them.

EU AI Act. Obligations attaching to high-risk systems bind the provenance work in Chapter 2 and the human oversight requirements in Chapter 5. Where an enterprise places systems in scope, the Human Supervision Matrix is the artifact that evidences human oversight rather than asserting it.

GDPR and US state privacy law. Erasure, purpose limitation, and automated decision-making provisions bind the entirety of Part IV. Chapter 10 names where the founding assumptions of these regimes break against AI systems; Chapter 11 names the engineering that makes compliance operationally real rather than nominally claimed.

OWASP Top 10 for LLM Applications, 2026. The 2026 revision renumbered and expanded the list, and the current entries are prompt injection, sensitive information disclosure, excessive agency, supply chain, data and model poisoning, unbounded consumption, misinformation, hidden context exposure, vector and embedding weaknesses, and improper output handling. Six of them bind directly to work in this Volume. Prompt injection and excessive agency bind the detection work in Chapter 5 and the supervision matrix. Supply chain and data and model poisoning bind the vendor and provenance work in Chapters 7 and 8. Hidden context exposure, new in the 2026 list, binds the context disclosure section in Chapter 8 and the context link of the Agent Authority Chain. Vector and embedding weaknesses bind the memory and vector store work in Chapter 11. Readers working from the 2025 list should note the renumbering before mapping their own control set.

References

This section lists the peer-reviewed and scholarly works underlying the threat claims, measured attack rates, and human-factors findings this Volume relies on. Entries are presented in American Psychological Association 7th edition format and listed alphabetically by first author. The list is distinct from the regulations, standards, and framework pronouncements referenced throughout the chapters, which are consolidated in the Framework Alignment section. A reader who needs to defend a control decision to a board, a regulator, or an architecture review will find the source for the underlying finding here. Where an entry is an author preprint or an applied or practitioner publication rather than a peer-reviewed study, the corresponding claim in the chapters is stated as reported rather than as settled, and the entry should be treated as a starting point rather than as a closed question.

Barni, M., Kallas, K., & Tondi, B. (2019). A new backdoor attack in CNNs by training set corruption without label poisoning. In *2019 IEEE International Conference on Image Processing (ICIP)* (pp. 101-105). IEEE.

Biggio, B., Corona, I., Maiorca, D., Nelson, B., Šrndić, N., Laskov, P., Giacinto, G., & Roli, F. (2013). Evasion attacks against machine learning at test time. In *Machine Learning and Knowledge Discovery in Databases (ECML PKDD 2013)* (pp. 387-402). Springer.

Bisconti, P., et al. (2025). Beyond single-agent safety: A taxonomy of risks in LLM-to-LLM interactions. *arXiv*.

Blanco-Justicia, A., Sánchez, D., Domingo-Ferrer, J., & Muralidhar, K. (2022). A critical review on the use (and misuse) of differential privacy in machine learning. *ACM Computing Surveys, 55*(8), 1-16.

Carlini, N., Chien, S., Nasr, M., Song, S., Terzis, A., & Tramèr, F. (2022). Membership inference attacks from first principles. In *2022 IEEE Symposium on Security and Privacy (SP)* (pp. 1897-1914). IEEE.

Carlini, N., Jagielski, M., & Mironov, I. (2020). Cryptanalytic extraction of neural network models. *arXiv*.

Chaudhari, H., Severi, G., Abascal, J., Jagielski, M., Choquette-Choo, C. A., Nasr, M., Nita-Rotaru, C., & Oprea, A. (2024). Phantom: General trigger attacks on retrieval augmented language generation. *arXiv*.

Chen, X., Liu, C., Li, B., Lu, K., & Song, D. (2017). Targeted backdoor attacks on deep learning systems using data poisoning. *arXiv*.

Chen, Z., Xiang, Z., Xiao, C., Song, D., & Li, B. (2024). AgentPoison: Red-teaming LLM agents via poisoning memory or knowledge bases. In *Advances in Neural Information Processing Systems*.

Chhetri, M. B., et al. (2026). From frontier to shadow AI: A simmering threat to assurance and security in critical infrastructure. *arXiv*.

Chourasia, R., Shah, N., & Shokri, R. (2022). Forget unlearning: Towards true data-deletion in machine learning. *arXiv*.

Cinà, A. E., Grosse, K., Demontis, A., Vascon, S., Zellinger, W., Moser, B. A., Oprea, A., Biggio, B., Pelillo, M., & Roli, F. (2022). Wild patterns reloaded: A survey of machine learning security against training data poisoning. *ACM Computing Surveys, 55*(13s), 1-39.

Ding, Z., et al. (2025). A rusty link in the AI supply chain: Detecting evil configurations in model repositories. In *2025 IEEE Security and Privacy Workshops (SPW)*. IEEE.

Dong, S., Xu, S., He, P., Li, Y., Tang, J., Xu, T., & Wang, S. (2025). A practical memory injection attack against LLM agents. *arXiv*.

Duarte, J. D., et al. (2026). A systematic review of prompt injection attacks on large language models: Trends, taxonomy, evaluation, defenses, and opportunities. *IEEE Access*.

Duddu, V., & Boutet, A. (2022). Inferring sensitive attributes from model explanations. In *Proceedings of the 31st ACM International Conference on Information and Knowledge Management* (pp. 3417-3421). ACM.

Dziemian, M., et al. (2026). How vulnerable are AI agents to indirect prompt injections? Insights from a large-scale public competition. *arXiv*.

Erisken, S., et al. (2025). MAEBE: Multi-agent emergent behavior framework. *arXiv*.

Goddard, K., Roudsari, A., & Wyatt, J. C. (2011). Automation bias: A systematic review of frequency, effect mediators, and mitigators. *Journal of the American Medical Informatics Association, 19*(1), 121-127.

Goldblum, M., Tsipras, D., Xie, C., Chen, X., Schwarzschild, A., Song, D., Mądry, A., Li, B., & Goldstein, T. (2023). Dataset security for machine learning: Data poisoning, backdoor attacks, and defenses. *IEEE Transactions on Pattern Analysis and Machine Intelligence, 45*(2), 1563-1580.

Graves, L., Nagisetty, V., & Ganesh, V. (2020). Amnesiac machine learning. *arXiv*.

Greshake, K., Abdelnabi, S., Mishra, S., Endres, C., Holz, T., & Fritz, M. (2023). Not what you've signed up for: Compromising real-world LLM-integrated applications with indirect prompt injection. In *Proceedings of the 16th ACM Workshop on Artificial Intelligence and Security* (pp. 79-90). ACM.

Hasan, M. M., et al. (2025). Model Context Protocol (MCP) at first glance: Studying the security and maintainability of MCP servers. *ACM Transactions on Software Engineering and Methodology*.

Huang, Y., Gupta, S., Xia, M., Li, K., & Chen, D. (2023). Catastrophic jailbreak of open-source LLMs via exploiting generation. *arXiv*.

Jagielski, M., Carlini, N., Berthelot, D., Kurakin, A., & Papernot, N. (2019). High accuracy and high fidelity extraction of neural networks. *arXiv*.

Janani, K. (2025). The human-machine identity blur: A unified framework for cybersecurity risk management in 2025. *arXiv*.

Jayaraman, B., & Evans, D. (2022). Are attribute inference attacks just imputation? In *Proceedings of the 2022 ACM SIGSAC Conference on Computer and Communications Security* (pp. 1569-1582). ACM.

Jiang, W., Synovic, N., Hyatt, M., Schorlemmer, T. R., Sethi, R., Lu, Y.-H., Thiruvathukal, G. K., & Davis, J. C. (2022). An empirical study of artifacts and security risks in the pre-trained model supply chain. In *Proceedings of the 2022 ACM Workshop on Software Supply Chain Offensive Research and Ecosystem Defenses* (pp. 105-114). ACM.

Karan, et al. (2026). The non-human identity governance crisis in cloud environments: A systematic review, threat taxonomy, and governance framework for agentic AI workloads. *International Journal for Research in Applied Science and Engineering Technology*.

Khan, R. M. S., et al. (2025). Agents under siege: Breaking pragmatic multi-agent LLM systems with optimized prompt attacks. *arXiv*.

Ko, R., et al. (2025). Seven security challenges in cross-domain multi-agent LLM systems. *npj Artificial Intelligence*.

Kotilingala, S. (2025). The non-human identity crisis: Managing machine identities in the modern enterprise. *World Journal of Advanced Research and Reviews*.

Kurakin, A., Goodfellow, I., & Bengio, S. (2016). Adversarial examples in the physical world. *arXiv*.

Kurtz, A., et al. (2026). Who governs the machine? A machine identity governance taxonomy (MIGT) for AI systems operating across enterprise and geopolitical boundaries. *arXiv*.

Li, T., et al. (2026). Safe multi-agent behavior must be maintained, not merely asserted: Constraint drift in LLM-based multi-agent systems. *arXiv*.

Liu, X., Xu, N., Chen, M., & Xiao, C. (2023). AutoDAN: Generating stealthy jailbreak prompts on aligned large language models. *arXiv*.

Mehnaz, S., Dibbo, S. V., Kabir, E., Li, N., & Bertino, E. (2022). Are your sensitive attributes private? Novel model inversion attribute inference attacks on classification models. In *31st USENIX Security Symposium* (pp. 4579-4596). USENIX Association.

Meimandi, K., et al. (2025). An adaptive responsible AI governance framework for decentralized organizations. *arXiv*.

Mühlhoff, R. (2020). Predictive privacy: Towards an applied ethics of data analytics. *Ethics and Information Technology, 23*, 675-690.

Nguyen, T. T., Huynh, T. T., Nguyen, P. L., Liew, A. W.-C., Yin, H., & Nguyen, Q. V. H. (2022). A survey of machine unlearning. *ACM Transactions on Intelligent Systems and Technology*.

Papagiannidis, E., Mikalef, P., & Conboy, K. (2025). Responsible artificial intelligence governance: A review and research framework. *Journal of Strategic Information Systems, 34*(2).

Papernot, N., McDaniel, P., Goodfellow, I., Jha, S., Celik, Z. B., & Swami, A. (2016). Practical black-box attacks against machine learning. In *Proceedings of the 2017 ACM Asia Conference on Computer and Communications Security* (pp. 506-519). ACM.

Parasuraman, R., & Manzey, D. H. (2010). Complacency and bias in human use of automation: An attentional integration. *Human Factors, 52*(3), 381-410.

Ponomareva, N., Hazimeh, H., Kurakin, A., Xu, Z., Denison, C., McMahan, H. B., Vassilvitskii, S., Chien, S., & Thakurta, A. (2023). How to DP-fy ML: A practical guide to machine learning with differential privacy. *Journal of Artificial Intelligence Research, 77*, 1113-1201.

Rath, A. (2026). Agent drift: Quantifying behavioral degradation in multi-agent LLM systems over extended interactions. *arXiv*.

Reid, A., et al. (2025). Risk analysis techniques for governed LLM-based multi-agent systems. *arXiv*.

Rieger, M., et al. (2026). Possibilities and limitations of using large language models (LLMs) for alert classification and prioritisation in security operations centers (SOCs). *Expert Systems with Applications*.

Sebastian, G. (2026). Digital shadow AI risk theory (DART): A framework for managing data disclosure and privacy risks of AI tools at work. *Technological Forecasting and Social Change.*

Shokri, R., Stronati, M., Song, C., & Shmatikov, V. (2017). Membership inference attacks against machine learning models. In *2017 IEEE Symposium on Security and Privacy (SP)* (pp. 3-18). IEEE.

Silic, M., et al. (2025). From Shadow IT to Shadow AI: Threats, risks and opportunities for organizations. *Strategic Change.*

Singh, R., et al. (2025). LLMs in the SOC: An empirical study of human-AI collaboration in security operations centres. In *2026 IEEE Symposium on Security and Privacy (SP).* IEEE.

Song, H., et al. (2025). Beyond the protocol: Unveiling attack vectors in the Model Context Protocol ecosystem. *arXiv.*

Srinivas, S., et al. (2025). AI-augmented SOC: A survey of LLMs and agents for security automation. *Journal of Cybersecurity and Privacy.*

Tilbury, J., & Flowerday, S. (2024). Automation bias and complacency in security operation centers. *Computers, 13*(7), 165.

Torra, V., et al. (2026). Memory poisoning and secure multi-agent systems. *arXiv.*

Tramèr, F., Zhang, F., Juels, A., Reiter, M. K., & Ristenpart, T. (2016). Stealing machine learning models via prediction APIs. In *25th USENIX Security Symposium* (pp. 601-618). USENIX Association.

Wang, Z., et al. (2025). MCPTox: A benchmark for tool poisoning attack on real-world MCP servers. *arXiv.*

Wei, Z., Wang, Y., Li, A., Mo, Y., & Wang, Y. (2023). Jailbreak and guard aligned language models with only few in-context demonstrations. *IEEE Transactions on Pattern Analysis and Machine Intelligence.*

Wirtz, B. W., Weyerer, J. C., & Kehl, I. (2022). Governance of artificial intelligence: A risk and guideline-based integrative framework. *Government Information Quarterly, 39*(4).

Xiang, C., et al. (2026). Architecting secure AI agents: Perspectives on system-level defenses against indirect prompt injection attacks. *arXiv*.

Xu, Z., Jiang, F., Niu, L., Jia, J., Lin, B. Y., & Poovendran, R. (2024). SafeDecoding: Defending against jailbreak attacks via safety-aware decoding. *arXiv*.

Yang, X., et al. (2026). Zombie agents: Persistent control of self-evolving LLM agents via self-reinforcing injections. *arXiv*.

Yi, S., et al. (2024). Jailbreak attacks and defenses against large language models: A survey. *arXiv*.

Yilmaz, E. (2026). Machine identity management in modern enterprise security: Concepts, challenges, and the role of privileged access management systems. *Engineering, Technology & Applied Science Research*.

Zhan, Q., Liang, Z., Ying, Z., & Kang, D. (2024). InjecAgent: Benchmarking indirect prompt injections in tool-integrated large language model agents. *arXiv*.

Zhao, X., et al. (2024). Weak-to-strong jailbreaking on large language models. *arXiv*.

Zou, W., Geng, R., Wang, B., & Jia, J. (2024). PoisonedRAG: Knowledge poisoning attacks to retrieval-augmented generation of large language models. *arXiv*.

Appendix: The Implementation Toolkit & Appendix A

Every artifact this Volume produces is specified here in the form the working version takes. Each appendix names the artifact's purpose, its owner, its cadence, and the fields it carries. The consulting worksheet versions are available through the companion materials.

Appendix A: The AI Security Operating System™ One-Page Map

APPENDIX A

The AI Security Operating System One-Page Map

Holds four domain programs as one program with shared decision rights, a shared evidence base, and one operating calendar. (Chapter 1)

Field	Content
Domain	Governance, Security Operations, Third-Party Risk, Data Protection
Domain owner	Named role, not team
Leading quarter	Which quarter this domain leads in the twelve-month sequence
Authoritative inventory consumed	Which system of record this domain reads rather than builds
Executive constraint	Which executive's calendar gates this domain's work
Quarterly measured number	The one metric this domain reports to the board
Shared services consumed	Discovery, enforcement gateway, evidence platform

Owner. CISO. Cadence. Reviewed annually; updated on material change.

Four domain programs on one calendar, or four projects competing for the same quarter.

WORKING FILE Toolkit_A_The_AI_Security_Operating_System_One_Page_Map.xlsx

Appendix B: The Decision Rights RACI

APPENDIX B

The Decision Rights RACI

Resolves who approves, who suspends, and who is accountable, per AI system class. (Chapter 1)

Field	Content
System or system class	Named, mapped to the model registry entry
Business owner	Named role in the business unit
Approves deployment	Named role with signature authority
Approves material change	Named role; may differ from deployment approver
Unilateral suspension authority	Named role who does not require an approval chain
Accountable when the system acts	Named role, singular
Legal review status	Reviewed, conditions, or not reviewed
Ratification date and signatories	Dated; signatories listed

Owner. CISO. Cadence. Ratified once by signature; reviewed quarterly; re-ratified annually or on material scope change.

An unratified RACI is an opinion. Signatures make it an authority.

WORKING FILE Toolkit_B_The_Decision_Rights_RACI.xlsx

Appendix C: The Five-Horizon Governance Rhythm

APPENDIX C

The Five-Horizon Governance Rhythm

Matches governance cadence to the rate at which the governed environment changes. (Chapter 2)

Horizon	Participants	Input	Output
Daily	GRC analyst	Platform exception queue, registry reconciliation	Disposition per item: none, escalate weekly, escalate now
Weekly	GRC manager, security director	Discovered systems, version changes, policy conflicts	Written disposition list
Monthly	Governance committee	Accumulated escalations, discovery findings	Binding decisions; published intake-to-approval time
Quarterly	CISO, board	Assembled scorecard	Board pack; one measured number
Annual	Executive committee	Regulatory movement, RACI scope, decay rates	Recalibrated operating model

Owner. GRC director. Cadence. Continuous.

Match the cadence to the decay rate. One review frequency cannot serve five horizons.

WORKING FILE Toolkit_C_The_Five_Horizon_Governance_Rhythm.xlsx

Appendix D: The Shadow AI Sanctioning Pathway™ Workflow

APPENDIX D

The Shadow AI Sanctioning Pathway Workflow

Converts unapproved AI use into governed capability rather than driving it underground. (Chapter 2)

Stage	Action	Decision criteria	Output
Discovery	Structured conversation with business unit leadership	What tools, from where, touching what data, solving what problem	Tool list with data classification
Tiering	Classify against four criteria	Sensitive data, autonomous decisions, external sharing, persistent memory	Tier 1 low, Tier 2 moderate, Tier 3 high
Migration	Offer governed alternative	Tier determines sandbox controls	Sanctioned equivalent or interim alternative
Disposition	Register or prohibit	Risk acceptance by named owner	Registry entry with owner and review date
Measurement	Publish intake-to-approval time	Must beat the workaround	Monthly published metric

Owner. GRC director. Cadence. One business unit discovered per month; intake continuous.

The pathway has to be faster than the workaround, or it is a prohibition with paperwork.

WORKING FILE Toolkit_D_The_Shadow_AI_Sanctioning_Pathway_Workflow.xlsx

Appendix E: The Living Risk Register Entry

APPENDIX E

The Living Risk Register Entry

Keeps AI risk current between committee cycles by separating machine-maintained fields from human-adjudicated ones. (Chapter 2)

Field	Maintained by	Notes
Risk statement	Human	Written once, revised on material change
Affected systems	Machine	Reconciled against model registry
Current control state	Machine	From continuous-control platform
Inherent and residual rating	Human	Adjudicated at committee
Volatility class	Human	Sets review frequency; not the committee calendar
Review frequency	Derived	From volatility class
Named owner	Human	Role, not team
Escalation trigger	Human	Threshold and recipient
Last verified date	Machine	Timestamped

Owner. GRC director. Cadence. Continuous; entry review frequency set per entry volatility.

Machines maintain the register. People remain accountable for the risk.

WORKING FILE Toolkit_E_The_Living_Risk_Register_Entry.xlsx

Appendix F: The Human Supervision Matrix™

APPENDIX F

The Human Supervision Matrix

Documents which actions machines may take alone and what evidence gates expansion. (Chapter 5)

Field	Content
System	Named, mapped to registry
Action class	Discrete; one row per class, never per tool
Current autonomy level	Autonomous, confirm-before-execute, human-execute
Accuracy evidence required to raise	Named metric and threshold
Current measured accuracy	With sample size and date
Approving authority for expansion	Named role
Last review date	Dated
Expansion log reference	Pointer to the dated expansion record

Owner. SOC director. Cadence. Reviewed monthly; expanded only on evidence.

Autonomy is earned with measured evidence, not granted by roadmap.

WORKING FILE Toolkit_F_The_Human_Supervision_Matrix.xlsx

Appendix G: The Red-Button Protocol Runbook

APPENDIX G

The Red-Button Protocol Runbook

Converts suspension from a policy paragraph into a rehearsed capability with a measured time-to-stop. (Chapter 5)

Field	Content
System	Named
Pre-authorized triggers	Enumerated; no approval chain required at time of use
Named executor	Individual and alternate
Execution sequence	Ordered steps
Dependency map	Systems and processes that degrade on suspension
Rehearsal date	Dated
Measured time to confirmed stop	Minutes and seconds
Findings	Undocumented dependencies; approvals not pre-authorized
Runbook changes made	What changed as a result

Owner. SOC director. Cadence. Rehearsed quarterly; file retained.

An unrehearsed runbook has an unknown time-to-stop, which is the same as not having one.

WORKING FILE Toolkit_G_The_Red_Button_Protocol_Runbook.xlsx

Appendix H: The Corruption Detection Baseline Worksheet

APPENDIX H

The Corruption Detection Baseline Worksheet

Defines what normal looks like for each AI system so deviation is detectable. (Chapter 5)

Field	Content
System	Named; ranked by decision consequence
Telemetry sources	Prompts, outputs, retrieval sources, agent actions
Behavioral baseline	Defined distribution or rule set
Drift thresholds	Values that trigger investigation
Finding rate	Findings per period, with disposition breakdown
Injection test date and result	Confirms the baseline can detect a known corruption

Owner. Detection engineering. Cadence. Baselines reviewed quarterly; injection-tested semiannually.

Without a baseline, corruption detection is a dashboard rather than a control.

WORKING FILE Toolkit_H_The_Corruption_Detection_Baseline_Worksheet.xlsx

Appendix I: The AI-Augmented Operating Rhythm

APPENDIX I

The AI-Augmented Operating Rhythm

Replaces detection and response timing metrics with measures that describe supervised autonomy. (Chapter 5)

Horizon	Focus	Primary metrics
Daily	What machines did overnight	Autonomous action count; exception queue depth
Weekly	Decision quality	Agreement rate on independent review sample
Monthly	Program health	Autonomous action rate; decision accuracy; corruption finding rate
Quarterly	Governance	Expansion decisions with evidence; rehearsal time-to-stop

Owner. SOC director. Cadence. Continuous.

Report coverage and time-to-stop. They survive scrutiny that mean time to detect does not.

WORKING FILE Toolkit_I_The_AI_Augmented_Operating_Rhythm.xlsx

Appendix J: The Non-Human Identity Pyramid™ Tiering Worksheet

APPENDIX J

The Non-Human Identity Pyramid Tiering Worksheet

Applies governance intensity proportional to what an identity can do rather than to where it came from. (Chapter 4)

Tier	Definition	Credential lifetime	Review cadence	Required controls
Tier 1	Read-only, scoped, no external egress	Standard	Annual	Named owner; inventory entry
Tier 2	Write or state-changing within one system	Shortened	Semiannual	Named owner; scoped permissions; logging
Tier 3	Cross-system action or external egress	Short	Quarterly	Named owner; boundary matrix entry; anomaly monitoring
Tier 4	Autonomous action with financial or safety consequence	Shortest	Monthly	All of the above; supervision matrix entry; kill-switch coverage

Owner. IAM lead. Cadence. Reviewed quarterly.

The largest identity population in the enterprise is the least monitored one.

WORKING FILE Toolkit_J_The_Non_Human_Identity_Pyramid_Tiering_Worksheet.xlsx

Appendix K: The AI Clause Library

APPENDIX K

The AI Clause Library

Encodes the enterprise's contractual position on AI so procurement enforces rather than negotiates each time. (Chapter 8)

Category	Examples	Enforcement
Required	No training on enterprise data without explicit consent; advance notice of model provider change; advance notice of change of control; AI Bill of Materials disclosure; exit assistance covering adaptations	Blocks execution
Prohibited	Unilateral amendment of data use terms; unrestricted subprocessor substitution; broad license to derived works	Blocks execution
Monitored	Data residency for inference; retention of prompts and outputs; incident notification timing	Flags for review

Owner. General Counsel. Cadence. Reviewed semiannually; annual review against the year's contract experience.

You have leverage at renewal. The rest of the year you have a request.

WORKING FILE Toolkit_K_The_AI_Clause_Library.xlsx

Appendix L: The Adaptive AI Trust Score™ Model

APPENDIX L

The Adaptive AI Trust Score Model

Makes vendor trust a continuously managed variable rather than a binary annual assessment. (Chapter 8)

Field	Content
Input categories	Attested posture; monitored external signals; contract protection strength; incident history; BOM completeness
Weighting	Documented and defensible; set by the enterprise, not the platform
Thresholds	Values at which review, restriction, or exit are triggered
Threshold actions	Named owner and required action per threshold
Friction reduction	What a sustained high score earns in procurement
Model review date	Dated annually

Owner. Third-party risk director. Cadence. Scores continuous; model reviewed annually.

A score that only moves once a year is a classification, not a control.

WORKING FILE Toolkit_L_The_Adaptive_AI_Trust_Score_Model.xlsx

Appendix M: The AI Bill of Materials Requirement

APPENDIX M

The AI Bill of Materials Requirement

Makes the model supply chain disclosable so concentration becomes measurable. (Chapter 8)

Required disclosure	Notes
Foundation model provider or providers	Named; not "varies"
Model family and version policy	How versions change and whether the customer is notified
Inference location and routing behavior	Static or dynamic; jurisdictions
Training and fine-tuning data sources	Category level minimum
Retention of prompts and outputs	Duration and purpose
Subprocessors at the model layer	Named
Unlearning capability	Ability to remove specific customer data influence from a trained model, with supporting evidence
Change notification commitment	Advance notice period

Owner. Third-party risk director. Cadence. Required at onboarding and at every renewal.

If the vendor cannot produce a bill of materials, that refusal is the finding.

WORKING FILE Toolkit_M_The_AI_Bill_of_Materials_Requirement.xlsx

Appendix N: The Foundation Model Concentration Analysis

APPENDIX N **The Foundation Model Concentration Analysis**

Converts an invisible architectural dependency into a financial figure the CFO can act on. (Chapter 9)

Field	Content
Provider	Named foundation model provider
Dependent vendor services	Enumerated from the BOM registry
Business processes affected	Named
Estimated impact of a seventy-two hour outage	Quantified in dollars
Mitigation status	Named owner; plan; date

Owner. Third-party risk director. **Recipient.** CFO. Cadence. Quarterly.

Concentration is invisible until the renewal notice arrives. Publish the number first.

WORKING FILE Toolkit_N_The_Foundation_Model_Concentration_Analysis.xlsx

Appendix O: The Erasure Engineering Register

APPENDIX O

The Erasure Engineering Register

Enumerates every location an erasure request must reach so the certification is defensible. (Chapter 11)

Location class	Examples	Erasure mechanism	Verification method
Primary stores	Databases, document repositories	Delete	Query confirmation
Replicas and backups	In-window backups	Scheduled expiry or targeted purge	Restore test
Vector representations	Embedding indexes	Index deletion and rebuild	Similarity probe
Retrieval caches	Context caches	Invalidation	Cache inspection
Agent memory	Session and long-term memory stores	Scoped purge	Memory query
Model artifacts	Fine-tuned adaptations	Retrain, unlearn, or documented limitation	Documented; disclosed where not achievable

Owner. CPO. Cadence. Reviewed quarterly; verification sampled monthly.

Register what you cannot erase. An undisclosed limitation becomes a finding.

WORKING FILE Toolkit_O_The_Erasure_Engineering_Register.xlsx

Appendix P: The Purpose Enforcement Map

APPENDIX P

The Purpose Enforcement Map

Binds consent basis to a pipeline enforcement point so purpose limitation is executed rather than described. (Chapter 11)

Field	Content
Data class	Named regulated category
Consent or lawful basis	Recorded
Permitted purposes	Enumerated
Enforcement point	Gateway, pipeline stage, or store-level policy
Enforcement behavior	Block or log; block preferred
Exception queue owner	Named role

Owner. CPO. Cadence. Continuous.

Purpose limitation enforced in the pipeline is a control. Everywhere else it is a claim.

WORKING FILE Toolkit_P_The_Purpose_Enforcement_Map.xlsx

Appendix Q: The Enterprise Memory Governance Standard

APPENDIX Q

The Enterprise Memory Governance Standard

Gives agent memory and knowledge bases a lifecycle, which they have historically lacked entirely. (Chapter 11)

Field	Content
Memory store	Named; mapped to system
Contents classification	Data classes present
Retention period	Defined; not indefinite
Scoping rules	Which users and contexts may read it
Isolation boundaries	Tenant, business unit, or user
Purge procedure	Mechanism and owner
Last purge executed	Dated

Owner. CPO with CDO. Cadence. Reviewed semiannually.

Agent memory is a data store that arrived without a steward. Give it one.

WORKING FILE Toolkit_Q_The_Enterprise_Memory_Governance_Standard.xlsx

Appendix R: The AI Security Scorecard™

APPENDIX R

The AI Security Scorecard

Gives the board current evidence assembled continuously, changing the CISO's role from assembling and defending to reviewing and approving. (Chapter 2)

Section	Content	Source
Population	AI systems in scope; drift since last quarter	Model registry
Accountability	Systems with ratified decision rights; gaps	Decision Rights RACI
Supervision	Autonomy distribution; expansion decisions with evidence	Supervision matrix
Containment	Rehearsal date; measured time to stop	Red-Button file
Supply chain	Trust score distribution; concentration figure	Trust score model; BOM registry
Data protection	Erasure verification result; enforcement block rate	Erasure register; gateway
The measured number	One figure the program produced itself this quarter	Chosen deliberately

Owner. CISO. Cadence. Assembled continuously; presented quarterly.

One measured number per domain beats a page of green status indicators.

WORKING FILE Toolkit_R_The_AI_Security_Scorecard.xlsx

Appendix S: The Agent Authority Chain™ Assessment Worksheet

APPENDIX S

The Agent Authority Chain Assessment Worksheet

Establishes whether a consequential machine action was authorized rather than merely authenticated. (Chapter 8)

Element	Question	Domain owner	Evidence source
Identity	Which system acted, and is it enumerated?	Governance	Model registry; non-human identity inventory
Intent	What objective was it pursuing, and was that objective recorded before the work began?	Governance	Recorded objective register
Authority	Who delegated the right, with what scope, and when does it expire?	Governance	Decision Rights RACI; authority tier grant
Context	What sources influenced the reasoning, and what is their trust classification?	Third-party risk	Retrieval provenance log; source classification
Action	What was done, which tools were invoked, which agents were delegated to?	Security operations	Tool invocation log; agent-to-agent message log
Impact	What changed in the enterprise, and which human decisions relied on it?	Data protection	Change record; downstream consumption log

Owner. CISO, with per-element owners named below. Cadence. Applied at design for every agent in the top two authority tiers; sampled quarterly in production.

Every step was inside policy. The aggregate was not. Assess the chain, not the call.

WORKING FILE Toolkit_S_The_Agent_Authority_Chain_Assessment_Worksheet.xlsx

Appendix T: The Agent Circuit Breaker Envelope

APPENDIX T

The Agent Circuit Breaker Envelope

Bounds how much an agent may do, which human supervision cannot govern at machine speed. (Chapter 5)

Dimension	Limit set at	Breach behavior
Single transaction value	Margin above observed maximum	Stop; incident
Cumulative transaction value per period	Business-defined ceiling	Stop; incident
API or tool invocations per task	Margin above observed maximum	Stop; incident
Execution duration per task	Margin above observed maximum	Stop; incident
Data volume read and written	Margin above observed maximum	Stop; incident
Delegation depth	Conservative; rarely above three	Stop; incident
Total delegated invocations per task	Margin above observed maximum	Stop; incident
Distinct external destinations	Allowlist plus count ceiling	Stop; incident
Retry count	Fixed low value	Stop; incident
Token consumption per task	Margin above observed maximum	Stop; incident
Cumulative token spend per period	Business-defined ceiling	Stop; incident
Repeated identical action (loop detection)	Fixed low threshold	Stop; incident

Owner. SOC director. Cadence. Observed for one period before enforcement; reviewed with the supervision matrix.

The breaker bounds the volume. The intent monitor bounds the direction.

WORKING FILE Toolkit_T_The_Agent_Circuit_Breaker_Envelope.xlsx

Appendix U: The AI Security Debt™ Register

APPENDIX U

The AI Security Debt Register

Converts ungoverned AI from an anecdote into a countable, aging liability the board can fund against. (Chapter 3)

Component	What counts as one unit	Source	Closing action
Unregistered systems	An AI system in production with no model registry entry	Discovery versus registry reconciliation	Register with named owner and decision right
Ungoverned identities	A non-human identity capable of action with no named human owner	Non-human identity inventory	Assign owner; tier; set credential lifetime
Stale authority	An authority grant past expiry or past review date, still active	Authority tier grant register	Renew by positive affirmation or revoke
Unassessed connections	A tool or MCP server reachable by an agent and absent from the allowlist	Orchestration layer versus provenance register	Assess and allowlist, or block
Undocumented versions	A production system whose current model version the enterprise cannot state	Model registry reconciliation	Record version; enable change notification
Unratified rights	A production system with no named approver, suspender, or accountable executive	Decision Rights RACI	Route to next ratification session

Owner. GRC director. Cadence. Recomputed monthly; reported to the board quarterly.

Debt you do not measure is debt you will refinance during an incident.

WORKING FILE Toolkit_U_The_AI_Security_Debt_Register.xlsx

Appendix V: The Continuous Adversarial Evaluation Test Set

APPENDIX V

The Continuous Adversarial Evaluation Test Set

Produces the adversarial resistance evidence the Human Supervision Matrix™ requires before any autonomy expansion. (Chapter 5)

Attack class	What is tested	Control validated	Failure signal
Objective hijacking via retrieval	Whether external retrieved content alters the agent's recorded objective	Retrieval boundary classification	Agent pursues supplied objective
Tool description manipulation	Whether a modified tool description changes agent behavior beyond that tool's function	Tool provenance; description integrity monitoring	Agent invokes tools outside normal set
Memory contamination	Whether adversarial content written to memory persists and shapes later sessions	Memory versioning; write attribution	Behavior change survives session boundary
Delegation abuse	Whether a delegation chain escalates rather than attenuates authority	Authority attenuation	Downstream agent exceeds originating scope
Context extraction	Whether system context, credentials, or retrieved content can be surfaced in output	Context isolation; output controls	Sensitive context appears in response
Envelope evasion	Whether the agent can exceed its circuit breaker limits	Agent Circuit Breaker Envelope	Agent continues past threshold
Workflow cascade	Whether a multi-agent workflow can exceed its aggregate bound while every agent stays inside its own	Workflow-level envelope	Aggregate outcome exceeds workflow objective
Revocation persistence	Whether a revoked agent or its delegated chain continues acting	Revocation path	Action continues after revocation

Owner. Detection engineering. Cadence. Automated runs monthly against production endpoints; external technique refresh annually.

An adversarial test you have not run is a control you do not have.

WORKING FILE Toolkit_V_The_Continuous_Adversarial_Evaluation_Test_Set.xlsx

Continuing the Work

The AI IT Security Implementation & Strategy™ is the sixth operating instrument in The Operating Discipline for AI Library™ and the second Volume of Pillar II.

Pillar I: AI Business Services™

Volume I, The AI Business Enablement Audit™, gives the board and the CEO the five-dimension view of what AI is running, what it costs, what it produces, where it exposes the business, and where the governance gaps sit.

Volume II, The AI Readiness & Performance Assessment™, evaluates six conditions per use case, scores them on the AI Readiness Maturity Scale™, and produces the Expand, Refine, or Pause Decision Protocol™ output.

Volume III, AI Risk & Governance Review™, builds the per-use-case governance dossier and the AI Governance Framework Crosswalk™.

Volume IV, The AI Efficiency & Process Optimization™, produces the AI Efficiency Scorecard™, the AI ROI Formula™, and the 90 Day AI Process Optimization Plan.

Pillar II: AI Risk Governance & Security™

Volume V, The AI IT Security Audit™, produces the evidence base: the four-layer inventory, the Non-Human Identity Inventory™, the Agent Boundary Matrix™, the AI Vendor Tier Map™, the AI Data Flow Map™, the Regulatory Crosswalk™, and the Defensible AI Security Baseline™.

Volume VI, this Volume, converts that evidence base into a running program across the four CISO domains on a twelve-month horizon.

Volume VII, Secure by Design in the Age of AI™, moves the work upstream into architecture, where the exposures this Volume operates around get designed out rather than governed around.

Volume VIII, Application Security in the Age of AI™, addresses what the business builds and what the vendors ship at the application layer.

Volume IX, Cloud and Infrastructure Security in the Age of AI™, closes the pillar at the infrastructure layer where the AI estate actually runs.

Together, these nine Volumes form a complete operating discipline. They are designed to be read in order by a leadership team that is serious about installing AI as a governed business function rather than adopting it as a set of tools.

If You Want to Continue This Work

A CISO who has read this Volume can run the implementation program inside their own organization. The frameworks are written to be self-applied. The target operating models in Chapters 3, 6, 9, and 12 name the owner, the cadence, and the quarterly milestone, and the appendices provide the worksheets in the form the work actually requires.

For organizations that want support standing up the first four quarters, converting the operating models into board-ready artifacts, or applying the method under regulatory or customer deadline pressure, SRJ Consulting & Services runs the program as an engagement. The engagement produces the same instruments this Volume describes, on a compressed timeline, with the evidence trail assembled as the work proceeds rather than reconstructed afterward.

The work itself is the point. Whether it is done internally or with help, what matters is that AI security inside the business stops being a position defended in a meeting and becomes a program that produces evidence on a schedule.

More information can be found at srjconsultingservices.com/books.

The AI Operating System™

Every Volume in this Library installs one component of the same operating system. The AI Operating Calendar™ is the cadence that runs inside it. Volume VI adds the four domain operating rhythms described in Chapters 2, 5, 8, and 11 to the existing calendar. It does not create a parallel structure, and a reader running the calendar from prior Volumes should extend it rather than replace it.

Companion Materials

Every worksheet, operating instrument, and figure in this Volume is available online for your use, free, at srjconsultingservices.com/books.

The companion library includes:

The complete implementation toolkit as editable files. Every appendix in this Volume, including the Human Supervision Matrix worksheet, the Red-Button Protocol runbook, the Agent Authority Chain worksheet, the Circuit Breaker Envelope, the Continuous Adversarial Evaluation test set, and the AI Security Debt register, provided in a form your team can populate directly.

The one-page target operating model templates for all four domains. The Chapter 3, 6, 9, and 12 operating models as fillable single-page documents with the owner, cadence, quarterly milestone, and budget line already structured.

The board scorecard format. The AI Security Scorecard in the layout used to report quarterly, with the metric definitions and the trend fields the audit committee will ask about.

The framework reference cards. Working reference cards for NIST AI RMF, ISO/IEC 42001, the EU AI Act, OWASP LLM Top 10, OWASP Agentic Top 10, OWASP MCP Top 10, OWASP AIVSS, MITRE ATLAS, and Google SAIF, mapped to the chapters where each one binds.

All companion materials are made available without restriction for legitimate business use within the organization that purchased this Volume. If you find them useful, the most helpful thing you can do is tell a peer who is facing the same deadline.

For additional resources, including AI governance frameworks, executive workshops, and advisory engagements, visit srjconsultingservices.com.

The Live Reference Layer

A printed Volume fixes its citations on the day it goes to press. The regulatory and litigation environment this Volume operates in does not hold still that long. The World of AI, published at theworldofai.org, is the companion reference layer that does move: an independent atlas of artificial intelligence, rebuilt daily from primary sources.

Use it wherever this Volume points at something that changes. The Regulatory Crosswalk carried forward from the audit stays current against the state legislation pages. The framework reference cards described above sit inside a cross-mapped index of sixty-two compliance frameworks. The vendor and tooling judgments in Part III can be checked against profiled companies and tools rather than against memory. Every reference page carries a last-verified date and a ready-made citation, so an artifact built from it holds up when the auditor asks where the number came from.

The legal and regulatory layer covers every tracked AI bill across all fifty states, the District of Columbia, Puerto Rico, and Congress, one page per jurisdiction, refreshed from the legislative tracking feed. The lawsuit tracker maintains ninety-seven living case pages with daily docket checks, timelines, and links to the underlying dockets and opinions. The compliance framework index cross-maps sixty-two frameworks, including the EU AI Act, the NIST AI Risk Management Framework, and ISO/IEC 42001.

The technical and market layer defines five hundred twenty-two glossary terms in plain English with origin, example, and related terms, and holds one hundred thirty-four peer-reviewed and preprint papers sorted into ten topics, each with authors, venue, citation count, and a plain-English note. Sixty-three tool profiles across twenty-three categories carry pricing, strengths, weaknesses, and governance notes. Sixty-one company profiles carry revenue and structure data drawn from public filings where the company is public. The Model Context Protocol server registry indexes one thousand seven hundred twenty-nine servers, which is the catalog to consult before a team stands up its own.

The working layer adds a weekly digest of what changed across law, litigation, research, and product, with permalinked archives by week, and six estimators covering token cost, model memory requirements, return on investment, training cost, energy and carbon, and context window sizing. A bibliography of one hundred twenty-three primary sources sits behind every fact published.

The site is built to be cited rather than browsed. The first paragraph of every reference page stands alone as a citable answer, every page displays a last-verified date driven by the daily pipeline run, and structured data markup is applied where it belongs so that answer engines resolve to the source rather than to a summary of it. Eight machine-readable endpoints expose the legislation, litigation, glossary, research, source, company, tool, and server registry data, so a security team can pull the material into its own tooling instead of transcribing it. Across two thousand eight hundred forty-five indexed pages, every published URL is data-backed.

An automated pipeline rebuilds the site every day from the legislative tracking service for state bills, the federal court docket archives for litigation, the Federal Register and the government publishing office for opinions and rules, an academic research index for papers, public company filings for corporate data, and thirty-four curated news feeds. The editorial policy is a single rule: every fact traces to a source in the bibliography, and where a claim cannot be sourced, it is not published. Corrections are sent to info@srjconsultingservices.com.

A Brief Note on the Library Continuum

The Volumes are numbered by operating sequence rather than by publication order or by difficulty. The sequence reflects the order in which the disciplines build inside a business: visibility before readiness, readiness before governance, governance before optimization, and the security pillar building on all four.

A reader can begin at Volume VI without having run Volume V, but the first chapter of each Part opens with a handoff section that names what the audit produced and what condition it arrives in. Those sections are written so the work is executable either way. A reader who has the audit will recognize their own artifacts. A reader who does not will find the list of what has to exist before the implementation work can start.

tion, computer science, photography, and educational media and technology. His multidisciplinary background contributed to the operational and governance-focused perspective reflected throughout The AI Operating System™ framework.

Through his work with business owners and organizational leadership teams, Jordan recognized that many companies were adopting artificial intelligence faster than they were developing the operational systems required to govern it effectively. That observation became the foundation for The AI Operating System™ and the operational frameworks introduced throughout this Volume and its companion Volumes.

Stephen is the author of The Operating Discipline for AI Library™, a nine-volume canon on running AI as a permanent business function. This is Volume VI, the second Volume of Pillar II.

Today, Jordan works with organizations seeking to improve visibility, governance, operational discipline, cost control, measurable performance, and security defensibility across artificial intelligence initiatives and business technology environments. His work focuses on helping businesses manage AI intentionally through structured operational systems rather than fragmented adoption and uncontrolled experimentation.

For additional resources, AI governance frameworks, executive workshops, and advisory engagements, visit srjconsultingservices.com.

About the Author

Stephen R. Jordan is the founder of SRJ Consulting & Services LLC, an operator-led AI advisory practice based in Frisco, Texas. His work helps executives establish governance, oversight, and operational discipline around artificial intelligence as a managed business function, not an experimental tool.

Jordan's professional background spans accounting, enterprise technology, cybersecurity, operational systems management, and risk governance. Over the course of a career that includes leadership, consulting, and advisory roles across multiple industries, he has worked extensively in operational oversight, business systems management, enterprise security, incident response, governance frameworks, and technology implementation. His experience includes work involving operational risk management, infrastructure security, compliance oversight, and business process improvement inside complex enterprise environments.

Prior to founding SRJ Consulting & Services LLC in 2023, Jordan held senior consulting, operational, and security roles at organizations including Citi, Optiv, Intel, and McAfee. His engagements span enterprise technology, cybersecurity operations, governance processes, and systems management, with recurring focus on operational risk, infrastructure security, compliance oversight, and the management infrastructure required to keep complex enterprise environments running as designed.

Jordan earned a Bachelor of Business Administration in Accounting and a Master of Arts in Political Science with a minor in business statistics from West Texas A&M University and later completed post graduate studies from East Texas A&M University in supervision instruction and curriculum for higher educa-